Land Legislation in
Mandate Palestine

Land Legislation in Mandate Palestine

VOLUME 4

ORDERS-IN-COUNCIL, ORDINANCES and PUBLIC NOTICES

Editor: Martin Bunton

an imprint of

CAMBRIDGE UNIVERSITY PRESS

Cambridge, New York, Melbourne, Madrid, Cape Town, Singapore, São Paulo

Cambridge University Press
The Edinburgh Building, Cambridge CB2 2RU, UK

Published in the United States of America by Cambridge University Press,
New York

www.cambridge.org
Information on this title: www.archiveeditions.co.uk

© Copyright in this edition including research, selection of documents, arrangement, contents lists and descriptions: Cambridge Archive Editions Ltd 2009

Cambridge Archive Editions is an imprint of Cambridge University Press.

Facsimiles of original documents including Crown copyright material are published under licence from The National Archives, London, England. Images may be used only for purposes of research, private study or education. Applications for any other use should be made to The National Archives Image Library, Kew, Richmond, Surrey TW9 4DU. Infringement of the above condition may result in legal action.

Subject to statutory exception and to the provisions of relevant collective licensing agreements, no reproduction of other parts of the work may take place without written permission of Cambridge University Press.

Every reasonable effort has been made to contact all copyright holders; in the event of any omission please contact the publisher.

First published 2009

Printed and bound by CPI Group (UK) Ltd, Croydon, CR0 4YY

British Library Cataloguing in Publication Data
Land Legislation in Mandate Palestine.
  1. Land tenure–Law and legislation–Palestine–History–
  20th century. 2. Land tenure–Law and legislation–
  Palestine–History–20th century–Sources. 3. Palestine–
  Politics and government–1917-1948.
  I. Bunton, Martin P.
  346.5'6940432-dc22

ISBN-13: 978-1-84097-260-3 (set) (hardback)
          978-1-84097-261-0 (volume 4)

Land Legislation in Mandate Palestine

CONTENTS

VOLUME 4, PART I:

ORDERS-IN-COUNCIL

Section 1 1

The Palestine Order-in-Council 1922, as amended by the Palestine (Amendment) Order-in-Council, 1923
Norman De Mattos Bentwich, *Legislation of Palestine, 1918–1925. Including the orders-in-council, ordinances, public notices, proclamations, regulations, etc., v. 1 Orders-in-council and ordinances.* (Alexandria, Whitehead Morris Limited, 1926, pp. 1–22)

VOLUME 4, PART II:

ORDINANCES, PUBLIC NOTICES, PROCLAMATIONS AND REGULATIONS

Section 1: 1918 25

Customs, taxes, tithes, etc., public notice, 27th February 1918
Government of Palestine, *Ordinances and Public Notices etc. issued by the Military Authorities and the Government of Palestine prior to January 1921.* (Jerusalem, Goldberg's Press, 1921, p. 126)

Proclamation organizing the courts, 24th June 1919
Norman De Mattos Bentwich, *Legislation of Palestine, 1918–1925. Including the orders-in-council, ordinances, public notices, proclamations, regulations, etc., v. 1 Orders-in-council and ordinances.* (Alexandria, Whitehead Morris Limited, 1926, pp. 605–610)

Proclamation establishing the courts in the sanjaks of Acre and Nablus, 1st November 1918
Norman De Mattos Bentwich, *Legislation of Palestine, 1918–1925. Including the orders-in-council, ordinances, public notices, proclamations, regulations, etc., v. 1 Orders-in-council and ordinances.* (Alexandria, Whitehead Morris Limited, 1926, pp. 612–613)

Proclamation prohibiting land transactions in the sanjak of Jerusalem, 1st November 1918
Norman De Mattos Bentwich, *Legislation of Palestine, 1918–1925. Including the orders-in-council, ordinances, public notices, proclamations, regulations, etc., v. 1 Orders-in-council and ordinances.* (Alexandria, Whitehead Morris Limited, 1926, pp. 613–615)

Proclamation prohibiting land transactions in the sanjaks of Acre and Nablus, 18th November 1918
Norman De Mattos Bentwich, *Legislation of Palestine, 1918–1925. Including the orders-in-council, ordinances, public notices, proclamations, regulations, etc., v. 1 Orders-in-council and ordinances.* (Alexandria, Whitehead Morris Limited, 1926, pp. 617–618)

Agricultural loans ordinance, 30th November 1918
Norman De Mattos Bentwich, *Legislation of Palestine, 1918–1925. Including the orders-in-council, ordinances, public notices, proclamations, regulations, etc., v. 1 Orders-in-council and ordinances.* (Alexandria, Whitehead Morris Limited, 1926, pp. 618–620)

Section 2: 1919 — 43

Transfer of land, public notice, 30th April 1919
Government of Palestine, *Ordinances and Public Notices etc. issued by the Military Authorities and the Government of Palestine prior to January 1921.* (Jerusalem, Goldberg's Press, 1921, p. 90)

Expropriation of land, public notice, 20th May 1919
Government of Palestine, *Ordinances and Public Notices etc. issued by the Military Authorities and the Government of Palestine prior to January 1921.* (Jerusalem, Goldberg's Press, 1921, p. 97)

Section 3: 1920 — 49

Leasing of state domains, 23rd January 1920
Government of Palestine, *Ordinances and Public Notices etc. issued by the Military Authorities and the Government of Palestine prior to January 1921.* (Jerusalem, Goldberg's Press, 1921, p. 98)

Cadastral survey ordinance, May 1920
Government of Palestine, *Ordinances and Public Notices etc. issued by the Military Authorities and the Government of Palestine prior to January 1921.* (Jerusalem, Goldberg's Press, 1921, pp. 124–125)

Land commission, public notice, 1st September 1920
Government of Palestine, *Ordinances and Public Notices etc. issued by the Military Authorities and the Government of Palestine prior to January 1921.* (Jerusalem, Goldberg's Press, 1921, p. 85)

Land transfer ordinance, September 1920
Moses Doukhan, ed., *Laws of Palestine, 1918–1925: Including the orders-in-council, ordinances, regulations, rules of court, public notices, proclamations, etc.* (Tel-Aviv, L.M. Rotenberg, 1933, pp. 297–301)

Acquisition of land for the army ordinance, 21st September 1920
Norman De Mattos Bentwich, *Legislation of Palestine, 1918–1925.*
Including the orders-in-council, ordinances, public notices, proclamations, regulations, etc., v. 1 Orders-in-council and ordinances. (Alexandria, Whitehead Morris Limited, 1926, pp. 644–646)

Correction of the land registers ordinance, 23rd September 1920. [As amended by correction of land registers (amendment) ordinance dated 27th September 1921 and by no.17 of 1922]
Norman De Mattos Bentwich, *Legislation of Palestine, 1918–1925.*
Including the orders-in-council, ordinances, public notices, proclamations, regulations, etc., v. 1 Orders-in-council and ordinances. (Alexandria, Whitehead Morris Limited, 1926, pp. 647–649)

Mahlul land ordinance, 1st October 1920
Government of Palestine, *Ordinances and Public Notices etc. issued by the Military Authorities and the Government of Palestine prior to January 1921.* (Jerusalem, Goldberg's Press, 1921, p. 93)

Woods and forests ordinance, October 1920
Norman De Mattos Bentwich, *Legislation of Palestine, 1918–1925.*
Including the orders-in-council, ordinances, public notices, proclamations, regulations, etc., v. 1 Orders-in-council and ordinances. (Alexandria, Whitehead Morris Limited, 1926, pp. 93–102)

Section 4: 1921 81

Mewat land ordinance, 16th February 1921
Norman De Mattos Bentwich, *Legislation of Palestine, 1918–1925.*
Including the orders-in-council, ordinances, public notices, proclamations, regulations, etc., v. 1 Orders-in-council and ordinances. (Alexandria, Whitehead Morris Limited, 1926, pp. 135–136)

Transfer of land ordinance, no. 2 of 1921, 4th April 1921
Moses Doukhan, ed., *Laws of Palestine, 1918–1925: Including the orders-in-council, ordinances, regulations, rules of court, public notices, proclamations, etc.* (Tel-Aviv, L.M. Rotenberg, 1933, pp. 301–302)

Land courts ordinance, 8th April 1921
Norman De Mattos Bentwich, *Legislation of Palestine, 1918–1925.*
Including the orders-in-council, ordinances, public notices, proclamations, regulations, etc., v. 1 Orders-in-council and ordinances. (Alexandria, Whitehead Morris Limited, 1926, pp. 150–152)

Surveyors' ordinance, 10th May 1921
Norman De Mattos Bentwich, *Legislation of Palestine, 1918–1925.*
Including the orders-in-council, ordinances, public notices, proclamations, regulations, etc., v. 1 Orders-in-council and ordinances. (Alexandria, Whitehead Morris Limited, 1926, pp. 653–654)

Demarcation of government lands, public notice, 10th November 1921
Norman De Mattos Bentwich, *Legislation of Palestine, 1918–1925. Including the orders-in-council, ordinances, public notices, proclamations, regulations, etc., v. 2 Regulations, public notices, proclamations, rules of court, agreements, and the royal instructions.* (Alexandria, Whitehead Morris Limited, 1926, pp. 397–398)

Transfer of land amendment ordinance, no. 2 of 1921, 8th December 1921
Moses Doukhan, ed., *Laws of Palestine, 1918–1925: Including the orders-in-council, ordinances, regulations, rules of court, public notices, proclamations, etc.* (Tel-Aviv, L.M. Rotenberg, 1933, pp. 302–303)

Section 5: 1922   97

Sand drifts ordinance, no. 15 of 1922
[CO 765/1]

Correction of land registers ordinance, no. 17 of 1922
[CO 765/1]

Land valuers ordinance, no. 18 of 1922
[CO 765/1]

Credit banks ordinance, no. 21 of 1922
[CO 765/1]

Section 6: 1923   121

Succession ordinance no. 4 of 1923
[CO 765/1]

Regulations governing assessment of tithes, July 1923
[CO 765/1]

Department of lands, notice, 18th July 1923
Moses Doukhan, ed., *Laws of Palestine, 1918–1925: Including the orders-in-council, ordinances, regulations, rules of court, public notices, proclamations, etc.* (Tel-Aviv, L.M. Rotenberg, 1933, p. 297)

Tax on land owned by companies, public notice
[CO 765/1]

Section 7: 1924   155

Expropriation of land ordinance, no. 5 of 1924
[CO 765/2]

Railway lands vesting ordinance, no. 17 of 1924, with order promulgating ordinances nos. 16, 17, 18 and 19 of 1924
[CO 765/2]

Charitable trusts ordinance, no. 26 of 1924
[CO 765/2]

Land courts ordinance, 1921, order 1924, with further amendment
[CO 765/2]

Woods and forests ordinance, 1920, order 1924
[CO 765/2]

Section 8: 1925   185

Jurisdiction of civil and religious courts, no. 3 of 1925
[CO 765/3]

Acquisition of land for the army and air force, no. 12 of 1925
[CO 765/3]

Land surveyors ordinance no. 14 of 1925
[CO 765/3]

Charitable trusts (amendment) ordinance, no. 24 of 1925
[CO 765/3]

Section 9: 1926   213

Forests ordinance, no. 5 of 1926
[CO 765/3]

Correction of land registers ordinance, no. 12 of 1926
[CO 765/3]

Public lands ordinance, no. 14 of 1926
[CO 765/3]

Expropriation of land ordinance, no. 28 of 1926
[CO 765/3]

Correction of land registers (amendment) ordinance, no. 42 of 1926
[CO 765/3]

Section 10: 1927   247

Commutation of tithes ordinance, no. 49 of 1927
[CO 765/3]

Section 11: 1928   257

Weights and measures ordinance, no. 2 of 1928
[CO 765/4]

Forests amendment ordinance, no. 8 of 1928
[CO 765/4]

Land settlement ordinance, no. 9 of 1928
[CO 765/4]

Commutation of tithes (amendment) ordinance, no. 27 of 1928
[CO 765/4]

Section 12: 1929   297

Land courts amendment ordinance, no. 7 of 1929
[CO 765/4]

Exemption from tithe ordinance, no. 13 of 1929
[CO 765/4]

Protection of cultivators ordinance, no. 27 of 1929
[CO 765/4]

Registration of land ordinance, no. 28 of 1929
[CO 765/4]

Transfer of land amendment ordinance, no. 30 of 1929
[CO 765/4]

Survey ordinance, no. 48 of 1929
[CO 765/4]

Section 13: 1930   321

Collection of taxes (amendment) ordinance, no. 7 of 1930
[CO 765/4]

Land settlement (amendment) ordinance, no. 18 of 1930
[CO 765/4]

Section 14: 1931   333

Protection of cultivators (amendment) ordinance, no. 3 of 1931
[CO 765/4]

Section 15: 1932   339

Land disputes (possession) ordinance, no. 12 of 1932
[CO 765/5]

Protection of cultivators (amendment) ordinance (No.1), no. 16 of 1932
[CO 765/5]

Expropriation of land (amendment) ordinance, no. 24 of 1932
[CO 765/5]

Land settlement (amendment) ordinance, no. 33 of 1932
[CO 765/5]

Section 16: 1933   357

Land settlement (amendment) ordinance, no. 22 of 1933
[CO 765/5]

Land law (amendment) ordinance, no. 25 of 1933
[CO 765/5]

Weights and measures (amendment) ordinance, no. 36 of 1933
[CO 765/5]

Protection of cultivators ordinance, no. 37 of 1933
[CO 765/5]

Co-operative societies ordinance, no. 50 of 1933
[CO 765/5]

Section 17: 1934   413

Protection of cultivators (amendment) ordinance, no. 7 of 1934
[CO 765/6]

Collection of taxes (amendment) ordinance, no. 16 of 1934
[CO 765/6]

Land disputes (possession) (amendment) ordinance, no. 19 of 1934
[CO 765/6]

Section 18: 1935   425

Rural property tax ordinance, no. 1 of 1935
[CO 765/6]

Land settlement (amendment) ordinance, no. 25 of 1935
[CO 765/6]

Rural property tax (amendment) ordinance, no. 26 of 1935
[CO 765/6]

Expropriation of land (amendment) ordinance, no. 30 of 1935
[CO 765/6]

[No selection for 1936]

Section 19: 1937   461

Land transfer (amendment) ordinance, no. 20 of 1937
[CO 765/8]

Land law (amendment) ordinance, no. 34 of 1937
[CO 765/8]

Section 20: 1938 467

Land transfer (amendment) ordinance, no. 16 of 1938
[CO 765/8]

Section 21: 1939 471

Land transfer (amendment) ordinance, no. 1 of 1939
[CO 765/9]

Land transfer (amendment) ordinance, no. 39 of 1939
[CO 765/9]

Land courts (amendment) ordinance, no. 46 of 1939
[CO 765/9]

Land (settlement of title) ordinance, no. 48 of 1939
[CO 765/9]

Section 22: 1940 489

'Land Transfers Regulations, 1940', *Supplement No. 2 to the Palestine Gazette Extraordinary No. 988 of 28th February 1940.* [Maps reproduced in facsimile in the Map Box.] [CO 733/418/12]

Section 23: 1941 507

Land transfer (fees) rules (amendment) ordinance, no. 11 of 1941
[CO 765/9]

Land law (amendment) ordinance, no. 39 of 1941
[CO 765/9]

Section 24: 1942 513

Rural property tax ordinance, no. 5 of 1942
[CO 765/10]

Public lands ordinance, no. 6 of 1942
[CO 765/10]

Forests (amendment) ordinance, no. 7 of 1942
[CO 765/10]

Land (settlement of title) (amendment) ordinance, no. 12 of 1942
[CO 765/10]

Land courts (amendment) ordinance, no. 14 of 1942
[CO 765/10]

Section 25: 1943 553

Land transfer (amendment) ordinance, no. 13 of 1943
[CO 765/10]

Land (acquisition for public purposes) ordinance, no. 24 of 1943
[CO 765/10]

Section 26: 1944 567

Rural property tax (amendment) ordinance, no. 11 of 1944
[CO 765/10]

Land (settlement of title) (amendment) ordinance, no. 18 of 1944
[CO 765/10]

Village administration ordinance, no. 23 of 1944
[CO 765/10]

Weights and measures ordinance, no. 24 of 1944
[CO 765/10]

Land registers ordinance, no. 30 of 1944
[CO 765/10]

Land courts (amendment) ordinance, no. 39 of 1944
[CO 765/10]

Section 27: 1945 613

Rural property tax (amendment) ordinance, no. 8 of 1945
[CO 765/10]

Land transfer (fees) rules (amendment) ordinance, no. 34 of 1945
[CO 765/10]

PART I : ORDERS-IN-COUNCIL

Section 1

THE PALESTINE ORDER-IN-COUNCIL, 1922,

AS AMENDED BY THE

PALESTINE (AMENDMENT) ORDER-IN-COUNCIL, 1923.

WHEREAS the Principal Allied Powers have agreed, for the purpose of giving effect to the provisions of Article 22 of the Covenant of the League of Nations, to entrust to a Mandatory selected by the said Powers the administration of the territory of Palestine, which formerly belonged to the Turkish Empire, within such boundaries as may be fixed by them;

And whereas the Principal Allied Powers have also agreed that the Mandatory should be responsible for putting into effect the declaration originally made on November 2, 1917, by the Government of His Britannic Majesty, and adopted by the said Powers, in favour of the establishment in Palestine of a national home for the Jewish people, it being clearly understood that nothing should be done which might prejudice the civil and religious rights of existing non-Jewish communities in Palestine, or the rights and political status enjoyed by Jews in any other country;

And whereas the Principal Allied Powers have selected His Majesty as the Mandatory for Palestine;

And whereas, by treaty, capitulation, grant, usage, sufferance and other lawful means, His Majesty has power and jurisdiction within Palestine.

Now, therefore, His Majesty, by virtue and in exercise of the powers in this behalf by the Foreign Jurisdiction Act, 1890, or otherwise, in His Majesty vested, is pleased by and with the advice of His Privy Council, to order, and it is hereby ordered as follows :—

PART I.

PRELIMINARY.

Title.

1. This Order may be cited as " The Palestine Order-in-Council, 1922."

The limits of this Order are the territories to which the Mandate for Palestine applies, hereinafter described as Palestine.

Definitions.

2. In this Order the word :—

" Secretary of State " means one of His Majesty's Principal Secretaries of State.

" The High Commissioner " shall include every person for the time being administering the Government of Palestine.

" Public Lands " means all lands in Palestine which are subject to the control of the Government of Palestine by virtue of Treaty, convention, agreement or succession, and all lands which are or shall be acquired for the public service or otherwise.

" The Mandate " means the Mandate for Palestine which was confirmed, and the terms of which were defined by the Council of the League of Nations on the 24th day of July, 1922.

" The High Commissioner in Council " means the High Commissioner acting by and with the advice of the Executive Council.

" Gazette " means the Official Gazette of Palestine.

" Person " includes corporation.

Words importing the plural or the singular may be construed as referring to one person or thing or to more than one person or thing, and words importing the masculine as referring to females (as the case may require).

Interpretation.

3.—(1) Where this Order or any Ordinance confers a power or imposes a duty, then, unless a contrary intention appears, the power may be exercised and the duty shall be performed from time to time as occasion requires.

(2) Where this Order or any Ordinance confers a power or imposes a duty on the holder of an office, then, unless a contrary intention appears, the power may be exercised and the duty shall be performed by the holder of the office for the time being or by a person duly appointed to act for him.

(3) Where this Order or any Ordinance confers a power to make rules, regulations or orders, then, unless a contrary intention appears, the power shall be construed as including a power, exercisable in the like manner and subject to the like approval and conditions (if any) to rescind, revoke, amend or vary the rules, regulations or orders.

(4) Expressions defined in this Order shall have the same respective meaning in any Ordinances, rules or regulations made under this Order, unless a contrary intention appears.

PART II.

EXECUTIVE.

4. His Majesty may, by a Commission under His Sign Manual and Signet, appoint a fit person to administer the Government of Palestine under the designation of High Commissioner and Commander-in-Chief or such other designation as His Majesty thinks fit, and the person so appointed is hereinafter referred to as the High Commissioner. Office of High Commissioner.

5. The High Commissioner shall do and execute in due manner all things that shall belong to the said office, according to the tenour of any Orders-in-Council relating to Palestine and of such Commission as may be issued to him under His Majesty's Sign Manual and Signet, and according to such instructions as may from time to time be given to him, for the purpose of executing the provisions of the Mandate, under His Majesty's Sign Manual and Signet, or by Order of His Majesty in Council or by His Majesty through one of His Principal Secretaries of State, and to such laws and ordinances as are now or shall hereafter be in force in Palestine. Powers of High Commissioner.

6. Every person appointed to fill the Office of High Commissioner shall, with all due solemnity, before entering on any of the duties of his office, cause the Commission appointing him to be High Commissioner to be read and published in the presence of the Chief Justice, or if the Chief Justice is not able to attend, in the presence of such other of His Majesty's Officers in Palestine as can conveniently attend, which being done, he shall then and there take before him or them the Oath of Allegiance in the form provided by an Act passed in the Session holden in the Thirty-first and Thirty-second years of the Reign of Her Majesty Queen Victoria, entitled, "An Act to amend the Law relating to Promissory Oaths," and likewise the usual oaths for the due execution of the Office of High Commissioner and for the due and impartial administration of justice, which oaths the said Chief Justice, or some other of His Majesty's Officers then present, is hereby required to administer. Publication of High Commissioner's Commission.

Succession to Government.	7. Whenever the office of High Commissioner is vacant, or if the High Commissioner become incapable, or be absent from Palestine, or be from any cause prevented from acting in the duties of his office, the person appointed to be Chief Secretary to the Government of Palestine, or if there be no such officer therein, or such officer be unable to act, then such person or persons as His Majesty may appoint under His Sign Manual and Signet and in default of such appointment the Senior Member of the Executive Council shall during His Majesty's pleasure administer the Government of Palestine, first taking the oaths hereinbefore directed to be taken by the High Commissioner and in the manner herein prescribed, which being done, the Chief Secretary or any other such Administrator as aforesaid is hereby authorised, empowered and commanded to do and execute during His Majesty's pleasure, all things that belong to the office of the High Commissioner according to the tenour of this Order, and according to His Majesty's Instructions as aforesaid, and the laws of Palestine.
Administrator.	
Oaths to be taken by the Administrator.	

Provided that the High Commissioner during his passage by sea from one part of Palestine to another, or when, in the exercise or discharge of any powers or duties by this Order in Council or otherwise conferred or imposed upon him, he is in any territories adjacent to or near to Palestine, shall not be considered to be absent from Palestine.

Appointment of Deputy to High Commissioner.	8. In the event of the High Commissioner having occasion at any time to be temporarily absent for a short period from the seat of Government, or, in the exercise or discharge of any powers or duties conferred or imposed upon him by His Majesty, or through one of His Majesty's Principal Secretaries of State, to visit any territories adjacent to or near to Palestine, he may by an instrument under the Public Seal of Palestine appoint the Chief Secretary, or if there be no such Officer or such Officer is absent or unable to act, then any other person to be his Deputy within any part of Palestine, during such temporary absence and in that capacity to exercise, perform and execute, for and on behalf of the High Commissioner during such absence but no longer, all such powers and authorities vested in the High Commissioner (except the power of pardon), as shall in and by such instruments be specified and limited, but no others. Every such Deputy shall conform to and observe all such instructions as the High Commissioner shall from time to time address to him for his guidance. Provided nevertheless that by the appointment of a Deputy as aforesaid the power and authority of the High Commissioner shall not be abridged, altered, or in any way affected otherwise than His Majesty may at any time think proper to direct.

9. The High Commissioner shall keep and use the Public Seal of Palestine for the sealing of all things whatsoever that shall pass the said Public Seal. *Public Seal.*

10. There shall be for the purpose of assisting the High Commissioner an Executive Council, which shall be composed of such persons and constituted in such manner as may be directed by any instructions which may from time to time be addressed to the High Commissioner by His Majesty under His Majesty's Sign Manual and Signet, and all such persons shall hold their places in the said Council during His Majesty's pleasure; and the said Executive Council shall observe such Rules in the conduct of business as may from time to time be contained in any such Instructions as aforesaid. *Executive Council.*

11. (1) The High Commissioner may, with the approval of a Secretary of State, by Proclamation divide Palestine into administrative divisions or districts in such manner and with such sub-divisions as may be convenient for purposes of administration, describing the boundaries thereof and assigning names thereto. *Definition of boundaries, formation of districts, etc.*

(2) If a question arises whether any place is or is not within any administrative division or district, and such question does not appear to be determined by any such Proclamation or other evidence, it shall be referred to the High Commissioner, and a certificate under his hand and seal shall be conclusive on the question and judicial notice shall be taken thereof.

12. (1) All rights in or in relation to any public lands shall vest in and may be exercised by the High Commissioner for the time being in trust for the Government of Palestine. *Public Lands.*

(2) All mines and minerals of every kind and description whatsoever being in, under, or on any land or water, whether the latter be inland rivers or seas or territorial waters, shall vest in the High Commissioner, subject to any right subsisting at the date of this Order of any person to work such mines or minerals by virtue of a valid concession.

13. The High Commissioner may make grants or leases of any such public land or mines or minerals or may permit such lands to be temporarily occupied on such terms or conditions as he may think fit subject to the provisions of any Ordinance. *High Commissioner empowered to make grants of land.*

Provided that such grant or disposition shall be in conformity either with some Order-in-Council or Law or Ordinance now or hereafter in force in Palestine, or with such instructions as may be addressed to the High Commissioner under His Majesty's Sign Manual and Signet, or through a Secretary of State, for the purposes of executing the provisions of the Mandate.

Appointment of officers.	14. The High Commissioner may, subject to the direction of the Secretary of State, appoint or authorise the appointment of such public officers of the Government of Palestine under such designations as he may think fit, and may prescribe their duties; and all such public officers, unless otherwise provided by law, shall hold their offices during the pleasure of the High Commissioner.
Suspension of public officers.	15. The High Commissioner may, subject to such instructions as may from time to time be given to him, upon sufficient cause to him appearing, dismiss or suspend from the exercise of his office any person holding any public office within Palestine, or subject as aforesaid, may take such other disciplinary action as may seem to him desirable.
Grant of pardon	16. When any crime or offence has been committed within Palestine, or for which the offender may be tried therein, the High Commissioner may, as he shall see occasion, grant a pardon to any accomplice in such crime or offence who shall give such information and evidence as shall lead to the conviction of the principal offender or of any such offenders if more than one; and further may grant to any offender convicted of any crime or offence in any Court or before any Judge, or Magistrate, within Palestine a pardon, either free or subject to lawful conditions, or any remission of such sentence passed on such offender, or any respite of the execution of the sentence, for such period as the High Commissioner thinks fit, and may, as he shall see occasion, remit any fines, penalties or forfeitures which may accrue or become payable in virtue of the judgment of any Court or Magistrate in Palestine.
Remission of fines.	

PART III.

LEGISLATURE.

Promulgation of Ordinances.	17. (1) (a) The High Commissioner shall have full power and authority, without prejudice to the powers inherent in or reserved by this Order to His Majesty and subject always to any conditions and limitations prescribed by any such instructions as may be given to him under the Sign Manual and Signet or through a Secretary of State, to promulgate such Ordinances as may be necessary for the peace, order, and good government of Palestine, provided that no Ordinance shall be promulgated which shall restrict complete freedom of conscience and the free exercise of all forms of worship save in so far as is required for the maintenance of public order and morals, or which shall tend to discriminate in any way between the inhabitants of Palestine on the ground of race, religion, or language.

(b) No Ordinance shall be promulgated by the High Commissioner until he has consulted the Advisory Council, as constituted on the date of the commencement of this Order, or such other advisory body as may after that date from time to time be constituted by him with the approval of a Secretary of State.

(c) No Ordinance shall be promulgated which shall be in any way repugnant to or inconsistent with the provisions of the Mandate, and no Ordinance which concerns matters dealt with specifically by the provisions of the Mandate shall be promulgated until a draft thereof has been communicated to a Secretary of State and approved by him, with or without amendment.

(d) No Ordinance shall be promulgated unless a draft of the same shall first have been made public for one calendar month at the least before the enactment thereof, unless immediate promulgation shall, in the judgment of the High Commissioner, be indispensably necessary in the public interest.

(e) His Majesty reserves to himself the right to disallow an Ordinance promulgated by the High Commissioner within one year of the date of promulgation, and to signify such disallowance through a Secretary of State. Every such disallowance shall take effect from the time when it shall be promulgated by the High Commissioner by notice in the Gazette.

(2) From and after a date to be fixed by the High Commissioner in Executive Council, by Proclamation in the Gazette, there shall be constituted a Legislative Council in and for Palestine as in this Order provided, and any advisory body then existing shall be dissolved. The powers of the High Commissioner as defined and limited by Clause (1) of this Article shall continue in force until a Legislative Council as provided above shall have been duly constituted, when Articles 18 to 34 of this Order shall apply.

18. The Legislative Council shall have full power and authority, without prejudice to the powers inherent in, or reserved by this Order to, His Majesty, and subject always to any conditions and limitations prescribed by any Instructions under the Sign Manual and Signet, to establish such Ordinance as may be necessary for the peace, order, and good government of Palestine, provided that no Ordinance shall be passed which shall restrict complete freedom of conscience and the free exercise of all forms of worship, save in so far as is required for the maintenance of public order and morals; or which shall tend to discriminate in any way between the inhabitants of Palestine on the ground of race, religion or language.

Powers of Legislative Council.

No Ordinance shall be passed which shall be in any way repugnant to or inconsistent with the provisions of the Mandate.

Constitution of Legislative Council.	19. The Legislative Council shall consist of 22 members in addition to the High Commissioner, of whom 10 shall be official members and 12 shall be unofficial members.
Official Members.	20. The official members of the Council shall be:—

The persons for the time being lawfully exercising the functions of the respective offices of—
- (a) Chief Secretary,
- (b) Attorney-General,
- (c) Treasurer,
- (d) Inspector-General of Police,
- (e) Director of Health,
- (f) Director of Public Works,
- (g) Director of Education,
- (h) Director of Agriculture,
- (i) Director of Customs,
- (j) Director of Commerce and Industry;

provided that if the High Commissioner is satisfied that any of the above persons is unable to attend a meeting of the Council he may summon in his place such other person holding public office in the Government of Palestine as he thinks fit, and such person shall for the purposes of that meeting be deemed to be an official member of the Council.

Unofficial Members.	21. The unofficial members of the Council shall be:—

Twelve persons to be elected in accordance with such Order-in-Council, Ordinance or other legislative enactment as may from time to time provide for elections to the Council.

Prorogation and dissolution of the Council.	22. The High Commissioner may at any time by Proclamation prorogue or dissolve the Council. The High Commissioner shall dissolve the Council at the expiration of three years from the date of the first meeting thereof.
General elections.	23. The first general election of members of the Legislative Council shall be held at such time not more than six months after the publication of the proclamation referred to in Article 17 (2) of this Order as the High Commissioner shall by Proclamation appoint. Within three months after the dissolution of the Council a date shall be fixed by the High Commissioner in Executive Council by Proclamation in the Gazette for the immediate holding of a general election.
No Ordinance to take effect until assented to.	24. No Ordinance shall take effect until either the High Commissioner shall have assented thereto and shall have signed the same in token of such assent, or until the assent of His Majesty thereto has been given by Order-in-Council or through a Secretary of State.

25. Subject to the provisions of the following Article, the High Commissioner may, according to his discretion and subject to any Instructions under the Sign Manual and Signet, declare that he assents to any Ordinance, or refuse his assent to the same. Assent to Ordinances.

26. The High Commissioner may reserve for the signification of the pleasure of His Majesty any Ordinance passed by the Legislative Council, and shall in any case so reserve any Ordinance which concerns matters dealt with specifically by the provisions of the Mandate. Reserved Ordinances.

An Ordinance so reserved shall take effect so soon as His Majesty has given his assent thereto either by Order-in-Council or through a Secretary of State, and the High Commissioner shall have signified such assent by notice in the Gazette.

27. His Majesty reserves to himself the right to disallow an Ordinance to which the High Commissioner has assented within one year of the date of the High Commissioner's assent thereto and to signify such disallowance through a Secretary of State. Every such disallowance shall take effect from the time when it shall be promulgated by the High Commissioner by notice in the Gazette. Disallowance of Ordinances.

28. No vote, resolution, or Ordinance for the appropriation of any part of the public revenue, or for the imposition of any tax or impost shall be proposed except by the High Commissioner, or by his direction. Financial measures.

29. The High Commissioner, or in his absence the Chief Secretary, or, in the absence of both the High Commissioner and Chief Secretary, some Member elected by the Council shall preside at the meetings thereof. President.

30. The Council shall not be disqualified from the transaction of business on account of any vacancies among the Members thereof, but it shall not be competent to proceed to the despatch of business unless ten Members be present. Quorum.

31. Every Member of the Legislative Council shall, before being permitted to sit or vote therein, take and subscribe the following oath before the President :— Oath to be taken by Members of Legislature.

> "I, A.B., do swear that I will be faithful and loyal to the Government of Palestine. So help me God."

Provided that any person authorised to make a solemn affirmation or declaration instead of taking an Oath may make such affirmation or declaration in lieu of such Oath.

Questions to be decided by majority of votes.	32. All questions in the Legislative Council shall be determined by a majority of the votes of Members present, including the President, or presiding Member, who shall in addition have and exercise a casting vote in case of an equality of votes.
Standing Rules and Orders.	33. The Legislative Council in its first Session, and from time to time afterwards as there shall be occasion, shall adopt Standing Rules and Orders, for the regulation and orderly conduct of its proceedings and the despatch of business, and for the passing, intituling and numbering of Ordinances and for the presentation of the same to the High Commissioner for his assent.

All such Rules and Orders shall be laid before the High Commissioner in Council, and being by him approved shall become binding and of force.

Privileges of Members.	34. It shall be lawful for the Council by Ordinance to define the privileges, immunities, and powers to be held enjoyed and exercised by the Council and the members thereof.

PART IV.

APPLICATION OF CERTAIN BRITISH STATUTES.

Foreign Jurisdiction Act, 1890.	35. The enactments in the First Schedule to the Foreign Jurisdiction Act, 1890, shall apply to Palestine, but subject to the provisions of this Order and to the exceptions, adaptations, and modifications following, that is to say :—

    (a) The High Commissioner is hereby substituted for the Governor of a Colony or British Possession, and the District Court is hereby substituted for a Superior Court or Supreme Court and for a Magistrate or Justice of the Peace of a Colony or British Possession.

    (b) For the portions of the Merchant Shipping Acts, 1854 and 1867, referred to in the said Schedule, shall be substituted Part XIII of the Merchant Shipping Act, 1894.

    (c) In Section 51 of the Conveyancing (Scotland) Act, 1874, and any enactment for the time being in force amending the same, the District Court is substituted for a Court of Probate in a Colony.

    (d) With respect to the Fugitive Offenders Act, 1881—

        (i) So much of the 4th, and 5th sections of the said Act as relates to sending a report of the issue of a warrant, together with the information, or a copy thereof, or to the sending of a certificate of committal and report of a case, or to the information to be given by a Magistrate to a fugitive, shall be excepted, and in lieu of such information the person acting as the Magistrate shall inform the fugitive that in the British Possession or Protectorate to which he may be conveyed he has the right to apply for a writ of *habeas corpus* or other like process.

(ii) So much of the 6th section of the said Act as requires the expiration of fifteen days before issue of warrant shall be excepted.

(iii) The High Commissioner shall not be bound to return a fugitive offender to a British Possession, unless satisfied that the proceedings to obtain his return are taken with the consent of the Governor of that Possession.

(iv) For the purposes of Part II of the said Act, Palestine, Cyprus, Egypt, the Ottoman Dominions, Persia, and Iraq shall be treated as one group of British Possessions.

Provided that nothing in this Article contained shall be taken to extend to Palestine the enactments mentioned in the Schedule to the Foreign Jurisdiction Act, 1913, or any of them.

36. Where under the Merchant Shipping Act, 1894, or any amending Act, anything is authorised to be done by, to, or before a British Consular officer, such thing may be done, in any place in Palestine by, to, or before such officer of the Government as the High Commissioner may appoint. [Acts done under Merchant Shipping Act, 1894.]

37. The Colonial Prisoners' Removal Act, 1884, shall apply to and take effect within Palestine as if it were part of His Majesty's dominions, subject as follows:— [Application of Colonial Prisoners' Removal Act, 1884.]

The High Commissioner is hereby substituted for the Governor of a British Possession.

PART V.

JUDICIARY.

38. The Civil Courts hereinafter described shall, subject to the provisions of this part of the Order, exercise jurisdiction in all matters and over all persons in Palestine. [Civil Courts.]

39. Magistrates' Courts shall be established in each district and sub-district as may be prescribed from time to time by Order under the hand of the High Commissioner. These Courts shall have the jurisdiction assigned to them by the Ottoman Magistrates Law of 1913, as amended by any subsequent law or Ordinance or Rules for the time being in force. [Magistrates' Courts.]

District Courts. 40. District Courts shall be established in such districts as may be prescribed from time to time by order under the hand of the High Commissioner, and every such court shall exercise jurisdiction—
(1) As a Court of First Instance :—
(a) In all civil matters not within the jurisdiction of the Magistrates' Courts in and for that district.
(b) In all criminal matters which are not within the jurisdiction of the Court of Criminal Assize.
(2) As an Appellate Court from the said Magistrates' Courts subject to the provisions of any Ordinances or Rules.

Court of Criminal Assize. 41. There shall be a Court of Criminal Assize which shall have exclusive jurisdiction with regard to offences punishable with death and such jurisdiction with regard to other offences as may be prescribed by Ordinances.

Land Courts. 42. The High Commissioner may by order establish Land Courts as may be required from time to time for the hearing of such questions concerning the title to immovable property as may be prescribed.

Supreme Court. 43. There shall be established a Court to be called the Supreme Court of which the constitution shall be prescribed by Ordinance. The Supreme Court sitting as a Court of Appeal shall have jurisdiction, subject to the provisions of any Ordinance, to hear appeals from all judgments given by a District Court in first instance or by the Court of Criminal Assize or by a Land Court.

The Supreme Court sitting as a High Court of Justice, shall have jurisdiction to hear and determine such matters as are not causes or trials, but petitions or applications not within the jurisdiction of any other Court and necessary to be decided for the administration of justice.

Appeal to Privy Council. 44. In civil matters when the amount or value in dispute exceeds £E.500 an appeal shall lie from the Supreme Court to His Majesty in Council. Every appeal shall be brought within such time and in such manner as may be prescribed by any rules of procedure made by His Majesty in Council.

Tribal Courts. 45. The High Commissioner may by order establish such separate Courts for the district of Beersheba and for such other tribal areas as he may think fit. Such courts may apply tribal custom, so far as it is not repugnant to natural justice or morality.

Law to be applied. 46. The jurisdiction of the Civil Courts shall be exercised in conformity with the Ottoman Law in force in Palestine on November 1st, 1914, and such later Ottoman Laws as have been or may be declared to be in force by Public Notice, and such Orders-in-Council, Ordinances, and regulations as are in force in Palestine at the date of the commencement of this Order, or may hereafter be applied or enacted; and subject thereto and so far as the same shall not extend or apply, shall be exercised in conformity with the substance of the common law, and the doctrines of equity in force in England, and with the powers vested in and according to the procedure and practice observed by or before Courts of Justice and Justices of the Peace in England, according to their respective jurisdictions and authorities at that date, save in so far as the said powers, procedure, and practice may have been or may hereafter be modified, amended, or replaced by any other provisions. Provided always that the said common law and doctrines of equity shall be in force in Palestine so far only as the circumstances of Palestine and its inhabitants and the limits of His Majesty's jurisdiction permit and subject to such qualification as local circumstances render necessary.

47. The Civil Courts shall further have jurisdiction, subject to the provisions contained in this Part of this Order, in matters of personal status, as defined in Article 51, of persons in Palestine. Such jurisdiction shall be exercised in conformity with any law, Ordinances or regulations, that may hereafter be applied or enacted and subject thereto according to the personal law applicable. *(Jurisdiction in personal status.)*

Where in any civil or criminal cause brought before the Civil Court a question of personal status incidentally arises, the determination of which is necessary for the purposes of the cause, the Civil Court may determine the question, and may to that end take the opinion, by such means as may seem most convenient, of a competent jurist having knowledge of the personal law applicable.

48. When any person has been sentenced to death, the Chief Justice shall transmit to the High Commissioner a copy of the evidence. The sentence shall not be carried into effect until confirmed by the High Commissioner. *(Confirmation of death sentence.)*

49. The Chief Justice may, with the approval of the High Commissioner, make rules for regulating the practice and procedure of the Supreme Court and of all other Civil Courts which are or may be established in Palestine. *(Rules of Court.)*

50. No action shall be brought against the Government of Palestine or any Department thereof, unless with the written consent of the High Commissioner previously obtained. *(Actions against Government.)*

The Civil Courts shall not exercise any jurisdiction in any proceeding whatsoever over the High Commissioner or his official or other residence or his official or other property.

51. Subject to the provisions of Articles 64 to 67 inclusive, jurisdiction in matters of personal status shall be exercised in accordance with the provisions of this Part by the Courts of the religious communities established and exercising jurisdiction at the date of this *(Jurisdiction of Religious Courts.)*

Definition of personal status. Order. For the purpose of these provisions matters of personal status mean suits regarding marriage or divorce, alimony, maintenance, guardianship, legitimation and adoption of minors, inhibition from dealing with property of persons who are legally incompetent, successions, wills and legacies, and the administration of the property of absent persons.

Moslem Religious Courts. 52. Moslem Religious Courts shall have exclusive jurisdiction in matters of personal status of Moslems in accordance with the provisions of the Law of Procedure of the Moslem Religious Courts of the 25th October 1333, A.H., as amended by any Ordinance or Rules. They shall also have, subject to the provisions of any Ordinance or of the Order of the 20th December, 1921, establishing a Supreme Council for Moslem Religious Affairs, or of any Orders amending the same, exclusive jurisdiction in cases of the constitution or internal administration of a Wakf constituted for the benefit of Moslems before a Moslem Religious Court.

There shall be an appeal from the Court of the Qadi to the Moslem Religious Court of Appeal whose decision shall be final.

Jewish Religious Courts. 53. The Rabbinical Courts of the Jewish Community shall have:—
(a) Exclusive jurisdiction in matters of marriage and divorce, alimony and confirmation of wills of members of their community other than foreigners as defined in Article 59.
(b) Jurisdiction in any other matter of personal status of such persons, where all the parties to the action consent to their jurisdiction.
(c) Exclusive jurisdiction over any case as to the constitution or internal administration of a Wakf or religious endowment constituted before the Rabbinical Court according to Jewish Law.

Christian Religious Courts. 54. The Courts of the several Christian communities shall have:—
(a) Exclusive jurisdiction in matters of marriage and divorce, alimony, and confirmation of wills of members of their community other than foreigners as defined in Article 59.
(b) Jurisdiction in any other matters of personal status of such persons, where all the parties to the action consent to their jurisdiction.
(c) Exclusive jurisdiction over any case concerning the constitution or internal administration of a Wakf or religious endowment constituted before the Religious Court according to the religious law of the community, if such exists.

Conflicts of law and jurisdiction. 55. Where any action of personal status involves persons of different religious communities, application may be made by any party to the Chief Justice who shall, with the assistance, if he thinks fit of assessors from the communities concerned, decide which Court shall have jurisdiction. Whenever a question arises as to whether or not a case is one of personal status within the exclusive jurisdiction of a Religious Court, the matter shall be referred to a Special Tribunal of which the constitution shall be prescribed by Ordinance.

56. The judgments of the Religious Courts shall be executed by the process and offices of the Civil Courts. Execution of judgments of Religious Courts.

57. Subject to the provisions of any Ordinance or Order establishing a Supreme Council for Moslem Religious Affairs, the constitution and jurisdiction of Religious Courts established at the date of this Order may be varied by Ordinance or Order of the High Commissioner. Change in composition of Religious Courts.

58. The Civil Courts shall exercise jurisdiction over foreigners, subject to the following provisions :— Jurisdiction over foreign subjects.

59. For the purpose of this part of the Order the expression "foreigner" means any person who is a national or subject of a European or American State or of Japan, but shall not include : Definition of foreigner.
   (i) Native inhabitants of a territory protected by or administered under a mandate granted to a European State.
   (ii) Ottoman subjects.
   (iii) Persons who have lost Ottoman nationality and have not acquired any other nationality.
The term "subject" or "national" shall include corporations constituted under the law of a foreign State, and religious, or charitable bodies, or institutions wholly or mainly composed of the subjects or citizens of such a State.

60. A foreigner accused of an offence punishable with imprisonment for a term exceeding fifteen days, or a fine exceeding £E.5 may claim to be tried by a British Magistrate. Any foreigner sentenced to imprisonment by a Palestinian Magistrate for an offence for which he cannot claim to be tried by a British Magistrate, may appeal to the District Court. Right of foreigners to claim trial by British Magistrate and other privileges.

61. A foreigner accused of an offence which is not triable by a magistrate may claim that his interrogation during the preliminary investigation shall be undertaken, and the question of his release on bail and committal for trial shall be decided, by a British Magistrate.

A warrant of search of the house of a foreigner shall be issued only by a British Magistrate.

62. A foreigner committed by a Magistrate for trial before the District Court or the Court of Criminal Assize may claim that the

Court shall consist of a single British Judge or contain a majority of British Judges.

63. In a civil case tried whether in first instance or on appeal by the District Court, a foreigner may claim that at least one member of the Court shall be a British Judge. In civil and criminal cases heard by the Supreme Court in its appellate capacity a foreigner may claim that the Court shall contain a majority of British Judges.

<small>Matters of personal status.</small>

64.—(1) Matters of personal status affecting foreigners other than Moslems shall be decided by the District Courts which shall apply the personal law of the parties concerned in accordance with such regulations as may be made by the High Commissioner, provided always that the Courts shall have no jurisdiction to pronounce a decree of dissolution of marriage until an Ordinance is passed conferring such jurisdiction.

(2) The personal law shall be the law of the nationality of the foreigner concerned unless that law imports the law of his domicile, in which case the latter shall be applied.

(3) The District Court, in trying matters of personal status affecting foreigners shall be constituted by the British President sitting alone. In trying matters of personal status affecting foreigners other than British subjects, the President may invite the Consul or a representative of the Consulate of the foreigner concerned to sit as an assessor for the purpose of advising upon the personal law concerned. In case of an appeal from the judgment in such a case the Consul or representative of the Consulate of the foreigner concerned shall be entitled to sit as an assessor in the Court of Appeal.

<small>Right to refer case to Religious Court.</small>

65. Nothing in the preceding article shall be construed to prevent foreigners from consenting to such matters being tried by the Courts of the Religious Communities having jurisdiction in like matters affecting Palestinian citizens.

The Courts of the Religious Communities other than the Moslem Religious Courts shall not, however, have power to grant a decree of dissolution of marriage to a foreign subject.

<small>Claim to be foreigner.</small>

66. Persons claiming to be treated as foreigners who do not in a criminal case make their claim on first appearance and in a civil case either on first appearance or in the first written pleading delivered to the Court, whichever be the earlier, shall forfeit their right so to claim. Nevertheless the claim may be made on appeal notwithstanding that it has not been made on first instance.

The burden of proof that they are entitled to be treated as foreigners shall be upon persons claiming the right aforesaid.

67. Notwithstanding anything in this Part of this Order, a Consul in Palestine may execute such non-contentious measures in relation to the personal status of nationals of his State as the High Commissioner, with the approval of the Secretary of State, may from time to time prescribe by regulation. *Powers of Consuls reserved.*

PART VI.

REMOVAL AND DEPORTATION.

68. Where an offender convicted before any Court is sentenced to imprisonment, and the High Commissioner, proceeding under Section 7 of the Foreign Jurisdiction Act, 1890, authority in that behalf being hereby given to him, considers it expedient that the sentence should be carried into effect outside Palestine, the place shall be a place in some part of His Majesty's Dominions out of the United Kingdom, the Government whereof consent that offenders may be sent thither under this Article. *Removal of prisoners.*

69. (1) Where it is shown by evidence on oath to the satisfaction of the High Commissioner, that any person is conducting himself so as to be dangerous to peace and good order in Palestine, or is endeavouring to excite enmity between the people of Palestine and the Mandatory, or is intriguing against the authority of the Mandatory in Palestine, the High Commissioner may, if he thinks fit, by order under his hand and official seal, order that person to be deported from Palestine to such place as the High Commissioner may direct. *Deportation of political offenders.*

(2) The place shall be a place in some part (if any) of His Majesty's Dominions to which the person belongs, or the Government of which consents to the reception of persons deported under this Order, or to some place under the protection of His Majesty, or in the country out of His Majesty's Dominions to which that person belongs.

70. An appeal shall not lie against an order of deportation made under this Order. *Appeal not to lie against deportation order.*

71. (i) If any person deported under this Order returns to Palestine without the permission in writing of the High Commissioner (which permission the High Commissioner may give), he shall be deemed guilty of an offence and liable on conviction to imprisonment for any period not exceeding three months with or without a fine not exceeding £E.50; and he shall also be liable to be again deported forthwith. *Penalty upon return, without permission, of deported person.*

(ii) The High Commissioner, by order under his hand and official seal, may vary or rescind any order of deportation under this Order.

Proceedings upon deportation.

72. (1) Where, under this Order, a person is to be removed or deported from Palestine he shall by warrant of the High Commissioner under his hand and seal, be detained, if necessary, in custody or in prison, until a fit opportunity for his removal or deportation occurs, and then, if he is to be deported beyond seas, be put on board one of His Majesty's vessels of war, or, if none be available, then on board some other British or other fit vessel.

(2) The warrant of the High Commissioner shall be sufficient authority to the person to whom it is directed or delivered for execution and to the commander or master of the vessel to receive and detain the person therein named, in the manner therein prescribed, and to remove and carry him to the place therein named, according to the warrant.

PART VII.

VALIDATION OF ORDINANCES AND INDEMNIFICATION.

Validation of Ordinances, etc., issued by Military Administration.

73. The Proclamations, Ordinances, Orders, Rules of Court, and other legislative acts made, issued, or done by the Commander-in-Chief of the Egyptian Expeditionary Force, or by the Chief Administrator of Occupied Enemy Territory or by Military Governors in Palestine, or any other officer of the Administration between October 1st, 1917, and June 30th, 1920, other than those set forth in the Schedule attached to this Order, shall be deemed to be and always to have been valid and of full effect, both during the military occupation and after the termination thereof, until repealed or superseded by the legislature established under this Order, notwithstanding that any such legislative act may have repealed or been inconsistent with the Law previously in force in Palestine; provided that in the future application of all such Proclamations, Ordinances, Orders, Rules of Court, and legislative acts the Government of Palestine shall be read for Occupied Enemy Territory Administration, High Commissioner for Chief Administrator, Governor of a District for Military Governor, and a Civil Court of competent jurisdiction for a Military Court or Military Magistrate.

The Proclamations, Ordinances, Orders, and Public Notices of the Military Administration which are set forth in the Schedule hereto are hereby cancelled and repealed, provided that any acts done thereunder before the passing of this Order shall be deemed to be and always to have been valid.

Validation of Ordinances, etc., issued since July, 1920.

74. (1) The Proclamations, Ordinances, Orders, Rules of Court and other legislative acts which have been issued or done by the High Commissioner or by any Department of the Government of Palestine on or after 1st July, 1920, shall be deemed to be and

always to have been valid and of full effect and all acts done thereunder and all prohibitions contained therein shall be deemed to be valid.

(2) The Proclamations, Ordinances, Orders, Rules of Court, and other legislative acts which have been issued or done by the High Commissioner or by any Department of the Government of Palestine on or after the 1st September, 1922, shall be deemed to be and always to have been valid and of full effect, and all acts done thereunder and all prohibitions contained therein shall be deemed to be valid.
(Art. 4 of the Amendment Order-in-Council, 1923.) Validation of Legislative Acts issued between September, 1922 and April, 1923.

75. All actions, prosecutions and legal proceedings whatsoever, whether civil or criminal, which might be brought or instituted in any of the Courts of Palestine against the High Commissioner, or the officer for the time being commanding the forces of His Majesty, or any public officer of Palestine, or against any person acting under them, or under their instructions, or under the instructions of any of them respectively in any command or capacity military or civil, for, or on account of, or in respect of, any acts, matters and things whatsoever, in good faith advised, commanded, ordered, directed or done as necessary for the suppression of hostilities, or the establishment and maintenance of good order and government in Palestine, or for the public safety and welfare of Palestine, or for the execution of any regulations issued under Martial Law between the date of the British occupation and the date of the commencement of this Order shall be discharged and become and be null and void. Indemnity for acts done under Martial Law.

Every such person as aforesaid by whom any such act, matter or thing shall have been advised, commanded, ordered, directed, or done for any of the purposes aforesaid shall be freed, acquitted, discharged, released and indemnified against all and every person whomsoever in respect thereof.

76. Every such act, matter or thing referred to in the preceding Article shall be presumed to have been advised, commanded, ordered, directed or done as the case may be, in good faith until the contrary shall be proved by the party complaining. Presumption of good faith.

77. Any sentence passed, judgment given, or order made by any Court Martial or Military Court constituted and convened by proper authority and under Martial Law, or pronounced by officers authorised to dispose of offences summarily under Martial Law, or passed, given or made by any Court established by the authority administering any part of Palestine in the occupation of His Majesty's Forces for the administration of justice within such territory, whether passed, given, or made during such occupation or after such occupation determined prior to the commencement Confirmation of sentences.

of this Order, shall be deemed to be and always to have been valid, and to be and always to have been within the jurisdiction of the Court and the sentences of all persons tried by any such Court shall be deemed to be sentences passed by a duly and legally constituted Court of Palestine.

Confirmation of orders of deportation.

78. All persons in Palestine who have been deported without the limits thereof under and by virtue of any of the foregoing sentences referred to in the last Article, or by virtue of any other order shall be deemed to have been and to be legally deported without the limits of Palestine. Any person who, having been deported as aforesaid, returns to Palestine without the permission in writing of the High Commissioner shall be guilty of an offence and shall on conviction be liable to imprisonment for a term which may extend to two years and shall also be liable to fine and shall further be liable to be again deported.

Arrests, etc., under Martial Law validated.

79. All persons who have been in good faith, and under proper authority during the existence of Martial Law arrested or detained, and all persons who have been similarly committed to gaol, and are there detained to await their trial, shall be deemed to have been lawfully arrested, committed to, and detained in gaol.

Interpretation of term "proper authority."

80. In all cases where any doubt arises whether any act, matter, or thing alleged to have been commanded, ordered, directed, or done under proper authority was done under such authority, it shall be lawful for the Chief Secretary for the time being to declare such act, matter, or thing to have been commanded, ordered, directed, or done under such authority, and such declaration, by any writing under the hand of the Chief Secretary shall in all cases be conclusive evidence as to such authority.

PART VIII.

GENERAL.

Officers and others to obey High Commissioner.

81. All His Majesty's officers, Civil and Military, and all other inhabitants of Palestine are hereby required and commanded to be obedient, aiding, and assisting unto the High Commissioner and to such person or persons as may from time to time, under the provisions of this Order, administer the Government of Palestine.

Official languages.

82. All Ordinances, official notices and official forms of the Government and all official notices of local authorities and municipalities in areas to be prescribed by order of the High Commissioner, shall be published in English, Arabic and Hebrew. The three

languages may be used in debates and discussions in the Legislative Council, and, subject to any regulations to be made from time to time, in the Government offices and the Law Courts.

83. All persons in Palestine shall enjoy full liberty of conscience, and the free exercise of their forms of worship subject only to the maintenance of public order and morals. Every religious community recognised by the Government shall enjoy autonomy for the internal affairs of the community subject to the provisions of any Ordinance or Order issued by the High Commissioner. *Freedom of conscience.*

84.—(1) From and after the constitution of the Legislative Council hereinbefore provided for, the High Commissioner shall confer upon all matters relating to the regulation of immigration with a Committee consisting of not less than one-half of the unofficial members of the Legislative Council, and provision shall be made by Order-in-Council for investing the said Committee with all such powers and authorities and otherwise for the constitution and conduct of the business of the said Committee, as may be necessary to carry this Article into effect. *Immigration.*

(2) In the event of any difference of opinion between the High Commissioner and the said Committee upon any such matter as aforesaid, the High Commissioner shall make a full report on the subject to a Secretary of State, whose decision thereon shall be final.

85. If any religious community or considerable section of the population in Palestine complains that the terms of the Mandate are not being fulfilled by the Government of Palestine, it shall be entitled to present a Memorandum through a member of the Advisory Council or other advisory body constituted under Article 17 (1) (b) of this Order or of the Legislative Council as the case may be to the High Commissioner. Any memorandum so submitted shall be dealt with in such manner as may be prescribed by His Majesty in conformity with the procedure recommended by the Council of the League of Nations. *Petition to League of Nations.*

86. This Order-in-Council shall not apply to such parts of the territory comprised in Palestine to the East of the Jordan and the Dead Sea as shall be defined by order of the High Commissioner. Subject to the provisions of Article 25 of the Mandate, the High Commissioner may make such provision for the administration of any territories so defined as aforesaid as with the approval of the Secretary of State may be prescribed. *Power to exclude territories to east of Jordan from application of any part of Order.*

87. The High Commissioner may by Proclamation in the Gazette at any time within one year from the date of the commencement of this Order, and provided he has previously obtained the approval *Power to vary this Order.*

of the Secretary of State, vary, annul, or add to any of the provisions of this Order in order to carry out the purposes of the same, and may provide for any other matters necessary in order to carry into effect the provisions thereof.

Power reserved to His Majesty to revoke, alter, or amend present Order.

88. His Majesty, His heirs and successors in Council, may at any time revoke, alter, or amend this Order.

Power of legislation, etc., reserved to the Crown.

89. There shall be reserved to His Majesty, His heirs, and successors, the right, with the advice of His or Their Privy Council, from time to time to make all such laws or ordinances as may appear to Him or Them necessary for the peace, order, and good government of Palestine in accordance with the Mandate conferred on Him.

Dates of operation of Order.

90. This Order shall commence and have effect as follows:—
(a) As to the making of any warrant or appointment, and the issue of instructions, and as to any other provisions necessary for bringing this Order into effect, immediately from and after the date of this Order.
(b) As to all other matters and provisions comprised and contained in this Order, immediately after this Order has been published and proclaimed within Palestine, and the date of such publication shall be deemed to be the date of the commencement of this Order.

SCHEDULE TO THE PALESTINE ORDER-IN-COUNCIL.

Enactment Repealed.	Date of Enactment.	Extent of Repeal
(1) Proclamation of the Commander-in-Chief declaring Martial Law	December 9th, 1917	The whole.
(2) Proclamation of the Commander-in-Chief concerning the relation of citizens with the Military Authorities ...	March 30th, 1918	The whole.
(3) Public Notice of the Military Governor, Jerusalem, concerning Banking Transactions	April 4th, 1918	The whole.
(4) Public Notice of the Chief Administrator concerning possession of Government property	May 11th, 1918	The whole.
(5) Public Notice of the Chief Administrator concerning possession of cartridge cases	July 20th, 1918	The whole.
(6) Proclamation of the Commander-in-Chief concerning dealing in Securities ...	November 17th, 1918	The whole.
(7) Notice by the Acting Chief Administrator concerning dealing in Securities ...	February 26th, 1919	The whole.

PART II : ORDINANCES, PUBLIC NOTICES, PROCLAMATIONS AND REGULATIONS

Section 1: 1918

No. 19.

Customs, Taxes, Tithes, etc.

The Public are hereby informed that all taxes in force under the Turkish Government, prior to the entry of that country into the War, will be re-established and collected.

All outstanding taxes for the Turkish Financial year 1333 will also be collected on pre-war rates.

Jaffa,
27th. February, 1918.

A. O. PARKER,
Lieut. Colonel,
Acting Administrator, O.E.T.

PROCLAMATION.

Establishment of Courts.*

WHEREAS, owing to the defection of the judges and officials, Civil Courts of Justice have been in abeyance in Enemy Territory occupied by the Egyptian Expeditionary Force, and it is proper and necessary to re-establish an administration of Justice : and

Whereas it is desirable for the better administration of Justice to define the jurisdiction of the Civil and Religious Courts and to modify in certain respects the constitution and procedure of the Civil Courts : and

Whereas certain Courts have been sitting during the Occupation and it is necessary to ratify their proceedings, and to make provision for appeals therefrom : and

Whereas certain enactments of the Ottoman Government imposing disabilities upon British and Allied subjects are inequitable and contrary to the principles of International Law, and it is proper to repeal the said enactments and to remove the said disabilities : and

Whereas for the relief of debtors and the protection of small landowners it is desirable to introduce measures in mitigation of the law of Execution :

Now, therefore, I, Major-General Sir Arthur Wigram Money, etc.,

Hereby Order as follows :—

1. This proclamation applies to all Ottoman Territory now occupied, or which may hereafter be occupied, by the Egyptian Expeditionary Force. *Preliminary.*

2. Subject to the provisions hereinafter contained, the Civil Courts shall be re-established as Courts of general jurisdiction, and will apply the Ottoman Law in force at the date of the Occupation, with such modifications as may be proper having regard to International Law and to the better administration of Occupied Territory. *Establishment of Courts.*

3. Magistrates' Courts shall be established in each kaza as may be required. As regards matter, these Courts shall have the jurisdiction assigned to them by the Ottoman Magistrates Law of 1913 as amended.

---

* Superseded by the Palestine Order-in-Council, 1922, and by the Courts Ordinance, No. 21 of 1924.

4. Courts of First Instance shall be established at Jerusalem and Jaffa and at such other places as may from time to time be prescribed.

The area of jurisdiction of the Court of First Instance at Jerusalem shall be the kazas of Jerusalem, Hebron and Beersheba.

The area of jurisdiction of the Court of First Instance at Jaffa shall be the kazas of Jaffa and Gaza.

These Courts shall hear cases on appeal from the Magistrates Courts.

Save as aforesaid, and subject to the provisions herein contained, the constitution of Courts of First Instance, and their jurisdiction as regards matter, shall be as laid down by Ottoman Law, provided always that they shall not hear civil cases within the jurisdiction of Magistrates' Courts.

5. Special Courts may be established in any kaza where there is no Court of First Instance. The constitution, and procedure of these Courts shall be as laid down by Rules of Court.

6. A Court of Appeal shall be established at Jerusalem. The Court shall be validly constituted by the presence of three judges, and shall decide by a majority of opinions, save when trying crime punishable by death, in which case it shall consist of four judges; and if no majority is obtained the accused shall be acquitted.

Save as aforesaid and subject to the provisions herein contained, the constitution of the Court of Appeal and its jurisdiction as regards matter shall be as laid down by Ottoman Law.

7. The right of recourse to the Court of Cassation is abolished.

Religious Courts and personal status.

8. Moslem Religious Courts will be established in each kaza and in such other places as may be deemed necessary. Subject to the provisions herein contained, the jurisdiction of these Courts shall be as it was before the Occupation.

9. The right of recourse from Moslem Religious Courts to the Sheikh ul Islam in Constantinople shall be abolished; and there shall be substituted therefor an appeal to a Court to be established.

10. The jurisdiction of the Courts of the Christian and Jewish Communities in matters of personal status of Ottoman subjects shall be as it was before the Occupation.

11. If in any case within the jurisdiction of any Religious Court the parties are members of different religious communities and one of them objects to the jurisdiction of the Religious Court, the case

shall be transferred to the Civil Court, which shall decide the case, applying such law as may appear to the Court to be just in the circumstances.

12. Matters of personal status affecting persons who are not Ottoman subjects may be decided by the Civil Courts, which shall apply the personal law of the parties concerned, provided always that :—

(a) The Civil Courts shall have no jurisdiction to pronounce a divorce ; and

(b) Nothing in this clause contained shall be construed to prevent those persons from consenting to their case being tried by the Courts of the religious communities having jurisdiction in like matters affecting Ottoman subjects.

13. When in any action properly brought before the Civil Courts a question of personal status arises, the determination of which is necessary for the purposes of the action, the Civil Courts may, notwithstanding the provisions of Clauses 8 and 10 hereof, determine the question and may, to that end, have recourse, whether by way of stating a case for opinion or by oral examination, to a competent jurist having knowledge of the personal law applicable.

14. The Courts re-established by this Proclamation shall have no jurisdiction to try actions :— _{Limitation of jurisdiction over persons.}

(a) Brought against the Occupied Enemy Territory Administration or any person employed thereunder in his official capacity ; or

(b) Brought by or against a person subject to Military law within the meaning of Sections 175 and 176 of the Army Act, except, in either case, with the consent in writing of the Chief Administrator.

15. Rules of Court made under this Proclamation shall define the expression " foreign subjects " ; and shall set out the manner in which the Court shall be constituted in proceedings to which a foreign subject is a party. _{Foreign subjects.}

16. The period between the last sitting of the competent Court under Ottoman Rule and the opening of the Courts re-established by this Proclamation shall not be reckoned in calculating the time within which opposition or appeal or application for review must be made from any judgment or order of an Ottoman Court passed before the Occupation, or in calculating the term of prescription or limitation of action if the term would have expired within the said period. _{Limitation and prescription.}

17. The Courts in deciding a civil or commercial action shall have regard to the inability of any party to assert or enforce any real or personal right during the war.

Payment of debts.

18. The term for the postponement of payments fixed by the Ottoman Laws of moratorium having expired in December, 1917, all debts have now become payable in full, and interest at the rates and on the conditions fixed in the said Laws will be payable on all debts hereby affected.

19. The enactment of the Ottoman Government entitled " A Provisional Law dated 24th November, 1914, concerning debts and contracts in cases in which one of the contracting parties is a subject of an enemy State or of a Power allied with an enemy State " is null and void throughout the occupied territory; and interest will be payable, as if this enactment had not been passed, on all debts due to British or Allied subjects on the same conditions and at the same rates as on debts due to Ottoman subjects.

20. The period for making protest in respect of negotiable instruments affected by the Ottoman Laws of Moratorium, whether on account of the instalments enforceable under those laws or on account of the balances due under such instruments, will be extended to the 1st August, 1918, and the period within which action must be brought to preserve rights of recourse will be extended to 1st August, 1918 or to the end of the fifteenth day following the date of protest, whichever is the later. These periods shall be applicable in the case of a negotiable instrument held by a British or Allied subject who was prevented by the Ottoman law of 24th November, 1914, aforesaid, from making a protest in respect of it in due time, or from bringing an action to preserve his rights of recourse.

Execution and bankruptcy.

21. Where it is shown to the satisfaction of the Court that owing to the war a judgment debtor or an insolvent is unable to pay his debts in full and has reasonable prospects, if given time, of paying, or that his property seizable in execution has considerably depreciated in value, the Court may order the postponement of execution or suspend proceedings in bankruptcy upon such terms as may seem to it just in the circumstances, provided always that these provisions shall not be applicable where the debt or debts were incurred since the occupation.

22. Until further notice the Court shall not order the sale of any land* in execution of a judgment or in satisfaction of a mortgage in any form, provided always that interest shall continue to run upon the debt at the rate fixed by the contract or, in the absence of such rate, at a rate to be fixed by the Court.

(*) Land includes all forms of immovable property. (Proclamation dated 20th July, 1918.)

23. Until further notice the Court shall not give any judgment deciding the ownership of land,* but this provision shall not prevent the Court from deciding in any action as to the possessory rights without prejudice to the question of ownership. Land.

24. The judgments or orders of any Court other than a Military Court which has been sitting in the Occupied Territory during the Occupation shall be deemed to have been validly passed, but an appeal may be brought to the proper Court within ten days of the date of this Proclamation from any such judgment or order when the value of the subject matter of the action was more than £E.10; or when the sentence exceeded two months' imprisonment, and the term of imprisonment has more than one month to run at the date of this Proclamation. Ratification of judgments and pending suits.

The Court in trying appeals brought under this clause shall not reverse any decision on the ground of mistake in or failure to observe the correct procedure unless it is of opinion that the mistake or failure has caused a miscarriage of justice.

25. Any judicial proceedings pending before a Court now sitting in the Occupied Territory, or which may have been begun before a Court sitting in Occupied Territory before the Occupation, may be continued before the Courts having jurisdiction under this Proclamation.

26. The Court may adopt any judicial proceeding which has taken place in a pending action, and, in particular, may accept any inquiry that has been made into a criminal matter as the preliminary investigation, provided that the Director of Public Prosecutions certifies that the case is fit to be tried.

27. Where owing to the absence of parties or records or documents the Court is unable to give a definitive judgment in any proceeding, it may make such provisional order as may, in the circumstances, seem just.

28. The general superintendence and control over all Civil Courts and Religious Courts in the Occupied Territory shall be vested in the Senior Judicial Officer, who, with the sanction of the Chief Administrator, may from time to time, make rules as to any of the following matters :— Superintendence and rules of Court.

   (a) The organisation, jurisdiction, procedure and business of the Courts ;

   (b) The functions and duties of the judges and officials of the Courts ;

---

*Land includes all forms of immovable property. (Proclamation dated 20th July, 1918.)

(c) The fees payable in the Courts or in connection with any proceedings of the Courts or their officials, and the costs, charges, and expenses to be allowed to parties, witnesses and others;

(d) The profession of advocates, legal practitioners and public notaries.

Rules made under this clause may annul or add to the provisions of this Proclamation or any Ottoman rules relating to the matters above-mentioned.

The Senior Judicial Officer may withdraw any action or proceeding pending in a Civil Court and refer it for disposal to any Civil Court which is competent to try it.

24*th June*, 1918.

PROCLAMATION.

Courts.*

WHEREAS, owing to the extension of Occupied Enemy Territory (South), it is necessary to make further arrangements for the organisation of Courts of Justice, and to supplement in certain particulars the provisions of the Proclamation of 24th June, 1918.

Now, therefore, I, Major-General Sir Arthur Wigram Money, etc.;

Hereby Order as follows:—

PRELIMINARY.

Application of Proclamation of June 24th, 1918, to Northern Palestine.

1. Subject to the modifications hereinafter contained, all the provisions of the Proclamation of June 24th, 1918, as amended by the Proclamation of July 26th, 1918, and all the Rules of Court issued in accordance with the Proclamation shall apply to the Sanjaks of Nablus and Acre as fully as they have applied to the Sanjak of Jerusalem.

Civil Courts.

2. Courts of First Instance shall be established at Nablus, Haifa, and Tiberias. The area of jurisdiction of the Court of First Instance of Nablus shall be the kazas of Nablus, Tulkarem and Jenin. The area of jurisdiction of the Court of First Instance of Haifa shall be the kazas of Haifa, Acre and Nazareth. The area of jurisdiction of the Court of First Instance of Tiberias shall be the kazas of Tiberias and Safad.

Courts of First Instance shall be validly constituted by a single British Judicial Officer. They shall hear cases on appeal from the Magistrates' Courts within their area of jurisdiction.

3. The Court of Appeal at Jerusalem shall hear appeals in civil and criminal cases from all Courts of First Instance in the Occupied Enemy Territory (South); provided that an Assize Court may be constituted in the Sanjak of Acre by any British Judicial Officer and any two judges eligible to sit as members of the Court of Appeal.

Religious Courts.

4. Moslem Religious Courts will be established in such kazas of the Sanjak of Nablus and Acre as the Senior Judicial Officer may appoint. The jurisdiction and law and procedure of these Courts shall be as they were before the promulgation of the Ottoman Laws of 25th October, 1333 (1917), concerning Family Rights and concerning procedure in the Religious Courts; provided that any cases heard or pending before the Courts at the time of the Occupation

in virtue of the said laws shall be deemed to have been validly entered.

5. The jurisdiction and law of the Courts of the Christian and Jewish Communities in the Sanjaks of Nablus and Acre in matters of personal status shall be as they were before the promulgation of the said Ottoman Laws.

6. An appeal shall lie from any final judgment already passed by a Moslem Religious Court in the Sanjak of Nablus and Acre to the Moslem Religious Court of Appeal; provided that the application is entered within twenty days of the publication of this Proclamation.

7. The provisions of Clause 16 of the Proclamation of June 24th, 1918, shall apply to the Courts re-established under this Proclamation. *Limitation and prescription.*

8. The term for the postponement of payment fixed by the Ottoman Law of Moratorium of 10th December, 1917, having expired in March, 1918, all debts incurred or payable in the Sanjaks of Nablus and Acre have now become payable in full; and interest at the rates and under the conditions fixed in the said laws will be payable on all debts thereby affected. *Payment of debts and bankruptcy.*

9. The provisions of Clause 20 of the Proclamation of June 24th, 1918, and of Clause 1 of the Proclamation of July 20th, 1918, shall apply to the whole of the Occupied Territory, and the provisions of Clauses 21 and 22 of the said Proclamation of June 24th, shall be substituted for those contained in Article 5 of the Ottoman Law of Moratorium of 10th December, 1917.

10. Any judicial proceedings pending before a Court now sitting in the Sanjaks of Nablus and Acre, or which may have been begun before the Court sitting in those Sanjaks before the Occupation, may be continued before the Courts having jurisdiction under this Proclamation.

1st November, 1918.

---

* Superseded by the Palestine Order-in-Council, 1922, and by the Courts Ordinance, No. 21 of 1924.

PROCLAMATION.

Land Transactions.*

WHEREAS the Ottoman Land Laws require that all sales, mortgages, transfers of mortgage or other dispositions of immovable property shall be registered in the Land Registry Office;

And whereas most of the registers of land in the Occupied Enemy Territory have been removed by the Turkish Authorities, and it has not yet been possible to re-establish and re-organise the Land Registry Offices, and in consequence no sale, mortgage, transfer of mortgage or other disposition made since the Occupation of the enemy territory has any validity;

And whereas it is expedient to limit the length of period for which leases may be granted, and to provide that prescription shall not run against the Occupied Enemy Territory Administration;

Now therefore, I, Major-General Sir Arthur Wigram Money, etc.

Hereby Order as follows :—

1. The expression " disposition " in this Proclamation means a sale, mortgage, transfer of mortgage, gift, dedication as waqf or other disposition of immovable property, and includes any agreement for a dispostion of immovable property.

2. All persons concerned are warned that until it is possible to re-establish and re-organise the Land Registry Offices owners of immovable property have no power to make dispositions of their immovable property, and that any disposition of immovable property which has taken place, or may hereafter take place, in contravention of this Proclamation is invalid, provided that a disposition already made with the written consent of a British Officer of the Administration shall be deemed to be valid subject to registration on the re-establishment of the Land Registry Offices.

3. If any person has paid money in respect of any invalid disposition or has parted with the possession of the property under an invalid disposition made since the date of the Occupation, he is at liberty to apply to the Courts within two months from the date of this Proclamation claiming repayment of the money paid, on giving up possession if he has been allowed to go into possession, or claiming possession of the property on repayment of the money paid to him.

4. If a mortgagor wishes and is entitled to repay the money due under a mortgage, the money may be repaid ; provided that the parties execute a document of discharge before a Notary Public, and that the documents of title in the hands of the mortgagee are handed over to the mortgagor in his presence.

5. No lease of immovable property shall be made for a period exceeding three years.

---

*Superseded by Land Transfer Ordinance, 1920.

6. Any order made by a Court in an action for the possession of immovable property shall be provisional only pending a land settlement. The Court in deciding such actions shall follow the rules laid down in the Magistrates' Law of 1913, as amended, unless, upon a consideration of all the relevant facts, it is of opinion that the strict application of those rules will result in injustice, in which case it may make such order as may seem just in the circumstances.

7. As from the date of the Occupation and until further notice, prescription in respect of immovable property shall not run against the Occupied Enemy Territory Administration.

8. This Proclamation shall apply to the Ottoman Sanjak of Jerusalem and the date of the Occupation shall, for the purposes of the Proclamation, be deemed to be 1st December, 1917.

9. Nothing in this Proclamation shall affect the right of the Occupied Enemy Territory Administration to buy, sell, mortgage or otherwise dispose of immovable property or to grant or take a lease for any period.

1st November, 1918.

PROCLAMATION.

Land Transactions.*

WHEREAS the Ottoman Land Laws require that all sales, mortgages, transfers of mortgage or other dispositions of immovable property shall be registered in the Land Registry;

And whereas it is not possible to re-organise at present the Land Registry Offices;

And whereas it is expedient to limit the length of period for which leases may be granted and to provide that prescription shall not run against the Occupied Enemy Territory Administration;

Now, therefore, I, Major-General Sir Arthur Wigram Money, etc.;

Hereby Order as follows :—

1. The expression "disposition" in this Proclamation means a sale, mortgage, transfer of mortgage, gift, dedication, waqf, or other disposition of immovable property and includes any agreement for the disposition of immovable property.

2. All persons concerned are warned that until it is possible to re-organise the Land Registry Offices, owners of immovable property have no power to make disposition of their immovable property, and that any disposition made in contravention of this Proclamation is invalid.

3. If a mortgagor wishes and is entitled to repay the money due under a mortgage the money may be repaid, provided that the parties execute a document of discharge before a Notary Public and that the documents of title in the hands of the Mortgagee are handed over to the Mortgagor in his presence.

4. No lease of immovable property shall be made for a period exceeding three years.

5. Any order made by a Court in an action for the possession of immovable property shall be provisional only pending a land settlement. The Courts in deciding such actions shall follow the rules laid down in the Magistrates' Law of 1913 as amended, unless upon a consideration of all the relevant facts it is of opinion that the strict application of those rules will result in injustice, in which case it may make such order as may seem just in the circumstances.

6. As from the date of the Occupation and until further notice, prescription in respect of immovable property shall not run against the Occupied Enemy Territory Administration.

7. This Proclamation shall apply to the (Ottoman) Sanjaks of Nablus and Acre, and the date of the Occupation shall for the purpose of this Proclamation be deemed to be 1st October, 1918.

8. Nothing in this Proclamation shall affect the right of the Occupied Enemy Territory Administration to buy, sell, mortgage, or otherwise dispose of immovable property or to grant or take a lease for any period.

18th November, 1918.

---

* Superseded by Transfer of Land Ordinance, 1920.

An Ordinance to provide for Agricultural Loans to Cultivators.*

WHEREAS it is expedient to assist landowners and cultivators to bring their land into cultivation, and to improve the already existing system of cultivation by making advances in money and kind from Government funds, and it is in consequence necessary to give the Government an effective security for such advances over the crops belonging to such landowners and cultivators.

It is hereby enacted as follows:—

1. Contracts made whether before or after the publication of this Ordinance with the Government in the form of Schedules A and B hereto annexed shall be deemed to be valid and may be executed according to the terms thereof.

2. The Government may take the crops made security for an advance, wherever they may be found, in satisfaction of their rights under the said contracts. The Government shall have a priority and preference over all creditors and claimants even though such creditors or claimants hold a mortgage over the lands, or a pledge or any other security over the crops.

3. A register of persons entering into contracts in terms of this Ordinance with the Government shall be kept at the offices of the District Administration, and shall be open to inspection by the public on such days and at such hours as the District Governor may direct.

30th November, 1918.

SCHEDULE A.

CONTRACT.

I/We agree (jointly and severally) to repay to (Governor on behalf of) the GOVERNMENT OF PALESTINE the sums appearing in the Schedule hereto, representing the advances made to me/us whether in money or kind by the Government of Palestine upon the date set out in the said Schedule.

And I/We further (jointly and severally) agree to pay interest at the rate of ten per cent. per annum upon the sums from time to time outstanding until the whole amount due under this Contract is repaid.

(a) The fuel shall be used solely for the purpose of irrigating my/our gardens and in the event of this fuel being used or disposed of for any other purpose a penalty not exceeding twice the value of the fuel so used or disposed of may be exacted by the Government of Palestine.

(b) The Government of Palestine has a right at any time to buy such part of my/our garden's crops at the then current requisitioning rates, or in the event of there being no requisitioning rates, at a price to be fixed by the Administration as may cover the then outstanding debt due to the Administration under this contract together with the cost (if any) of picking, removing and disposing of the part of the crops so bought.

(c) For the purpose of protecting or exercising its rights under this contract, the Government of Palestine may, without having recourse to the Law Courts and without giving notice, seize the whole or any part of my/our garden's crops wheresoever situated and whether gathered or not.

(d) I/We will not enter into any contract of sale of my/our garden's crops without the consent in writing of the Government of Palestine; and this contract shall operate as an assignment to the Administration of any benefit accruing to me/us under any contract of sale of the said crops or any part of them, whether made with or without consent of the Administration.

This contract is made in duplicate, one copy in English and the other in Arabic. In case of dispute the English copy shall prevail.

SCHEDULE B.

Contract.

I/We agree (jointly and severally) to repay to (Governor on behalf of) the Government of Palestine the sums appearing in the Schedule annexed representing advances made to me/us in money or in kind by the Government of Palestine upon the dates set out in the said Schedule.

And I/we further (jointly and severally) agree to pay interest at the rate of   per cent. per annum upon the amounts from time to time outstanding until the whole amount due under this contract is repaid.

(a) The animals and seeds or cash advanced shall be used solely for the benefit of my/our land and for the improvement of the state of agriculture thereon. In the event of any of the said animals or any portion of the said seeds or any of the implements purchased with the cash so advanced being used for any other purpose, or being sold without the consent of the State or given in writing, a penalty not exceeding twice the total value of the said animals or seeds or implements may be exacted by the Government of Palestine, and such sale shall be null and void.

(b) The Government of Palestine has a right at any time to requisition all or any portion of my/our crops or stock or implements and pay for them at a price to be fixed by the Administration. The amount to be requisitioned shall not in any case be more than sufficient to repay the debt outstanding to the Administration for the full amount of the said advances, interest and all necessary expenses.

(c) For the sake of protecting its rights under this contract the Government of Palestine may at any time without recourse to the Law Courts and without giving notice, enter into possession of my/our land, and reap and sell all or any of the crops thereon, and may seize and sell the whole or any part of such crops, wheresoever situated, in order to cover the said advances, interest and expenses.

(d) I/We will not enter into any contract of sale of my/our crops without the consent in writing of the Government of Palestine and this contract shall operate as an assignment to the Administration of any benefit accruing to me/us under any sale of the said crops or any part of them.

(e) This contract is made in duplicate, one copy in English and the other in Arabic. In case of dispute the English copy shall prevail.

---

*This Ordinance is now obsolete.

Section 2: 1919

No. 115.

Public Notice.

Transfer of Land.

NOTICE IS HEREBY GIVEN, that whereas Proclamations Nos. 75 and 76, dated November 18th., 1918, prohibited any agreement for a transfer of immovable property till the Land Registries are re-established, and an agreement made in breach of this provision is null and void, any promissory note or other instrument acknowledging a debt which is proved to have been given since the promulgation of this Notice on account of an invalid transaction in immovable property will be null and void, and the person to whom such a note or instrument was given may further be liable to prosecution.

Jerusalem,
30th. April, 1919.

A. W. MONEY,
Major-General,
Chief Administrator.

NOTE: See Section 11 of Land Transfer Ordinance 1920.

No. 117.

Public Notice.

NOTICE IS HEREBY GIVEN that where it is necessary to expropriate land for a public purpose, the Ottoman Law of Expropriation of 21st. December, 1329, will be applied, subject to the following amendments:—

1. THE CHIEF ADMINISTRATOR of Palestine shall be substituted for the highest civil officer of the Vilayet, as the person whose consent is required to the scheme of expropriation.

2. The Governor of the district shall exercise the powers of nominating arbitrators given to the general councils of the Vilayet in Article 4 of the said Law.

3. An appeal to the Court of Appeal shall be substituted for the right of recourse to the Court of Cassation given to the landowner under Article 8 of the said Law.

Jerusalem
20th., May, 1919.

A. W. MONEY,
Major General,
Chief Administrator.

Section 3: 1920

Leasing of State Domains.

1. Mahlul lands are leased annually, the land being placed out to auction and the highest bidder obtaining the privilege of possession, under the terms of the published Agreement for the leasing of State Domains (vide Official Gazette No. 7 of 16.10.19).

2. In cases where the outgoing tenants have established rights of cultivation through long tenure, such rights should be respected providing a fair and reasonable rent is obtained for the land. The interests of tenants who have longstanding and traditional rights to a particular holding should be carefully considered.

When Mahlul lands are placed out to auction, a notice will be issued for the information of the Public which will enumerate the rights and privileges of communities or tribes over such lands and having particular reference to water rights.

3. The above instructions are also applicable to Awqaf Lands.

Ref. 4666 — FR
of the 23.1.20.

Ordinance.

WHEREAS it is proposed to initiate a Cadastral Survey commencing in the Districts of Gaza and Beersheba, and

WHEREAS it is necessary to facilitate the demarcation of boundaries and the making of Surveys,

IT IS HEREBY ORDERED AS FOLLOWS :—

1. Any authorised Official of the Government of Palestine shall have power at any reasonable time to enter upon any lands of whatever tenure for the purpose of executing any Survey work or any work incidental thereto, and shall for such purpose have power to make any enquiries, fix any stone, post pillar or other boundary or Survey mark in or upon the land and to dig up any ground for the purpose of fixing the same.

2. The Administration shall not be responsible for any ordinary damage reasonably caused to any property by the act of any authorised Survey or demarcation official in the execution of his duty. But compensation shall be paid in respect of any extraordinary damage caused. The value of such damage shall be assessed after consultation by the District Governor, whose decision regarding the validity of the claim shall be final.

3. A District Governor may by written order require any persons in his District who own or occupy or are employed on or interested in any land, or who are in a position to give any information regarding the boundaries of any land, or in whose possession or power any document relating to such boundaries is alleged to be

(a) to attend before the demarcation or Survey Officer at a fixed time and place,
(b) to point out the boundaries of the land.
(c) to give any information required for the purpose of the demarcation or Survey.
(d) to produce any document in his power relating to such boundaries.

4. A District Governor may order the owner or occupier of any land in his District within a reasonable time to be fixed by him,

(a) to demarcate his land, and for the purpose of such demarcation to erect such stones, pillars, posts or other boundary or land marks as the said officer may direct.
(b) to clear any boundary or other line.
(c) to provide labor or otherwise assist in the demarcation or Survey of his land.

5. If any person fails to obey any such order of the District Governor, the Demarcation or Survey Officer shall after enquiry mark out the boundaries of the land, and may cause proper boundary marks to be erected at the cost of the owner or occupier.

6. An owner of land on which any survey or demarcation mark has been erected shall be responsible for the maintenance and for the protection thereof from tampering or obliteration, and if such mark shall be upon a common boundary the owners of

the property on each side thereof shall be held jointly responsible. In the case
marks erected upon village or public lands the Mukhtars of the village shall likebe held responsible. All owners and occupiers of land and Mukhtars shall further
held responsible for informing the District Governor of any land or boundary n
which is in bad repair or which has been obliterated.

7. Any person failing to obey the order of a District Governor or commit
any contravention under this Ordinance shall be liable on conviction before a Magisl
to imprisonment not exceeding one year or to a fine not exceeding £. E. 50 o
both these penalties; and shall in addition be liable to pay to the Survey Departm
any expenses arising out of his default. Further any person who obstructs an off
of the Survey Department in the execution of his duty may be dealt with under
116 of the Ottoman Penal Code.

Jerusalem, May 1920.

L. J. BOLS
Major-General
Chief Administrator.

NOTE.: The above Ordinance is amended by Public Notice of 6.2.21.
To be read in conjunction with Public Notice 166 of July 20th. and Ordin:
No. 9 of May 3rd. 1922.

Public Notice.

The Land Commission.

As announced in his speech before the Assemblies at Jerusalem and Haifa the High Commissioner is appointing a Commission to enquire into different questions concerning Land Settlement. The Commission will in the first place ascertain the area and nature of the various kinds of land which are at the disposal of the Government. There is at present great uncertainty on these points. The Turkish Government kept records of the Mudawara Land but no proper check appears to have been preserved of the Mahlul and Mewat Land. The Commission will consider what steps should be taken to obtain an accurate record of these areas, and to make the best disposition of them in the interests of the country. The Sand Dunes and a large part of the bare hill-tops, it is believed, can be reclaimed by planting trees. The Commission will examine this question, and advise what can be done to secure the profitable use of land that is now left waste.

The Commission has also to report upon what lands in the country are available for closer settlement, by which is meant a more intensive cultivation of the soil by larger agricultural population. Large areas at present in all parts of Palestine are imperfectly cultivated and could be made to produce a very much greater yield if more cultivators were settled on them. The Commission will advise the High Comissioner on the measures that should be taken by the Government to secure the greater productivity of the country. At the same time it will make recommendations as to the measures to be taken to protect the interests of the persons who are at present tenants or occupants of these lands. There are large areas of Government lands which have been leased or occupied for a long period by particular tribes and cultivators of particular districts, and the rights of these people will be protected. The Commission will advise also on the measures to be taken to prevent land owners selling land which is now cultivated by tenants without making arrangement protecting the interest of their tenants.

The Commission will also act as an advisory body to the High Commissioner upon any questions concerning settlement of land which may be referred to him including proposals for disposition of parts of the Government lands.

The Commission will travel about the different parts of the country and take evidence on the spot from the land owners and tenants and from any other person who may be able to give useful information about land questions. Those who desire to give evidence will appear personally, and any land owner or other person can be represented before the Commission by an Advocate.

Official Gazette No. 26
1.9.20.

LAND TRANSFER ORDINANCE.

WHEREAS an Ordinance of 18th November 1918 prohibited all dispositions of immovable property pending the re-establishment of the Land Registry Offices; and

WHEREAS Land Registry Offices have been re-established and in order to meet the needs of the people it is desirable that transactions having in view the immediate use and cultivation of land be permitted; and

WHEREAS it is necessary to take measures to prevent speculative dealings in land and to protect the present occupants; and

WHEREAS a Land Settlement Court is shortly to be established which will adjudicate on all titles, and in the meantime no guarantee of title can be given by the administration, and

WHEREAS it is intended to introduce legislation to secure the orderly planning of towns in Palestine and the erection of buildings on land in the neighbourhood of towns will be subject to the control of the administration; and

WHEREAS the administration is taking measures to facilitate the establishment of Credit Banks in Palestine which will have power to lend on the security of immovable property, and pending the consideration of the establishment of such Banks it is desirable to continue the prohibition of sales of land in satisfaction of a mortgage or execution of a judgment.

IT IS HEREBY ORDERED AS FOLLOWS.—

1 This Ordinance applies to all immovable property the subject of the Land Law of 7 Ramadan 1274, as well as to mulk land, all forms of wakf land and every other form of immovable property, and shall, so far as it applies, cancel the provisions of the Ordinance of 18th November, 1918.

2. In this Ordinance and in all regulations made hereunder, unless there is something repugnant in the context, the word "disposition" means a sale, mortgage, gift, dedication of Wakf of every discription and any other disposition of immovable property except a devise by will or a lease for a term not exceeding 3 years. It includes the transfer of mortgage and a lease containing an option by virtue the term may exceed 3 years.

The word "Court" shall include any Civil or Religious Court competent to deal with actions concerning land, as well as any Land Settlement Court which may be established.

The word "land" shall include houses, buildings and things permanently fixed in the land.

3. No disposition of immovable property will be valid until the provisions of this Ordinance have been complied with.

4. Any person wishing to make a disposition of immovable property must first obtain the written consent of the Administration

In order to obtain this consent, a petition must be presented through the Land Registry Office to the Governor of the District in which the land is situated, setting out the terms of the disposition intended to be made and applying for his consent to the disposition. The petition must be accompanied by proof of the title of the transferor, and must contain an application for registration of a deed to be executed for the purpose of carrying into effect the terms of the disposition. The petition may also include a clause fixing the damages to be paid by either party who refuses to complete the disposition if it is approved.

5. If the application for registraton is made by an agent or nominee on behalf of a principal, the agent or nominee shall make full disclosure in his petition of the principal for whom he is acting, and the immovable property disposed of shall be registered in the name of the principal.

If at any time it appears to a Court or a Registrar that immovable property has been registered under this Ordinance otherwise than in accordance with the foregoing provision, the Court or Registrar shall inquire into the case and make a report to the High Commissioner, who may impose upon any of the parties concerned penalties by way of fine or forfeiture not exceeding one fourth of the value of the property.

6.[1]) The consent of the Administration will be given through the Governor of the District in which the land is situated, provided that he is satisfied that the person acquiring the property fulfils the following conditions

(a) He must be resident in Palestine

(b) He shall not obtain under this Ordinance property exceeding either in value £P. 3000 or in area 300 dunoms in the case of agricultural land and 30 dunoms in the case of urban land.

(c) He intends himself to cultivate or develop the land immediately.

The Governor shall also withhold his consent unless he is satisfied that in the case of agricultural land either the person transferring the property, if he is in possession, or the tenant in occupation, if the property is leased, will retain sufficient land in the District or elsewhere for the maintenance of himself and his family. The Governor may refer to the High Commissioner any case in which he withholds his consent.

7.[2]) The District Governor shall withhold his consent to a disposition of any immovable property, if the land has been sold or otherwise disposed of within a year, and the intending transferor fails to give satisfactory reason for wishing again to dispose of it

8[2]) Except in cases complying with the conditions set out in Sec. 6. hereof, all dispositions shall be referred to the High Commissioner for his consent, which he may give or withhold in his absolute discretion.

The High Commissioner may refer the application for any such disposition to any Commission which may be appointed by him to report upon the closer settlement of the land.

He may consent to the transfer of larger areas of land than may be transferred with the assent of the District Governor, where he is satisfied that the transfer will be in the public interest or will serve some purpose of recognised public utility. The Ottoman Law of the 22nd Rabi El-Awal, 1331

[1]) R.—See O. G No. 60 of 1 2.1922.
[2]) A.—See O G No 60 of 1 2 1922

concerning the right of a corporation to own immovable property, shall remain in force provided that the High Commissioner may authorise any banking company to take a mortgage of land and any commercial company registered in Palestine to acquire such land as is necessary for the purpose of its undertaking, and may subject to the above conditions consent to the transfer of land to any corporation.

9. After the title has been examined and the consent of the Administration has been obtained, a deed shall be executed in the form prescribed by Rules made in accordance with Sec 16 hereof, and shall be registered in the Land Registry.

No guarantee of title or of the transaction is implied by the consent of the Administration and the registration of the deed.

A person acquiring land under this Ordinance will be subject to any registration which may hereafter be introduced by the Government of Palestine for regulating the right of building and the development of land in or in the neighbourhood of a town

10 No mortgage shall be accepted for registration unless it complies with the terms of the Provisional Law for the mortgage of immovable property of 16 Rabia Tani 1331 and the amendments of the Law

11 Every disposition to which the written consent of the Administration has not been obtained shall be null and void, provided that any person who has paid money in respect of a disposition which is null and void may recover the same by action in the Courts.

Nothing in this Section shall affect the operation of Public Notice No. 115 dated 30th April 1919 concerning promissory notes given on account of an invalid transaction in immovable property.

12. If any person is a party to any disposition of immovable property which has not received the consent of the Administration and either enters into possession or permits the other party to enter into possession of the immovable property, whether by himself or any person on his behalf, he shall be liable on conviction by a Court to payment of a fine not exceeding one-fourth of the immovable property

13. When any immovable property passes operation of a will or by inheritance, the legatees or heirs, as the case may be shall be jointly and severally responsible for the registration of the immovable property in the name of legatees or heirs within a year of the death The registration shall be made upon the certificate of a competent Court stating that the person or persons acquiring registration are entitled as legatees or heirs or upon a certificate signed by the Mukhtar or Imam and two notables

14.[1]) The provisions of the Proclamation of 24th June 1918 preventing the Courts from ordering the sale of immovable property in execution of a

---

[1]) A—O G. No. 41 of 15 4 1921

judgment or in satisfaction of a mortgage shall remain in force till further order.

15.¹) The provisions of Art 23 of the Proclamation of 24th June, 1918 preventing the Courts from giving any judgment deciding the ownership of land shall remain in force, provided that

(1) The Courts may hear actions for the partition of land in accordance with the Law of 14th Moharram 1332

(2) The Legal Secretary may in a special case allow an action concerning the ownership of land to be heard.

16 The High Commissioner may establish a Land Registry Office in such places as may seem desirable and in consultation with the Financial Secretary may appoint such number of registrars and assistant registrars as may be necessary

The general superintendence and control over all land Registry Offices in Palestine shall be vested in the Legal Secretary, who with the sanction of the High Commissioner may from time to time make rules as to any of the following matters Subject to consultation with the Financial Secretary on the Subject of fees as in sub-section (f) below,

(a) The organization, procedure and business of the Land Registry Offices

(b) The functions and duties of the registrar and other officials of the Land Registry Office

(c) The mode in which the register is to be kept

(d) The forms to be used for deeds and documents.

(e) The requirements for attestation and official verification of the execution of deeds

(f) The fees payable for or in connection with registration

(g) The appointment of attorneys

(h) Any other matter or thing, whether similar or not to those above mentioned, in respect of which it may be expedient to make rules for the purpose of carrying this Ordinance into effect.

17 This Ordinance shall be called "The Transfer of Land Ordinance 1920"

September, 1920 O G No 28 of 1 10 1920

Acquisition of Land for the Army Ordinance.†

WHEREAS, during the Military Occupation, the British Army has occupied land and houses and other premises in Palestine for military purposes and has built railways and reservoirs on the land and carried out other works of public utility :

And whereas it is necessary to define the rights of the British Army in the land or premises so occupied, and to provide for the expropriation of land on which such improvements have been carried out and of other land which the Military Authorities may desire to occupy permanently :

It is hereby Ordered as follows :

1. The British Army in Palestine may continue, with the consent

---

* Repealed by Section 12 (i) of the Credit Banks Ordinance, 1922.

† Repealed by the Acquisition of Land for the Army and Air Force Ordinance, 1925.

of the High Commissioner, to occupy for military needs during a period not exceeding two years from the ratification of Peace with the Ottoman Empire or from the declaration of the British Mandate over Palestine, whichever shall be the earlier event, any land or premises of which they have taken occupation during the war, on condition of paying compensation to the owners to be assessed in the manner hereafter mentioned. Notice shall be given to the owner, or his representative, and to the High Commissioner, of any land or premises which it is desired so to occupy and of the term and the purpose of occupation, and the High Commissioner shall decide whether and for what period the occupation is to be allowed.

2. The Government of Palestine may on behalf of the British Army expropriate any land required for the permanent use of the Army. The consent of the High Commissioner shall be obtained to any expropriation, and the High Commissioner in giving his consent will have regard to all the circumstances of the case.

3. Where land is required for the permanent use of the Army, written notice shall be given to the owner that the Military Authorities desire to expropriate it, and an entry shall be made in the Land Registry of the District that the land is so required. No dealing in such land shall thereafter be permitted until the expropriation proceedings are completed, or the High Commissioner has refused his consent to the expropriation.

4. A notice shall be published in the Official Gazette, and in one Arabic and one Hebrew newspaper circulating in the District, and shall also be posted in the Governorate, the District Court, and the Land Registry of the District, and served on the Mukhtars of the village or quarter in which the land is situated, stating that the High Commissioner has approved the expropriation of the land, and requiring anybody who claims any interest in the land to put in a claim at the Governorate within 15 days from the date of the advertisement or notification.

5. Compensation for the use of the land occupied by the Army and the price of the land expropriated for the Army shall, in default of agreement, be assessed by a Permanent Arbitration Board which shall be nominated by the High Commissioner. The Board shall be composed of five members, one representative each of the Army in Palestine, of the Department of Agriculture and the Department of Public Works, and two Palestine civilians one of whom shall be the President of the Board.

The owner and any person interested in the land and a representative of the Army shall be entitled to appear before the Board either personally or through an advocate. The Board shall fix the value of the land to be occupied or expropriated having regard to its condition and value prior to the British Occupation, and without taking account of the improvements on or about the land made during the Occupation by the British Army. When the land to be expropriated is not occupied by the Army, the Board shall fix the price according to the value of neighbouring land of similar character, without taking account of any special value which the land required may have for military purposes.

6. The decision of the Board shall be final and shall be registered in the District Court and also in the Land Registry Office of the District.

The District Court shall decide any claim of a person other than the registered owner to receive any part of the whole of the purchase money or compensation, and an appeal shall lie from its decision to the Court of Appeal.

The procedure laid down by the Law of Expropriation which shall be in force in Palestine, as regards the disposal of the compensation, shall be followed.

7. The land expropriated shall be registered in the name of the Palestine Government on behalf of His Majesty's Secretary of State for War.

If at any time the land so required is not wanted by the Government either for military or other purposes, the former owner shall have the right of pre-emption on paying the sum awarded as compensation together with the value of any improvements made upon the land.

8. The word "land" in this Ordinance includes all water rights on, over or under the land, buildings, trees and easements.

9. The High Commissioner may delegate his powers under this Ordinance to any person or persons he may appoint.

10. This Ordinance shall be known as the "Acquisition of Land for the Army" Ordinance, and shall be substituted, so far as its provisions apply, for the Ottoman Law of Expropriation.

21st September, 1920.

An Ordinance to make provision for entering on the Land Registers interests in land registered in another name.*

WHEREAS, notwithstanding the provisions of Articles 1 and 4 of the Ottoman Provisional Law regulating the right to dispose of Immovable Property, dated 5th Jamad Awal, 1331, forbidding dispositions of land otherwise than through the Land Registry, many cases exist in which a person other than the registered owner or his heir claims an interest in registered land, whether as owner, mortgagee or otherwise ; and

Whereas it is desirable that, pending the decision of the Land Settlement Court as to the validity of any interest so claimed, the same should not be prejudiced by any registered disposition of the land ;

And whereas Article 4 of the same Law provides that no action of Nam Mustaar (land registered through a nominee) shall be heard in respect of immovable property owned by virtue of title deeds, whether Mulk or Miri ; but the Law granted a period of two years in which application could be made to correct the register ;

And whereas the Ottoman Provisional Law of 22nd Rabi El-Awal, 1331, provided that immovable property which had been owned by charitable institutions and corporations under a borrowed name might be correctly registered if application was made within six months from the date of the promulgation of the Law ;

And whereas owing to the occurrence of the war it was impossible in many cases for persons to make application for correction of the register ;

And whereas it is desirable that a further opportunity should be given to a person or corporation claiming to be the owner of the land registered in another's name, to make application for correcting the register :

It is hereby ordered as follows :

1. Any person claiming any interest in registered land, otherwise than as being the registered owner or mortgagee or the heir of such registered owner or mortgagee, may apply to the Court for an order that an entry be made in the register relating to such land to the effect that the applicant claims an interest therein, and the Court after hearing all parties may at its discretion order such entry to be made. Such entry shall specify the nature of the interest claimed

---
*This Ordinance has now lapsed. It is published as amended by the Correction of Land Registers Amendment Ordinance, 1921, and the Correction of Land Registers Amendment Ordinance, 1922.

and shall include short particulars of the proofs produced in support of such claims.

2.—(1) No such order shall be made by the Court unless the applicant shall produce to the Court either :—

(a) A non-appealable judgment of a competent Court establishing his right to the land as owner or mortgagee, or giving him possession thereof pending decision of the question of ownership ; or

(b) A private document ; or

(c) Evidence of payment of Werko Tax in respect of the lands in question for a period of 3 years immediately preceding the date of application.

(2) Such order shall not be made in respect of any application founded upon a transaction invalidated by the provisions of Proclamations Nos. 75 and 76 dated 18th November, 1918.

3. Where any immovable property is registered in the name of a person who is alleged to hold on behalf of, or as the nominee of, any other person or corporation, the person or corporation claiming to be the beneficial owner may within one year of the date of the issue of this Ordinance apply to the Court for an order stating that such person or corporation is entitled to be registered as owner in the place of the person at present registered. The applicant must produce documentary evidence to prove that the registered owner holds the property in the capacity of trustee or nominee, and the Court after hearing both parties, if the registered owner does not oppose the application, shall order the register to be corrected on such terms as it thinks fit.

If the registered owner opposes the application, the Court shall hear the application in accordance with the foregoing sections, and shall at its discretion order such entry to be made in the register as is thereby provided.

(Section 1 of Correction of Land Registers Amendment Ordinance, No. 17, 1922).

4. No application to correct the register on the grounds mentioned above shall be entertained after 10th July, 1924.

(Section 2 of the Amendment Ordinance, No. 17, 1922).

5.—(1) Any application under this Ordinance shall be made to the Director of Lands who may refer it at his discretion either to the District Court or to the Land Court in the district. Such application shall contain particulars of any document which the applicant intends to produce in support of his application, and the names of any witnesses whom he proposes to call.

(2) The application shall also state the name of the person who is registered as the owner or the mortgagee of the land, and whether

such person is living, and, if not, the name of his heir upon whom notice of the application is to be served.

6. The decision of the District Court or the Land Court as to making or refusing the order applied for, shall be final and shall not be subject to appeal.

7. Whether such application shall be successful or not, all fees, costs, and expenses of all parties in connection with such application shall be paid by the applicant.

8. Subject as aforesaid, the provisions of the Civil Procedure Code and any amendments thereof for the time being in force, whether as to service of documents, summons of witnesses, hearing, opposition or otherwise, shall apply to any such application, whether made to the Land Court or to the District Court.

9. The fees payable on such application shall be one-half per cent. on the value of the land as it appears in the Werko Register. *(Section 3 of the Amendment Ordinance, 1921).*

10. This Ordinance shall be known as the "Correction of the Land Registers Ordinance, 1920."

23rd September, 1920.

No. 186.

Mahlul Land Ordinance.

WHEREAS by the Land Code Miri Land reverts to the Government on failure of heirs of the holder or on non-cultivation during 3 years, and,

WHEREAS as a result of the Cadastral Survey all lands which through failure of heirs or non-cultivation during 3 years have become Mahlul, will become known in due course, but it is necessary that the Administration obtain forthwith a complete record of all such lands;

IT IS HEREBY ORDERED AS FOLLOWS :—

1. Every person who at any time previous to the issue of this Ordinance has taken possession of any land which owing to failure of heirs or non-cultivation became Mahlul is required to inform the Administration within 3 months of the date of this Ordinance.

No action will be taken against any person who has held such lands and who complies with the requirements of this Article. The Administration will in proper case lease the land to the person who has possessed it.

The right of inheritance will be determined according to the Provisional Law of the 3rd of Rabi El Awal 1331 relating to the inheritance of immovable property.

2. Every Mukhtar of a town, village or mazraa is required to inform the Administration within 3 months of all Mahlul lands of which at any time previous to the issue of this Ordinance illegal possession was taken, stating the names of the persons who have so taken possession.

3. Any person who having taken possession of Mahlul lands fails to inform the Administration will be liable to a fine of £E. 50 or imprisonment not exceeding 3 months or both these penalties.

Any Mukhtar who having reason to know of such illegal possession fails to inform the Administration in accordance with Art. 2 will be liable to a fine of £E. 25 or imprisonment not exceeding one month or both these penalties.

4. This Ordinance shall be known as the "Mahlul Land Ordinance 1920".

Government House
Jerusalem
1st. October, 1920.

HERBERT SAMUEL
High Commissioner
for Palestine.

Ordinance to provide for the regulation of Forest Lands and the protection of Trees.*

PART I.

PRELIMINARY.

1. This Ordinance may be cited as the "WOODS AND FORESTS ORDINANCE, 1920." Short title.

2. From the date on which this Ordinance comes into operation, the Laws, Regulations and Instructions mentioned in the Schedule hereto are repealed. Repeal of Laws.

3. In this Ordinance, unless there be something repugnant in the subject or context :— Interpretation.

> "Forest Land" means all land bearing forest trees, whether standing in masses or scattered about and land covered with shrub and brush wood which may serve for the purpose of fuel or for making charcoal or for any like use, and all land on which are plantations of young forest trees, grown either naturally or by the hand of man ;
>
> "Tree" includes shrubs and brush-wood ;
>
> "Fruit tree" includes every fruit-producing tree that is cultivated for domestic purposes and every tree that is customarily grafted ;
>
> "Timber," includes trees, fallen or felled, and all wood whether cut up or fashioned for any purpose or not ;
>
> "Forest Produce," includes the following when found in or brought from a forest, that is to say : Minerals, stones, surface soil, trees, timber, grass, creepers, leaves, flowers, fruits, seeds, roots, bark, honey, charcoal, resin and gum ;
>
> "Cattle," includes sheep, goats, camels, horses, mules and donkeys ;
>
> "Forest Officer," means any person whom the High Commissioner may from time to time appoint by name, or as holding an office, to carry out any of the purposes of this Ordinance, or to do anything required by this Ordinance.

---

*This Ordinance has since been repealed by 5 of 1926.

PART II.

FOR DETERMINING THE LIMITS OF FORESTS UNDER THE PROTECTION, CONTROL AND MANAGEMENT OF THE GOVERNMENT.

Forest lands not private property are State forests.

4. (1) All forest lands in Palestine, except such as are the private property of any person or persons or body corporate, are under the protection, control and management of the Government and are in this Ordinance referred to by the expression " State forests " ; provided that the net revenue arising from any forest land hereby defined to be a State forest and which may not actually be the property of the Government, shall be accounted for and paid to the persons and communities (if any) who have actually been in occupation of such forest land.

(2) Any question arising as to whether any forests or parts of forests belong to any community, shall be decided in the same manner as is provided for the delimitation of State forests under this Ordinance.

Private forests may be placed under Government protection.

5. The owner of any forest may place the same under the protection, control and management of the Government, subject to such conditions with regard to the payment of expenses and the termination of protection, control and management as the Government and the owner may agree to.

Government may control private forest land.

6.—(1) When and wherever it may be deemed advisable in the public interest, the High Commissioner may authorise the forest officer to enter into possession of, protect, control and manage forest lands which are the private property of persons or communities, subject to the provisions of Section 4 as to the payment of the net revenue to the owners.

(2) The forest officer may issue to the owners of private forest lands orders and regulations for the protection, control and management of these forest lands.

(3) When and wherever it may be deemed advisable in the public interest, the High Commissioner may authorise the forest officer to enter into possession of and control unused lands fitted for afforestation which are the private property of persons or villages or communities, provided that the net revenue arising from any such land after afforestation shall be paid to the persons or villages or communities who were in possession of such land.

(4) Where a grant of waste land (Mewat) has been made by the Palestine Government to any person on the condition that he afforests it, the High Commissioner may authorise the forest officer to enter

into possession of and manage such land if, in the opinion of the forest officer, within two years from the grant of the concession, proper steps have not been taken to plant the land.

7. So long as any forest shall be under the protection, control and management of the Government, it shall be deemed to be a State forest and shall be subject to all the laws, rules and regulations affecting State forests, provided always that it shall not be necessary to delimit any private forest lands under the provisions of this Ordinance. *Effect of placing private forests under Government protection.*

8. No right shall hereafter be acquired in or over any State forest except under a grant or contract made by or on behalf of the Government. *No future right to be acquired over State forests.*

9.—(1) As soon as conveniently may be after the passing of this Ordinance, there shall be appointed one or more commissions to ascertain and determine the limits of the State forests.

(2) Every such commission shall be appointed by the High Commissioner and shall consist of not less than three persons.

(3) For the purpose of delimiting State forests every such commission shall have all the powers and authorities which by the Survey Ordinance, 1920, are vested in the Director of Surveys, and all boundary marks erected or laid down by any such commission shall be deemed to be boundary marks erected or laid down under the provisions of such Ordinance.

10. Wherever the limits of any State forest or any part thereof shall have been determined in manner aforesaid the commission by whom the same has been determined shall draw up a report describing the limits so determined, and shall deposit with the District Commissioner of the District a copy thereof, and a notice shall be posted in every village in the immediate neighbourhood of the forest so delimited stating that the report has been deposited and that all persons objecting to the delimitation therein stated to have been made must carry in their objection thereto within three months from the date of such notice. *Publication of report of commission.*

11. Every objection shall be brought before the District Court in the same manner as a civil action and as though the party objecting was plaintiff and the party seeking to support the report was defendant, and the decision of every such Court on any such objection may be appealed from in the same manner and subject to the same restrictions as though it was a decision in any ordinary civil action. *Hearing of objections.*

12. At the expiration of three calendar months from the deposit of any such report as aforesaid, the delimitation of any State forest as described in the report shall, except so far as it may have been objected to, be binding and conclusive on all persons. *Determination to become final after three months.*

Delimitation not to hinder claims to adjacent forest land.

13. The delimitations of any State forest shall not operate to hinder the Government from claiming as State forest any forest land situated in the same neighbourhood as, but outside the limits of, any State forest actually delimited.

PART III.

THE MANAGEMENT OF STATE FORESTS.

Acts prohibited in State forests.

14. Whoever does any of the following acts on forest land declared to be under the protection, control and management of the Government by notification issued under Section 10 or under the provisions of Sections 5 and 6 hereof, except with the authority in writing of the forest officer or his representative duly authorised therefor:—

(a) Removes timber lying in such forests, felled either before the issue of the notification or at any time by or on account of the Government ;

(b) Fells, cuts, lops or burns any tree, strips off the bark or leaves from or otherwise damages any tree ;

(c) Extracts or collects resin, gum or other substance ;

(d) Extracts or removes stones, minerals, leaves, cones or other products of the forest ;

(e) Burns lime or manufactures charcoal, tar or pitch ;

(f) Sets fire to the forest or kindles a fire without taking due precaution to prevent its spreading ;

(g) Leaves burning any fire kindled within or in the vicinity of the forest ;

(h) Pastures cattle or permits cattle to trespass ;

(i) Clears or breaks up land for cultivation or any other purpose ;

shall be liable to a fine not exceeding £E.50 or to be imprisoned for a period not exceeding six months, or to both penalties, and may be charged in addition such compensation for the damage done to the forest as the convicting Court may direct to be paid.

Collection of firewood permitted.

15. Nothing in Section 14 shall prohibit the collection and removal from forests, other than closed forest areas, of dead and dry wood or brush wood to be used solely for firewood, for use of the inhabitants of villages who have been accustomed to supply their wants in this respect from the forests in the vicinity of their villages. Such privileges shall not, however, extend to the removal of roots or stumps or the felling of standing timber or the cutting of branches even though the same be dead.

16. Inhabitants of villages in the vicinity of forests who have been in the habit of supplying their wants from the neighbouring forests, and of obtaining timber for house building, domestic and agricultural purposes, shall apply for permission to fell and remove such timber in the manner hereinafter provided. *Inhabitants of neighbouring villages to apply for timber as provided.*

17. Persons eligible for grants under Section 16 and desirous of felling trees for their own use, for purpose specified in that paragraph, shall submit in writing to the District Commissioner of the District through the Mukhtar of the village, an application supported by a declaration of the Mukhtar that such grant is necessary stating :— *Form and manner of application.*

(a) The use for which the timber is required ;

(b) The girth, height, number and kind of trees required ;

(c) The place where it is desired to fell the same ;

(d) And the period requisite to remove the trees.

18. After due enquiry, having regard to the maintenance of the forest, the forest officer shall issue an order sanctioning or refusing such application in whole or in part. In the case of sanction, such order shall take the form of a permit which shall be issued in triplicate, two copies of which shall be forwarded to the forester in charge of the forest in which the felling is to take place, who shall, with as little delay as possible, proceed to the forest with the grantee, and mark the trees specified in the permit, and shall deliver one copy of the permit, to the grantee, retaining another for his own guidance and check, and the third copy shall remain with the issuing officer. *Order on application for grant of timber.*

19. It shall be the duty of the grantee to keep the permit constantly with him when working in the forest and produce it when required to do so. The non-production of the permit shall make the felling an infringement of Section 14 (b). *Production of permit when required.*

20. The use of the timber so granted for another purpose than that specified in the permit shall entail its forfeiture. *Timber to be forfeited when used for other than specified purpose.*

21. All trees felled and not removed within the period specified in the permit shall be forfeited, and any further action on the part of the grantee or anyone in his employ in removing or felling the timber shall be deemed to be an infringement of Section 14 (a) or (b) as the case may be. The issuing officer may, at his discretion, on sufficient cause for delay being shewn, extend the permit for such further time as he may deem proper. *Action after expiry of permit an infringement of Section 14*

Return of permits to office of issue.

22. Immediately after the date of the expiration of the permit, whether the total number of trees have been felled and removed or not, the copies held by grantee and forester respectively shall be returned to the office of issue. The forester shall enter on his copy the number of trees felled and removed.

Timber forfeited to be in charge of forest officer.

23. All timber forfeited under Sections 19 and 20 shall be in charge of the forest officer and may be sold or disposed of by him on account of the Government at his discretion.

Felling for purposes and by persons other than those specified in section 15.

24. The felling of timber on forest lands declared to be under the protection, control and management of the Government, for purposes or by persons other than those specified in Section 15, shall be at the discretion of the forest officer. In the case of sanction, the procedure and provisions of Sections 17, 18, 19, 20 and 21 shall be observed. Operations for the felling and removal of such timber shall be carried out according to rules made by the forest officer, and any contravention of such rules shall be deemed an infringement of Section 14 (*b*) of this Ordinance.

Cases in which the extraction of resin is allowed.

25. The extraction and collection of resin from pine trees may be allowed at the discretion of the forest officer, from the following trees :—

(*a*) Such as have already been subjected to the process ;

(*b*) Such as are destined to be felled within six years from the commencement of the extraction ; and

(*c*) Such as have a girth of six feet or more at four feet from the ground.

Rules for collection of gum and resin.

26. No gum or resin shall be extracted from any trees save those duly marked by the forest officer or his representative duly authorised for the purpose. Operations for the extraction and collection of gum or resin shall be carried out according to rules made by the forest officer, and any contraventions of such rules shall be deemed an infringement of Section 14 (*b*) of this Ordinance.

Erection of kilns only on approved spots.

27. Whenever the burning of lime, tar, pitch or charcoal within the forests has been permitted under Section 14, the erection of kilns for such purposes shall not be proceeded with until spots upon which such may be established shall have been pointed out by the forester, and the establishment of kilns within the forests upon other than the specified spots shall be deemed an infringement of Section 14 (*c*), whether fire has been commenced or not.

28. Whoever may have erected a kiln for any of the purposes specified in Section 26, and shall not have taken due precautions against the spread of fire therefrom into the forests, either by clearing a space of ground around the kiln, or other effectual means, or by keeping men constantly on watch, shall on fire so spreading, be deemed to have committed an offence under Section 14 (*f*) of this Ordinance. *Spread of fire from kilns an offence.*

29. The pasturage of cattle prohibited under Section 14 (*h*) of this Ordinance may be permitted when, with regard to the maintenance of the forest, it is, in the opinion of the forest officer, admissible, in such condition as the District Commissioner of the District may determine. *Pasturage of cattle permitted.*

30. Every year in the month of March, the Mukhtar of each village desiring to pasture its flocks under Section 28 of this Ordinance shall submit to the District Commissioner of the District a statement in writing, shewing the number and description of the cattle and the places in which it is desired to graze them, and provided such areas are available, the District Commissioner of the District, with the advice of the forest officer shall designate the tracts to which the cattle may be admitted, and fix the period during which they may be grazed. *Statement of cattle to be submitted by Mukhtar.*

31. The cattle belonging to the inhabitants of each village granted the privilege of grazing shall be placed under the charge of a separate herd, who shall, whenever grazing cattle in the forest, carry with him the order authorising the grazing and shall shew it whenever required and if he fails to do so the cattle so grazing shall be considered as trespassing under Section 34 of this Ordinance. *Cattle to be in charge of herds.*

32. In the event of fire breaking out in the forest through the negligence of any herd, the permission to pasture accorded to the village to which the herd belongs shall be at once rescinded, and it shall be at the discretion of the District Commissioner of the District, acting with the advice of the forest officer, to renew it or not. *Forfeiture of permit.*

33. Permission to cattle dealers and strangers to pasture cattle in the forests may be granted or refused at the discretion of the District Commissioner of the District, and on such conditions as he may determine in consultation with the forest officer. *Provision for grazing of strangers' cattle.*

34. If any cattle be found in the forests without the necessary permission, or not in the charge of a herd as specified, or having the necessary permission, is found on other land than that designated in the permission, the owner shall be liable to a fine not exceeding five piastres for each head of cattle so found, and to pay in addition compensation for any damage done. *Grazing without or contrary to terms of permission.*

H2

Closed forest areas. **35.** When for the better maintenance of the forest, or for the protection of young trees, or for any other purpose, it may in the opinion of the forest officer be desirable to exclude the public from any forest or part of a forest under the protection, control and management of the Government, notification of the position and boundaries of such forest or part of a forest shall be published in the Official Gazette, and such forest or part of a forest shall be known as a "closed forest area." Copy of the notice shall be posted prominently in villages in the neighbourhood of the "closed forest area."

Penalties for trespass or grazing in closed forest areas. **36.** Any person trespassing or grazing or allowing cattle to graze in a "closed forest area" after publication and posting of the notice shall be deemed guilty of an offence under this Ordinance and shall be liable to a fine not exceeding £E.10, or to imprisonment not exceeding one month, or both, and shall in addition pay compensation for any damage done.

Persons bound to assist in the extinction of fires. **37.** All persons having any right or privilege in a forest in which fire may have broken out, and the inhabitants of the neighbouring villages, shall be bound to assist in its extinction, and any person refusing so to assist shall be deemed guilty of an offence under this Ordinance punishable by a fine not exceeding five pounds, or imprisonment not exceeding fourteen days, or both, and may be deprived of his right or privilege for a space of from one to five years.

PART IV.

FOR THE BETTER PROTECTION OF FRUIT TREES.

Procedure for obtaining permit to fell trees. **38.** Applications to fell olive, carob or other fruit trees whether growing in State forests or in the forests that are the property of an individual or of a community or communities, or on cultivated land, shall be addressed in writing to the forest officer, and shall be accompanied by a statement setting forth :—

(a) The reasons and grounds on which the application is based ;

(b) The number, position, age and variety of the trees which it is desired to fell ;

(c) The purpose to which the timber is to be put, and, if it is to be sold, the name and address of the purchaser.

Penalties for cutting without permit. **39.** Whoever, except with the permission in writing from the forest officer, fells, cuts, lops, burns or removes olive, carob or other fruit producing trees shall be deemed guilty of an offence under this Ordinance, and on conviction shall be liable to a fine not exceeding £E.50 or to be imprisoned for a term not exceeding six months or to both.

40. Wood shall be deemed to be removed within the meaning of this Ordinance when it is being transported to any place of sale or disposal. *Wood in transit deemed to be removed.*

41. Any olive, carob, or other fruit producing tree which may have been cut or removed without permission, or for which a permit has not been produced on demand by a person duly authorised thereto, shall be liable to seizure and confiscation, as provided for by Section 43 of this Ordinance. *Confiscation and disposal of wood removed or cut without permit.*

PART V.

PENALTIES AND PROCEDURE.

42. An offence against this Ordinance may be tried by any Civil Court of competent jurisdiction; and such Court shall, in every instance where a fine is inflicted, be empowered to award any portion thereof not exceeding one-half to the persons upon whose information the conviction may be obtained. *Jurisdiction.*

43. Any forest produce in respect of which an offence has been committed, and all tools, carts and cattle used in committing any such offence, may be seized by any officer of the forest service or police officer, and any officer seizing any property under this section shall report such seizure to the District Commissioner and all such forest produce, tools, carts and cattle shall be liable to confiscation; such confiscation may be in addition to any other punishment prescribed for the offence. *Seizure of property liable to confiscation.*

44. Any officer of the forest service or police officer shall have authority to arrest without warrant any persons found committing any act prohibited by this Ordinance, or against whom there is reasonable suspicion of his having committed or having been concerned in any such act. *Power to arrest without warrant.*

45. Every officer of the forest service and every police officer shall prevent and may interfere for the purpose of preventing the commission of any offence under this Ordinance. *Power to prevent commission of an offence.*

46. Any person who obstructs, hinders or assaults any officer of the forest service or police officer in the execution of this Ordinance shall be deemed to have committed an offence, and shall be liable on conviction to a fine not exceeding £E.50, or to be imprisoned for a period not exceeding six months or to both. *Obstruction to execution of Ordinance.*

Wrongful seizure or arrest.

47. Any officer of the forest service or police officer who unnecessarily and vexatiously seizes any property under any section of this Ordinance, and so arrests any person under Section 44 shall be punished with a fine not exceeding £E.50, or with imprisonment not exceeding six months, or with both.

Wilful and malicious injury to trees.

48. Any person who wilfully and maliciously burns, strips the bark off, cuts or uproots any tree or shrub situated on Government or private lands shall be liable to imprisonment not exceeding three years and may also be ordered to pay compensation to the owner thereof in respect of any tree or shrub injured or destroyed.

Operation of other laws not barred.

49. Nothing in this Ordinance shall be deemed to prevent any person being prosecuted under any other law for any act which constitutes an offence against this Ordinance, or being liable under any such law to any higher punishment or penalty than that provided by this Ordinance, provided that no person shall be punished twice for the same offence.

October, 1920.

Section 4: 1921

An Ordinance to amend the Provisions of the Ottoman Land Law concerning "Mewat" Land.

1. This Ordinance may be cited as the "MEWAT LAND ORDINANCE, 1921." Short title.

2. The following paragraph shall be substituted for the last paragraph of Article 103 of the Ottoman Land Law :— Amendment of Article 103 of the Ottoman Land Law.

> Any person who, without obtaining the consent of the Government, breaks up or cultivates any waste land, shall obtain no right to a title deed for such land, and further will be liable to be prosecuted for trespass.

3. Any person who has already cultivated such waste land without obtaining authorisation shall notify the Registrar of the Land Registry within two months of the publication of this Ordinance and apply for a title-deed. Notification of Mewat land cultivated.

16th February, 1921.

TRANSFER OF LAND ORDINANCE,

No 2 of 1921.

WHEREAS Art. 14 of the Transfer of Land Ordinance 1920 temporarily maintains the provisions of Article 22 of the proclamation of June 24th, 1918, preventing the Courts from ordering the sale of immovable property in execution of a judgement or in satisfaction of a mortgage, and

WHEREAS grave hardship is caused in many cases to creditors and mortgagees owing to the prohibition against enforcing their claims, and it is expedient to modify the provisions of the said Article of the Ordinance.

Be it enacted by the High Commissioner for Palestine, after consultation with the Advisory Council, as follows. —

(1) Notwithstanding anything in the said articles of the Proclamation of June 24th, 1918 and the Transfer of Land Ordinance 1920, the Courts may order the sale of immovable property in execution of a judgement or in satisfaction of a mortgage.

(2) Application for sale should be made to the President of the District Court, who may order postponement of the sale if he is satisfied (a) that the debtor has reasonable prospects of payment if given time or (b) that having regard to all the circumstances of the case, including the needs of the creditor, it would involve undue hardship to sell the property of the debtor.

(3) This Ordinance may be cited as the Transfer of Land Ordinance No. 2, 1921.

April 4th, 1921. O G No 41 of 15 4 1921

An Ordinance to establish Courts for the settlement of the Title to Land, and to define their powers.

Short title.
1. This Ordinance may be cited as the "LAND COURTS ORDINANCE, 1921."

Construction.
2. In this Ordinance the word "land" shall include houses, buildings, and things permanently fixed in the land.

Constitution of and superintendence over Land Courts.
3.—(1) The High Commissioner may by order to be published in the Official Gazette establish a Land Court for such districts as may seem desirable, and may appoint such officers as may be necessary for the Courts. The constitution and the area of jurisdiction of the Court shall be specified in the order.

(2) The general superintendence and control over the Land Courts shall be vested in the Chief Justice,* who, with the sanction of the High Commissioner, may from time to time make rules as to any of the following matters :—

    (a) The Constitution, organization and procedure of the Land Courts;

    (b) The mode in which the records of the Courts shall be kept;

    (c) The forms to be used for applications and documents;

    (d) Fees payable for or in connection with land cases;

    (e) The appointment of attorneys;

    (f) Any other matter or thing in respect of which it may be expedient to make rules for the purpose of carrying this Ordinance into effect.

*See Notice published in Gazette of 1st September, 1922.

4. The Land Court shall have the following powers :— *Powers of Land Court.*

(*a*) To call for and record all claims to rights in or over Mulk and Miri and every other class of land ;

(*b*) Where claims to ownership, mortgage, or other registrable rights in or over land are accepted by the Land Court as valid and undisputed, to direct the registration of same in the Land Registry, and to demarcate the boundaries of the land over which such rights extend ;

(*c*) Where claims to such rights are accepted by the Court as valid and are undisputed except with regard to the boundaries, to give a decision as to the boundaries and to demarcate them in accordance with the decision ;

(*d*) Where there is a dispute as to the ownership of the land or any rights in or over the land, to hear the case and give a judgment ;

(*e*) To decide upon any dispute arising out of the partition of lands held in undivided ownership.

(*f*) To enquire into any case where an application is made under the Correction of Land Registers Ordinance, 1920, and to give a judgment whether such correction shall be made ;

(*g*) To hear and decide disputes as to the possession of State lands other than Miri land and to demarcate boundaries in accordance with the decision.

5. An appeal shall lie from the judgment of the Land Court to the Court of Appeal on conditions to be prescribed in Rules of Court made under this Ordinance. *Right of Appeal.*

6. The Land Department shall carry out the instructions of the Land Court as regards the registration of any rights to ownership, mortgage, or any other registrable rights, and shall issue title deeds in accordance with such instructions. *Registration following decision of Court.*

7.—(1) The Land Court may, with the consent of the parties, refer to arbitration any dispute arising before it in any matter under this Ordinance. Subject to the powers hereinafter set out as to remitting or setting aside the award, the Land Court shall, within six months of its issue, authenticate the award ; and the award when so authenticated shall have the effect of a judgment of a Court and shall be executory. *Reference to arbitration.*

(2) Before authenticating an award, the Land Court may remit it to the arbitrators for reconsideration on the following grounds :— *Grounds for reviewing awards.*

(*a*) If there is some defect patent on the face of the award ;

(b) If the Land Court is satisfied that the arbitrators have made a mistake;
(c) If material evidence, which could not with reasonable diligence have been discovered before the award was made, has since been obtained.

(3) The award may be set aside on the following grounds:—
(a) If the decision has been procured by fraud or the production of forged documents, or by the concealment of material documents;
(b) If there has been misconduct on the part of the arbitrators.

Powers to summon witnesses, etc.

8. The Land Court shall have power in the discharge of its duties under this Ordinance to summon any person to attend before it, to take evidence on oath, to require the production of any document or thing, to enter upon any lands and to set up any boundary or survey marks.

Law and procedure.

9.—(1) The Land Court will apply the Ottoman Law in force at the date of the British Occupation as amended by any Ordinances or Rules of Court issued since the Occupation; provided that the Courts shall have regard to equitable as well as to legal rights to land, and shall not be bound by any rule of the Ottoman Law prohibiting the Courts from hearing actions based on unregistered documents.

(2) The procedure to be followed by the Land Court shall, subject to any Rules of Court, be that laid down in the Code of Civil Procedure as amended. Provided that the Court shall not be bound by the rules of evidence contained in that Code or in the Civil Code.

Saving for jurisdiction of Magistrates and District Courts.

10. Nothing in this Ordinance shall derogate from—
(a) The power of Magistrates' Courts to hear actions concerning possession of land, or concerning the partition of land in accordance with the Law of 14th Moharram, 1332 A.H., or
(b) The power of the Chief Justice to allow an action concerning ownership of land to be heard by any District Court.

Order to demarcate land.

11.—(1) The Land Court may order the landowner or occupier of any land, within a reasonable time:
(a) To demarcate his land, and for the purpose of such demarcation to erect such stones, pillars, posts or other boundary or landmarks as they may direct;
(b) To demarcate any boundary or other line.

(2) If any person fails to obey such order, the Court may, after enquiry, mark out the boundary of the land and cause proper boundary lines to be erected at the cost of the owner or occupier.

8th April, 1921.

Surveyors Ordinance.*

WHEREAS it is expedient to regulate the profession of surveyors in Palestine :—

1. No person shall engage in private practice as a Surveyor in Palestine unless he has previously obtained a licence to practise as a Surveyor.

2. Application for a licence to practise as a Surveyor shall be addressed to the Director of Surveys, who may grant a licence on being satisfied either :—

(a) That the applicant has passed the examination of any approved institute of Surveyors or similar institution, or is by examination qualified to practise as a Surveyor ; or

(b) That the applicant is otherwise a fit person by reason of his knowledge to practise as a Surveyor in Palestine.

Every applicant for a licence to practise as a Surveyor shall pay to the Department of Surveys a fee of £E.2.

3. Whoever practises as a Surveyor in Palestine without having obtained a licence to practise shall be punishable with a fine not exceeding £E.50, or, in case of a second offence, with a fine not exceeding £E.100 in respect of each transaction in which he has engaged.

No prosecution, however, shall be instituted in respect of any act done within one month from the date of publication of this Ordinance, unless the person practising as Surveyor has failed within such period to apply for a licence.

4. No person who is not in possession of a licence to practise as a Surveyor granted under the Ordinance shall be entitled to sue in any Court of Law for a fee payable in respect of a survey made by him or any plan drawn by him.

5. The Director of Surveys may, upon being satisfied that the holder of a licence under this Ordinance has been guilty of unprofessional conduct as a Surveyor, at any time cancel the licence granted to him. Forthwith upon such cancellation, the Director of Surveys shall notify the same to the person whose licence is cancelled, and shall at the same time forward a brief statement of his reasons for cancellation.

6. Any person whose licence is cancelled may, within three months of the date of cancellation, apply to the President of the District Court in Jerusalem for an order that the Director of Surveys shall show cause to the District Court why the licence should not be restored. An order to show cause shall not be granted unless, in the opinion of the President, there is ground for believing that the licence has been cancelled for insufficient reasons.

Upon an order to show cause being granted, the District Court, after hearing the Director of Surveys, may either confirm the cancellation of the licence or order its restoration. The costs of the application shall be in the discretion of the Court.

7. A list of Surveyors licensed to practise and a note of the cancellation of any licence will be published in the Official Gazette.

8. This Ordinance shall be known as the Surveyors Ordinance, 1921.

May 10th, 1921.

*Repealed by Section 8 of the Land Surveyors Ordinance, 1925.

Demarcation of Government Lands.

1. In order to ascertain and demarcate unused Government Lands with a view to securing the cultivation and afforestation thereof, the Demarcation Commissions constituted under the Woods and Forests Ordinance, 1920, will henceforth demarcate :—

   (a) Mewat lands ;

   (b) Mahlul lands ;

   (c) Lands subject to the rights of Tapu (Mustehiki Tapu) ;

   (d) Any other Government lands.

2. An inspector of the Land Department will be appointed as a member of each Demarcation Commission.

3. The Commission will also demarcate all lands within a Municipal or Town Planning area for which no title is held and which have never been cultivated. All lands so demarcated will be registered as Government lands.

4.—(1) The Commission will demarcate as Mewat lands vacant lands for which no title is held and which are not allotted to the inhabitants of any place or village, and lie so far from the last house of a place or village that the voice of a man cannot be heard therefrom.

(2) Persons who have cultivated Mewat land will be issued with a Kushan for the cultivated area on payment of Bedl Misl in accordance with the terms of the Mewat Land Ordinance, 1921.

(3) Bedl Misl shall be paid within three months of the granting of the application for a Kushan.

5. Persons who have cultivated Mahlul land and notified the Government in accordance with the provisions of the Mahlul Land Ordinance, 1920, will, in proper cases, be granted a lease of the cultivated area

6. Claimants to land subject to the right of Tapu who give satisfactory reasons for non-cultivation, such as are set out in Article 68 of the Ottoman Land Code, or disabilities arising from the war, or inability to obtain agricultural loans, may be granted remission of the Tapu value provided they cultivate during the next sowing season.

7. The Commission in consultation with village representatives will, where possible, recommend the setting aside of an area as Metroukeh for villages which have no grazing land.

8. A list of the areas demarcated by the Commission as Government lands will be sent to the Mukhtars and posted up in the village. Any person who contests the demarcation shall send in his objection thereto, within three months from the date of such notice, to the Director of the Land Department, Jerusalem.

9. If the Director of the Land Department does not admit the objection, he will submit it to the Land Court, which shall hear the action as though the party objecting were plaintiff and the Land Department were defendant.

10th November, 1921.

TRANSFER OF LAND AMENDMENT ORDINANCE,

No 2 of 1921.

(A verbal amendment has been made in the Ordinance as published in Official Gazette No. 57 and it is therefore reprinted).

WHEREAS the Transfer of Land Ordinance 1920 contains provision to prevent speculative dealing in land and to protect the present occupants of land, and

WHEREAS it is desired to enlarge the power of disposition and to remove certain of the restrictions therein contained but it is still necessary to protect the present occupants of land,

Be it Hereby Enacted by the High Commissioner for Palestine, after Consultation with the Advisory Council, as follows:

1. Article 6 and 7 of the Land Transfer Ordinance 1920 and Article 8 up to the words "public utility" shall no longer be applied. The words "to the Director of Land Registries" shall be inserted after the word "presented" in Art. 4 of said Ordinance, and the words "to the Governor" shall be deleted from that Article. The words "Director of Land Registries" shall be substituted in the last sentence of Article 8 for "High Commissioner"

2. The consent of the Administration to a disposition shall be given by the Director of Land Registries or the Registrar of the District or Sub-District who shall be satisfied only that the transferor has a title, provided that in the case of agricultural land which is leased he shall also be satisfied that the tenant in occupation[1]) will retain sufficient land in the district or elsewhere for the maintenance of himself and his family.

3. This Ordinance shall be read together with the Transfer of Land Ordinance 1920, without prejudice to any transactions already carried out or commenced under that Ordinance.

4. This Ordinance shall be known as the Transfer of Land Amendment Ordinance No 2, 1921.

December 8th, 1921 O. G. No 60 of 1.2 1922.

Section 5: 1922

Orders-in-Council, Ordinances and Public Notices

GOVERNMENT OF PALESTINE.

Ordinance No. 15 of 1922.

SAND DRIFT ORDINANCE 1922.

No. 15.

WHEREAS it is desirable to make provision whereby the drifting of sand over land fit for cultivation may be checked and land covered by sand drifts may be made available for cultivation,

1922

BE IT ENACTED BY THE HIGH COMMISSIONER FOR PALESTINE, AFTER CONSULTATION WITH THE ADVISORY COUNCIL, AS FOLLOWS:—

Definition.

1. In this Ordinance and in any regulations made thereunder "sand drift" means a deposit of sand blown upon land; "tax payer" means any male person of not less than 18 years of age resident in a village and assessed to pay werko within the limits of a village or within its lands.

Chief Forest Officer to have Power to Publish Sand Drift Notice.

2. In any case in which the Chief Forest Officer is of opinion that sand has drifted or is likely to drift over land available for cultivation in such a manner as injuriously to affect agriculture, he may cause to be published in the Official Gazette a Notice giving particulars of the situation, extent, and boundaries of the land affected or likely to be affected by the sand drift and stating that steps will be taken under this Ordinance to stop the sand drift or to reclaim any land covered by sand drift. The Notice shall be published in conspicuous places in the neighbourhood, and shall be posted also at the office of the Governor of the District.

Provisions as to Registered Lands.

3. (i) A copy of the Notice shall be served upon every person in whose name the land or any part thereof or any interest therein is

— 2 —

registered, and the copy shall be accompanied by a request to him to cooperate with the Government in carrying out such works as may be necessary to stop the sand drift or to reclaim land covered by sand drift.

(ii) If the address of any such person is not known, the Chief Forest Officer may apply to the President of the District Court who shall make such order for substituted service as he thinks fit.

(iii) The cooperation of any person in works under this Ordinance shall be upon such terms as may be arranged, and in default of arrangement, upon such terms as the Director of Agriculture may, in view of all the circumstances, decide to be equitable.

(iv) If any person declines to cooperate in the work after having been required to do so by the Director of Agriculture, then

(a) if the land in respect of which he is registered is covered by sand drift, any interest which he may have therein shall be extinguished and shall vest in the Government, and

(b) if the land in respect of which he is registered is threatened by sand drift, such land shall be deemed to be charged with such part of the cost of any protective works as may be fixed in the order of the Director of Agriculture as if the land had been mortgaged as security for the same upon the date of the order.

(v) There shall be deemed to be refusal to cooperate within the meaning of this Article if within one month after service of the order of the Director of Agriculture the person served has not in writing accepted cooperation upon the terms of the order.

(vi) If within two months of the publication of the Notice a person produces evidence to the Chief Forest Officer that he cultivated the land for at least three years prior to the covering of the land by sand drift, and he further gives a written undertaking to cooperate in the work of reclaiming the land, the Chief Forest Officer shall refer his claim to the Director of Land Registries, who, if he is satisfied that the claimant has a right to be registered, shall register the interest. All further proceedings shall conducted as though the interest had been registered at the date of the Notice The decision of the Director of Land Registries shall be final.

(vii) The Director of Land Registries shall, upon the application of the Chief Forest Officer, make such entries in the Land Registers as may be required for carrying out the provisions of this Article.

(viii) If a person has agreed to cooperate under this Ordinance and fails to do so in whole or in part, the loss or damages thereby incurred by the Government shall be recoverable from him as a civil debt.

Extinguishment of Unregistered Interest.
4. Every unregistered interest in land included in any Notice in respect of which no claim has been sent to the Chief Forest Officer within two months of the date of publication, or the holder of which fails to give an undertaking to cooperate in the reclamation of the land, shall be deemed to be extinguished, unless the interest

(a) is the subject of an application for registration at the date at which this Ordinance comes into force, or

(b) is the subject of litigation instituted before the date at which this Ordinance comes into force wherein the title to such land is the matter in dispute.

— 4 —

Invitation to Villages to Co-operate.	5. Subject to the provisions of Article 3 of this Ordinance, the Chief Forest Officer may, after the expiration of two months from the date of the publication of the Notice in the Official Gazette, under Article 2, summon a meeting of the tax payers of the village adjacent to which the land affected by the sand drifts described in the Notice is situate, for the purpose of ascertaining their views as to the measures to be taken and shall cause notice of the date of the meeting to be posted in conspicuous places in the village at least 10 days before such date. A notice of every such meeting together with an invitation to be present thereat shall be forwarded to every important land owner in the neighbourhood
Proceedings at Meeting.	6. The Chief Forest Officer shall preside at the meeting and shall take down in writing the names of the inhabitants present. He shall explain to the persons present the nature of the steps proposed to be taken for the purpose of checking the inroads of sand drifts or for the purpose of reclaiming the land covered by sand drift, and shall in particular explain the provisions of this Ordinance so far as they concern the result of the resolution of the meeting.
Resolution of Meeting and Effect Thereof.	7. Where at any such meeting it is resolved by a majority of not less than two-thirds of the tax payers there present that the work of checking the inroad of sand drift or reclamation of land covered by sand drift, shall be undertaken by the village the following provisions shall forthwith come into effect with respect to that village:
	(i) Every male inhabitant over the age of 15 years shall be thenceforth obliged to contribute in each year such number of days labour not exceeding six, at such times as the Chief Forest Officer may require for the purpose of any

— 5 —

work directed to be done by the Chief Forest Officer to check the inroad of sand drifts in the neighbourhood or to reclaim land covered by sand drift, or in lieu thereof shall be liable to contribute the sum of P.T.20 in respect of each day on which he has failed to do or provide the labour.

(ii) It shall be duty of the Mukhtar of the village, at the request of the Chief Forest Officer to provide from among persons subject to the obligation of labour under this Article such number of labourers upon any day or for any work required by the Chief Forest Officer in accordance with and subject to the provisions of this Article.

Payment of Contribution.

8. Money contribution payable under this Ordinance shall be paid to the Mukhtar, who shall account to the Chief Forest Officer for the same.

Contributions shall be recoverable by proceedings before a Magistrate at the suit of the Mukhtar and in default, at the suit of the Chief Forest Officer or any person authorised by him.

Use of Reclaimed Land, etc.

9. Where a village has, under this Ordinance resolved to carry out any work, and in consequence of the execution of such work any land has been reclaimed or any shrubs or trees have been planted, such land and trees and shrubs shall be hereafter applied as Matruke Land for the benefit of the inhabitants of the villages which carried out the work, subject, nevertheless, to any arrangement made with a registered or unregistered owner under the provisions of Article 3 hereof, and subject to the regulations of the Chief Forest Officer.

Regulations.

10. The Chief Forest Officer may, with the approval of the High Commissioner, from time to time make rules for any of the following purposes, that is to say,

— 6 —

i. as to the plantation of any land as to which a notice has been published in pursuance of this Ordinance, and as to the manner in which any trees or shrubs planted are to be cultivated, watered, or protected;

ii. as to the erection and maintenance of protective works required to check the inroad of sand in connection with any land as to which a notice has been published in pursuance of this Ordinance;

iii. as to duties of the Mukhtars of villages under this Ordinance.

iv. as to any other matter which requires regulation under this Ordinance.

Lands to be Deemed State Forests.
11. All lands in respect of which work has been executed in pursuance of this Ordinance shall be deemed to be a State Forest under the protection and control of the Government within the meaning of Chapter III, IV, and V of the Wood and Forests Ordinance 1920.

Government May Carry Out Works.
12(i) The Government may carry out any works for the purpose of checking encroachment by sand drift or of reclaiming land covered by sand drift upon land included in any Notice under this Ordinance notwithstanding any refusal or failure of any person to cooperate or the refusal of any village to undertake the work, or may arrange with any person, company, or corporation for the execution of the work.

(ii) In any case in which the Government undertakes works for the purpose of checking encroachments by sand drift or of reclaiming land covered by sand drift in respect of land not included in a Notice published under this Ordinance or arranges with any other person

— 7 —

for the execution of such work an invitation to cooperate shall be given to any person who would be entitled to cooperate under the provisions of Article 3 hereof.

Citation.   13. This Ordinance may be cited as the SAND DRIFT ORDINANCE 1922.

Date.   14. This Ordinance shall come into force on the 1st day of August 1922.

HERBERT SAMUEL,
High Commissioner.

GOVERNMENT OF PALESTINE

Ordinance No. 17 of 1922.

CORRECTION OF LAND REGISTERS AMENDMENT ORDINANCE 1922.

No. 17.

1922.

WHEREAS the Correction of Land Registers Amendment Ordinance 1921 prolongs the period within which application may be made for the correction of land registers till 1st September 1922,

AND WHEREAS it is desirable to extend further the period within which such application may be made.

BE IT ENACTED BY THE HIGH COMMISSIONER FOR PALESTINE, AFTER CONSULTATION WITH THE ADVISORY COUNCIL, AS FOLLOWS:—

Extension of Period for Application.

1. The period within which an application for the correction of the registers in accordance with the provisions of the Correction of Land Registers Ordinance 1920, may be made is extended to two years from the date of this Ordinance.

Applications.

2. The Director of Land Registries may refer any such application, at his discretion, either to the District Court or to the Land Court in the District.

Citation.

3. This Ordinance may be cited as the CORRECTION OF LAND REGISTERS AMENDMENT ORDINANCE 1922.

July 10th, 1922.

WYNDHAM DEEDES,
Acting High Commissioner.

GOVERNMENT OF PALESTINE.

ORDINANCE No. 18 of 1922.

LAND VALUERS ORDINANCE.

No. 18

1922

WHEREAS it is expedient to regulate the profession of land valuers in Palestine.

BE IT ENACTED BY THE HIGH COMMISSIONER FOR PALESTINE, AFTER CONSULTATION WITH THE ADVISORY COUNCIL, AS FOLLOWS:—

Prohibition of Practice without Licence.

1. No person shall engage in private practice as a land valuer in Palestine unless he has previously obtained a licence so to practise.

Procedure on Application for Licence.

2. Applications for a licence to practise shall be addressed to the Director of Surveys, who may grant a licence on being satisfied that the applicant

(i) is above the age of 25 years, and

(ii) (a) has carried on practice as a land valuer in Palestine for a period of 3 years preceding the promulgation of this Ordinance; or

(b) has, during not less than three years, been engaged in land valuation whilst in the employ of any person practising as a valuer in Palestine, and is fitted by his knowledge of the principles of land valuation; or

(c) is either in possession of a diploma from a recognised professional institution of a foreign country, or has passed an examination approved by the Director of Surveys, with reference to the principles of land valuation.

Applications for Licences.

3. Any person applying for a licence on either of the grounds specified in para (ii) (a) or (b) of the preceding Article shall produce to the Director of Surveys a certificate to that effect signed by the Governor of the District in which he has practised or has been employed.

2

Every applicant for a licence to practise as a land valuer shall pay to the Department of Surveys a fee of two pounds Egyptian (£E.2).

A licence shall be valid for a period of 5 years only. At the end of that period the Director of Surveys shall be entitled to impose a fresh test or any fresh conditions for the renewal of the licence.

Unlicensed Valuer not Entitled to sue for Fees.
4. No person who is not in possession of a licence to practise as a Land Valuer granted under this Ordinance shall be entitled to sue in any Court of Law for a fee payable in respect of a valuation of land or any interest therein made by him.

Any person who holds himself out to be a licensed valuer, or practises as such in Palestine, when he has not been licensed, shall be punishable with a fine not exceeding £E.50.

Cancellation of Licence.
5. (i) The Director of Surveys may, upon being satisfied that the holder of a licence under this Ordinance has been guilty of unprofessional conduct as a valuer, at any time cancel the licence granted to him. The Director of Surveys shall notify the cancellation to the person whose licence is cancelled, and shall at same time forward a brief statement of his reasons for cancellation.

(ii) Any person whose licence is cancelled may, within three months of the date of cancellation, apply to the President of the District Court of Jerusalem for an order that the Director of Surveys shall show cause to the District Court why the licence should not be restored. An order to show cause shall not be granted unless in the opinion of the President there is ground for believing that the licence has been cancelled for insufficient reasons.

Upon an order to show cause being granted, the District Court, after hearing the Director of Surveys, may either confirm the cancellation of the licence or order its restoration. The costs of the application shall be in the discretion of the Court.

Publication of Names of Valuers.

6. A list of Land Valuers licensed to practise and a note of the cancellation of any licence shall be published in the Official Gazette.

Citation.

7. This Ordinance shall be known as the LAND VALUERS ORDINANCE 1922.

15th August 1922

HERBERT SAMUEL,
High Commissioner.

GOVERNMENT OF PALESTINE.

ORDINANCE No. 21, OF 1922.

CREDIT BANKS ORDINANCE 1922.

No. 21.

WHEREAS it is desirable to facilitate the operations of Credit Banks lending money on immovable security, and to provide more expeditious remedies for the enforcement of loans on mortgage and further to make provision for the supervision by the Government of the operations of such Banks,

1922.

BE IT ENACTED BY THE HIGH COMMISSIONER FOR PALESTINE, AFTER CONSULTATION WITH THE ADVISORY COUNCIL, AS FOLLOWS:—

Definition of Credit Bank.

1. The provisions of this Ordinance shall apply only to Companies incorporated as, or authorized to act as, Credit Banks in Palestine.

i. A Company incorporated as a Credit Bank shall mean a Company registered under the Companies Ordinance 1921 which is described by its name as a Credit or Mortgage or Agricultural Bank, and which has as its principal object the lending of money on the security of immovable property.

ii. A Company authorized to act as a Credit Bank shall mean a Company registered as aforesaid which has been authorized by the High Commissioner to carry on the business of a Credit Bank. Applications for such authorization shall be made to the Registrar of Companies.

iii. The Registrar of Companies shall from time to time keep the Inspectors appointed under this Ordinance informed of the name and principal Office of every Company incorporated as, or authorized to act as, a Credit Bank in Palestine.

2

Sale of Mortgage Property out of Court.

2. (i) Notwithstanding the provisions of the Proclamation of June 24th, 1918, and the Transfer of Land Ordinance No.2, 1921, land within a Municipal Area or within a townplanning area, where it exists, which has been mortgaged to a Credit Bank may be sold by order of an Execution Officer without an order of Court, provided that such Officer shall, before ordering the sale, satisfy himself that three months notice in writing to pay the debt has been given by the mortgagee to the mortgagor, and default in payment has been made.

(ii) Notwithstanding anything contained in the Provisional Law of Mortgages of 15th February 1328 (A.H.), if the highest bid offered at the Auction is less than the debt due to the bank, the bank may make a higher bid not less than the debt, interest and costs and shall thereafter be entitled

(a) to have the property registered provisionally in their name as purchasers, and

(b) to obtain an order for possession under Article 10 of the said Provisional Law:

(c) when in possession under such order, to lease the property for a period not exceeding one year.

Provided that no disposition of the property other than a lease made in accordance with the provisions of this Article shall be valid against the mortgagor unless an order of the Court has been made in manner hereinafter provided.

(iii) If at any time before an order of the Court is made, the mortgagor pays the debt due to the Bank including interest and expenses, the Bank shall, at the expense of the mortgagor, re-transfer the property into his name, if it has been already registered in the name of the Bank, and vacate possession in favour of the mortgagor, if an order for possession has been obtained.

3

(iv) At any time not less than 6 months from the date of the sale, the Bank may apply to the District Court of the district in which the property is situated for an order for vesting the property, and the Court shall, if it is satisfied that the mortgagor is not able to repay the debt and interest, make an order for vesting the property upon such terms as it thinks fit; and upon such order being made the Bank shall be deemed to be owner of the property as purchasers under the sale by auction.

Mortgage of Leasehold Property.

3. (i) Notwithstanding anything contained in the Provisional Law of the Mortgage of Immovable Property of 15th February A.H. 1328, a leasehold interest for a period of more than five years in any immovable property may, subject to any covenant as to transfer or mortgage in the lease contained, be mortgaged to a Credit Bank, and every such mortgage shall be made in accordance with the provisions of the said Law for the Mortgage of Immovable Property as if such leasehold interest were deemed to be immovable property within the meaning of that Law, and the remedies of the Mortgagee, by way of sale or otherwise under this Ordinance or any other Law shall be applicable to a mortgage of leasehold property to the same extent as the same are applicable to the mortgage of any other interest in immovable property.

(ii) The remedies of the mortgagee by sale or otherwise shall be exerciseable without it being necessary to obtain the prior consent of the lessor provided that a written notification of the proposed mortgage was served upon him not less than fifteen days before the execution of the mortgage.

Conditions of Loans by Credit Banks.

4. (i) Every loan on immovable security advanced by a Credit Bank shall be repayable by instalments, and the time of payment shall be fixed with regard to the borrower's circumstances.

4

(ii) A Credit Bank shall accept payment of the whole outstanding loan or of any part thereof, not less than one-fourth of the original loan, before the date stipulated for payment, whether such repayment be made by the mortgagor or by a third party, subject to payment of a commission to the Bank which shall in no case exceed six calendar months interest on the sum so paid in advance. If the mortgagor gives three months notice to the Bank of his intention to repay, the commission payable shall not exceed three calendar months interest on the sum so repaid in addition to the interest accrued due at the date of repayment.

(iii) In the case of every loan made by a Credit Bank on the security of Agricultural property there shall be an implied condition for the relief of borrowers in a bad season either by postponement of all outstanding instalments for the year, or by spreading the instalments for the year over the remaining years of the term.

In the event of any mortgagor claiming that the season has been a bad one, the Executive Council of the Government of Palestine acting with the advice of the Director of Agriculture and after calling such evidence as it may think fit, shall cause a list to be prepared showing in what Districts and Sub-Districts, if any, the season shall be deemed to be a bad season for the purposes of this sub-section.

If, after the publication of this list, either the mortgagor or the mortgagee shall represent that the decision arrived at is inequitable in any particular case, the Executive Council shall cause the matter to be adjudicated upon by such officer of the Government or other person as they may think fit. If the adjudicator shall find that the application was unfounded, frivolous or vexatious, the person making it shall be liable to pay all the expenses involved by the adjudication.

(iv) Every loan made by a Credit Bank shall be made upon a Certificate of value of the property signed by a valuer licensed in accordance with the provisions of the Land Valuers Ordinance 1922.

The regulations of a Credit Bank upon the matters dealt with in this Article shall be submitted to the Treasurer for his approval.

Inspectors of Credit Banks.

5. (i) The High Commissioner may appoint one or more Officials of the Government of Palestine to act as Inspectors of Credit Banks.

(ii) The Inspectors of Credit Banks shall at all times have access to the books and other documents of the Banks. It shall be their duty from time to time to make such investigations as they think fit for the purpose of ascertaining that the Bank is conducting its business in accordance with the provisions of this Ordinance and in accordance with the provisions of its Memorandum, Articles of Association or Statutes regulating the conduct of its operations.

(iii) Inspectors shall be entitled to call for the production of any books or documents relating to the banking business which they may deem necessary, and to examine any officer or agent of the Bank in relation to its business whether upon oath or otherwise

(iv) Any officer or agent of the Bank who refuses to produce, or who fails upon any inspection to produce any relevant book or document, or to answer any question relating to the affairs of the Bank put by an Inspector, shall be liable to a fine not exceeding £E.50 in respect of each offence.

(v) Any officer or agent of the Bank who, in the course of an investigation under this Article wilfully makes a false statement on oath shall be liable to the same punishment as though he had given false evidence at a judicial hearing.

Report by Inspector	6. A report as to the conduct of the business of every Credit Bank in Palestine shall be rendered annually by the Inspector to the High Commissioner. Every Credit Bank shall be entitled upon its application to receive a copy of such report so far as it refers to its own operations.
Inspector may Apply for Winding-up.	7. If, in the opinion of the Inspector, any Credit Bank is not conducting its business in accordance with the provisions of this Ordinance or with the provisions of its Memorandum, Articles, and Statutes, it shall be competent for the Inspector to make application to the proper Court for an order for the winding-up of the Bank.
Expense of Investigation.	8. The expenses of, or incidental to, any investigation conducted by the Inspector, including such fees to be paid to the Inspector as may be from time to time authorized by the High Commissioner, shall be paid by the Bank.
Disclosure by Inspectors.	9. An Inspector appointed under this Ordinance who, otherwise than in accordance with his duty, discloses any fact which may have come to his knowledge in the course of his enquiries, shall be liable to the penalties from time to time provided by the Penal Codes for the disclosure of professional secrets.
Restrictive Conditions may be Imposed by High Commissioner.	10. Upon the application for registration under the Companies Ordinance 1921 of any Company of which the principal object is the lending of money on the security of immovable property, or upon the application by any Banking Company for authorization to act as a Credit Bank within the meaning of this Ordinance, the grant of the certificates of incorporation or of such authorization shall be made subject to such provisions for the better securing of the financial stability of the Bank as the High Commissioner may think fit, and in particular, the High Commissoner may require

that any or all of the following restrictions on the operations of the Bank shall be prescribed:—

i. Loans shall not be made on other than the first mortgage.

ii Uninsured buildings shall not be accepted as security.

iii. The amount of any loan shall not exceed, except with the approval of the Director of Agriculture, 25 per cent. of the value of the security in the case of plantations, or 50 per cent. in the case of unplanted land, or, except with the approval of the Director of Commerce and Industry, 50 per cent. in the case of industrial loans, or 75 per cent. in the case of buildings whether urban or rural.

Statement to be Lodged by Credit Banks.

11. Where in the opinion of the Inspector appointed under this Ordinance any Company incorporated as a Credit Bank in Palestine is not carrying on any other business in Palestine except that of making advances on the security of immovable property, the Inspector may require that the statement of the assets and liabilities of the Companies lodged with the Registrar of Companies in accordance with the provisions of Article 5 of the Banking Ordinance 1921 and Article 1 of the Banking Ordinance 1922, shall be in such form as he may prescribe, and the lodging of a statement in the prescribed form shall in such case be deemed to be in substitution for the statement required to be lodged under the aforesaid provisions.

Repeals.

12. (i) Articles 5 and 6 of the Credit Banks (Facilities) Ordinance 1920 are hereby repealed.

(ii) The provisions of the Credit Banks (Facilities) Ordinance shall be henceforth deemed to be applicable only to Companies which are Credit Banks as defined by this Ordinance.

(iii) Credit Banks shall be entitled to borrow money on debentures or otherwise, subject.

8

nevertheless, to the provisions of Articles 65 to 69 of the Companies Ordinance 1921. Debentures issued by a foreign Banking Company authorized to act as a Credit Bank under this Ordinance shall not affect assets in Palestine unless the debentures have been issued in conformity with the provisions of the said Articles.

Citation.

13. This Ordinance may be cited as the CREDIT BANKS ORDINANCE 1922, and shall be read in conjunction with the Credit Banks (Facilities) Ordinance 1920.

Date.

14. This Ordinance shall come into force on the 15th day of October 1922.

HERBERT SAMUEL,
High Commissioner.

Section 6: 1923

GOVERNMENT OF PALESTINE

Ordinance No. 4 of 1923.

SUCCESSION ORDINANCE.

No. 4.

1923.

WHEREAS it is provided by Articles 52, 53 and 54 of the Palestine Order-in-Council, 1922, that Moslem Religious Courts shall have exclusive jurisdiction in matters of personal status of Moslems, and that the Courts of non-Moslem Religious Communities shall, with certain limitations, have jurisdiction in matters relating to the succession to deceased members of those Communities,

AND WHEREAS it is desirable to make provision for the succession on death to persons in cases where the Courts of the Religious Communities do not exercise such jurisdiction, and otherwise to provide for the succession to persons dying possessed of immovable or movable property in Palestine,

BE IT ENACTED BY THE HIGH COMMISSIONER FOR ALESTINE, AFTER CONSULTATION WITH THE ADVISORY COUNCIL, AS FOLLOWS:—

Part I — Jurisdiction of Civil Courts.

Exclusive Jurisdiction of Civil Courts.

1. (i) The Civil Courts shall have exclusive jurisdiction in all matters relating to the succession to, and the confirmation of wills of, every Palestinian citizen and any other person not being a foreigner within the meaning of this Ordinance, provided that such citizen or other person was not at the

— 2 —

date of his death either a Moslem or a member of one of the religious communities specified in the 1st Schedule hereto and of such other communities as may from time to time be specified by the High Commissioner.

(ii) They shall also have exclusive jurisdiction in all cases in which a dispute arises as to the succession to, or the will of, a foreigner other than a Moslem.

(iii) They shall have jurisdiction concurrently with the Courts of the specified Religious Communities in matters relating to the succession to members of the specified Religious Communities other than foreigners, except where exclusive jurisdiction is by this Ordinance conferred upon the Courts of the Community.

Rules to be applied by the Civil Courts in distributing successions.

2. Subject to the provisions of Article 19, a Civil Court shall distribute successions within its jurisdiction according to the rules set forth in this Article.

(i) Where the deceased was a member of one of the specified religious Communities and was not a foreigner, the provisions of Article 9 hereof shall apply.

(ii) Where the deceased was a Palestinian citizen and was not a member of one of the specified religious communities, the provisions of the Ottoman Law shall apply, subject to any testamentary disposition made by the deceased.

(iii) Where the deceased was either a foreigner or, not being a foreigner within the meaning of this Ordinance, was neither a Palestinian citizen nor a member of one of the specified religious communities, the following rules shall apply.

— 3 —

(a) Mulk land and movables of the deceased shall be distributed in accordance with the National Law of the deceased.

(b) The validity in form of any will left by the deceased and his capacity to make testamentary disposition shall be determined in accordance with his National Law. Provided that if the will is made in Civil Form under this Ordinance it shall in all cases be held valid.

(c) Where the National Law imports the Law of the Domicile or the Religious Law or the Law of the situation of an immovable, the Law so imported shall be applied. If the National Law imports the Law of the Domicile and the latter provides no rules applicable to the person concerned, the law to be applied shall be his National Law.

Civil Courts may refer succession to Religious Court.

3. In any case in which the deceased was a foreigner, the President of the competent District Court may, upon the application of any person having interest, and if he deems it just and convenient, refer to the appropriate Religious Court the administration and distribution of the estate of such person provided that

(a) he was at the time of his death a member of one of the said Religious Communities;

(b) the law of such community would be applicable to the distribution of his estate according to his National Law.

Where the estate with reference to which such an order is made includes immovable property, a memorandum thereof shall be forthwith entered at the Land Registry

— 4

at the instance of the President of the District Court, and the Director of Land Registries shall, by the effect of such entry, be restrained from making any entries in the Register in respect of the interest of any persons therein except by order of the Court of the Community to which the succession is referred.

Part II. Jurisdiction of Religious Courts.

Exclusive Jurisdiction of Moslem Courts.

4. i) The Moslem Religious Courts shall have exclusive jurisdiction as to all matters relating to succession upon death to the estate of a Moslem, whether under a will or otherwise.

ii) Where the deceased Moslem was a foreigner of any other than the Sunni rite, it shall be competent for his heirs to petition the High Commissioner, who may direct the constitution of a special Moslem Court for the determination of any questions relating to the succession, or may otherwise make provision therefor.

Exclusive Jurisdiction of Christian and Jewish Courts.

5. i) The Courts of each of the specified Religious Communities shall have exclusive jurisdiction to confirm a will made by any member of the Community not being a foreigner within the meaning of this Ordinance.

ii) The certificate of the Court of the community confirming a will shall be deemed to be conclusive evidence that the will is valid in form and that the testator had capacity to make the will and was not affected by mistake, fraud or undue influence, but confirmation by a Court

Concurrent jurisdiction of Courts of the Communities.

shall not make valid any disposition of property thereby which is contrary to law.

6. i) The Courts of each of the specified Religious Communities shall have jurisdiction in matters relating to the intestate succession upon death to persons who at the date of their death were members of the Community.

ii) Subject to the provisions of Article 19, the estates of such persons shall be administered and distributed in accordance with the law of the Community. Provided that the Court of the Community may, upon being invited so to do by any person beneficially interested in such estate, regulate its distribution in accordance with the provisions of the Ottoman Law, subject, nevertheless, to any testamentary disposition made by the deceased, so far as such disposition is permitted.

Transfer to Civil Courts.

7. i) The President of a District Court may, upon the application of any person interested in the estate of a deceased person and if he deems it just or convenient make an order prohibiting the Court of any of the specified Religious Communities from taking cognizance of, or from dealing further with, the succession of any deceased person, and from the date of such order the administration and distribution of the estate shall be within the exclusive jurisdiction of the Civil Courts, and any proceedings which may be pending shall be forthwith transferred to the District Court.

Provided that no such order shall be made where the estate has already been

— 6 —

distributed under the order of the Courts of the Community,

And provided further that no such order shall affect any proceedings taken in a Religious Court solely with a view to the confirmation of a will.

ii) Where the property includes in the succession immovables, a memorandum of every such order shall be forthwith entered in the Land Register at the instance of the Court making the order, and the Director of Land Registries shall, by the effect of such entry, be restrained from making any entries in the Register in respect of the interests of persons in the estate, except by order of the President of the District Court.

Persons Entitled to make Applications to Civil Courts.

8. The following persons shall be deemed to be persons interested in the estate of a deceased person within the meaning of Article 7:

a) Any person who, upon the distribution of the estate by a Civil Court, would be entitled to any share therein;

b) an executor or beneficiary under a will made by the deceased.

c) A creditor of any beneficiary who has renounced his share in the succession

Part III.
Estates Administered and Distributed by Civil Courts.

Distribution by Civil Courts in certain cases.

9. In the administration and distribution of the estate of a deceased person who was a member of any of the specified Religious Communities and was not a foreigner, the Civil Courts shall apply the following rules to regulate the distribution

of his Mulk and movable property.

i. Any restriction upon the power to testamentary disposition recognised by the law of the Community of which the deceased was a member at the time of his dead shall be applied.

ii. Any part of the property of the deceased which is by the law of such Community to be reserved for any particular person or class of persons shall be distributed in accordance with that Law.

iii. Subject to the foregoing provisions, the property shall be distributed in accordance with the testamentary dispositions made by the deceased.

iv. In default of testamentary dispositions, or in so far as such dispositions do not extend, the property shall be distributed in accordance with the provisions of the Ottoman Law contained in the 2nd Schedule hereto.

Wills in Civil Form.
10. The Civil Courts shall hold a will to be valid in Civil Form if it complies with the following conditions: —

i. The will is a) in writing;

b) signed or sealed at the end thereof by the testator or by some other person by his direction in the presence of two witnesses at least, present at the same time, who have attested the will in the presence of the testator;

c) The witnesses were persons who had attained the age of 18 years and were of sound mind at the time of the execution of the will.

ii. The testator was not under the age of 18 years at the time of the execu-

— 8 —

tion of the will or suffering from mental infirmity, or otherwise incapable of making a will according to the law governing his personal status applicable to him in Palestine.

iii. The testator was not induced to make the will by fraud or by the exercise of undue influence.

Witnesses not to be Beneficiaries. 11. No person shall be entitled to take any interest under a will in Civil Form if he is one of the attesting witnesses thereof.

Probate of will. 12. i) No will made in Civil Form shall be deemed to be valid unless it has been proved before a District Court. Probate thereof may be granted to an executor appointed by the will, or if the executor appointed has died or renounced Probate or is incompetent, to a beneficiary thereunder or to any other fit person.

ii) Probate shall not be granted until there has been filed with the Probate Officer of the Court a) an inventory of the movable property of the deceased verified by the oath of the applicant, and b) an inventory of the Mulk Land of the deceased (if any) certified by the Director of Land Registries.

iii) In any case in which the will affects Mulk Land, the Probate Officer shall forthwith upon Probate being granted, register the Probate at the Land Registry. Such registration shall have the effect specified in Article 7, para (ii) hereof.

Appointment of Administrator. 13. i) The District Court or any judge thereof may in any case, where it appears to be just and convenient, appoint an ad-

— 9 —

ministrator to administer the estate of any deceased person of which the administration and distribution is within the jurisdiction of the Civil Court.

ii) Such administrator may be appointed on the application of any person entitled to an interest in the estate, and the Court or judge may nominate any such person or any other person whom it may think fit, to be administrator, provided that a creditor shall not be appointed administrator unless there is reasonable probability that the estate is insolvent.

iii) Every administrator shall, within such time as the Court may direct, file in the Court an inventory of the property of which the deceased died possessed, verified by oath and certified, so far as regards interests in immovable property, by the Director of Land Registries.

iv) The person to whom Probate of a will has been granted in accordance with the provisions of Article 12 shall be deemed to be an administrator and have the powers of an administrator under this Ordinance.

Duties of Administrator.

14. It shall be the duty of an administrator to administer the estate of the deceased according to law. He shall with all convenient speed

a) collect and get in the property of which the deceased died possessed;

b) pay the funeral and testamentary expenses and all the just debts of the deceased;

c) have the property of the deceased valued if it appears to be necessary so to do and distribute the residue according to law reducing legacies and bequests proportionately. if it appears that the testator affected to dispose by will of property belonging to him in excess of the limits allowed by the law applicable to him, or if there is a deficiency of assets.

Powers of Administrator.   15.   In any case in which an administrator has been appointed by the Court, the following provisions shall apply :

i) The administrator shall be entitled to sell, mortgage or pledge, in due course of administration, any part of the property included in the estate for the purpose of paying debts and costs of administration or of satisfying legacies, provided that in the case of the sale or mortgage of immovable property the consent of the Court or a judge has been first obtained.

ii) The administrator shall be entitled in due course of administration :

a) To institute in his own name and on behalf of the estate any proceedings with a view to the recovery of debt or the liquidation of any claim due to the estate ;

b) to compromise or settle any debt or claim on behalf of the estate ;

c) to enter into any contract on behalf of the estate, provided that no such contract with respect to immovable property other than a lease at the full rent for a period not exceeding one year shall be valid unless the consent of the Court or a judge has first been obtained.

iii) All proceedings with respect to any property, interest, debt, claim or liability of the deceased shall, except with the leave

— 11 —

of the Court or judge, be brought by or against the administrator only.

Court to give Directions. 16. The Court or a judge thereof may, upon the application of an administrator, give such directions as may from time to time be required as to the administration of the estate.

Liability of Administrator. 17. An administrator shall be personally liable at the instance of persons beneficially entitled, for any wrong committed by him in the course of his administration.

Exclusion of Moslem Succession. 18. The provisions of this Part of the Ordinance shall not apply to successions to Moslems.

Part IV. Miscellaneous.

Succession to Miri Land. 19. Every Court having jurisdiction in matters of succession shall in all cases determine the rights of succession to Miri land in accordance with the provisions of the Ottoman Law set forth in the Second Schedule hereto, and the said provisions shall be applied notwithstanding any disposition made or power of attorney given by the deceased intended to take effect after death whether by way of will or otherwise.

Minor Heirs. 20. Where it appears that any person under the age of 18 years is or may become a person interested in the estate of a deceased person other than a Moslem, the President of a District Court may, upon the application of the person having the custody of the minor, or of any other person interested in his welfare, make such order as he deems fit for the protection of

— 12 —

the interest of the minor, and in particular, orders may be made under this Article

a) authorising the sale or lease of the share or part thereof of any minor heir or beneficiary;

b) directing the application and investment or re-investment of any such share or income of the sale of any such share;

c) directing payments to be made out of capital or income for the maintenance or otherwise for the benefit of the minor;

d) appointing any person to represent such minor in any proceedings;

e) transferring to the Civil Courts the administration and distribution of any estate in which a minor is interested, in any case in which there is jurisdiction to make such order in accordance with the provision of Article 7 hereof.

The powers under paras (a), (b) and (c) of this Article may, subject to the law of the Community, be exercised by the Court of a Community with reference to the property of any minor the administration of which is within the jurisdiction of such Court.

Determination of Questions of Personal Status. 21. For the determination of any question as to whether any person is a member of a class or possesses a character or quality whereby he is entitled to share in a succession, the Civil Courts shall apply the following rules:

a) If the claimant is a Moslem or a member of one of the specified Communities, the Moslem Law or the Law of the Community shall apply;

b) If such claimant is a foreigner, his National Law shall be applied in accordance with the rules laid down in Article 2 (iii) (c);

c) In any other case, the Courts shall apply such rules as appear to be just and equitable under the circumstances.

d) The Court shall in all cases determine any question of personal status in favour of legitimacy if the claimant would be deemed to be legitimate under the law governing the personal status of the deceased from whom succession is claimed. No change of religion or nationality on the part of the claimant or the deceased shall be taken into account.

No Incapacity Arising from Nationality or Religious Belief.

22. i) No person shall be deemed to be under a legal incapacity to take any share in a succession to property in Palestine or to take under a will by reason only of his nationality or religious belief.

ii) Where under the law then applicable in Palestine, any person has been excluded from a share in the succession to a person who has died possessed of property in Palestine, since the 31st day of December 1918, by reason only of his nationality or religious belief, the person so excluded or his heirs may apply to the District Court, who, upon such application and upon consideration of all the circumstances, may make such order as they think fit reopening the succession and granting to the applicant such share in the succession as may, under the circumstances, appear equitable, provided that the share so granted shall in no case exceed the share to which

— 14 —

such person would have been entitled under the then existing law if he had not been excluded therefrom by reason of his nationality or religious belief, and provided also that no such applicant shall be entitled to receive any sum in respect of rent, interest or profits arising from the share to which he is admitted by the order of Court between the date at which the succession opened and the date of the order.

Proceedings in the Land Registry. 23. i) Any person claiming to be entitled to any share in immovable property forming part of a succession, may apply to the Director of Land Registries to enter his name upon the Register in respect of his interest, and such entry shall be made accordingly upon payment of the prescribed fees and upon production to the Director

A. Where the deceased was a Moslem, of an Ilam Sharia from the competent Religious Court;

B. In any other case

a) of an order of the President of the competent District Court in any case in which there has been registered at the Land Registry a memorandum of an order under Article 7 para (ii) hereof, or the Probate of a will;

b) of an order of the President of the competent District Court in any case in which the deceased was a foreigner as to whose succession no order to refer had been made in pursuance of Article 3 hereof; and in any case in which the deceased was not, at the time of his death, a member of one of the specified religious communities.

— 15 —

c) In any other case, of an order of the competent Court of the Community of which the deceased was a member at the date of his death.

ii) The Director of Land Registries may refuse to make any entry upon the Register in pursuance of an Ilam Sharia or other order of a Religious Court in any case in which he has reason to believe that the persons thereby entitled to be entered as heirs are not the only heirs of the deceased, unless such order is stated on the face of it to contain the names of all persons then known to be the heirs of the deceased.

iii) Where an application for entry on the Register is supported by an Ilam Sharia or other order of a Religious Court and the Director of Land Registries entertains a doubt whether the Court had jurisdiction to make the order, he may require the parties to refer the matter to the competent authority for determining cases of conflict and shall enter on the Register a note of their application and reference.

Rules. 24. The Chief Justice may, with the approval of the High Commissioner, make rules as to the following matters :—

i) The rights of creditors and the administration of the estates of deceased persons other than Moslems;

ii) Procedure to be followed in obtaining probate or grant of administration, and security to be given by administrators;

iii) Publication of advertisements and notices by executors and administrators of intention to proceed to distribution of the assets;

— 16 —

iv) Procedure to be followed by an administrator in the administration of the estate;

v) Remuneration of administrators;

vi) Accounts to be rendered by, and discharge of, executors and administrators;

(vii) Procedure to be followed in the Land Registry in connection with entries on the Register of the name or names of any persons entitled to a share in the immovable property forming part of any succession;

(viii) Investment of, and dealing with, the share or interests of minors;

(ix) rocedure to be followed in ayn proceedings under this Ordinance;

(x) Fees to be paid in connection with grants of probate and administration or otherwise under this Ordinance;

(xi) Any other matter requiring regulation under this Ordinance.

Competence of Courts.
25. The jurisdiction of the Civil Courts under this Ordinance shall be exercised by the District Courts. The Chief Justice, with the approval of the High Commissioner, shall, by order published in the Official Gazette, define the jurisdiction to be exercised by each District Court, and subject thereto such jurisdiction shall be exercised by the District Court of the District within which the deceased resided at the date of his death

Definitions.
26. In this Ordinance the following words and expressions shall have the following meanings:—

i. "Estate" includes all movable property comprised in a succession.

17.—

ii. "Immovable property" includes Miri Land and Mulk Land as hereinafter defined.

iii. "Miri Land" includes Mevkafe and all other land to which the Ottoman Law, relating to the Succession to Immovable Property dated 3rd Rabi El Awal 1331 A.H. is by its terms expressed to apply, as also any registered interest in such land.

iv. "Mulk Land" includes all heritable land or interests therein not being Miri land as defined by this Article.

v. "Movable property" includes all property other than immovable property as defined by this Article, and in particular includes any standing or growing crops or produce though not severed from the soil or tree.

vi. "Will" means a legal declaration in writing of the intentions of the testator with respect to the disposal of this property after the death, and includes a codicil.

vii. "Codicil" means an instrument in writing made in relation to a will explaining, adding to, or revoking all, or any part of a disposition.

viii. "Executor" means a person to whom the execution of the will of the deceased person is confided by appointment therein.

ix. "Probate" means an instrument in writing issuing out of a Civil Court declaring that the will of a person has been duly proved.

x. "Civil Court" means a Court established by, and sitting under the authority

— 18 —

of, the Government of Palestine, but does not include a Religious Court.

xi. "Court of a Community" means a Court sitting in virtue of the jurisdiction conferred upon the authorities of a Religious community, but does not include a Moslem Religious Court.

xii. "Religious Community" and "Community" means a community specified in the 1st Schedule to this Ordinance of such other community as may from time to time be specified by the High Commissioner.

xiii. "Foreigner" means any person who is a foreigner within the meaning of Article 59 of the Palestine Order-in-Council, 1922.

xiv. "The Ottoman Law" shall mean the provisional Law relating to the Succession to Immovable Property dated 3 Rabi El Awal A.H. 1331 as set forth in the 2nd Schedule hereto.

Citation.   27. This Ordinance may be cited as the SUCCESSION ORDINANCE, 1923.

March 8th., 1923.   HERBERT SAMUEL
High Commissioner.

THE FIRST SCHEDULE.

The Eastern (Orthodox) Community.
The Latin (Catholic) Community.
The Gregorian Armenian Community.
The Armenian (Catholic) Community.
The Syrian (Catholic) Community.
The Chaldaean (Uniate) Community.
The Jewish Community.

№ 20

THE SECOND SCHEDULE.

Provisional Law relating to the Inheritance of Immovable Property.

3rd Rabi'ul Awwal 1331 — 27th February, 1328.

Art 1. On the death of a person, the Miri and Wakf land held by him are transferred to a person or persons according to the following degrees. These are called "ashab haqq al intiqal".

Art 2. The heirs of the first degree are the descendants of the deceased, i.e. his children and grandchildren. The right of succession within this degree belongs in the first place to the children and then to the grandchildren who are their descendants and then to the children's grandchildren. Therefore, when a man dies, the descendants of his surviving descendants lose their right of succession, as it is through this surviving descendant that they are related to the deceased. If a descendant dies before the deceased, his descendants represent him and take the share which he would have taken. If all the children of the deceased die before him the share of each will pass to his descendants who are through him related to the deceased. If any of the children of the deceased have died without descendants, the right of succession will be conferred upon the other children and their descendants only. The same rules will be applied where there are several descendants. Sons and daughters, grandsons and granddaughters have equal rights.

Art 3. The heirs of the second degree are the parents of the deceased and their descendants. If both parents survive, they share equally. If either of the parents have died, his or her descendants represent according to the rules mentioned in

— 21 —

the previous article. If the deceased parent has no descendants, the surviving parent, father or mother, will alone have the right. If both parents have predeceased him, the share of the father will pass to his descendants and that of the mother to her descendants. If either dies without descendants, his or her share will pass to the descendants of the other.

Art 4. The heirs of the third degree are the grandfathers and grandmothers of the deceased and their descendants. If all the grandparents on both sides are alive, they will share equally. If one has predeceased, his descendants will represent him in accordance with the rules already mentioned. The share of a grandparent who has no descendants will pass to the grandparent who is his or her spouse. If the spouse is also dead, this share passes to his or her descendants. If all the grandparents on one side, whether paternal or maternal, and their descendants have predeceased, then the right of succession passes to the grandparents on the other side and their descendants. The rules relating to the first degree of heirs apply to descendants in this article who succeed to their parents or grandparents.

Art 5. The descendant, whether of the first, second or third degree, who acquires a right of succession through more than one source, retains them all.

Art 6. If there is a person in any of the degrees mentioned with a prior right, the others in the later degrees will have no right of succession; but if the deceased leaves children or grandchildren and his father and mother or either of them are still alive, then a share of one-sixth will be given to the latter.

If the deceased is survived by his or her spouse, the surviving spouse will have the right to succeed to a share. If the heirs are of the first degree, this share will be one quarter. If the heirs are either of the second degree or are the grandparents of the deceased, the share will be a half. If in accordance with article

— 22 —

4, descendants of a grandparent succeed with any of the grandparents, their share will also be taken by the spouse. If there are no heirs of the first or second degree or no grandparents surviving, the spouse alone succeeds.

Art 7. The provisions of the foregoing articles apply also to waqf musaqqafat and mustaghillat whether let on ijara wahida kadima or ijaratain or mustaghillat of muqata'a kadima.

GOVERNMENT OF PALESTINE.

PALESTINE

ORDER.

(Gazetted 1st July, 1923).

I APPOINT

Mr. F. M. Goadby, Chairman,
Mr. W. J. Johnson,
Mr. L. W. Charley, O. B. E.,
Mr. S. Ginsberg,
Aref Pasha Dajani,
Mr. S. Hoofien,
Mr. E. Shelley, and
Said Eff. El Husseini,

to be members of a Committee to enquire into the present system of taxation of the non-agricultural population, and to recommend measures for

(1) adapting the Ottoman Law of Income Tax (Temettu) to conform with the present economic conditions;

(2) revising the registers of persons liable to pay House and Land Tax (Werko), so as to bring them up to date.

HERBERT SAMUEL,
High Commissioner.

15th June, 1923.

GOVERNMENT OF PALESTINE.

PALESTINE

REGULATIONS GOVERNING ASSESSMENT OF TITHES.

(1st July, 1923).

COMMISSIONS of Assessment to estimate tithable crops will be appointed by the District Governor, and shall consist of two members, as under:- *(Members of Commissions of Assessment.)*

    (i) One paid member selected from nominations by the local Agricultural Committee and two local Agriculturists;

    (ii) One unpaid member from the village, selected from nominations by the Mukhtars and notables.

The Commission will therefore consist of one paid member for the whole area, and one unpaid member for each village.

A paid member shall not be appointed to assess crops in an area in which he has any agricultural interests or in which he is resident. Each such member shall not receive payment in excess of £E. 1 per diem, or exceeding £E. 35 for the whole period of assessment.

District Governors will arrange, whenever posible, for a District Clerk or Tax Collector to accompany each Commission. No clerk may be specially engaged for the purpose without the prior approval of the Treasurer. Temporary clerks shall not receive payment in excess of PT. 50 per diem, or exceeding £E. 15 for the period of assessment.

2. Inspection of assessments will be carried out, whenever possible, by District Administrative Officers of the senior service or in certain cases by Mudirs El Mal. No inspector may be specially engaged for the purpose without the prior approval of the Treasurer. Each such inspector shall not receive payment in excess of £E. 1 per diem nor exceeding £E. 40 for the period of assessment. The Inspectors will test assessments and will settle disputes concerning assessments between members of Commissions or between Commissions and Cultivators. *(Inspector of Assessment)*

A paid Inspector shall not be appointed to assess crops in an area in which he has any agricultural interest or in which he is resident.

3. The number of Commissions of Assessment for each district will be determined by the Treasurer, in consultation with the District Governor. District Governors will forward their recommendations to the Treasurer at least one month before estimations are due to commence, together with the following particulars:- *(Number of Commissions of Assessment.)*

    (i) The area to be served by each Commission;

    (ii) The number of villages and threshing floors in each area; and.

    (iii) The estimated number of days required to complete the assessment of crops in each area.

Separate Commissions may be appointed to supervise threshing by machines and to assess the results.

Particulars to be published in the Official Gazette.

4. District Governors will forward to the Treasurer, in the prescribed form and at least fourteen days before the estimations are due to commence, a list of approved Commissions showing:-

(i) The area to be served by each Commission;

(ii) The kinds of crops each Commission will assess;

(iii) The names of the members of each Commission; and

(iv) The names of the Inspectors appointed in each District.

These particulars will be published in the Official Gazette.

Method of Assessments.

5. Cereal crops will be estimated on the threshing floor before they are winnowed or threshed. Fruit and vegetables will be estimated before they are gathered. Where, however, it is desired to thresh by machine before assessment, permission must be obtained, in writing, beforehand from the District Governor.

When crops are ready for assessment, the Mukhtar of the village shall notify the District Officer in writing of the number of stacks and plots of each kind of crop awaiting assessment.

The assessment of cereal crops shall take place within twenty-five days of the date of notification by the Mukhtar that the crops are awaiting assessment. If the Commission of Assessment has not visited the village within fourteen days of the receipt of such notification, a second notification shall be sent to the District Officer within two days. If no assessment has commenced by the twenty-fifth day, the Mukhtar and Elders of the village will assess the crops and notify their assessment to the District Officer.

Inspection of cereal crops shall take place within ten days of the assessment or notification of assessment by the Mukhtar. The period of inspection may be extended with the consent of the Treasurer.

In the case of fruit and vegetables, the dates of assessment and inspection shall be determined by the District Governor. In the event of assessment not taking place within a reasonable time, having regard to the nature of the crop, the Mukhtar and the Elders of the village are at liberty to assess the crops, and will notify the District Officer of such assessment.

Amendment of Assessments.

6. In the event of an alleged under or over-assessment by a Commission, or by the Mukhtar and Elders of a village, the Inspector may amend the assessment in agreement with the cultivators. Should the cultivators demand a re-assessment, the Inspector may order such re-assessment to be made at the expense of the cultivator.

The District Governor or the Inspector is empowered at any time to order a re-assessment of the whole or part of any crop; and the Treasurer may, independently, order re-assessment by a Treasury Inspector.

— 3 —

7. The Commission of Assessment will record, in the prescribed form, the assessment of the crops on each threshing floor or plot, or the result obtained after threshing by machine. The form should be prepared in triplicate. One copy will be handed to the Mukhtar, one copy will be posted in the village, and one copy will be retained by the Commission. The Inspector, after having made any necessary amendments, will countersign the Mukhtar's copy, and the copy posted in the village; and will send the Mukhtar's copy to the District Governor.
Registration and Notification of Assessments.

8. The standard form of weight measurement for cereals will be the kilogramme.
Standard Weights.

9. The local Mamour of Awkaf, or his representative, will accompany the Commission when the assessment of crops on Mazbutah Wakf lands is to be undertaken. The Mutawelli, or his representative, will accompany the Commission during the assessment of crops of Mulhaka Wakf lands. Objections to assessment made by the local Mamour of Awkaf or the Mutawelli will be dealt with by the Inspector.
Wakf Tithes.

The number of kirats assigned to each Wakf will be recorded in the Register.

10. A written permission to thresh cereals or to gather fruit and vegetables, or to remove from the threshing floor cereals threshed by machine, must be obtained from the Inspector of Assessment.
Permits to thresh, gather or remove machine-threshed cereals.

11. Tithes will be collected in cash and not in kind.
Collection of tithes.

12. Redemption prices will be based on local market prices.
Redemption Prices.

The redemption prices of all cereals, citrous fruits, olives, olive oil, melons and grapes will be determined by the Treasurer in consultation with District Governors, and the redemption prices of all other fruits and vegetables will be fixed by the District Governor in consultation with local Committees.

District Governors will forward to the Treasurer a statement, in the prescribed form, showing the total quantities of all cereals, fruits and vegetables assessed in each of their Sub-Districts, the local market prices and the redemption prices fixed by them or recommended for adoption by the Treasurer.

District Governors will notify the public by public notice of all redemption prices, and any complaints must be submitted to the District Governor within ten days of the publication of the redemption prices.

13. As soon as the redemption price is fixed, the amount due by each cultivator will be computed by the District Governor, and lists of amounts due forwarded to the Mukhtar of each village. Separate lists (coloured yellow) will be prepared and forwarded in respect of amounts due for tithes assigned to Awkaf. A copy of each list will be forwarded to the Treasurer.
Tithe Bills.

Separate lists (coloured blue) will be prepared for amounts

— 4 —

due in respect of rental tithes. A copy of each list will be forwarded to the Mukhtar of each village and to the Director of Lands. A copy will not be required by the Treasurer.

Method of Payment.

14. Amounts of piastres 500 or over may be paid in three equal instalments, the first instalment within one month, the second instalment within two months and the third instalment within three months of the date of fixing the redemption price. Amounts of over piastres 100, and under piastres 500 will be paid in two equal monthly instalments; and amounts of piastres 100 and under will be paid within one month in one instalment.

Amounts due from villagers will be collected by the Mukhtars, who will issue receipts from books of counterfoil forms bearing printed consecutive numbers. Mukhtars will bring in their collections to the nearest Sub-Accountant (District Administrative Officer) weekly at least, or at more frequent intervals to avoid unduly large sums being held by them.

The Sub-Accountant will prepare a schedule in support of his receipt voucher, showing the serial number of the receipt issued by the Mukhtar, the name of the taxpayer and the amount.

Separate receipt vouchers and schedules will be prepared for rental tithes and tithes assigned to Awkaf. Receipts in respect of tithes assigned to Awkaf will be credited to a separate deposit account and will be refunded on the written request of the Director General of Awkaf.

Amounts due from Institutions, Companies, or Committees may be paid direct to the nearest District Administration Officer.

Stamp duties.

15. Stamp duty will not be required on receipts issued in respect of tithes.

Remuneration to Mukhtars.

16. When the tithes have been satisfactorily collected and accounted for to the Sub-Accountant, the Mukhtar will be entitled to remuneration of 2 per cent. on the collections by him within due date. In the Beersheba District, Sheikhs of Beduin Tribes are entitled to remuneration of 3 per cent. of their total collections within due date.

Arrears of Tithes.

17. District Governors will furnish, half-yearly, at the end of June and December, to the Treasurer, for transmission to to the Auditor, a statement of arrears of tithes.

Cancellation of Regulations.

18. The regulations for the Assessment of Tithes published in Official Gazette No. 67, dated the 15th May, 1922, are hereby cancelled.

S. S. DAVIS,
Treasurer

June 5th, 1923.

APPROVED

HERBERT SAMUEL,
High Commissioner.

June 6th, 1923.

NOTICE
DEPARTMENT OF LANDS

NOTICE is hereby given that the Department of Land Registries, which is now amalgamated with the Department of Lands of the Government of Palestine, succeeded on the first day of July 1920 to all the functions of and was substituted for the Daftr Khakani of the former Ottoman Government in Palestine.

July 18th, 1923

GOVERNMENT OF PALESTINE

PUBLIC NOTICE.

Tax on Land Owned by Corporations.

Notice is hereby given that as from the beginning of the financial year 1923—4 the Government of Palestine will apply the provisions of Article 5 of the Ottoman Law dated 22nd Rabi El Awal, 1331, concerning the right of corporate bodies to own immovable property.

The Article states that corporate bodies registered as the owners of immovable property shall pay an annual tax on all such property as long as it remains in their possession. The tax shall be in the case of Miri and Miri Wakf land P.T. 1 per 1000, and in the case of Mulk land P. T. $1/_2$ per 1000 of its estimated value. An annual payment of P. T. 10 per 1000 will be payable in respect of wakf property which is transferred to a corporate body by way of Ijary Wahide or Ijaretein, The fee payable in respect of such wakf property will be accounted to the Administration of Wakfs where a Moslem Wakf is concerned.

The annual tax will be payable by all corporate bodies owning land whether religious or local communities or cooperative Societies.

January 7th, 1923.

HERBERT SAMUEL
High Commissioner.

Section 7: 1924

EXPROPRIATION OF LAND ORDINANCE, No. 5 OF 1924

Herbert Samuel

GOVERNMENT OF PALESTINE.

PALESTINE

EXPROPRIATION OF LAND ORDINANCE
No. 5 of 1924.

AN ORDINANCE TO AMEND THE PUBLIC NOTICE WITH REGARD TO EXPROPRIATION OF LAND ISSUED BY THE CHIEF ADMINISTRATOR IN MAY, 1919.

BE IT ENACTED by the High Commissioner of Palestine with the advice of the Advisory Council thereof:

Public Notice of May 1919 does not affect purposes of expropriation.
1. The Public Notice dated the 20th May, 1919, concerning the expropriation of land for public purposes shall not be deemed to restrict the purposes for which land may be expropriated outside Municipal areas. Section 1 of the Ottoman Law of Expropriation of the 21st. Jamada al-Ula 1296 as amended by the law of the 17th Nisan 1330, shall continue to be in force with regard to the purposes of such expropriation.

Procedure of Expropriation to follow law of 1332 A.H.
2. Subject to the provisions of the Acquisition of Land for the Army Ordinance 1920 and the Town Planning Ordinance 1921, the procedure of expropriation for all purposes shall be that prescribed by the Ottoman Law of the 7th. Rabi' al-Awal 1332 as amended by the said Public Notice.

Citation
This Ordinance may by cited as the Expropriation of Land Ordinance, 1924.

HERBERT SAMUEL
High Commissioner.

13th February, 1924.

RAILWAY LANDS VESTING ORDINANCE, No. 17 of 1924

Herbert Samuel

GOVERNMENT OF PALESTINE.

RAILWAY LANDS VESTING ORDINANCE
No. 17 of 1924.

AN ORDINANCE TO VEST IN THE PALESTINE GOVERNMENT LAND OCCUPIED BY THE PALESTINE RAILWAYS.

BE IT ENACTED by the High Commissioner for Palestine with the advice of the Advisory Council thereof:—

1. This Ordinance may be cited as the Railway Lands Vesting Ordinance 1924. *Short title.*

2. The word "Land" shall include houses, buildings and things permanently fixed in the land, and any water rights and easements on, over, or under the land. *Definition of land.*

3. Where prior to the commencement of this Ordinance any lands outside a municipal area have been occupied by the British Army or by the Palestine Railways and are used as railway premises as defined in the Railway Ordinance, 1922, the land shall be vested in the High Commissioner on behalf of the Government of Palestine, and shall be so registered in the Land Registers. *Vesting of Railway lands.*

Where land has become so vested the following provisions shall apply.

4. (1) If the land occupied consisted only of a strip traversed by a single line and the area immediately adjacent thereto, and was agricultural land neither built upon, nor planted with fruit or olive trees or other quasi-permanent crops, nor irrigated by artificial means, no compensation shall be payable. Provided that where the land so occupied was a large proportion of the land belonging to the owner and it is established that hardship would be caused if no compensation were paid, the High Commissioner may grant such compensation as having regard to all the circumstances of the case he shall think fit. *Compensation payable and assessment of compensation.*

(2) In other cases, if a claim for compensation is made by any person as owner of the land, the assessment of compensation shall be referred, in default of agreement, to the Permanent Arbitration Board constituted under Section 5 of the Acquisition of Land for the Army Ordinance, 1920, which shall act in accordance with the provisions of that Section. Provided that in assessing the amount of compensation it shall take into account:

(a) any compensation that may have been paid by the Army or the Central Claims Bureau since the occupation by way of rent or indemnity or otherwise; and

(b) any increase in the value of the adjoining land belonging to the claimant owing to the laying of the railway;

and shall reduce the amount of compensation to be paid by the amount so paid by the Army or the Central Claims Bureau or

— 2 —

such increase in value or both, and if the amount so paid or such increase in value, or both, are equal to or exceed the value of the land occupied, no compensation shall be payable.

(3) No claim for compensation shall be considered unless it is presented to the Railway Administration within six months from the date of this Ordinance.

Expropriation of land within a municipal area.

5. Any land occupied prior to the commencement of this Ordinance for railway premises within a municipal area shall be expropriated in accordance with the provisions of the Acquisition of Land for the Army Ordinance 1920, subject to the proviso contained in Section 4 (2) hereof.

In the absence of any Order defining a municipal area, the High Commissioner may by Public Notice define the area which for the purpose of this Ordinance shall be deemed to be a municipal area.

June 15th, 1924.

HERBERT SAMUEL
High Commissioner.

ORDER PROMULGATING ORDINANCES Nos. 16, 17, 18 & 19 OF 1924

Herbert Samuel

PALESTINE.

GOVERNMENT OF PALESTINE.
PROMULGATION OF ORDINANCES.
ORDER.

(Gazetted June 15th, 1924).

1. The Copyright Ordinance, No. 16 of 1924, is hereby promulgated in the form in which the draft was published in the Gazette of May 1st, 1924, and shall be in force as from the date of publication of this Order.

2. The Railway Lands Vesting Ordinance, No. 17 of 1924, is hereby promulgated in the form in which the draft was published in the Gazette of May 1st, 1924, subject to the following amendments, and shall be in force as from the date of publication of this Order:

(1) At the end of Section 3, the words "subject to the following provisions" shall be omitted and the following paragraph shall be added;

"Where land has become so vested, the following provisions shall apply".

(2) The following paragraph shall be added at the end of Section 5. "In the absence of any Order defining a municipal area, the High Commissioner may by Public Notice define the area which for the purpose of this Ordinance shall be deemed to be a municipal area".

3. The Extradition Ordinance, No. 18 of 1924, is hereby promulgated in the form in which the draft was published in the Official Gazette of May 15th, 1924, subject to the following amendments, together with the Schedules that were published in the Official Gazette of June 1st 1924, and shall be in force as from the date of publication of this Order:

(1) The preamble to the Ordinance shall be omitted.

(2) Section 2(e) shall read:

"Magistrate includes any person holding a Magisterial Warrant, and any judge of a Distrisct Court or Land Court."

4. The Werko Tax and Municipal House Rate Validation Ordinance, No. 19 of 1924, is hereby promulgated in the form in which the draft was published in the Gazette of May 15th, 1924, and shall be in force as from the date of publication of this Order.

HERBERT SAMUEL
High Commissioner.

June 5th, 1924.

CHARITABLE TRUSTS ORDINANCE, No. 26 OF 1924.

Herbert Samuel

GOVERNMENT OF PALESTINE.

CHARITABLE TRUSTS ORDINANCE

No. 26 of 1924

WHEREAS by Sections 52, 53, and 54 of the Palestine Order in Council 1922 it is provided that the Moslem Religious Courts, the Courts of the Christian Communities and the Rabbinical Courts shall have jurisdiction in respect of Wakfs or Religious Endowments constituted before such Courts in accordance with the law thereof;

AND WHEREAS it is desirable to make provision for the regulation of Charitable Trusts established in Palestine otherwise than in conformity with Religious Law;

BE IT ENACTED by the High Commissioner for Palestine, with the advice of the Advisory Council thereof: -

1. This Ordinance may be cited as the Charitable Trusts Ordinance 1924. *(Short Title)*

2. (1) Property is held in trust for charitable purposes in any case in which there is an obligation annexed to the ownership thereof and arising out of a confidence reposed in and accepted by the owner or declared and accepted by him that while the ownership is nominally vested in the owner, such property and the income and proceeds thereof shall be exclusively used and enjoyed for charitable purposes. *(Definition of trust.)*

(2) For the purpose of this Ordinance the term charitable purposes shall include all purposes for the benefit of the public or any section of the public within or without Palestine of any of the following categories: *(Charitable purposes.)*

(a) for the relief of poverty;

(b) for the advancement of education or knowledge;

(c) for the advancement of Religion or the maintenance of religious rites or practices;

(d) for any other purpose beneficial or of interest to mankind not falling within the preceding categories.

3. (1) Subject to the provisions of Section 37, no trust in relation to immovable property is valid unless declared by the last will of the author of the trust or of the trustee or by a non-testamentary instrument in writing signed by the author of the trust or the trustee and notarially executed. *(Creation of trust of immovable property.)*

Price P.T. 2. On sale at the Stationery and Printing Office, Russian Buildings, Jerusalem.

Printed by the Greek Convent Press & Azriel Press, Jerusalem.

Palestine No. 26 of 1924

— 2 —

Of movable property.
(2) No trust in relation to movable property is valid unless declared by the last will of the author of the trust or of the trustee, or by a non-testamentary instrument in writing signed by the author of the trust or the trustee, or unless the ownership of the property is transferred to the trustee by delivery.

Creation of trust.
4. Subject to the provision of Section 3, a trust is created when the author of the trust indicates with reasonable certainty

    (a) an intention on his part to create a trust;

    (b) the purpose of the trust;

    (c) the trust property; and

    (d) (unless the trust is declared by will or the author of the trust is himself to be the trustee) transfers the trust property to a trustee.

Acceptance of trust.
5. The acceptance of the trust by the trustee may be shown by words or acts indicating with reasonable certainty such acceptance.

Trustee to execute trust.
6. (1) The Trustee is bound to fulfil the purpose of the trust and to obey the directions of the author of the trust at the time of its creation except as modified by any scheme settled by the Court for the administration of the trust in accordance with Section 30 hereof.

Trustee to protect title of trust property.
(2) A trustee is bound to maintain and defend all such suits and to take such other steps as, regard being had to the nature and amount or value of the trust property, may be reasonably requisite for the preservation of the trust property and the assertion or protection of the title thereto.

Care required from trustee.
7. A trustee is bound, subject to the provisions of the instrument of the trust, to deal with the trust property as carefully as a man of ordinary prudence would deal with such property if it were his own; and in the absence of a contract to the contrary, a trustee in so dealing is not responsible for the loss, destruction or deterioration of the trust property.

Investment of trust money.
8. Where the trust property consists of money and cannot be applied immediately or at an early date to the purposes of the trust, the trustee is bound, subject to any direction contained in the instrument of trust, to invest the money in any of the following securities and in no others:

Palestine No 26 of 1924

— 3 —

(a) In bonds debentures, stock, promissory notes or other securities of the Government of Palestine.

(b) In a first mortgage of immovable property situated in Palestine;

Provided that the value of the property exceeds by one-third, or if consisting wholly or mainly of buildings, exceeds by one-half the amount of the mortgage.

(c) In any security, other than immovable securities, authorised as a trustee investment by the Law of England for the time being.

(d) In any other security expressly authorised by the instrument of trust or by any regulation which the High Commissioner in Executive Council may from time to time prescribe in that behalf.

Nothing in this Section shall apply to investments made before this Ordinance comes into force, or shall be deemed to preclude in any case in which the trust property does not exceed £E. 200, deposit thereof in a Bank.

9. Where the trustee commits a breach of trust he is liable to make good the loss which the trust property has sustained, provided always that the Court may, upon the application of the trustee, relieve the trustee of any liability for breach of trust if it is of opinion that he has acted honestly and ought fairly to be excused for the breach of trust and for omitting to obtain the directions of the Court in the matter in which he has made such breach. **Liability for breach of trust.**

10. Subject to the provisions of Sections 6 and 7 one trustee is not, as such, liable for a breach of trust committed by his co-trustee; **Non—liability for co-trustee's default.**

Provided that, in the absence of an express declaration to the contrary in the instrument of the trust, a trustee is so liable

(a) where he has delivered trust property to his co-trustee without seeing to its proper application; or

(b) where he allows his co-trustee to receive trust property and fails to make due enquiry as to the co-trustee's dealings therewith, or allows him to retain it longer than the circumstances of the case reasonably require; or

(c) where he becomes aware of a breach of trust committed or intended by his co-trustees and either actively conceals it, or does not within a reasonable time take proper steps to protect the charitable interest.

A co-trustee who joins in signing a receipt for trust property, if he proves, or if it otherwise appears that he has not received the same, is not answerable by reason of such signature only, for loss or misapplication of the property by his co-trustee.

Right to reimbursement of expenses.

11. Every trustee may reimburse himself or pay or discharge out of the trust property all expenses properly incurred in or about the execution of the trust, or the realisation, preservation or benefit of the trust property.

Power to lease and sell.

12. (1) A trustee shall not be entitled to sell or mortgage the whole or any part of immovable trust property save with the sanction of the Court or judge and subject to such conditions as the Court or judge may direct.

(2) Every lease made by a trustee shall be made to take effect in possession upon execution or within not more than three months thereafter. It shall be made at the best rent which can reasonably be obtained.

(3) Except with the permission of the Court or judge, no trustee shall lease any immovable trust property for a term of more than three years.

(4) Any sale, mortgage, or lease effected otherwise than in conformity with this Section shall be void.

Trustee cannot renounce after acceptance.

13. A trustee who has accepted a trust cannot afterwards renounce it save with the permission of the Court or judge.

Trustee cannot delegate.

14. A trustee cannot delegate his office or any of his duties either to a co-trustee or to a stranger unless

(a) the delegation is in the regular course of business; or

(b) the delegation is permitted by the instrument of the trust; or

(c) the Court or judge so directs.

The appointment of an advocate or agent or proxy to do an act merely ministerial and involving no independent discretion is not a delegation within the meaning of this Section.

Palestine No. 26 of 1924

— 5 —

15. Where there are more trustees than one, all must join in the execution of the trust, except where the instrument of the trust otherwise directs or except when on good cause shown the Court otherwise directs. *Co-trustees cannot act singly.*

16. In the absence of express directions to the contrary contained in the instrument of trust or of an order of a Court or judge, a trustee has no right to remuneration for his trouble, skill and loss of time in executing the trust. *Trustee may not charge for services.*

17. A trustee may not use or deal with the trust property for his own profit or for any other purpose unconnected with the trust. *Trustee may not use trust property for his own benefit.*

18. No trustee, and no person who has within one year ceased to be a trustee, may, without the permission of the Court or judge, buy or become mortgagee or lessee of the trust property or any part thereof; and such permission shall not be given unless the proposed purchase, mortgage or lease is manifestly for the advantage of the trust. *Trustee may not obtain interest in trust property.*

19. Save where the instrument of the trust provides the contrary, a trustee having power to invest trust money on mortgage or personal security must not invest it on a mortgage by, or on the personal security of, himself or one of his co-trustees. *Co-trustees may not lend to one of themselves.*

20. The office of a trustee is vacated by his death or by his discharge from his office. *Office how vacated.*

21. A trustee may be discharged from his office only as follows: *Discharge of trustee.*

(a) by the extinction of the trust; or

(b) by the completion of his duties under the trust; or

(c) by such means as may be prescribed by the instrument of the trust or by any scheme under this Ordinance; or

(d) by the appointment under this Ordinance of a new trustee in his place; or

(e) by the Court.

22. Whenever any person appointed a trustee disclaims, or any trustee, either original or substituted, dies, or is absent from Palestine for such a continuous period and in such circumstances that, in the opinion of the Court, it is desirable, in the ineterest of the trust, that his office should be declared *Appointment of new trustee on death, etc.*

vacant, or is declared insolvent or desires to be discharged from the trust, or refuses, or is or becomes, in the opinion of the Court, unfit or personally incapable to act in the trust, or accepts an inconsistent trust, a new trustee may be appointed in his place by

(a) the person nominated for that purpose by the instrument of trust (if any); or

(b) if there be no such person, or no such person able and willing to act, the author of the trust, if he be alive and competent to act, or the surviving or continuing trustee or trustees for the time being or (with the consent of the Court) the retiring trustees, if they all retire simultaneously or (with the like consent) the last retiring trustee.

Every such appointment shall be by writing under the hand of the person making and shall be notarially executed.

On an appointment of a new trustee, the number of trustees may be increased.

The provisions of this Section relative to a trustee who is dead include the case of a person nominated trustee in a will but dying before the testator; and those relative to a continuing trustee include a refusing or retiring trustee if willing to act in the execution of the power.

Appointment by Court.

23. Whenever any such vacancy or disqualification occurs and it is found not reasonably practicable to appoint a new trustee under the preceding Section or where for any other reason the due execution of the trust is or becomes impracticable, the Attorney General or any person benefiting by the purpose of the trust, may without instituting a suit, apply by petition to the Court for the appointment of a trustee or a new trustee and the Court may appoint a trustee or a new trustee accordingly. If the Public Trustee is appointed, the Court may direct that he shall act alone and that any continuing trustee shall be discharged, or that he shall act together with the continuing trustee as may be deemed most convenient in the interest of the trust.

Vesting of trust property in new trustee.

24. Whenever any new trustee is appointed under or in pursuance of this Ordinance, all the trust property for the time being vested in the surviving or continuing trustee or trustees or in the representatives of any trustee and all the rights of suits in relation thereto of the trustee in whose place the appointment is made, shall become vested in such new trustee, either

Palestine No. 20 of 1924

— 7 —

solely or jointly with the surviving or continuing trustees or trustee as the case may require.

Every new trustee so appointed and every trustee appointed by a Court either before or after the passing of this Ordinance shall have the same powers, authorities and discretion and shall in all respects act as if he had been originally nominated a trustee by the author of the trust.

25. On the death or discharge of one of several co-trustees, the trust survives, and the trust property passes to the others, unless the instrument of trust expressly declares otherwise. Survival of trust.

26. A trust is extinguished Trust how extinguished.

(a) when its purpose is completely fulfilled; or

(b) when its purpose becomes unlawful; or

(c) subject to the powers of the Court under Section 28, when the fulfilment of its purpose becomes impossible by destruction of the trust property or otherwise; or

(d) when the trust, being revocable, is expressly revoked.

27. No trust can be revoked by the author of the trust save by permission of the Court, and no such revocation shall defeat or prejudice what the trustees may have duly done in the execution of the trust. Revocation of trust.

28. The Court shall have the same powers for the establishment, regulation, protection, and adaptation of all charitable trusts as are exercised for the time being with reference to "charitable trust" within the meaning of English Law by the Court of Justice in England. General powers of the Court.

29. In case of any alleged breach of any trust, or whenever the direction of the Court is deemed necessary for the administration of any such trust, the Attorney General or two or more persons having an interest in the trust, and having obtained the consent in writing of the Attorney General, may institute an action to obtain a decree Actions for carrying into effect trusts for public charity

(a) removing any trustee or trustees of the charity and, if necessary, appointing new trustees thereof; or

(b) directing accounts and enquiries; or

Palestine No. 26 of 1924

— 8 —

(c) declaring what proportion of the trust property or of the interest therein shall be allocated to any particular object of the trust ; or

(d) authorising the whole or any part of the trust property to be let, sold or mortgaged or exchanged ; or

(e) settling a scheme for the management of the trust; or

(f) granting such further or other relief as the nature of the trust may require.

Nothing in this Section shall be deemed to preclude the trustee or author of any trust from appying to the Court by action or otherwise for such direction or relief as he may be entitled to obtain under the general provisions of this Ordinance, or for the purpose of invoking the assistance of the Court for the better securing the objects of the trust, or for regulating its administration or succession to the trusteeship, and upon any such application the Court may make such order as it may deem equitable.

Special powers of Court.
30. In settling any scheme for the management of a trust (without prejudice to its general powers) the Court shall have the powers following :

(a) To provide for the periodical auditing of the accounts of the trust property by auditors appointed by or subject to the approval of the Court, or otherwise as the Court may deem expedient.

(b) To provide for the visitation of the charity.

(c) To provide for the settlement of the remuneration of the trustee ;

Provided that no such remuneration shall, except with the consent of the Court, in any case exceed ten per centum of the gross income of the trust.

(d) To devote any surplus income that may be available after the reasonable satisfaction of the objects of the trust to the extension of such objects, or if the Court see fit, to purposes of education.

(e) To make such adaptation of the trust purposes as may be necessary to carry out the wishes of the author of the trust as nearly as practicable where it is not possible to carry out those wishes in the exact manner of the trust.

Palestine No. 26 of 1924

— 9 —

31. In the following cases, that is to say: Prescription.

(a) in the case of any claim against a trustee founded upon any fraud or fraudulent breach of trust to which the trustee was party or privy; or

(b) in the case of any claim to recover trust property, or the proceeds thereof still retained by a trustee, or previously received by the trustee and converted to his use:

the claim shall not be held to be barred or prejudiced by any provisions relating to prescription of right or limitation of action, but the Court may entertain such action notwithstanding the lapse of any period of prescription or limitation if it is of opinion that in all the circumstances of the case it is in the interest of justice that it should be entertained.

Save as aforesaid, the defence that the right or claim is barred by prescription or by a period of limitation of the actions shall be available for a trustee in any action or legal proceeding in the like manner and to the like extent as it would have been available if he had not been a trustee.

32. (1) In the following cases, namely,

(a) where it is uncertain in whom the title to any trust property is vested; or

(b) where a trustee or any other person in whom the title to trust property is vested has been required in writing to transfer the property by or on behalf of a person entitled to require such transfer, and has wilfully refused or neglected to transfer the property for twenty-eight days after the date of the requirement, the Court may make an order (in this Ordinance called a "vesting order") vesting the property in any such person in any such manner or to any such extent as the Court may direct.

(2) A vesting order under any provision of this Ordinance shall have the same effect as if the trustee or other person in whom the trust property was vested had executed a transfer to the effect intended by the order. Devolution of trust property.

33. (1) Where, whether before or after the commencement of this Ordinance, it is declared or intended in any instrument of trust that the trustee of the trust shall be the Public Trustee or any person for the time being holding or acting in any public office, or holding or acting in any office Vesting orders.

Palestine No. 26 of 1924

— 10 —

or discharging any duty in any public institution or association, or religious community, or where any property comes into or is in the possession or ownership of any such person in any of the aforesaid capacities upon any trust, the title of the trust property shall devolve from time to time upon the person for the time being holding or acting in any such office, or discharging such duty without any conveyance, vesting order, or other assurance otherwise necessary for vesting the property in such person.

(2) Where, whether before or after the commencement of this Ordinance, in the case of any charitable trust or in the case of any trust for the purpose of any public or private association (not being an association for the purpose of gain), a method for the appointment of new trustees is prescribed in the instrument of trust (other than nomination referred to in Section 22), or by any rule in force, or in the absence of any such prescribed method is established by custom, then upon any new trustee being appointed in accordance with such prescribed or customary method, and upon the execution of

the memorandum referred to in the next succeeding sub-section, the trust property shall become vested without any conveyance, vesting order, or other assurance in such new trustee and the old continuing trustees jointly or if there are no old continuing trustees, in such new trustee wholly.

(3) Every appointment under the last preceding sub-section shall be made to appear by a memorandum under the hand of the person presiding at the meeting, or other proceeding at which the appointment was made, and attested by two other persons present at the said meeting or proceeding. Every such memorandum shall be notarially executed.

Transfer of securities.
34. (1) Where any trust property comprises any stocks or any shares or securities transferable in any book kept by any company or society or any shares in any ship registered under the law relating to merchant shipping, an instrument, memorandum or order of appointment of a trustee or a vesting order shall not take effect so far as it relates thereto until notice in writing of such instrument or order shall have been given to the person or authority in charge of the register or book and upon

such notice in writing being given, and on reasonable proof being furnished that such stocks, shares or securities form part of the said trust property, the new trustee or the person in whom the property is vested under this order shall be entitled to the transfer into his name of any such stoks, shares or securities, and to the receipt of all devidends, interest or other sums due or to become due, in respect of any such stoks, shares or securities.

Palestine No. 26 of 1924

— 11 —

(2) Where immovable property is registered in the names of trustees, the Director of Land Registries shall, upon production of any instrument or order, of appointment of new trustees or of a vesting order, and upon being satified that the property fors part of the trust property, make all necessary entries in the Land Register upon payment of such fees as may be prescribed.

35. If at any time the post of Public Trustee is created by Ordinance in Palestine, the Public Trustee may be appoined a trustee of any trust under this Ordinance. In any case in which the Court or judge is empowered to appoint a trustee of any trust, the Public Trustee shall be appointed, unless the circumstancess are tuch as to render suh appointmedt inconvenient.

Pulic Trustee.

36. The High Commissioner in Council may, in his discretion, by Order, on the application of the trustees, of any charitable trust, authorise the incorporation of the said trustees, and upon the publication of the said Order the said trustees of the charity and their successors for the time being shall be constituted a corporation under such style and subject to such conditions as may be specified in the Order.

Incorporation of trustee.

37. Notwithstanding anything in this Ordinance, if the Court is of opinion upon the evidence of documents laid before it or proved custom that any property in Palestine is held by the owner thereof under an obligation that the use of such property and the proceeds and income thereof shall be devoted to charitable purposes, the Court may declare such property to be held in trust for the purpose of this Ordinance and the provision of this Ordinance shall apply theteto as though the truts had been created in accordance therewith:

Trust created by construction of documents or practice.

Provided that where the trust was created under foreign law the Court shall in exercising junisdiction with reference thereto apply the law under wish it was created so far as such law is not contrary to the public policy of Palestine or to the policy of this Ordinance.

38. (1) Where property in Palestina is held in trust for charitable purposes by a Foreign Corporation, such Corporation shall be recognised as the trustee of the property for the purpose of this Ordinance upon registration of the Corporation with the Registrar of Companies in accordance with Section 40 and following of the Companies Ordinance 1921.

Foreign Corporations.

(2) For the purpose of registration, the Members of the Committee of Management of the Corporation or other

Palestine No. 26 of 1924

— 12 —

persons authorised to control its affairs shall be deemed to be the Directors.

(3) Where property in Palestine is held on trust by a Foreign Corporation and the Corporation has failed to register, the Attorney General may apply to the Court for the appointment of trustee as though there was no existing trustee, and the Public Trustee shall be appointed trustee.

Limitation of power to hold land.

39. (1) Where immovable property is devised, transferred or otherwise comes to be held upon trust for charitable purposes, the trustees thereof shall within one year from the date at which such trust was registered apply to the Court or judge under Section 42 of this Ordinance for an order for sale and such order shall be made accordingly.

(2) The Attorney General may at any time, if satisfied that immovable property is held subject to a trust for charitable purposes make application to the Court or judge for an order for sale thereof.

(3) The provisions of this Section shall apply to immovable property held by any limited company in respect of which a licence has been granted under Section 22 of the Companies Ordinance 1921, unless the company is recognised as having purposes of public utility by certificate of the High Commissioner under Section 8 of the Companies Ordinance 1921.

(4) The provisions of this Section shall not apply in the following cases:
(a) where the immovable property consists of houses or buildings in, or required for, the occupation of the trustee for the purposes of the trust; or
(b) where the permission of the High Commissioner has been obtained; or
(c) where the immovable property was at the date when this Ordinance came into force held upon a charitable trust within the meaning of this Ordinance; or
(d) where the immovable property is acquired by the trustees in substitution for property sold by them.

Application of English law.

40. All matters with reference to any trust, or with reference to any obligation in the nature of a trust arising or resulting by the implication or construction of law, for which no specific provision is made in this or any other Ordinance, shall be determined by the principles of equity for the time being in force in the High Court of Justice in England.

Palestine No. 26 of 1924

— 13 —

41. The Chief Justice may, with the approval of the High Commissioner, make rules   **Rules.**

(a) as to the procedure to be observed in any proceedings under this Ordinance; and

(b) as to the jurisdiction of the Courts or judges thereof under this Ordinance.

42. Subject to any rules under this Ordinance,   **Jurisdiction.**

(a) the competent Court in any proceedings under this Ordinance shall be the District Court of the district in which any part of the subject-matter of the trust is held or situate;

(b) where it is provided that any application may be made to or order made by the Court or a judge, such application may be made to or order made by the competent District Court or the President thereof.

43. Nothing in this Ordinance shall affect property devoted to charitable purposes which is the subject of a wakf or religious endowment constituted before a Religious Court in accordance with the provisions of the Palestine Order in Council, 1922.   **Ordinance does not refer to wakf or religious endowments.**

1st October, 1924.

G.F. CLAYTON
Officer Administering the Government.

LAND COURTS ORDINANCE 1921

Herbert Samuel

GOVERNMENT OF PALESTINE.

PALESTINE.

LAND COURTS ORDINANCE 1921. — ORDER.

ORDER

(Gazetted March 1st. 1924).

In accordance with the powers vested in me by Article 1 of the above-mentioned Ordinance, I hereby appoint :

(a) The President of the District Court at Haifa and one or more judges of such District Court to be the Land Court in the Northern District except in the Sub-District of Nazareth.

(b) The President of the Samaria District Court and one or more judges of such District Court to be the Land Court for the Sub-District of Nazareth.

(c) Mr. R. C. Tute and Abdel Aziz Eff. Daoudi to constitute the Land Court for the division of Jaffa and the Sub-District of Gaza ;

(d) Mr. F.O.J. Ongley and Ishak Eff. Budeiri to constitute the Land Court for the division of Jerusalem and the Sub-Districts of Hebron and Beersheba.

HERBERT SAMUEL
High Commissioner.

26th, February, 1924.

LAND COURTS ORDINANCE 1921

Herbert Samuel

GOVERNMENT OF PALESTINE

LAND COURTS ORDINANCE, 1921 — ORDER.

PALESTINE.

ORDER

(Gazetted May 15th, 1924)

In accordance with the powers vested in me by Article 1 of the above-mentioned Ordinance, I hereby appoint Mr. R.C. Tute, in the place of Mr. F.O.J. Ongley, to constitute with Ishak Eff. Budeiri the Land Courts for the Division of Jerusalem and the Sub-Districts of Hebron and Beersheba as well as for the Division of Jaffa and the Sub-District of Gaza.

May 8th, 1924.

HERBERT SAMUEL
High Commissioner.

WOODS AND FORESTS ORDINANCE 1920

Herbert Samuel

GOVERNMENT OF PALESTINE

WOODS AND FORESTS ORDINANCE 1920 — ORDER.

PALESTINE.

ORDER.

(Gazetted May 15th. 1924).

Order Constituting Demarcation Commissions.

In pursuance of the power vested in me by Article 9 of the Woods and Forests Ordinance, 1920, I hereby declare that:

1. Every Demarcation Commission created by that Ordinance shall be constituted of

   (1) a Chairman who shall be a Senior Officer of the Department of Agriculture or of the Department of Lands or the Department of Surveys, or a Senior British Officer of the District Administration.

   (2) at least two members each of whom shall be an Inspector or Sub-Inspector of the Department of Agriculture, or an Inspector or Sub-Inspector of the Department of Lands or the Department of Surveys, or a District Officer of the District Administration.

2. The Demarcation Commissions of which the constitution is prescribed by the preceding paragraph shall be the commissions entitled to exercise the powers and functions created by the Public Notice entitled Demarcation of Government Lands, dated 10th November, 1921, which was published in Official Gazette No. 56 of 1st December, 1921.

3. The Order appointing Demarcation Commissions under the Woods and Forests Ordinance, 1920, published in Official Gazette dated 15th November, 1920, and the Public Notice entitled Demarcation of Government Forests and Government Lands dated 22nd March, 1922, which appeared in Official Gazette dated 1st April, 1922, are hereby cancelled.

HERBERT SAMUEL
High Commissioner.

May 6th. 1924.

Section 8: 1925

SANCTIONED.

JURISDICTION OF CIVIL AND RELIGIOUS COURTS ORDINANCE No. 3 OF 1925.

Herbert Samuel

GOVERNMENT OF PALESTINE.

JURISDICTION OF CIVIL and RELIGIOUS COURTS ORDINANCE
No. 3 of 1925

AN ORDINANCE TO DEFINE MORE EXACTLY THE JURISDICTION OF THE CIVIL AND RELIGIOUS COURTS WITH REGARD TO QUESTIONS OF WAKF AND TO APPLICATIONS FOR DIYET.

BE IT ENACTED by the High Commissioner for Palestine with the advice of the Advisory Council thereof:

Citation.

1. This Ordinance may be cited as the Jurisdiction of Civil and Religious Courts Ordinance 1925.

Conversion of non-Moslem Wakfs created before Moslem Religious Court into charitable trusts on application of authorised persons within one year of commencement of Ordinance.

2. Where a non-Moslem Wakf has been constituted before a Moslem Religious Court prior to the promulgation of the Palestine Order in Council, 1922, the dedicator of such a Wakf, or, if the dedicator is dead, the guardian of the Wakf, or, in case there is more than one, a majority of the guardians of the Wakf nominated in the Wakf Deed may, within one year of the date of the commencement of this Ordinance, apply to the Civil Court for an Order to tran-form the Wakf into a trust under the provisions of the Charitable Trusts Ordinance, 1924; and the Court may thereupon declare that the property shall be held in trust in accordance with the provisions of the said Ordinance as though the charitable endowment had been created in accordance therewith.

Jurisdiction with regard to constitution of non-Moslem Wakfs created before Moslem Religious Court.

3. In default of such an application, or where such an application has been refused by the Civil Court,

(a) An action or other proceeding concerning the constitution or validity of such a Wakf shall be brought before the Civil Court, unless all the parties concerned shall agree to submit the question at issue to the Moslem Religious Court. It shall be competent to the parties to such an action or other proceeding in a Civil Court to obtain by agreement a stay of proceedings in the said Court at any time before judgment for the purpose of removing such action or other proceeding into a Religious Court and bring such action or other proceeding anew in the Religious Court.

Jurisdiction with regard to administration of such Wakfs.

(b) An action or other proceeding concerning the administration of such a Wakf shall be brought before the Court of the Religious Community of which the dedicator of the Wakf was a member. If the dedicator did not belong to

Palestine No. 3 of 1925

— 2 —

a Religious Community, or if there is no established Court of the Community, the action or proceeding shall be brought before the Civil Court, which shall apply the general principles of equity.

Reference to Special Tribunal of conflicts of jurisdiction about Wakf.	4. When conflict arises between a Civil and a Religious Court upon a question whether a matter is one of Wakf within the exclusive jurisdiction of a Religious Court, the matter shall be referred to the Special Tribunal referred to in Article 55 of the Palestine Order in Council 1922.
Actions of ownership or possession of immovable property to be tried by Civil Court.	5. Every action or other proceeding concerning the ownership or possession of immovable property shall be decided by a Civil Court notwithstanding any claim by any party or person that the land is Wakf.
Jurisdiction in cases of Diyet.	6. The Moslem Religious Court shall have jurisdiction in cases of application for blood-money on account of homicide or injury to a member (Diyet) where all the parties concerned are Moslems. In other cases the Civil Court shall exercise the jurisdiction, unless all the parties agree to refer the application to the Moslem Religious Court.

A Criminal Court may, if it sees fit, in any case in which a prosecution for homicide or injury to a member is brought, and at the request of a person entitled to Diyet, award any sum not exceeding £E. 250 as compensation in lieu of Diyet, and shall not be bound in making such award by the rules of the Sharia Law. The amount awarded shall be recoverable as a civil debt. Where an order has been made under this provision no further claim for Diyet shall be brought before a Moslem Religious Court.

March 1st, 1925.

HERBERT SAMUEL
High Commissioner.

ACQUISITION OF LAND FOR THE ARMY AND AIR FORCE
ORDINANCE No. 12 OF 1925.

GOVERNMENT OF PALESTINE

ACQUISITION OF LAND FOR THE ARMY AND AIR FORCE ORDINANCE 1925.

No. 12 of 1925.

An Ordinance to make provision for the acquisition of land for the service of His Britannic Majesty's Army and Air Forces in Palestine and for the assessment of compensation for land so acquired.

BE IT ENACTED by the High Commissioner for Palestine with the advice of the Advisory Council thereof:

1. This Ordinance may be cited as the Acquisition of Land for the Army and Air Force Ordinance 1925 and shall come into force on the 15th May, 1925. *Short title and commencement.*

2. In this Ordinance the following words shall, unless the context otherwise requires, have the following meanings:— *Definitions.*

"Land" shall include any building, tree or anything fixed in the land and any portion of the sea, or shore, or a river; and any easement in or over land including the right to fire over it and other rights of user and any right of interference.

"The Officer Commanding" shall mean the officer of His Britannic Majesty's Army or Air Force commanding the Army or the Air Force as the case may be, or both such forces if they be under a single command.

"The Board of Arbitration" means the Board constituted by this Ordinance.

3. Subject to the provisions of this Ordinance it shall be lawful for the Officer Commanding to treat and agree with the owner or owners of any land required for the purposes of the Army or the Air Force either for the absolute purchase thereof or for the possession or use thereof for a definite period or during such time as the exigence of such service shall require, or for the acquisition of any easement in or over land including the right of firing over it and other rights of user and any right of interference. *Officer Commanding may treat for the acquisition of land etc.*

4. (1) If the Officer Commanding shall fail to come to terms with the owner or owners of any land required under the preceding Section he shall (a) submit to the High Commissioner for his approval the Notice or Notices to treat referred *In default of agreement Notice to treat to be approved by High Commissioner.*

Printed by the Greek Convent Press and Azriel Press, Jerusalem.

Palestine No. 12 of 1925.

— 2 —

Contents and service of Notice to treat.
to in the next succeeding sub-section, and the High Commissioner shall have power to withhold approval or to grant approval with such modifications as he shall think fit and the Officer Commanding shall thereafter (b) cause a Notice or Notices to treat in the form approved by the High Commissioner in the preceding sub-section to be served on the owners or lessees or reputed owners or lessees and on the occupiers of the land to which such Notice or Notices relate.

(2) Every such Notice shall specify the land concerned and shall state that the Officer Commanding is willing to treat as to the compensation or rent to be paid for the purchase or possession or the use of such land or for the easement to be acquired or as to the compensation for the damage to be sustained by reason of the restraint as to any right incidental to ownership which it is intended to prohibit or restrict.

(3) Every such Notice shall demand from the persons on whom it is served particulars in writing of the interest of each such person in the lands and of the claims made in respect thereof, with a statement of the amount which he may be willing to receive as compensation and the details of the compensation claimed.

(4) Every such Notice shall be served personally on the said persons or left at their last known usual place of abode. In case any such persons are absent from Palestine or cannot be found, the notice shall be served on the Mukhtar of the village or quarter, and affixed upon some conspicuous part of the lands, and advertised in a newspaper circulating in the District.

Officer Commanding may agree to compensation to be payable.
5. The amount of compensation to be paid for the lands specified in the Notice to treat may be determined by agreement between the Officer Commanding and the parties having any interest in such lands respectively.

Procedure on failure to agree to compensation.
6. If for 15 days after the service of any such Notice as aforesaid any person on whom the same is served fails to state the particulars of his claim in respect of any land to which such Notice relates or to treat with the Officer Commanding as to the amount of compensation to be paid or if the Officer Commanding and such person do not within such 15 days agree as to the amount of such compensation,

(a) it shall be lawful for the Officer Commanding to enter into immediate possession of the lands referred to in such Notice,

Palestine No. 12 of 1925.

— 3 —

Provided that if the owners or occupiers refuse to allow the Officer Commanding to enter into such possession the Officer Commanding may apply to the President of the District Court in whose jurisdiction the land is situated who if he is satisfied that the Officer Commanding is entitled to possession under this Section shall issue an order under his hand commanding possession to be delivered; and

(b) the amount of such compensation shall be settled by the Board of Arbitration in accordance with the provisions hereinafter contained.

7. The compensation payable for land specified in the Notice to treat shall in default of agreement be determined by an Arbitration Board which shall consist of three members, viz:— _{Constitution of Board to assess compensation.}

(a) the President of the Land Court or the President of a District Court as President,

(b) an officer of the Army or Air Force and
(c) an inhabitant of Palestine } Assessors.

The assessors shall be nominated by the High Commissioner. The President shall have power to summon witnesses to appear before the Board to give evidence on such relevant matters as he may think fit.

Any person who is dissatisfied with the award of the Board of Arbitration shall be entitled within 15 days of the notification of that award to appeal to the High Commissioner. The decision of the High Commissioner shall be final.

The President shall direct the manner in which the cost of the arbitration including the fee payable to any Palestinian assessor shall be borne.

8. The owners, occupiers and any other person who proves to the Board that he has an interest in the land specified in the Notice to treat shall be entitled to appear before the Board either personally or by an advocate. _{Right of audience.}

Any person who desires to appear shall submit particulars of his claim prior to the assembling of the Board.

9. In assessing compensation the Board of Arbitration shall act in accordance with the following rules:— _{Rules for assessment of compensation.}

Palestine No. 12 of 1925.

— 4 —

(1) No allowance shall be made on account of the acquisition being compulsory.

(2) The value of land shall, subject as hereinafter provided, be taken to be the amount which the land if sold in the open market by a willing seller might be expected to realise;

Provided that the Board in assessing such amount shall assess the same according to the value of the land on the said basis at the time when the same were or under the provisions of this Ordinance could have been entered upon by the Officer Commanding without regard to any improvements or works made by the Army or the Air Force therein; and

Provided further that the Board of Arbitration in assessing such amount shall be entitled to consider all returns and assessments of capital or rental value for taxation made or acquiesced in by the claimant.

(3) The special suitability or adaptability of the land for any purpose shall not be taken into account if it is a purpose to which it could be applied only in pursuance of statutory powers or for which there is no market apart from the special needs of a particular purchaser or the requirements of the Army or the Air Force or of any Government Department or any local or public authority;

Provided that any bona fide offer for the purchase of the land made before the passing of this Ordinance which may be brought to the notice of the Board of Arbitration shall be taken into consideration.

(4) Where the land is, and but for the compulsory acquisition would continue to be devoted to a purpose of such a nature that there is no general demand or market for land for that purpose, the compensation may it the Board of Arbitration is satisfied that reinstatement in some other place is bona fide intended, be assessed on the basis of the reasonable cost of such equivalent reinstatement.

(5) The provisions of sub-section (2) shall not affect the assessment of compensation for disturbance or any other matter not directly based on the value of land.

(6) In assessing the rent to be paid for possession or use of land the Board of Arbitration shall assess the same on the basis that the said rent shall be a reasonable return to the owner on the capital value of the land assessed in accordance with the provisions of the preceding sub-sections hereof.

Palestine No. 12 of 1925.

— 5 —

(7) The Board of Arbitration shall assess the compensation to be paid by way of damage for the imposition of any restraint on the exercise of any rights incidental to ownership on the basis of the amount by which the value of the land assessed in accordance with the preceding sub-sections hereof shall have been diminished by reason of the imposition of such restraints.

10. (1) If part only of any lands comprised in any lease or mortgage or otherwise subject to any rent or any annual or other payment or incumbrance be acquired or occupied under this Ordinance such rent, payment or incumbrance may be apportioned by agreement between the Officer Commanding and the persons entitled thereto or to the lands subject thereto, or in case no such agreement be made the same shall be apportioned ᵇ the Board of Arbitration. *Provision for apportionment of rents and incumbrances.*

(2) After such apportionment such apportioned part only of such rent, payment or incumbrance shall be payable out of the residue of the said lands, and all conditions, agreements, powers and remedies in respect of such rent, payment or incumbrance shall remain in force in respect of the residue of the said lands.

11. (1) Where any damage has been sustained by reason of any works done in or upon lands acquired or occupied under this Ordinance in accordance with Section 15 (b) and such damage has not been agreed upon or otherwise determined prospectively, compensation shall be paid when the works have been done and shall be determined by the Board of Arbitration in the manner prescribed under this Ordinance or as near thereto as circumstances admit. *Compensation to be payable in respect of lands injuriously affected by any works done on land acquired under this Ordinance.*

(2) In determining the amount of compensation payable regard shall be had to any increase in the value of the land by reason of any improved drainage and other advantages derived from any such works.

12. (1) Where the Officer Commanding has made an unconditional offer in writing of any sum as compensation to any claimant and the sum awarded by the Board of Arbitration to that claimant does not exceed the sum offered the Board shall unless for special reasons they think proper not to do so, order the claimant to bear his own costs and to pay the costs of the Officer Commanding so far as they were incurred after the offer was made. *Provision as to costs.*

(2) If the Board of Arbitration are satisfied that a claimant has failed to comply with the demands of the Officer

Palestine No. 12 of 1925.

— 6 —

Commanding as set forth in Section 4 (3) in sufficient time to enable the Officer Commanding to make a proper offer, the foregoing provisions of this Section shall apply as if an unconditional offer had been made by the Officer Commanding at the time when in the opinion of the Board sufficient particulars should have been furnished and the claimant had been awarded a sum not exceeding the amount of such offer.

(3) Where a claimant has made an unconditional offer in writing to accept any sum as compensation and has complied with the provisions of Section 4(3) hereof and the sum awarded is equal to or exceeds that sum the Board of Arbitration shall unless for special reasons they may think proper not to do so, order the Officer Commanding to bear his own costs and to pay the costs of the claimant so far as they were incurred after the offer was made.

(4) Subject as aforesaid the costs of an arbitration shall be in the discretion of the Board of Arbitration who may direct to and by whom and in what manner those costs shall be paid;

Provided that such costs shall be in accordance with the scale that may be prescribed under Section 23 hereof.

(5) Where the Board of Arbitration orders the claimant to pay the costs or any part of the costs of the Officer Commanding, the Officer Commanding may deduct the amount so payable by the claimant from the amount of compensation due to him.

Officer Commanding may pay compensation into the Court if persons entitled thereto cannot be found or fail to make out a title.

13. The Officer Commanding may in any case, at or after the expiration of three months from the time at which the compensation for any lands has been agreed upon or otherwise ascertained, if the persons entitled thereto cannot be found, or if the persons claiming to be entitled shall fail to make out a title thereto, pay such compensation to the District Court in whose jurisdiction the lands are situated, and such payment shall discharge the Officer Commanding from all liability in respect of the money so paid.

Lands taken to be vested in the High Commissioner on behalf of Secretary of State for War or President Air Council.

14. The lands required to be taken under this Ordinance shall from and after the payment of the compensation for the same be vested in the High Commissioner for the interest acquired therein on behalf of His Britannic Majesty's Principal Secretary of State for War or the President of the Air Council respectively according as such lands were taken for Army or Air Force purposes.

Palestine No. 12 of 1925.

— 7 —

15. From and after the service of any Notice to treat requiring any lands to be kept free from buildings and other obstructions the following restrictions, powers and consequences shall attach with reference to such lands:- _{Restriction and powers with respect to lands required to be kept free from buildings.}

(a) No building or other obstruction shall be made or erected thereon in contravention of the restrictions specified in the Notice to treat without the prior consent of the Officer Commanding.

(b) It shall be lawful for the Officer Commanding at any time after the expiration of fourteen days from the service of such Notice to enter and pull down any present or future building or structure thereon and to cut down or remove any of the trees thereon and to remove or alter any of the banks, fences, hedges and ditches thereon and to make underground or other drains and generally to level and clear the said lands and do all such acts for levelling and clearing the same as may be deemed necessary or proper by the Officer Commanding for the purpose of giving effect to the restrictions specified in the Notice to treat but in such manner that evidence of the boundaries of the lands held by different owners may be preserved.

16. If in any case after the service of a Notice to treat by the Officer Commanding it appears to him expedient to withdraw such Notice either in respect of the whole or any part of the lands it shall be lawful for him to do so by giving a further Notice and thereupon the lands comprised in the Notice of withdrawal shall be wholly discharged from the effect of the Notice to treat and the Officer Commanding shall be wholly discharged from any obligation in respect of the lands comprised in the Notice of withdrawal and from the obligation to make compensation in respect thereof, without prejudice to any claim of any owner, lessee or occupier for compensation for such damage as he may have sustained in consequence of the service of the Notice to treat, the amount of such damage to be determined in like manner as other compensation under this Ordinance: _{Power of Officer Commanding to withdraw Notices to treat.}

Provided that every notice of withdrawal shall be approved by the High Commissioner and shall be given within three months after the service of the Notice to treat or within six weeks after the delivery by the claimant of the claim specified in Section 4 (3), whichever date shall be the later.

17. It shall be lawful for the Officer Commanding, without taking any legal proceeding (a) to stop up or divert or alter the level of any public or private road, sewer, drain or _{Power to divert roads, etc.}

Palestine No. 12 of 1925.

— 8 —

pipe if he deems it necessary for any of the works contemplated to be done on any land acquired or occupied under this Ordinance;

Provided that he shall (if necessary) first have made, opened or laid down another good and sufficient road, sewer, drain or pipe in lieu of that stopped up or diverted;

and (b) for the like reasons to alter the course or level of any river, stream or watercourse;

Provided that he shall pay compensation to be determined in the manner prescribed in this Ordinance for any damage sustained by reason of the exercise of such power.

Limitation of the term of any compulsory lease or the term of any renewed lease.

The High Commissioner shall not authorise the compulsory grant of any lease of which the term exceeds 21 years nor the grant or renewal of any lease for a period which, together with the period of occupation then expired, exceeds 21 years.

Power of the owner of any land occupied during such period as the exigence of the service shall require to apply to the High Commissioner that the land be vacated or purchased after 20 years of occupation.

19. (1) When land has been occupied by the Army or the Air Force on account of the exigencies of the services for a period of twenty years, the owner or owners may thereafter apply to the High Commissioner for an order directed to the Officer Commanding either to vacate or to purchase such land within one year of the date of the order. The High Commissioner shall grant or refuse the application as he shall think fit.

(2) If the High Commissioner grants the application and the Officer Commanding shall decide to purchase such land and shall fail to agree upon the compensation to be paid he shall comply with the provisions of Section 4 hereof and such compensation shall be determined in accordance with the provisions of this Ordinance.

(3) When land has been occupied by the Army or the Air Force on account of the exigencies of the service and the Officer Commanding vacates the land he shall be entitled to remove all buildings, erections or other improvements erected or made thereon during the period of occupation making such compensation to the owners of the land for the damage which may have been done by the erection of such buildings or otherwise as may be agreed between him and the said owners or as in default of agreement may be assessed by the Board of Arbitration.

Power of the Officer Commanding to sell land no longer required for Army or Air Force purposes.

20. (1) If at any time the land acquired for the service of the Army or the Air Force is, in the opinion of the Officer Commanding, no longer required for such purposes, and if the Government of Palestine does not desire to acquire the land from the Officer Commanding on such terms as may be agreed, it shall be lawful for the Officer Commanding to treat and agree with any person for the sale to him of any such land;

Palestine No. 12 of 1925.

— 9 —

Provided that if the former owner of the land from whom the Officer Commanding acquired it for the service of the Army or Air Force is still alive he shall have the right of pre-emption on paying the sum agreed or awarded as compensation together with the value of any improvement made upon the land since its occupation by the Army or Air Force, such value to be determined, in default of agreement between the parties, by the Director of Public Works.

The right of pre-emption shall be exercised within one month of notice to the previous owner by the Officer Commanding of the intended sale. The notice shall be served in the manner provided for serving a Notice to treat in Section 4 hereof.

(2) It shall be lawful for the Officer Commanding when selling any lands under this Section, to sell subject to the condition that they are forever thereafter to be kept free from all buildings and other obstructions to or from buildings or other obstructions of a kind specified in the condition and if the lands are sold subject to such condition, the restrictions, powers and the consequences referred to in Section 15 shall attach with reference to such lands.

21. (1) The High Commissioner acting on the request of the Officer Commanding may make regulations regarding the use of land acquired or occupied under this Ordinance for the purposes to which it is appropriated and for securing the public against danger arising from that use with power to prohibit all intrusion on the land and all obstruction of the use thereof.

Power of High Commissioner at the request of the Officer Commanding to make Regulations as to use of land held for Army or Air Force purposes and securing the safety of the public.

(2) Where any land the use of which can be regulated by regulations abuts on any sea or where any flying, rifle or artillery practice is or can be carried on over any sea-shore from any such land regulations may be made in relation to any such sea or shore as if they were part of the land, provided that if any regulation injuriously affects or obstructs the exercise of any private rights in or over any such sea or shore, that person shall be entitled to compensation which in case of difference shall be assessed by the Board of Arbitration.

(3) Where any regulations made under this Section permit the public to use the land for any purpose when not used for the Army or Air Force purposes to which it is appropriated, such regulations may also provide for the preservation of order and good conduct on the land and for the prevention of nuisances, obstructions and encroachments thereon, and for the prevention of any injury to the same or to anything growing or erected thereon.

Palestine No. 12 of 1925.

— 10 —

(4) The High Commissioner shall cause such draft regulations to be published in the Official Gazette at least fifteen days before they come into force, and any persons who desire to raise objections to any of the said regulations may do so to the office of the District Governor in whose district the lands are situated. The District Governor shall cause such objections to be forwarded to the office of the Chief Secretary and the High Commissioner shall consider such objections before approving the regulations.

(5) All regulations approved by the High Commissioner shall be published in the Official Gazette, and he shall take such steps as appear to him necessary to make them known to all persons in the locality and shall cause boundaries of the area to which the regulations apply to be marked provided that if the regulations apply to any sea or the shore thereof and the boundaries of the area cannot in the opinion of the High Commissioner be conveniently marked those boundaries shall be described in the regulations.

(6) If any person commits an offence against any regulation he shall be liable on conviction to a fine not exceeding five pounds Egyptian and may be removed by any constable or officer authorised from the area to which the regulation applies and may be arrested without warrant and any vehicle, animal, vessel or thing found in the area in contravention of any regulation may be removed by any constable or such officer and on due proof of such contravention be declared by the Court to be forfeited to the Government of Palestine.

Application of Ordinance to Wakf lands.
22. In the application of this Ordinance to Wakf land the trustee, (mutawalli) of any wakf, or in the absence of any trustee, the Administration of Wakfs, shall have all the powers and be subject to all the obligations imposed herein upon the owner or occupier of land, and the price of the land shall be handed to the Treasury of the Awkaf in the name of the wakf property concerned.

High Commissioner may make regulations.
23. The High Commissioner may make regulations prescribing:

(a) the forms to be used under this Ordinance;

(b) the scale of costs in respect of arbitration under this Ordinance;

(c) the means by which claims for several interests in the same land shall be heard at the same time;

Palestine No. 12 of 1925.

— 11 —

(d) the fees to be paid to the Palestinian assessors of the Arbitration Tribunal.

24. The Acquisition of Land for the Army Ordinance 1920 is hereby repealed; Repeal.

Provided (a) that such repeal shall not prejudice or annul any sale, purchase, lease, agreement, award or any other act, matter or thing made, done or affected under the said Ordinance or the determination of any question of compensation where before the date of the commencement of this Ordinance such question has been referred to the Permanent Arbitration Board created by the Ordinance hereby repealed;

And (b) that where land has been expropriated under the said Ordinance for the use of the Air Force and has been registered in the name of the Palestine Government on behalf of His Majesty's Secretary of State for War, that registration shall be corrected and the land shall henceforth be vested in the High Commissioner for the interest acquired therein on behalf of the President of the Air Council.

May 15th, 1925   HERBERT SAMUEL
High Commissioner.

SANCTIONED.

LAND SURVEYORS ORDINANCE No. 14 OF 1925.

Herbert Samuel

GOVERNMENT OF PALESTINE.

AN ORDINANCE TO REPEAL THE SURVEYORS ORDINANCE, 1921, AND TO MAKE OTHER PROVISIONS IN LIEU THEREOF.

No. 14 of 1925.

BE IT ENACTED by the High Commissioner for Palestine, with the advice of the Advisory Council thereof:—

Short Title.

1. This Ordinance may be cited as the Land Surveyors Ordinance, 1925.

Extent of Ordinance.

2. The terms "surveyor" and "survey" in this Ordinance refer to the surveying of land.

Practising surveyors to be licensed

3. (1) The High Commissioner may, on the advice of the Director of Surveys, grant licences to persons desiring to practise the profession of surveying in Palestine, and no person may practise that profession unless he is in possession of a licence so granted.

(2) The name and address of every person to whom a licence is granted shall be published in the Official Gazette upon the issue of the licence.

Suspension and cancellation of licence.

4. (1) Where it appears to the High Commissioner upon complaint of the Director of Surveys or of any person aggrieved that the holder of a licence to practise has proved himself incapable or grossly negligent in the performance of his duties as Surveyor or has been guilty of any offence involving moral turpitude, or has persistently failed to comply with the Regulations made under this Ordinance, the High Commissioner may cancel the licence to practise or direct that it shall be suspended for such time as may be fixed by him: Provided that no order of cancellation or suspension shall be made unless the surveyor complained against has had an opportunity of being heard in his own defence.

(2) A person whose licence has been cancelled or suspended in pursuance of this Section shall be deemed not to be the holder of a licence to practise under this Ordinance and shall forthwith deliver the cancelled or suspended licence to the Director of Surveys.

(3) Every order of cancellation or suspension shall be published in the Official Gazette.

Printed by the Greek Convent Press and Azriel Press, Jerusalem.

Palestine No. 14 of 1925.

— 2 —

5. No survey or plan purporting to have been prepared after the date of the commencement of this Ordinance shall be receivable at a Land Registry unless it has been prepared and signed by a surveyor licensed to practise in Palestine or is a copy of such plan or survey signed as being a true copy by a licensed surveyor. Plans receivable at Land Registry.

6. (1) Any person who practises or professes to practise as a surveyor in Palestine not being the holder of a licence to practise shall be punishable with a fine not exceeding £E. 50 in respect of each transaction in which he was engaged. Penalties and disqualification.

(2) Any person against whom an order for cancellation or suspension has been made who fails to deliver up his licence to the Director of Surveys within fourteen days of the order shall be punishable with a fine not exceeding £E.20

(3) No person who is not the holder of a licence to practise as a surveyor shall be entitled to sue in any Court of Law for any remuneration in respect of a survey made by him or any plans drawn by him.

7. The High Commissioner in Executive Council may make, and when made, vary or revoke Regulations: Regulations.

(a) prescribing the conditions on which licences may be granted, the form of licences to be granted, and the fees payable in respect thereof;

(b) as to the method in which surveys shall be executed and plans shall be made;

(c) as to the filing by surveyors with the Director of Surveys of copies of plans prepared by them;

(d) as to any other matter requiring regulation under this Ordinance.

8. The Surveyors Ordinance 1921 is hereby repealed: Provided that such repeal shall not affect the validity of any licence to practise granted thereunder; but the provisions of this Ordinance shall apply thereto as if the licence had been granted under this Ordinance. Repeal.

June 1st, 1925

HERBERT SAMUEL
High Commissioner.

CHARITABLE TRUSTS (AMENDMENT) ORDINANCE, No. 24 OF 1925.

GOVERNMENT OF PALESTINE

CHARITABLE TRUSTS (AMENDMENT) ORDINANCE

No. 24 of 1925.

An Ordinance to amend the Charitable Trusts Ordinance, 1924

BE IT ENACTED by the High Commissioner for Palestine, with the advice of the Advisory Council thereof:—

1. This Ordinance may be cited as the Charitable Trusts (Amendment) Ordinance, 1925, and shall be construed as one with the Charitable Trusts Ordinance, 1924, (hereinafter called the principal Ordinance) and it may be cited together with the principal Ordinance as the Charitable Trusts Ordinance, 1924-25. *Short title and construction.*

2. Section 3 of the principal Ordinance shall be construed as if it had been originally worded as follows: *Amendment of Section 3 of the principal Ordinance.*

Subject to the provisions of Section 37

(a) No trust in relation to immovable property is valid unless declared by the last will of the author of the trust or of the trustees or by a non-testamentary instrument in writing signed by the author of the trust or the trustees and notarially executed. *Creation of trust of immovable property.*

(b) No trust in relation to movable property is valid unless declared by the last will of the author of the trust or of the trustee, or by a non-testamentary instrument in writing signed by the author of the trust or the trustee, or unless the ownership of the property is transferred to the trustee by delivery. *Of movable property.*

3. The word "exchange" shall be inserted after the word "sell" in sub-section (1) and after the word "sale" in sub-section (4) of Section 12 of the principal Ordinance. *Amendment of Section 12.*

4. Section 25 of the principal Ordinance is hereby repealed; and the following provisions shall be substituted therefor: *Alteration of Section 25.*

(1) Trust property shall be deemed to be vested in all the trustees jointly.

(2) Where trust property consists of stock, shares, or securities or of immovable property or any interest therein or of any other property transferable in any book or register, it shall be registered in the names of all the trustees.

Printed by the Greek Convent Press and Azriel Press, Jerusalem.

Palestine No. 24 of 1925.

2

(3) On the death or discharge of one of co-trustees, the trust survives and the trust property remains vested in the surviving or continuing trustees unless the instrument of trust expressly declares otherwise.

(4) Where trust property transferable in any book or register is registered in the names of two or more co-trustees and is expressed to be so registered upon a joint account, the registering authority shall upon proof of the death or discharge of any trustee amend the register accordingly and the trust property shall continue registered in the names of the surviving or continuing trustees or trustee only.

(5) Where upon the death of any trustee any interest in the trust property or in any part thereof has by the effect of any law regulating succession to property become vested in any person or persons who have not been appointed trustees thereof, such person or persons shall, pending any appointment of new trustees, hold such property upon the trust declared and shall be liable for any breach of trust as though they had been duly appointed trustees and had accepted the trusteeship.

Amendment of Section 32.

5. (1) Sub-section (1) of Section 32 of the principal Ordinance is hereby repealed and the following provisions shall be substituted therefor.

(1) In the following cases, namely,

(a) where it is uncertain in whom the title to any trust property is vested; or

(b) where a trustee or any other person in whom the title of trust property is vested has been required in writing to transfer the property by or on behalf of a person entitled to require such transfer, and has wilfully refused or neglected to transfer the property for twenty-eight days after the date of the requirement; or

(c) where a trustee or other person in whom the trust property is vested is a minor or is out of Palestine or cannot be found; or

(d) where it is otherwise convenient to vest the trust property in any other person;

the Court may make an Order (in this Ordinance called a vesting Order) vesting the property of any such person in any such manner or to any such extent as the Court may direct.

Palestine No. 24 of 1925.

(2) There shall be added to Section 32 the following sub-section:—

(3) Where a vesting Order may be made under this Section, the Court may, if it is more convenient, appoint a person to transfer the property; and a transfer by that person in conformity with the Order shall have the same effect as an Order under this Section, and every person so appointed shall for the purpose of all transactions, proceedings and formalities incidental to the transfer, have all the power and capacities of the trustee or other person in whom the trust property was vested and shall be deemed to be the authorised attorney of such trustee or other person for the purpose aforesaid.

6. (1) Sub-section (1) of Section 34 of the principal Ordinance is hereby repealed. *Repeal of Section 34 (1).*

(2) The marginal note of Section 34 shall read "Registration of immovable trust property".

7. The term "Public Trustee of Charities" shall be substituted for the term "Public Trustee" wherever the same occurs in Section 35 of the principal Ordinance. *Amendment of Section 35.*

8. The following paragraph shall be added to Section 37 of the principal Ordinance: *Addition to Section 37.*

"In dealing with any property alleged to be subject to a charitable trust, the Court shall not be debarred from exercising any of its powers by the absence of evidence of the former constitution of the trust if it shall be of opinion in all the circumstances of the case that the trust in fact exists or ought to be deemed to exist."

9. Sub-section (3) of Section 38 of the principal Ordinance shall read as follows:— *Amendment of Section 38 (3).*

(3) Where property in Palestine is held on trust by a foreign corporation and the corporation has failed to register, the Attorney General may apply to the Court for the appointment of a trustee as though there were no existing trustee.

10. Section 39 of the principal Ordinance shall be construed as though it had been originally enacted with the alterations and additions following:— *Amendment of Section 39.*

(a) The words "such property became subject to the trust" replaced the words "such trust was registered" in sub-section (1).

Palestine No. 24 of 1925.

— 4 —

(b) The words "Mulk immovable property" replaced the words "the immovable property" in paragraph (c) of sub-section (4).

(c) The words "which was not subject to the provisions of this Section" were added to paragraph (d) of the same sub-section.

Amendment of Section 41.

11. A paragraph shall be added to Section 41 of the principal Ordinance as follows:—

"(c) as to the fees to be charged in respect of any proceeding under this Ordinance."

Amendment of Section 43.

12. The words "nor be construed to validate a devise of Miri land for charitable purposes" shall be added to Section 43 of the principal Ordinance.

G. S. SYMES
Officer Administering the Government.

1st August, 1925

Section 9: 1926

FORESTS ORDINANCE, No. 5 OF 1926.

The first day of March, One thousand nine hundred and twenty-six.

GOVERNMENT OF PALESTINE.

FORESTS ORDINANCE

No. 5 of 1926.

AN ORDINANCE TO REPEAL THE WOODS AND FORESTS ORDINANCE, 1920, AND TO MAKE OTHER PROVISION IN LIEU THEREOF.

PART I.

BE IT ENACTED by the High Commissioner for Palestine with the advice of the Advisory Council thereof:—

1. This Ordinance may be cited as the Forests Ordinance, 1926. *Short title.*

2. In this Ordinance, unless the context otherwise requires:— *Definitions.*

"Forest Land" means all land bearing trees whether naturally or under cultivation.

"Tree" means trees in all stages of their growth, palms, bamboos, shrubs and brushwood and stumps.

"Fruit Tree" means every fruit producing tree that is cultivated for domestic purposes and every tree that is customarily grafted.

"Timber" includes trees, fallen or felled and all wood whether cut up or fashioned for any purpose or not.

"Forest Produce" means the following when found in or brought from forest land:—

Timber, charcoal, resin, gum, gutta percha, wood oil, natural varnish, grass, creepers, climbers, soil-binding plants, leaves, fruits, seeds, roots, bark, fibres, reeds, all other parts or produce of trees and plants, peat, surface soil and minerals other than minerals within the meaning of any Ordinance regulating the working of minerals.

Palestine No. 5 of 1926.

— 2 —

"Take" in connection with forest produce, includes felling or carrying away of timber, and cutting, collecting, gathering, or removing any other forest produce.

"Cattle" means bull, ox, cow, steer, heifer, buffalo, horse, pony, mule, ass, camel, sheep, goat, pig, and the young of the same.

"Forest Officer" means any Officer whom the High Commissioner may from time to time appoint, by name or as holding an office, to carry out any of the purposes of this Ordinance.

"Person" includes any company, corporation or society or any village community or communities.

"Prescribed" means prescribed by this Ordinance or by any Regulations made hereunder.

PART II.

Forest Reserves.

Definition of forest reserves.
3. The High Commissioner may by proclamation to be published in the Gazette, bring any forest lands not being private property under the control and management of the Government as forest reserves. On the issue of any such proclamation, the provisions of this Ordinance shall apply to any forest lands therein specified.

Right not to be alienated without sanction.
4. (1) No right in or over any forest reserve which has been exercised for the first time since July, 1920, or which may hereafter be exercised shall be deemed to have been duly acquired unless it has been acquired under or in pursuance of a grant or contract made by or on behalf of the Government of Palestine.

(2) No right in or over any forest reserve shall be alienated by way of grant, lease, mortgage or other disposition without the sanction of the High Commissioner;
Provided that when such right is appurtenant to any land or building it may be sold or otherwise alienated with such land or building without such sanction.

PART III.

The Management of Forest Reserves.

Offences in connection with forest reserves.
5. (1) Any person who does, or causes, or knowingly permits any other person to do, any of the following acts in any forest reserve, save in accordance with the conditions of a licence granted under this Ordinance, or in virtue of the provisions of Section 6 hereof, namely:

Palestine No. 5 of 1926.

— 3 —

(a) takes any forest produce;

(b) uproots, burns, strips off the bark or leaves from, or otherwise damages any tree;

(c) sets fire to any grass or herbage, or kindles a fire without taking due precautions to prevent its spreading;

(d) smokes or lights a fire in any part of a forest reserve within which, or at a time when, smoking or the lighting of fires is prohibited by an order of the High Commissioner;

(e) pastures cattle or permits cattle to trespass;

(f) digs, cuts or turns the soil;

(g) trespasses in any part of a forest reserve in which trespass shall be prohibited by an order of the High Commissioner or during any period specified in an order of the High Commissioner;

(h) constructs any dam or weir across any river or stream or otherwise obstructs the channel of any river or stream; or

(i) resides or erects any building in any forest reserve

shall be liable on conviction to a fine not exceeding £E. 100 or to imprisonment for a period not exceeding twelve months, or to both penalties and may be ordered to pay in addition such compensation for damage done as the Court may direct.

(2) Any person who purchases forest produce, knowing or having reason to believe that such forest produce was taken from a forest reserve in contravention of the provisions of this Ordinance shall be liable on conviction to the like penalties.

6. (1) Nothing in Section 5 contained shall prohibit the collection and removal from forest reserves (other than closed forest areas) of dead and dry wood or brush-wood to be used solely for firewood for the use of inhabitants of villages who have been accustomed to supply their wants in this respect from the forests in the vicinity of their village but such inhabitants shall not remove roots, or stumps, or fell standing timber or cut branches.

Collection of firewood permitted.

Palestine No. 5 of 1926.

— 4 —

Villages requiring forest produce (other than firewood) to apply as provided.
(2) Inhabitants of villages who have hitherto obtained forest produce other than dead or dry wood or brushwood collected in accordance with the preceding sub-section in virtue of any legal right or custom from forest reserves within the boundaries or in the vicinity of their village, for house building, domestic and agricultural purposes may continue to exercise such rights or customs subject to the following conditions:—

They shall submit in writing to the Forest Officer an application for permission to collect such forest produce which shall be supported by a declaration of the Mukhtar that the application is reasonable and shall contain the following particulars:—

(a) the amount, kind and description of the forest produce required;

(b) the purpose for which the same is required;

(c) the place whence it is desired to extract the same; and

(d) the period requisite to remove the same.

(3) After due enquiry, and having regard to the maintenance of the forest, the Forest Officer shall sanction or refuse such application in whole or in part and, if he sanctions it, issue a licence in the form prescribed.

(4) The licensee shall produce his licence for inspection whenever required to do so by a Police Officer or Forest Officer or Administrative Officer.

Licence may be cancelled and forest produce forfeited.
(5) If a licensee fails to observe any of the conditions laid down or perform any act prescribed in his licence, his licence may be cancelled by a Forest Officer and the forest produce in respect of which he has failed to observe the conditions or to perform the act may be forfeited.

Forest produce forfeited may be sold.
(6) Any forest produce forfeited in pursuance of this Section may be sold by the Forest Officer and the proceeds accounted to the Government.

Extraction of forest produce by other persons and for other purposes.
7. The extraction of forest produce by persons or for purposes other than those specified in the preceding Section may be authorised by a licence issued by a Forest Officer, subject to such conditions as may be specified in the licence.

Palestine No. 5 of 1926.

— 5 —

8. All persons enjoying any right in a forest reserve in which fire breaks out, and the inhabitants of all villages, within a distance of 5 kilometres from the scene of the fire, shall be bound to assist in its extinction, and any person refusing so to assist shall be liable on conviction to a fine not exceeding £E. 5 or imprisonment not exceeding fourteen days, or both penalties and may be deprived of his right for a period not exceeding one year. Persons bound to assist in the extinction of fires.

9. Notwithstanding anything in this Ordinance contained, a Forest Officer may by licence authorise the inhabitants of villages or members of tribes in the vicinity of forest reserves to pasture their cattle therein on the following conditions:— Provisions as to grazing rights.

(a) Every year, before a date to be notified locally by the Forest Officer, the Mukhtar of each village or Sheikh of a tribe desiring to pasture its cattle shall submit to the Forest Officer a statement in writing showing the number and description of cattle and the place in which it is desired to graze them and, if suitable areas are available, the Forest Officer may grant a licence in the form prescribed which shall designate the tracts to which the cattle may be admitted and fix the period during which they may be grazed.

(b) Cattle belonging to the inhabitants of any village or tribe shall be placed under the charge of a herd who shall at all times carry with him the licence relating to such cattle and shall produce it when required by a Forest Officer or Police Officer or Administrative Officer.

10. The Forest Officer may in his discretion grant licences to persons other than those mentioned in the preceding Section to pasture cattle in a forest reserve subject to the payment of such fees as may be prescribed by Regulation under this Ordinance, and to such conditions as may be specified in the licence. Provision for grazing of strangers' cattle.

11. If any cattle be found in a forest reserve in respect of which a licence has not been obtained or if they are not in charge of a herd, or if their presence in the forest reserve is contrary to the conditions of the licence, the owner of the cattle shall be liable on conviction to a fine not exceeding P.T. 5 for each head of cattle, and may be ordered to pay, in addition, such compensation for any damage done as the Court may direct. Grazing without or contrary to the terms of a licence.

12. If fire breaks out in a forest reserve and it is proved that the fire was due to the negligence of any herd, the herd shall be liable on conviction to a fine not exceeding £E. 10 or Liability for fire.

Palestine No. 5 of 1926.

to imprisonment for a period not exceeding three months or to both penalties; and the inhabitants of the village or the members of the tribe or the persons employing the herd, as the case may be, may be ordered to pay such compensation for any damage caused by the fire as the Court may direct.

Closed forest areas.

13. When, for the better maintenance of the forest, or for the protection of young trees, or for any other purpose it may be desirable to exclude the public from any forest reserve, or part of a forest reserve the High Commissioner may by notice published in the Gazette declare the forest or part thereof, the position and boundaries of which shall be described in such notice, to be a closed forest area. If such forest or such part thereof be within the boundaries of any village land, a copy of the notice shall forthwith be posted in such village.

Grazing or trespass in closed forest areas.

14. Any person trespassing or grazing cattle or allowing cattle to graze in a closed forest area after the publication and, if necessary, the posting of such notice, shall be deemed to be guilty of an offence against this Ordinance, and shall be liable on conviction to the penalties prescribed in Section 5 hereof.

Produce of forest land over which private ownership is established.

15. Where a claim is established to the ownership of forest land that has been under the control and management of the Government as a forest reserve, no revenue that has been derived from forest produce of the land prior to the establishment of such ownership shall be recovered from the Government.

PART IV.

The Protection of Trees.

Power to declare trees protected.

16. The High Commissioner may, by notice published in the Gazette, declare that the trees described therein shall be protected throughout Palestine or in any District or part of a District for the period specified in such notice and thereupon no person shall fell any such trees or remove the timber thereof save in accordance with a licence granted under Section 17.

Prohibition to fell protected trees, etc., save under licence.

17. No person shall fell any olive or carob or other tree protected by notice under Section 16 hereof, wherever growing, or remove the timber thereof unless he shall first have obtained from the Forest Officer a licence to do so in the form prescribed.

Penalties for felling, etc., without permission.

18. Any person who save in accordance with a licence granted by a Forest Officer, fells any olive or carob or any protected tree or removes any timber of such tree shall be liable on conviction to a fine not exceeding £E. 50 or imprisonment for a period not exceeding 6 months, or to both penalties.

Palestine No. 5 of 1926.

— 7 —

19. (1) Any person who wilfully and maliciously burns, strips the bark off, cuts, uproots or otherwise injures any tree shall be liable on conviction to imprisonment for a period not exceeding three years and may also be ordered to pay such compensation to the owner thereof in respect of any tree injured or destroyed as the Court may direct. *Wilful and malicious injury to trees.*

(2) Any person who by negligence allows animals to cause damage to any tree shall be liable on conviction to a fine not exceeding £E. 5 or to imprisonment for a period not exceeding fifteen days or to both penalties, and the owner of the animals may be ordered to pay such compensation for the damage caused as the Court may direct. If the animals belong to more than one owner, all the owners may be ordered jointly and severally to pay compensation for the damage caused by such animals. *Damage to trees by animals.*

PART V.

Control over Private Forest Land.

20. (1) The High Commissioner may, when he thinks fit in the public interest, authorise a Forest Officer to take under his protection forest lands which are private property, and in respect of which it appears that the destruction of trees is diminishing or likely to diminish the water supply, or is injuring the agricultural conditions of neighbouring lands, or imperilling the continuous supply of forest produce to the village communities contiguous to such lands. Every such authorisation shall be published in the Gazette. Measures necessary for the protection of such forest lands, as determined by the Forest Officer whose decision shall be final, shall be carried out by or at the cost of the owner of the forest land who shall repay to the Government any reasonable expenditure incurred for this purpose. *Protection of private forest lands for special purposes.*

(2) So long as any forest land shall be under the protection of the Government, it shall be deemed to be a forest reserve within the meaning of any provision of this Ordinance or of any Regulations hereunder affecting forest reserves.

PART VI.

Miscellaneous.

21. Where a fine is inflicted for an offence under this Ordinance, the Court imposing the fine may award any portion thereof not exceeding one half to the person upon whose information the conviction was obtained. *Power of Court to order payment of reward.*

Palestine No. 5 of 1926.

— 8 —

Forfeiture.

22. In addition to any fine or term of imprisonment imposed under this Ordinance or any Regulation hereunder the Court may order that the forest produce, instrument or means in respect of which or by which the offence has been committed be forfeited and disposed of as the Court may direct; and may order that any licence or permit held under this Ordinance by the person convicted shall be forfeited.

Arrest of suspected persons.

23. It shall be lawful for any Forest Officer to arrest without a warrant any person who may be reasonably suspected of having been concerned in any offence under this Ordinance, if such person refuses to give his name and residence or gives a name or address which is believed to be false, or if there is reason to believe that he will abscond;

Provided that any person so arrested shall be taken before a Magistrate or to the nearest police station without unnecessary delay.

Onus of proof as to possession of forest produce.

24. The onus of proof that any forest produce has not been taken in contravention of this Ordinance shall lie upon the person in whose possession the same is found.

Appointment of station for forest produce.

25. (1) The High Commissioner may by notice to be published in the Gazette appoint places to be defined in such notice as stations to which any person removing any forest produce from any forest land for the purpose of trade shall bring such produce.

Government not liable for loss in respect of produce at station.

(2) The Government shall not be responsible for any loss or damage which may occur to any forest produce while at such stations.

Regulations.

26. (1) The High Commissioner may make and when made may vary or revoke, Regulations to carry out the objects and purposes of this Ordinance, and in particular:

(a) designating the Forest Officers by whom licences may be granted and cancelled under this Ordinance and prescribing the form, duration and conditions of such licences;

(b) prescribing the methods to be employed in the extraction, conversion and removal of forest produce from forest reserves and from privately owned forests;

(c) prescribing the fees to be paid on the application for and the grant of any licences;

Palestine No. 5 of 1926.

— 9 —

(d) prescribing the fees to be paid in respect of the removal of forest produce of forest reserves or the forest produce extracted from private forests for purposes of trade;

(e) requiring the holders of licences to render returns and accounts, and to submit their books for inspection;

(f) providing for the management and protection of forest reserves;

(g) regulating the transit of any forest produce to an appointed station and providing for the examination and marking of forest produce in transit;

(h) regulating the marking of timber and the manufacture, use and possession of marking instruments.

(2) Any person who is convicted of a breach of the Regulations under this Ordinance shall be liable on conviction to a fine not exceeding £E. 100 or to imprisonment not exceeding six months, or to both penalties.

27. (1) The Woods and Forest Ordinance, 1920, is hereby repealed, provided that this repeal shall not affect the validity of any licence, permit, certificate or document made, granted or issued thereunder. — Repeal.

(2) Any other laws or regulations concerning forestry shall no longer be applicable in Palestine. — Other law not to apply.

1st March, 1926.

PLUMER, F. M.
High Commissioner.

CORRECTION OF LAND REGISTERS ORDINANCE, No. 12 OF 1926.

The first day of March One thousand nine hundred and twenty-six

GOVERNMENT OF PALESTINE.

CORRECTION OF LAND REGISTERS ORDINANCE

No. 12 of 1926.

An Ordinance to make further provision for the correction of the Land Registers.

BE IT ENACTED by the High Commissioner for Palestine, with the advice of the Advisory Council thereof :—

1. This Ordinance may be cited as the Correction of Land Registers Ordinance, 1926. — *Short title.*

2. In this Ordinance :— — *Definitions.*

"Land" includes anything attached to the earth or permanently fastened to anything attached to the earth, but does not include minerals.

"Director" means the Director of Lands.

"Official Registers" means the Land Registers of the Government of Palestine.

"Unofficial Land Books" means any books or registers other than the official registers in which a record of title to land or rights in land has been kept.

"Person" includes any corporate body.

3. (1) Any person, Village Committee, or Local Council having in his or their possession any unofficial land book shall within three months from the date of this Ordinance deliver such book to the Director and shall receive an acknowledgement of its delivery. — *Unofficial land books to be delivered to Government.*

(2) No unofficial land book which has not been delivered to the Director within the said period of three months shall be pleaded or given in evidence in any Court as affecting any land. — *Unofficial land book not delivered not to be given in evidence.*

Printed by the Greek Convent Press and Azriel Press, Jerusalemm. on behalf of the Government of Palestine.

Palestine No. 12 of 1926.

— 2 —

Entry in unofficial land book not to be given in evidence.
(3) No entry made in an unofficial land book subsequent to the date of promulgation of this Ordinance in the Gazette, shall be pleaded or given in evidence in any Court as affecting any land.

Restoration of books.
(4) The Director shall subject to any regulations made hereunder, restore any unofficial land book to the person, Committee, or Council which has delivered it, provided that he receives a copy of such book.

Penalties for possession.
(5) Any person, Village Committee, or Local Council found in possession of any such book after three months from the date of this Ordinance, save in the circumstances provided in the preceding sub-section, shall be liable to a fine not exceeding £E. 500.

Power to apply for correction of official registers where transaction recorded in unofficial books.
4. (1) Where an unofficial land book has been delivered to the Director, any person who has an interest recorded in such book may apply to the Director for the registration of the interests in the official registers; and, notwithstanding anything in the Ordinance of the Chief Administrator dated the 18th of November, 1918, concerning the disposition of immovable property, or in the Transfer of Land Ordinance, 1920, and any amendment thereof, any sale, mortgage, lease, partition, or other transaction in land which, prior to the date of this Ordinance has been recorded in an unofficial land book shall not be deemed to be null and void for the reason only that it was not recorded in the official registers.

(2) The application shall be supported by such evidence relating to the interest claimed as the Director may require.

Exclusion of land which is the subject of final judgment.
5. No application under this Ordinance shall be entertained in respect of any interest in land which could have been registered in the official registers in pursuance of the final judgment of a competent Court.

Procedure on application to register.
6. (1) Every application under this Ordinance shall be published for a period of four months in such manner as may be prescribed by regulation hereunder; and the unofficial land books and any maps or plans concerned, and all documentary evidence offered in support of such application, shall be open for inspection during that period by any officer of the Department of Lands or by any person claiming an interest in the land to which the application relates.

Palestine No. 12 of 1926.

— 3 —

(2) If the land is registered in the official registers, notice of the application shall be served by the applicant upon the registered owner if he is in Palestine, and shall be communicated to him by registered letter if he is out of Palestine. If the registered owner has no known address or if he is registered as the owner of an undivided share of the land, notice of the application may be given by publication in a newspaper or elsewhere as may be prescribed by the Director.

(3) If it appears from the unofficial land books that any person other than the applicant has a recorded interest in the land, notice of the application shall be communicated to him in like manner.

(4) The Director may in any appropriate case extend the period within which notice of an adverse claim may be received.

7. The Director may require any person who has a mortgage or charge recorded in the unofficial land books in respect of land which is the subject of an application to produce for his inspection any documents relating to the mortgage or charge, and if required, to deliver to him copies thereof. *Mortgagee to produce documents for inspection.*

8. (1) If no adverse claim is made within four months of the publication of the application, or such extended time as the Director may prescribe, the Director may order that the interest claimed shall be registered in the official registers in the name of the applicant, on payment of the fee prescribed herein. *Order for registration where no adverse claim.*

(2) If the applicant or his immediate predecessor in title is registered in respect of the land in the official registers or if the interest claimed by the applicant is other than ownership, the applicant shall pay the fee prescribed under the appropriate head of the schedule of fees issued under the Land Transfer Ordinance, 1920. If the applicant or his immediate predecessor is not registered in respect of the land in the official registers and the interest claimed is that of ownership, the fee payable shall be that prescribed in the said schedule for the issue of a certificate of registration when property does not appear in the registers.

9. (1) If a person having an interest registered in the official registers or the unofficial land books makes objection to the registration within the said period of four months, or any *Procedure where objection raised to registration.*

Palestine No. 12 of 1926.

— 4 —

extension thereof duly made by the Director, the Director shall notify the applicant for registration and require him to refer his application within 30 days of such notification to the Land Court of the district in which the land is situate. If the applicant fails to refer his application to the Land Court within such period, no change shall be made in the registration in the official registers.

(2) If any other person claiming an interest in the land makes objection to the registration within the same period, and notifies the Director thereof in the manner prescribed by Regulation, the Director shall require the person objecting to refer his claim forthwith to the Land Court; and if such person fails to refer the claim within 30 days, the Director shall proceed as if the objection had not been raised.

Powers of the Land Court where objection made to registration.
10. (1) Where an application is referred to the Land Court under the preceding Section, the Court may, notwithstanding anything in the enactments mentioned in Section 4 hereof, have regard to all the circumstances of the case, and make such order in the matter as shall be just and equitable.

(2) The fees payable on an action in the Land Court shall be those prescribed for a possessory action in respect of the land.

Director may retain documents.
11. Where an order has been made for registration in the official registers under this Ordinance, whether by the Director, or by the Land Court, the Director may retain possession of any documents produced in support of the application for registration.

Power reserved in case of a land settlement.
12. If at any time a land settlement is instituted in Palestine, the officer conducting the settlement in an area in which transactions have been recorded in the unofficial land book shall give notice to any person who has an interest recorded in the unofficial land book as well as to the owner registered in the official registers that he proposes to determine the title to the land and is prepared to receive any claim; provided that no such notice shall be given where an objection to registration under this Ordinance has been referred to a Land Court.

Regulations.
13. The High Commissioner in Executive Council may make, and when made, may vary or revoke, Regulations for the purpose of giving effect to this Ordinance, and in particular, in the following matters: —

Palestine No. 12 of 1926.

— 5 —

(a) As to the form of application for and objection to registration.

(b) As to the manner of the publication of the application.

(c) As to the form of notice of publication and proof of service thereof.

(d) As to the fees to be paid on an application under this Ordinance and on registration.

(e) As to the restoration of any unofficial land books when the registration has been completed.

1st March, 1926.

PLUMER, F. M.
High Commissioner.

PUBLIC LANDS ORDINANCE, No. 14 OF 1926.

The first day of April, One thousand nine hundred and twenty-six.

GOVERNMENT OF PALESTINE.

PUBLIC LANDS ORDINANCE

No. 14 of 1926.

An Ordinance to delegate to the Director, Department of Lands, the power to sign certain leases of State Domains.

WHEREAS Article 13 of the Palestine Order in Council, 1922, provides that the High Commissioner may make grants or leases of any public lands or may permit such lands to be temporarily occupied on such terms or conditions as he may think fit subject to the provisions of any Ordinance;

AND WHEREAS it is expedient to make provision for the delegation of certain of these powers.

BE IT ENACTED by the High Commissioner for Palestine with the advice of the Advisory Council, thereof:-

1. This Ordinance may be cited as "The Public Lands Ordinance, 1926". *Short title.*

2. The Director, Department of Lands, may subject to any general or special directions from the High Commissioner execute for and on behalf of the High Commissioner any lease or licence of or for the occupation of public lands the term of which does not exceed three years and the annual rental of which does not exceed £E. 50. *Power of the Director of Lands to execute certain leases and licences on behalf of the High Commissioner.*

1st. April, 1926.

PLUMER, F. M.
High Commissioner.

Printed by the Greek Convent Press and Azriel Press, Jerusalem,
on behalf of the Government of Palestine.

EXPROPRIATION OF LAND ORDINANCE, No. 28 OF 1926.

The first day of August, One thousand nine hundred and twenty-six.

GOVERNMENT OF PALESTINE.

EXPROPRIATION OF LAND ORDINANCE

No. 28 of 1926.

An Ordinance to repeal certain laws regarding the compulsory acquisition of land required for undertakings of a public nature and for the assessment of compensation for land so acquired and to make other provisions in lieu thereof.

BE IT ENACTED by the High Commissioner for Palestine, with the advice of the Advisory Council thereof:—

1. This Ordinance may be cited as the Expropriation of Land Ordinance, 1926. *Short title.*

2. In this Ordinance, unless the context otherwise requires, the following words shall have the following meanings:— *Definitions.*

"Land" includes land of any category or tenure and any building, tree or other thing fixed in the land and any portion of the sea, or shore or a river and any easement in or over land or water.

"The Court" means the Land Court within whose jurisdiction the land is situated.

"Undertaking" means an undertaking of a public nature which shall have been certified by the High Commissioner to be an undertaking within the meaning of this Ordinance.

"The promoters" means the Government or a Municipality or a Local Council or other local authority, or any person, whether a company or a private person, executing or about to execute an undertaking as above defined.

3. It shall be lawful for the High Commissioner to certify that any works of a public nature which are being or are about to be carried out by promoters are an undertaking within the meaning of this Ordinance and thereupon, subject to the provisions of this Ordinance, it shall be lawful for the promoters of the undertaking to treat and agree with the owner or owners of any land required by them for the undertaking and with all persons having an interest in such lands either for the absolute purchase thereof or for the possession or use thereof for a definite period, or for the acquisition of any easement required for the purpose of the undertaking. *Promoters may treat for the acquisition of land etc.*

Printed by the Greek Convent Press and Azriel Press, Jerusalem, on behalf of the Government of Palestine.

Palestine No. 28 of 1926

— 2 —

Persons under disability may sell etc. to promoters.

4. It shall be lawful for all persons entitled to any such lands or any interest therein to sell, lease or otherwise dispose of the same or any interest therein to the promoters of the undertaking, and to enter into all necessary agreements for that purpose; and in particular any company or trustee, guardian, curator or other person representing any person under disability may, by force of this Ordinance and notwithstanding anything to the contrary in any law, memorandum or articles of Association or other document, sell, lease or otherwise dispose of such lands or interest therein and enter into any necessary agreements for that purpose.

In default of agreement, notice to treat to be approved by High Commissioner.

5. (1) If the promoters of an undertaking shall fail to come to terms with the owner or owners of, or any other person having an interest in, any land required for the undertaking, they may submit to the High Commissioner for his approval the notice or notices to treat referred to in the next succeeding subsection and the High Commissioner shall have power to withhold or to grant approval with such modifications as he may think fit and the promoters shall thereupon cause the notice or notices to treat in the form approved by the High Commissioner to be served in the prescribed manner on the person indicated in sub-section 4 of this Section.

Contents of notice to treat.

(2) Every such notice shall state the particulars of the land and the interest therein so required and that the promoters are willing to treat as to the compensation or rent to be paid for the purchase or possession or the use of such land or for the easement to be acquired and as to the compensation for the damage that may be caused by the undertaking.

(3) Every such notice shall demand from the person on whom it is served particulars in writing of the interest of such person in the land and of the claims made in respect thereof, with a statement of the amount which he may be willing to receive as compensation or rent and the details of the compensation or rent claimed.

Service of notice to treat.

(4) Every such notice shall be served on all the persons interested in the land required to be taken or on such of them as shall after enquiry be known to the promoters and shall be served personally on the said persons or left at their respective last known or usual places of abode in Palestine, or, in the case of a Company, at the principal office of business thereof in Palestine, or, if no such office can after enquiry be found, on some principal official of such Company. In case any such persons are absent from Palestine or cannot be found, the notice shall be served on the Mukhtar of the village or quarter in which the land referred to is situated, and shall be affixed upon some conspicuous part of the lands, and advertised in a newspaper circulating in the district.

Palestine No. 28 of 1926.

— 3 —

6. The amount of compensation to be paid for the land specified in the notice to treat may be determined by agreement between the promoters and the parties having any interest in such lands respectively. *Promoters may agree to compensation payable.*

7. If within 15 days after the service of any such notice as aforesaid the person on whom the same is served fails to state the particulars of his claim in respect of any land to which such notice relates or to treat with the promoters as to the amount of compensation to be paid or if the promoters and such persons do not within 15 days agree as to the amount of such compensation, *Procedure on failure to treat or agree as to compensation.*

(a) it shall be lawful for the promoters to enter into immediate possession of the lands referred to in such notice;

provided that if the owners or occupiers refuse to allow the promoters to enter into such possession the promoters may apply to the President of the Court who, if he is satisfied that the promoters are entitled to possession under this Section, shall issue an order under his hand commanding possession to be delivered and

provided also that where the land is being acquired by any body or person other than the Government, the President may direct that such sum as he shall deem proper shall be lodged in Court before the issue of such order.

(b) The amount of compensation to be paid by the promoters in respect of land into the possession of which they may have entered in pursuance of this Section, shall be determined in accordance with the provisions hereinafter contained.

8. The amount of such compensation shall, in default of agreement, be determined by the Land Court in whose jurisdiction the land is situated. *Land Court to assess compensation.*

9. (1) The owners and occupiers and any other person who proves to the Court that he has a registrable interest in the land specified in the notice to treat shall be entitled to appear before the Court either personally or by an advocate. *Right of audience.*

(2) Any such person who desires to appear shall submit to the Court particulars of his interest in the land and of his claim to compensation prior to appearance.

10. In assessing compensation, the Court shall act in accordance with the following rules:- *Rules for assessment of compensation.*

Palestine No. 28 of 1926.

— 4 —

(1) No allowance shall be made on account of the acquisition being compulsory.

(2) The value of the land shall, subject as hereinafter provided, be taken to be the amount which the land if sold in the open market by a willing seller might be expected to realise.

Provided that the Court in assessing such compensation shall assess the same according to the value of the land on the said basis at the time when the same was or under the provisions of this Ordinance could have been entered upon by the promoters without regard to any improvements or works made thereon subsequent to such date by the promoters or the owners or any other person, and

Provided further that the Court in assessing such compensation shall be entitled to consider all returns and assessments of capital or rental value for taxation made by or acquiesced in by the claimant.

(3) The special suitability or adaptability of the land for any purpose shall not be taken into account if it is a purpose to which it could be applied only in pursuance of powers derived from legislation or for which there is no market apart from the special needs of a particular purchaser or the requirements of the promoters.

Provided that any bona fide offer for the purchase of the land made before the passing of this Ordinance which may be brought to the notice of the Court shall be taken into consideration.

(4) Where the land is and but for the compulsory acquisition would continue to be devoted to a purpose of such a nature that there is no general demand or market for land for that purpose, the compensation may, if the Court is satisfied that reinstatement in some other place is bona fide intended, be assessed on the basis of the reasonable cost of such equivalent reinstatement.

(5) In assessing the rent to be paid for the lease of land, the Court shall assess the same on the basis that the said rent shall be a reasonable return to the owner on the capital value of the land assessed in accordance with the provisions of the preceding sub-sections hereof.

(6) The court shall assess the compensation to be paid by way of damage for the imposition of any easement or other restraint on the exercise of any rights incidental to ownership on the basis of the amount by which the value of

Palestine No. 28 of 1926.

— 5 —

the land assessed in accordance with the preceding sub-sections hereof shall have been diminished by reason of the imposition of such easement or restraint.

(7) The Court shall also have regard to

(a) the damage (if any) caused by the severance of the land acquired from other land belonging to the person entitled to compensation by reason of the undertaking; and

(b) the enhancement or depreciation in value of other land belonging to the person entitled to compensation by reason of the undertaking;

(8) Such enhancement or depreciation in value shall be set off against or added to the amount of the value of the land and the damage thereto assessed by the Court under the provisions of this Ordinance.

11. Any person who is dissatisfied with the award of the Court shall, if the amount awarded exceeds £E. 200, be entitled within 15 days of the notification of that award to appeal to the Supreme Court sitting as a Court of Appeal. *Right of appeal.*

12. (1) If part only of any lands comprised in any lease or mortgage or otherwise subject to any rent or any annual or other payment or incumbrance be acquired under this Ordinance, such rent, payment or incumbrance may be apportioned by agreement between the promoters and the persons entitled thereto or to the land subject thereto, or in case no such agreement be made the same shall be apportioned by the Court. *Provision for apportionment of rents and incumbrances.*

(2) After such apportionment the apportioned part only of such rent, payment or incumbrance shall be payable out of the residue of the said lands, and all conditions, agreements, powers, and remedies in respect of such rent, payment or incumbrance shall remain in force in respect of the residue of the said lands.

13. (1) Where any damage has been sustained by reason of any undertaking executed in or upon lands acquired under this Ordinance and such damage has not been agreed upon or otherwise determined prospectively, compensation shall be paid when the works have been done and shall be determined by the Court in the manner prescribed under this Ordinance or as near thereto as circumstances admit. *Compensation to be payable in respect of lands injuriously affected by any undertaking executed on land acquired under this Ordinance.*

(2) In determining the amount of compensation payable regard shall be had to any increase in the value of the land by reason of any improved drainage and other advantage derived from the undertaking.

Palestine No. 28 of 1926.

Provision as to costs.

14. (1) Where the promoters have made an unconditional offer in writing of any sum as compensation to any claimant and the sum awarded by the Court to that claimant does not exceed the sum offered the Court shall, unless for special reasons they think proper not to do so, order the claimant to bear his own costs and to pay the costs of the promoters so far as they were incurred after the offer was made.

(2) If the Court is satisfied that a claimant has failed to comply with the demands of the promoters as set forth in Section 5 (3) in sufficient time to enable the promoters to make a proper offer, the foregoing provisions of this Section shall apply as if an unconditional offer had been made by the promoters at the time when in the opinion of the Court sufficient particulars should have been furnished and the claimant had been awarded a sum not exceeding the amount of such offer.

(3) Where a claimant has made an unconditional offer in writing to accept any sum as compensation and has complied with the demands of the promoters set out as aforesaid and the sum awarded is equal to or exceeds that sum, the Court shall, unless for special reasons it may think proper not to do so, order the promoters to bear their own costs and to pay the costs of the claimant so far as they were incurred after the offer was made.

(4) Subject as aforesaid the costs of any proceedings shall be in the discretion of the Court who may direct to and by whom and in what manner those costs shall be paid.

Provided that such costs shall be in accordance with the scale that may be prescribed under Section 24 hereof.

(5) Where the Court orders the claimant to pay the costs or any part of the costs of the promoters, the promoters may deduct the amount so payable by the claimant from the amount of compensation due to him.

Promoters may pay compensation into Court if persons entitled thereto cannot be found or fail to make out a title.

15. At or after the expiration of three months from the time at which the compensation for any lands has been agreed upon or otherwise assessed, the promoters may, if the persons entitled thereto cannot be found, or if the persons claiming to be entitled shall fail to make out a title thereto, or if, for any like reason, the promoters shall be unable to obtain a valid discharge for the payment of such compensation or any part thereof, pay such compensation to the Court and such payment shall discharge the promoters from all liability in respect of the compensation awarded to the extent of the amount so paid.

Palestine No. 28 of 1926.

— 7 —

16. If in any case after the service of a notice to treat it appears to the promoters expedient to withdraw such notice either in respect of the whole or any part of the lands it shall be lawful for them to do so by giving a further notice and thereupon the lands comprised in the notice of withdrawal shall be wholly discharged from the effect of the notice to treat and the promoters shall be wholly discharged from any obligation in respect of the lands comprised in the notice of withdrawal and from the obligation to make compensation in respect thereof, without prejudice to any claim of any owner, lessee or occupier or other person having a registrable interest in such land for compensation for such damage as he may have sustained in consequence of the service of the notice to treat, the amount of such damage to be determined in like manner as other compensation under this Ordinance. *Power of promoters to withdraw notices to treat.*

Provided that every notice of withdrawal shall be approved by the High Commissioner and shall be given within three months after the service of the notice to treat or within six weeks after the delivery by the claimant of the claim for compensation or rent referred to in Section 5 (3) whichever date shall be later.

17. The lands required to be taken under this Ordinance shall from and after payment of the compensation for the same be vested in the High Commissioner on behalf of the Government of Palestine if the Government is the promoter, and in the promoters if any other authority or person is the promoter: and a certificate of the Court that the compensation awarded by them has been duly paid in accordance with the provisions hereof shall be sufficient authority to the Director of Lands to cause the necessary entries to be made in the Land Registers. *Lands taken to be vested in High Commissioner or promoters on payment of compensation.*

18. (1) It shall be lawful for the promoters without taking any legal proceeding, *Power to divert roads etc.*

(a) to stop up or divert or alter the level of any public or private road, sewer, drain or pipe if they deem it necessary for any of the works contemplated to be done on any land acquired under this Ordinance; provided that they shall first have obtained the written authority of the High Commissioner to do so and, if he so requires, shall have made, opened or laid down another good and sufficient road, sewer, drain or pipe in lieu of that stopped up or diverted; and

(b) for the like reasons to alter the course or level of any river, stream or water-course; provided that they shall first have obtained the like authority.

Palestine No. 28 of 1926.

— 8 —

(2) The promoters shall pay compensation to be determined in the manner prescribed in this Ordinance for any damage sustained by reason of the exercise of the powers conferred on them by this Section.

Limitation of the term of any compulsory lease or the term of any renewed lease.

19. The High Commissioner shall not authorise the compulsory grant of any lease of which the term exceeds 21 years nor the renewal of any lease for a period which, together with the period of occupation then expired, exceeds 21 years.

Power of the promoters to sell land no longer required.

20. (1) If at any time land acquired by promoters or any part thereof is, in the opinion of such promoters, no longer required for the purposes of the undertaking for which it was acquired, it shall be lawful for the promoters to treat and agree with any person for the sale to him of any such land;

Provided that if the former owner of the land from whom the promoters acquired it is still alive he shall have the right of pre-emption on paying the sum agreed or awarded as compensation together with the value of any improvement made upon the land since its occupation by the promoters, such value to be determined, in default of agreement between the parties, by the Court.

(2) The right of pre-emption shall be exercised within one month of notice to the previous owner by the promoters of the intended sale. The notice shall be served in the manner provided for serving a notice to treat in Section 5 hereof.

Application of Ordinance to Wakf lands and other like lands.

21. (1). In the application of this Ordinance to land dedicated as Wakf, the trustee (Mutawalli) of any wakf, or in the absence of any trustee, the Awkaf Administration, shall have all the powers and be subject to all the obligations imposed herein upon the owner of the land, and the compensation for the land shall be paid to the trustee (Mutawalli) of the wakf, or, in the absence of any such trustee, to the Treasury of the Awkaf in the name of the wakf property concerned.

(2) In the application of this Ordinance to land subject to other religious, charitable or the like trusts, the person or authority responsible for the administration of such land shall have all the powers and be subject to all the obligations imposed herein upon the owner of the land, and the compensation for the land shall be paid to him.

Gratuitous expropriation for widening roads.

22. Where any land is taken under this Ordinance by the Government or a Municipality for the purpose of widening any existing road or part of it, the amount by which the road is

Palestine No. 28 of 1926.

widened on each side of the centre line of the road shall be equal unless the alignment of the road is altered. The owner of the land expropriated shall not be entitled to compensation unless the area taken exceeds one-quarter part of the total area of the plot which he owns. Provided that, if it is established that hardship would be caused if no compensation were paid, the High Commissioner may in his discretion grant such compensation as, having regard to all the circumstances of the case, he shall think fit. If the area taken from any owner exceeds one-quarter part of the total area of the plot owned by him, compensation shall be paid in accordance with the provisions of this Ordinance.

Betterment charge where land taken for making or widening roads.

23. (1) Where by the taking of any land under this Ordinance for the purpose of making a new road or of widening an existing road in a Municipal or Town Planning area, any land is increased in value, the promoter of the undertaking of which the making of such road is a part shall, if he be a Department of the Government or a Municipality and if he makes a claim for that purpose within one year of the execution of the work, be entitled to recover from any person whose property is so increased in value a contribution towards the cost of the work not exceeding one fourth of the amount of that increase:

Provided that, where a contribution is imposed under this Section, compensation shall be paid for any land taken for the purpose of widening a road: and the amount of compensation may be set off against the contribution due under this Section.

(2) Any question whether any land is increased in value within the meaning of this Section and as to the amount of such increase shall in default of agreement be determined by a single arbitrator to be appointed by the Chief Justice.

(3) In default of agreement the contribution due from the owner towards the cost of the work shall be payable in not less than four equal annual instalments, and shall be recoverable as a civil debt by the promoter from the owner of the land for the time being.

High Commissioner may make regulations.

24. The High Commissioner may make, and when made, may vary and revoke Regulations prescribing:

(a) The forms to be used under this Ordinance;

(b) the scale of costs in respect of the award of compensation under this Ordinance;

Palestine No. 28 of 1926.

— 10 —

(c) the means by which claims for several interests in the same land shall be heard at the same time;

(d) the fees to be paid in arbitration proceedings under Section 23 (2) hereof;

(e) generally, for the application of this Ordinance.

25. Nothing in this Ordinance shall affect the provisions as to expropriation contained in the Town Planning Ordinance, 1921, the Mining Ordinance, 1925, and the Acquisition of Land for the Army and Air Force Ordinance, 1925. Saving any other laws concerning expropriation.

26. (1) The following Ottoman Laws shall cease to have effect in Palestine: Repeals.

(a) Regulations for Expropriation for Public Purposes dated the 21st Jamad el Awal, 1296, as amended by the law of 17th Nissan, 1330.

(b) The Provisional Law as to Expropriation for Municipalities dated the 7th Rabi Awal, 1332.

(2) The Expropriation Ordinance, 1924, the Public Notice concerning expropriation dated the 20th May, 1919, and Section 20 of the Antiquities Ordinance, 1920, are hereby repealed.

Provided that the operation of this Section shall not prejudice or annul any sale, purchase, award or any other act, matter or thing made, done or effected under the said laws, notices or Ordinances or the determination of any question of compensation where before the date of the commencement of this Ordinance such question has been referred to the appropriate authority created by the enactments which hereby ceased to have effect or are repealed.

1st August, 1926

PLUMER, F. M.
High Commissioner.

CORRECTION OF LAND REGISTERS (Amendment) ORDINANCE, No. 42 OF 1926.

The sixteenth day of November, One thousand nine hundred and twenty-six.

GOVERNMENT OF PALESTINE.

CORRECTION OF LAND REGISTERS (AMENDMENT) ORDINANCE.

No. 42 of 1926.

An Ordinance to amend the Correction of Land Registers Ordinance, 1926.

BE IT ENACTED by the High Commissioner for Palestine with the advice of the Advisory Council thereof:

Short Title and Interpretation.

1. This Ordinance may be cited as the Correction of Land Registers (Amendment) Ordinance, 1926; and the Correction of Land Registers Ordinance, 1926 (hereinafter referred to as the Principal Ordinance) and this Ordinance may together be cited as the Correction of Land Registers Ordinance, 1926.

Order for registration where no adverse claim.

2. Section 8 of the Principal Ordinance is hereby repealed and the following shall be substituted therefor:

"If no adverse claim is made within four months of the publication of the application, or such extended time as the Director may prescribe, the Director may order that the interest claimed shall be registered in the official registers in the name of the applicant, on payment of such fees as may be prescribed by Regulation hereunder".

PLUMER, F. M.
High Commissioner.

16th. November, 1926.

Section 10: 1927

COMMUTATION OF TITHES ORDINANCE, No. 49 OF 1927.

The sixteenth day of December, One thousand nine hundred and twenty-seven.

COMMUTATION OF TITHES ORDINANCE

No. 49 of 1927.

An Ordinance for Commutation of Tithes.

BE IT ENACTED by the High Commissioner for Palestine, with the advice of the Advisory Council thereof:-

1. This Ordinance may be cited as the Commutation of Tithes Ordinance, 1927. *Short title.*

2. In this Ordinance, the following words shall, unless the context otherwise requires, have the following meanings: *Definitions.*

"Crops" include the produce of fruit trees;

"Fruit tree" means a fruit-producing tree the fruit of which is subject to tithe at the date on which this Ordinance becomes operative within the boundaries of a village;

"Land" includes fruit trees and an undivided interest in land;

"Reputed owner" means a person who is in receipt of the rents or profits of land in such circumstances that he is the reputed owner of the land, whether or not he is in possession thereof or is the registered owner thereof;

"Village" includes a town and a tribal area.

3. The High Commissioner may, by Order published in the Official Gazette, declare that, in lieu of the tithe payable by cultivators under the law in force relating to the payment of tithe at the date on which this Ordinance becomes operative in virtue of such Order, there shall be payable annually by the reputed owners of lands within the boundaries of the village or villages prescribed in such Order a fixed amount in money (hereinafter called "commuted tithe") which shall be assessed and paid in accordance with the provisions of this Ordinance. *Power of High Commissioner to order tithe in certain village to be commuted to a fixed money payment.*

4. As soon as any such Order shall have been made, the District Commissioner of the District in which any village or tribal area affected by the Order is situate, shall constitute a Committee for every such village or tribal area (hereinafter referred to as "the Assessment Committee") consisting of the Mukhtars and such notables of the village as may be appointed by the District Commissioner, if the village is not in a tribal area, and of tribal sheikhs if the Order affects a tribal area. Provided that the District Commissioner may appoint on the Committee a reputed owner who is not an inhabitant of the village or a representative of such owner. *District Commissioner to appoint Assessment Committee.*

— 380 —

Palestine No. 49 of 1927.

District Commissioner to inform Assessment Committee of amounts of tithe assessed as payable during a period of years prescribed by the Order.

5. (1) The District Commissioner shall inform the assessment Committee of

(a) the average aggregate amount of tithe assessed as payable during a period of years which shall be prescribed by the Order in respect of crops grown within the boundaries of the village other than the produce of fruit trees, and of

(b) the average aggregate amount of tithe assessed as payable during the like period on the produce of fruit trees within the boundaries of the village.

Provided that where, during the period of years prescribed by the Order, a new village has been established, or the tithes of two or more villages have been assessed together and it is impossible to establish the aggregate amount of tithe assessed in respect of the crops and product of fruit trees within the boundaries of the new village or each of such villages, the Disctrict Commissioner shall estimate the average aggregate amount of tithe for each such village, and shall inform the Assessment Committee accordingly.

Assessment Committee to prepare a list of reputed owners.

(2) The Assessment Committee shall thereupon prepare a list (hereinafter called the "assessment list") containing

(a) the names of the persons who are the reputed owners of lands, other than lands planted with fruit trees, within the boundaries of the village, and

(b) the names of the persons who are the reputed owners of fruit trees and of lands planted with fruit trees within the boundaries of the village.

Assessment Committee to apportion among reputed owners the amounts referred to in subsection (1).

(3) The Assessment Committee shall apportion

(a) the amount referred to in subsection (1) (a) hereof among the persons referred to in subsection (2) (a) hereof in the proportion of the potential productivity in terms of wheat of the lands respectively in the reputed ownership of such persons, if such lands are divided (Mafruz), and, if such lands are undivided (Musha'a), in the proportion of the respective shares in the reputed ownership of such persons: provided that, in a tribal area, such apportionment shall be made in accordance with tribal customs, and

(b) the amount referred to in subsection (1) (b) hereof among the persons referred to in subsection (2) (b) hereof in the proportion of the actual average amount of tithe payable during the period of years prescribed by the Order in respect of the produce of the fruit trees respectively in the reputed ownership of such persons, provided that, if it shall

Palestine No. 49 of 1927.

not be possible to determine accurately the actual average amount of tithe so payable by such person, apportionment shall be made on the basis of the annual productivity of the trees as estimated by the Assessment Committee.

6. Every Assessment Committee shall publish the assessment list containing the names of the persons liable to pay commuted tithe and the amount payable by every such person in such form, manner and place and for such period as may be prescribed by the High Commissioner by Regulations under this Ordinance. *Assessment list to be published.*

7. One or more Revising Committees shall be constituted by the District Commissioner concerned for the purpose of hearing objections to assessment lists prepared for villages in his District and of revising such lists; and each Committee shall consist of such persons as may be appointed by the District Commissioner and shall hear objections to and revise such lists as may be prescribed by him. *Revising Committee to be appointed.*

8. (1) Every person whose name appears in an assessment list shall have a right of objection to the Revising Committee appointed for the purpose by the District Commissioner on the ground that he is aggrieved by reason of the unfairness or incorrectness of the apportionment made, or by reason of the insertion or incorrectness of any matter in the assessment list, or by reason of the omission of any matter therefrom. *Right of objection to assessment list.*

(2) Every such objection shall be made in such manner and within such period as may be prescribed by the High Commissioner by Regulations issued under this Ordinance and shall be heard by the Revising Committee in accordance with Regulations issued in like manner.

9. The Revising Committee shall, within 30 days after the publication of the assessment list under Section 6 hereof, revise the assessment list in accordance with this Ordinance. When they have finally approved such assessment list, they shall sign at the foot thereof a declaration of approval and certificate of compliance with this Ordinance; and the list so signed shall be published in accordance with Regulations issued by the High Commissioner under this Ordinance. *Revising Committee to revise, approve and publish assessment list.*

10. (1) Any person whose name appears in an assessment list published by the Revising Committee under the preceding Section may, if he feels aggrieved by any decision of the Revising Committee on an objection made to them, appeal to the District Commissioner whose decision shall be final. *Right of appeal against revised assessment list.*

Palestine No. 49 of 1927.

(2) Every such appeal shall be made in such manner and within such period as may be prescribed by the High Commissioner by Regulations issued under this Ordinance, and shall be heard by the District Commissioner in accordance with Regulations issued in like manner.

Commuted tithe to be an annual tax payable in instalments.

11. Commuted tithe shall be payable in respect of every period of twelve calendar months following the date of the Order made under Section 3, and shall be paid to such persons and in such instalments as may be prescribed by the High Commissioner by Regulations issued under this Ordinance.

Provided that the High Commissioner may by any Order made under Section 3 declare that this Ordinance shall be applicable as from a date to be specified therein not prior to the last assessment for tithe made in respect of crops grown within the boundaries of the village to which such Order relates.

Commuted tithe in revised assessment list to be paid notwithstanding pending appeal.

12. (1) Notwithstanding any appeal being pending under Section 10 hereof, every person whose name appears in any assessment list published under Section 9 hereof shall be liable to pay, in accordance with Section 11 hereof, the amount for which he is assessed in such list.

(2) If an appeal under Section 10 hereof succeeds, the amount of commuted tithe from the payment of which the appellant is relieved shall be distributed by the District Commissioner among the other reputed owners in the proportion of the amounts of commuted tithe payable by them respectively according to the assessment list published under Section 9 hereof; and every such reputed owner shall be liable to pay the amount so added to the amount for which he was originally assessed as if such additional amount has been included in the amount appearing in the list aforesaid, but shall not be entitled to object or appeal against the addition to his liability so made. Provided always that the High Commissioner may in his discretion waive the distribution amongst the other reputed owners of the amount of the commuted tithe from the payment of which an appellant is relieved.

(3) Any sum paid by a successful appellant on account of any commuted tithe from the payment of which he has been relieved as a result of his appeal shall be refunded to him.

Commuted tithe to be recoverable as a Government tax.

13. Commuted tithe shall be deemed to be a Government tax within the meaning of the Ottoman Law for the Collection of Taxes of 1325 A.H., and any law or Ordinance amending the same, and shall be recoverable by any of the means set out in Chapter III of such law and in accordance with the provisions thereof.

Palestine No. 49 of 1927.

14. (1) Prior to the expiration of every period of twelve calendar months in respect of which commuted tithe is payable, and not later than a date to be prescribed by the High Commissioner by Regulations issued under this Ordinance, the District Commissioner shall appoint a Committee constituted in the same manner as the Committee referred to in Section 4 hereof for the purpose of revising the list of reputed owners liable to pay commuted tithe and, subject to no increase being made in the aggregate amount of tithe, reapportioning the aggregate amount of commuted tithe payable; and such Committee shall take account of any changes in reputed ownership which have occurred by reason of death, sale, partition and otherwise, since the publication of the assessment list then in force, and shall amend accordingly such list of reputed owners and reapportion the amounts payable by them in accordance with the provisions of Section 5 hereof. *Annual reapportionment and revision thereof.*

(2) The assessment list as amended shall be published in like manner as the assessment list referred to in Section 6 hereof and shall be revised in accordance with Section 9 hereof, and any person whose name appears in such list shall have a right of objection and appeal in respect of any change effected by such reapportionment or revision in the assessment list in force immediately prior to such reapportionment or revision, on the same grounds and subject to the same conditions as are set out in Sections 8 and 10 hereof respectively.

(3) The provisions of this Ordinance shall apply in respect of such amended and revised list as if it had been an original list published and revised under Sections 6 and 9 hereof respectively.

15. Any inhabitant of a village to which this Ordinance applies who receives within the boundaries of such village any crops from any place outside the boundaries of such village in order to assist the evasion of the payment of tithe on such crops shall be liable, on conviction by a Magistrate, to a fine not exceeding £P. 50 or to imprisonment for a period not exceeding three months, or to both such penalties. The crops so received shall be forfeited by order of the Magistrate. *Offences.*

16. The High Commissioner may make, and when made, may vary or revoke Regulations concerning any of the following matters:- *Power of High Commissioner to make Regulations.*

(a) The form and contents, and the method, place, and period of publication of assessment lists prepared by Assessment and Revising Committees;

(b) The period within which an objection under Section 8 shall be made and the mode of such objection and the procedure to be followed in the hearing of any such objection

— 303 —

Palestine No. 49 of 1927.

(c) The period within which an appeal under Section 10 shall be made and the mode of such appeal and the procedure to be followed in the hearing of any such appeal;

(d) The manner in which commuted tithe shall be paid;

(e) The remuneration of the clerk of the Assessment Committee and of the unofficial members of the Revising Committee;

(f) The records to be kept and the contents thereof and the persons by whom such records shall be kept;

(g) Generally, to give effect to the provisions of this Ordinance.

Power of High Commissioner to revoke an Order for commutation of tithes.

17. The High Commissioner may by Order revoke any Order made under this Ordinance, either wholly or in so far as it relates to a particular village; and thereupon the law relating to the payment of tithe in force at the date of such revocation shall become applicable to the crops grown after such date within the boundaries of the village or villages affected by such revocation; provided that the making of such Order of revocation shall not affect the collection of any commuted tithe due at the date thereof, and all proceedings for the recovery of all sums so due may be taken as if such Order of revocation had not been made.

Power of High Commissioner to postpone or remit payment of commuted tithe.

18. The High Commissioner may authorise postponement of payment of commuted tithe in whole or in part, or the remission thereof in whole or in part, for such period as he thinks fit, in the event of a total or partial failure of crops, or for the reason that land formerly planted with rotation crops has been planted with fruit trees, or for any other reason which may seem to him to be just and reasonable.

Reputed owner to have right of indemnity in respect of commuted tithe against tenant under a subsisting cultivation agreement.

19. (1) Every reputed owner who has, prior to the date on which this Ordinance becomes operative in virtue of an Order made under Section 3, entered into an agreement, whether oral or in writing, for the cultivation of land in his reputed ownership on the terms that the tenant shall pay the tithe, shall have, if such agreement is or was subsisting at such date, a right of indemnity against the tenant of such land in respect of any and every amount of commuted tithe paid by such owner during the continuance of such agreement, notwithstanding anything to the contrary contained therein.

— 394 —

Palestine No. 49 of 1927.

(2) Every occupant of State Domain in virtue of a lease, express or implied, shall pay an amount equal to the amount of the commuted tithe due on the land, in addition to any rental prescribed in the lease, as if he were the reputed owner of the land. Application to tenant of State Domain.

20. The provisions of any law, Ordinance or Regulation regarding the collection of tithe shall cease to be applicable to crops grown within the boundaries of a village to which this Ordinance may be applied as from the date on which the Ordinance becomes operative in such village in virtue of an Order made under Section 3, provided that the making of such Order shall not affect the collection of any tithe assessed on or prior to such date and all proceedings for the recovery of all sums thereby due may be taken as if such Order had not been made. Law relating to collection of tithe not to be applicable in villages to which Ordinance is applied.

21. Nothing in this Ordinance shall affect the liability to Mukata'a tax on land previously subject to the payment of tithe, which is built upon. Liability to pay Mukata'a tax not affected.

16th December, 1927.

PLUMER F. M.
High Commissioner.

Section 11: 1928

WEIGHTS AND MEASURES ORDINANCE, No. 2 of 1928.

The fifteenth day of February, One thousand nine hundred and twenty-eight.

— 2 —

WEIGHTS AND MEASURES ORDINANCE

No. 2 of 1928.

An Ordinance to provide for the introduction of a system of Metric Weights and Measures.

BE IT ENACTED by the High Commissioner for Palestine, with the advice of Advisory Council thereof:-

1. This Ordinance may be cited as the Weights and Measures Ordinance, 1928. *Short title.*

2. In this Ordinance:- *Definitions.*

"Metric Weights and Measures" means the weights and measures specified in Section 3 hereof with their decimal multiples and divisions.

"Inspector" means an Inspector of metric weights and measures under this Ordinance.

"Weighing Machine" includes any balance, scale, beam, steelyard, counterpoise and every other machine for determining weight.

3. The standards of measure and weight shall be:- *Standards of measures and weights.*

(a) the metre as the measure of length. The length of the metre is the length of the standard International Metre;

(b) the kilogramme as the standard of weight. The weight of the kilogramme is the weight of the standard International Kilogramme;

(c) the litre as the standard of capacity. The capacity of the litre is the capacity of the standard International Litre;

(d) the square metre; and

(e) the standard dunum, consisting of 1000 square metres, as standard measures of surface.

4. (1) The High Commissioner shall, as occasion may require, procure standard metric weights and measures which shall be verified at the Standard Department of the Board of Trade in England before being brought into use. *Standards to be procured and kept.*

Palestine No. 2 of 1928.

(2) The weights and measures so procured shall be the Palestine standards of weights and measures, and shall for all purposes be conclusively deemed to be true and accurate.

(3) The standards shall be kept at such Department of the Government as the High Commissioner may from time to time determine, under the care of an officer to be appointed by the High Commissioner to be the keeper of the standards, and shall be re-verified at the Standard Department of the Board of Trade from time to time as the High Commissioner may direct.

Secondary standards to be kept.

5. (1) The High Commisioner shall procure such copies of the standards, or any of them, as he shall think fit, and shall provide for verifying the same, and shall cause such copies to be authenticated as secondary standards in such manner as he may think fit.

(2) Judicial notice shall be taken of every secondary standard so authenticated.

(3) The High Commissioner may at any time cancel any secondary standard and direct that the same be no longer used as such.

(4) One complete set at least of such secondary standards shall be kept at the office of each Sub-District, and shall serve as a local standard for the purpose of comparison for all metric weights and measures used within the Sub-District.

Production of secondary standards.

6. The Officer in charge of a Sub-District shall, upon reasonable notice being given and upon payment of the fees prescribed by Regulation hereunder, produce the secondary standards at the place where they are kept to any person who makes written application for their production.

Inspectors of weights and measures.

7. (1) The High Commissioner may appoint such persons as he may think fit to be Inspectors of Weights and Measures under this Ordinance. Any Police Officer of the rank of Inspector and upwards shall have the power of an Inspector. An officer of a Municipality may be appointed as Inspector within a Municipal Area.

(2) An Inspector may at all reasonable times inspect all metric weights and measures and weighing machines which are used by any person for trade or are on any premises for use in trade, and may compare the same with the secondary standards; and may seize and detain any such weight, measure

Palestine No. 2 of 1928.

or weighing machine which he deems to be used contrary to any of the provisions of this Ordinance. He may, for the purpose of such inspection, enter any place where he has reasonable cause to believe that any such weight, measure or weighing machine is kept for trade.

(3) Any person who neglects or refuses to produce for inspection all metric weights, measures or weighing machines in his possession or on his premises, or refuses to admit the Inspector to examine the same, or otherwise obstructs or hinders the Inspector, shall be liable on conviction to a fine not exceeding LP. 5.

8. (1) An Inspector shall examine every metric weight and measure which is of the same denomination as one of the secondary standards and is brought to him for the purpose of verification, and shall compare it with such secondary standard. If he shall find it is just and not already stamped and marked, he shall stamp and mark it in the prescribed manner. Verification of weights and measures.

(2) The Inspector shall deliver to the person producing to him such weight or measure or weighing machine a certificate of justness which shall remain in force from the day on which it is given for a period not exceeding one year.

(3) Fees shall be payable for verification and stamping in accordance with Regulations made under this Ordinance; provided that any person who at the date on which this Ordinance comes into force is in possession of metric weights and measures may, within a period of six months, produce them to the Inspector in order that they may be verified and stamped, and no fees shall be charged for such verification and stamping.

(4) Where the Inspector is an officer of a Municipality, the fees shall be payable to the Municipality.

9. From the date at which this Ordinance comes into force metric weights and measures shall be used for the purpose of all transactions entered into by any Department of the Government or any Municipal or Local Council. Metric weights, etc to be exclusively used by Government.

10. The area of any land concerning which any right, disposition or contract shall be recorded in any register of the Government or any Municipal or Local Council, shall be expressed therein in terms of the standard measure of surface; provided that nothing herein shall affect the validity of any right, disposition or contract in or concerning land which is Application to land transactions.

— 5 —

Palestine No. 2 of 1928.

at the date of this Ordinance defined according to dunums which are not standard dunums, or according to any other existing measure of surface.

Comparison between metric and customary weights and measures.

11. The customary weights and measures in use at the date of this Ordinance shall be deemed to be equivalent to the metric weights and measures according to the table contained in the Schedule hereto.

Power of High Commissioner to make metric system compulsory.

12. If, at any time within five years from the date at which this Ordinance comes into force, the High Commissioner is of the opinion that it is desirable to prohibit the use of any weights and measures other than metric weights and measures, he may, by Order in Executive Council, declare that, from a date to be notified in the Official Gazette, the use of any weight or measure other than a metric weight or measure shall be unlawful, and thereupon any contract or dealing in any work or goods, disposition of land or other thing which is to be carried out, done or made by weight or measure shall be deemed to be carried out, done or made according to metric weights and measures, and otherwise shall be void. Provided that the High Commissioner may in such notice make such reservations from and exceptions to the application of the metric system of weights and measures as he may think fit.

Use of illegal metric weights, etc.

13. (1) Any person who uses for the purpose of any sale, contract or dealing, or has in his possession for use in trade, any metric weight or measure or weighing machine which is false or unjust shall be liable on conviction to a fine not exceeding LP. 20 or, in the case of a second or subsequent offence, to a fine not exceeding LP. 50.

(2) Where any weight, measure or weighing machine is found in the possession of any person carrying on trade, or in or upon the premises of any person which are in use for trade, such person shall be deemed, until the contrary is proved, to have such weight or measure or weighing machine in his possession for use in trade.

Dealing in unjust weights, etc.

14. Any person who knowingly makes or sells or causes to be made or sold any unjust metric weight or measure or weighing machine, shall be liable on conviction to a fine not exceeding LP. 50, and in respect of a second or subsequent offence to a fine not exceeding LP. 100 or to imprisonment for a period not exceeding six months.

Forgery of marks.

15. Any person who forges or counterfeits or causes to be forged or counterfeited or knowingly assists in forging or counterfeiting any stamp or mark used for stamping or marking

any weight or measure or weighing machine under this Ordinance, shall be liable on conviction to a fine not exceeding LP. 50 or to imprisonment for a period not exceeding six months.

16. Any person who knowingly sells or disposes of any metric weight, measure or weighing machine with any forged or counterfeited stamp or mark thereon shall be liable on conviction to a fine not exceeding LP. 20 or to imprisonment for a period not exceeding three months. *Dealing in counterfeit weights.*

17. Every metric weight or measure or weighing machine which is found to be false or unjust, or which has thereon any forged or counterfeited stamp or mark shall be forfeited, and may at any time be seized by any Inspector. *Forfeiture of counterfeit weight, etc.*

18. Where an Inspector has reasonable cause to believe that an offence against this Ordinance has been committed in respect of any metric weight or measure or weighing machine, he may seize the same; and upon conviction of any person of an offence in relation thereto, such weight or measure or weighing machine may be forfeited. *Seizure of weights and forfeiture.*

19. The High Commissioner in Executive Council may make, and when made may vary or revoke, regulations for all or any of the following purposes :- *Power to make regulations.*

(a) prescribing the fees to be paid on the verification, stamping and marking of metric weights and measures;

(b) prescribing the limits of error to be allowed on verification and to be tolerated on inspection, either generally or in respect of any trade;

(c) generally, for the due carrying into effect of this Ordinance.

G. S. SYMES
Officer Administering the Government.

15th February, 1928.

— 7 —

Palestine No. 2 of 1928.

SCHEDULE.

Customary weights and measures with their equivalents in metric and British weights and measures.

Measures of Length and Surface.

1 dra'=24 quirats.
1 dra' or pic=67.75 cm.=26.67 inch (Cloth measure).
1 dra' or pic=75.80 cm.=29.84 inch (Building and land measures).
1 dunum=1600 sq. pics=0.193 ares=1099.5056 sq. yards.

Weights.

1 dram (dirhem)=3204.804 milligrams=49.459 grains.
1 okka=400 dirhems=1281.957 grams=2.827 lbs.
1 rotl=12 oqias.
1 kantar=100 rotls.

(South) 1 rotl=900 dirhems=2.884 kilos=6.360 lbs.
1 kantar=225 okkas=288.450 kilos=635.922 lbs.
1 oqia=75 dirhems=240.637 grams=0.530 lbs.

(North) 1 rotl=800 dirhems=2.564 kilos=5.653 lbs.
1 kantar=200 okkas=256.400 kilos=565.250 lbs.
1 oqia=66.667 dirhems=213.659 grams=0.471 lbs.

Measures of Capacity. *

1 saa=2 rubeiyas=9.00 litres=1.980 gallons.
1 jarrah (olive oil)=29.53 litres=52.00 pints.
(South) (Wheat) 1 keile=22.464 kilogs.=49.518 lbs.
(South) (Barley) 1 keile=19.656 kilogs.=43.328 lbs,
(Oil Measure) 1 jarrah=16 okkas=20.511 kilogs.=45.227 lbs.

* Averages only. Different equivalents exist in different parts of Palestine.

FORESTS AMENDMENT ORDINANCE, No. 8 OF 1928.

— 23 —

FORESTS AMENDMENT ORDINANCE

No. 8 of 1928.

An Ordinance to amend the Forests Ordinance. *No. 5 of 1926.*

BE IT ENACTED by the High Commissioner for Palestine with the advice of the Advisory Council thereof:-

1. This Ordinance may be cited as the Forests Amendment Ordinance, 1928; and the Forests Ordinance, No. 5 of 1926 (hereinafter called the Principal Ordinance), and this Ordinance may together be cited as the Forests Ordinance 1926-28. *Short title.*

2. Section 22 of the Principal Ordinance shall be cancelled, and the following shall be substituted therefor:-

(1) Any Forest Officer or Police Officer may seize any forest produce, instrument, or means of transport in respect of which or by which he has reasonable grounds for believing that an offence under the Ordinance has been committed, and retain the same until the Court or an officer exercising the power of compounding an offence under this Ordinance has given directions as to its disposal. *Seizure of suspected forest produce, etc. for forfeiture.*

(2) In addition to any fine or term of imprisonment imposed under the Ordinance or any Regulations thereunder, the Court may order that such forest produce, instrument or means of transport shall be forfeited; and may further order that any licence or permit held under the Ordinance by the person convicted shall be forfeited.

3. The following Sections shall be added in Part VI of the Principal Ordinance:-

(1) In a prosecution for an offence under this Ordinance any report signed by a Forest Officer may be accepted as evidence unless the accused person desires that the Officer shall attend as a witness; or the Court considers his attendance necessary. *Acceptance of written report as evidence.*

(2) The Director of Agriculture and Forests or any Forest Officer not below the grade of Sub-Inspector empowered in that behalf by the High Commissioner, may accept from any person reasonably suspected of having committed an offence under this Ordinance a sum by way of compensation for the offence which may have been committed; and if any forest produce, instrument or means of transport in respect of which or by which the offence has been committed has been seized, may *Power to compound offences.*

— 24 —

Palestine No. 8 of 1928.

either confiscate such produce, instrument or means of transport or may release it on payment of its value as estimated by the Officer, or on payment of any less sum, or without payment. On such payment being made, the accused person, if in custody, shall be discharged and no further proceedings shall be taken against him in respect of such offence.

Addition to Section 26. Licences for sale, purchase, etc. of forest produce.

4. (1) The following shall be added to Section 26 of the Principal Ordinance as paragraphs (c) and (d):-

(c) prohibiting the sale, purchase and export of forest produce or of any specified kind of forest produce by any person other than the holder of a licence or permit granted under this Ordinance;

(d) prescribing the manner in which, and the persons to whom, applications shall be made for the grant of licences and permits to sell, purchase or export forest produce.

(2) Paragraphs (c) - (h) of Section 26 shall be renumbered as paragraphs (e) - (j).

PLUMER F. M.
High Commissioner.

30th May, 1928.

LAND SETTLEMENT ORDINANCE, No. 9 OF 1928.

— 25 —

LAND SETTLEMENT ORDINANCE.

No. 9 of 1928.

An Ordinance to provide for the Settlement of Land and Registration of title thereon.

BE IT ENACTED by the High Commissioner for Palestine with the advice of the Advisory Council thereof:-

INTRODUCTORY.

1. This Ordinance may be cited as the Land Settlement Ordinance, 1928. <small>Short title.</small>

2. In this Ordinance, unless the context otherwise requires- <small>Definitions.</small>

"Block" means a subdivision of the land of a village which contains one or more parcels and forms a unit of survey and registration.

"Parcel" means a continuous unit of land within a block which is owned by a person or body of persons.

"Disposition" means any transaction of whatever nature by which the rights of persons in or over land are affected or a charge is created or affected, but does not include an agreement to transfer or charge land.

"Commissioner of Lands" means the officer appointed by the High Commissioner to exercise general direction and control over settlement and registration under this Ordinance.

"District Commissioner" includes a Deputy District Commissioner and an Assistant District Commissioner.

"Instrument" includes any deed, judgment, order or other document requiring or capable of registration under this Ordinance.

"Land" includes any rights arising out of land, buildings and things permanently fixed to land, an undivided share in land, and any interest in land which requires or is capable of registration under this Ordinance.

"Existing Register" means a Register of title to land existing prior to the Settlement.

"New Register" means a Register of title to land established under this Ordinance.

— 26 —

Palestine No. 9 of 1928.

"Registrar" includes an Assistant Registrar and any person duly authorised by the Director of Lands to act for the Registrar.

"Settlement Officer" includes any person duly authorised to act for a Settlement Officer for any specified purpose.

"Village" means any of the villages specified in the Proclamation under the Palestine Order in Council which was published in the Gazette of the 1st of June, 1924, or any Proclamation amending the same; and includes a tribal area and also village lands within or abutting on a municipal area.

"Village Settlement Committee" includes a Settlement Committee for any tribal area.

"Transfer of land or of a charge" means the passing of land or of a charge from one person to another by act of the parties or by Order of the Court.

"Claimant" includes any tribe or group of persons.

"Land Court" means the Land Court of the District in which is situate the land which is the subject matter of the action or application.

Settlement order.

3. (1) Whenever it appears expedient to the High Commissioner that a settlement of the rights in land in any area and registration thereof shall be effected, the High Commissioner shall publish in the Gazette an Order, hereinafter called a Settlement Order.

(2) The Order shall state the situation and limits of the area, hereinafter called the settlement area, within which the settlement of rights to land and registration thereof shall be effected and shall declare that, after a period to be defined in the Order, the demarcation of parcels and presentation of claims may begin in any village within the settlement area.

Appointment of Settlement Officers, Assistant Settlement Officers and process servers.

4. (1) On or after the publication of the Order mentioned in the previous Section, the High Commissioner shall appoint a Settlement Officer, and one or more Assistant Settlement Officers as may be necessary for carrying out the settlement of land.

(2) A Settlement Officer may appoint such number of process servers as may be approved.

Notice by Settlement Officer to villages.

5. (1) The Settlement Officer shall cause preliminary notice of the intended survey settlement and registration of rights in any village to be published at the office of the District Commissioner of the District within which the village lies, and at the

Palestine No. 9 of 1928.

District Office of the Sub-District, and at convenient places in the neighbourhood of the village. A copy of the notice shall be sent to the Land Court, and to the Director of Lands.

(2) The notification shall be published not less than 30 days before demarcation of the parcels and presentation of claims shall begin; and shall contain :—

(a) directions as to the demarcation of the boundaries of land and the presentation of claims;

(b) notice of the consequences of and penalties for failure to present claims in due time and to demarcate the parcels claimed;

(c) such instructions as the Settlement Officer may think fit for obtaining assistance and information.

6. Save as provided herein, no action concerning rights to land in any village in which notification of the settlement has been published shall be entered in any Land Court or Civil Court. Any action entered before the notification is published shall, if possible, be heard and decided before the settlement is begun in the village, or, by leave of the Court, any such action may be withdrawn. Provided that nothing herein shall prevent the Land Court or Civil Court completing the hearing of an action pending at the date the notification of settlement was published. Where an action is withdrawn, no fee shall be payable in respect of the hearing of an action concerning the same matter before the Settlement Officer. *Staying actions after publication of notice.*

7. Not less than ten days before the begining of the settlement, the Settlement Officer shall publish in a village notified in accordance with Section 5 hereof a notice, hereinafter callled the settlement notice, which shall state such particulars as may be prescribed by Regulation under this Ordinance. *Publication of Settlement Office.*

8. During the course of the settlement, the Settlement Officer shall publish from time to time a notice recording the progress of the settlement and stating the order in which the work will be continued. The notice shall be published in the Office of the Sub-District, in the village in which the settlement is being conducted, and at the office or camp of the Settlement Officer. *Notice of progress to be published.*

9. Subject to the provisions of this Ordinance, the Settlement Officer in execution of his duties, may— *General powers of Settlement Officer.*

(a) publish notices ordering the attendance at any time and place of claimants to land in the settlement area:

— 28 —

Palestine No. 9 of 1928.

(b) order any claimant or any person included in the Schedule of Rights referred to in Section 30 hereof to mark out the boundaries of the land affected by his claim or specified in the Schedule of Rights in such manner and before such date as he may direct; and in default of compliance may cause such boundaries to be marked at the expense of such person;

(c) issue summonses, notices or orders requiring the attendance of any person or the production of any documents that he may deem necessary for carrying out the settlement, and administer oaths in any enquiry made for the purpose of the settlement;

(d) dispense with the attendance of any person or the production of any document;

(e) make a copy of any document produced, or endorse or stamp such document;

(f) authenticate any document signed and attested before him;

(g) extend the time prescribed herein for the performance of any act to be done under this Ordinance.

_{Settlement Officer to have judicial powers.}

10. (1) The Settlement Officer shall have power to hear and decide any dispute with regard to the ownership or possession of land in a settlement area and may make such order as to costs in any such matter as he thinks fit.

(2) The Chief Justice may from time to time with the approval of the High Commissioner make Rules of procedure to be followed in any judicial proceeding by a Settlement Officer.

(3) A Settlement Officer shall apply the Land Law in force at the date of the hearing of the action, provided that he shall have regard to equitable as well as legal rights to land, and shall not be bound by any rule of the Ottoman Law or by any enactment issued by the British Military Administration prohibiting the Courts from hearing actions based on unregistered documents or by the rules of evidence contained in the Code of Civil Procedure or the Civil Code.

Appointment of religious judges to assist Settlement Officer in matters of personal status.

11. (1) Upon the application of the Commissioner of Lands, the Supreme Moslem Council shall appoint a Kadi of the Sharia Court, or a person approved by the Government to exercise within the settlement area the functions of a Kadi of the Sharia Court of first instance, who shall issue certificates of succession to Moslems, decide any disputes as to succession, and carry out any other matters of the personal status of Moslems.

— 20 —

Palestine No. 9 of 1928.

(2) Upon the like application the Court of any Community which exercises jurisdiction in accordance with the Succession Ordinance, 1923, shall appoint a judge of a Religious Court of the Community, who shall issue certificates of succession and carry out any other matter of personal status which is within the jurisdiction of the Religious Court of the Community.

(3) The Settlement Officer in trying any claim to land as Wakf land shall invite a Kadi or person appointed to act as Kadi or a religious judge appointed under this Section to sit as an assessor for the purpose of advising him upon the law of Wakf involved.

12. The Settlement Officer shall settle any doubt or dispute as to the boundaries of a village or block within the settlement area, and where any parcel is detached from the rest of the land of the village to which it belongs, he may, subject to the approval of the High Commissioner, include any such parcel in the land of another village which it adjoins. For these purposes he may exercise any of the powers of a District Commissioner prescribed in the Survey Ordinance, 1920 or any Ordinance substituted therefor. *(Settlement of village blocks and boundaries.)*

13. (1) Upon the application of the Commissioner of Lands, the District Commissioner of the District in which a village within the settlement area is situated shall constitute a Committee for such village, hereinafter called the Village Settlement Committee, and shall determine or vary from time to time the composition of the Committee. *(Village Committees.)*

(2) The Village Settlement Committee shall be chosen by the District Commissioner from amongst persons nominated by the inhabitants of the village and the reputed owners of land within the village. In default of such nomination, the District Commissioner shall appoint such persons as he thinks fit as members of the Village Settlement Committee.

(3) The District Commissioner may issue an order for remuneration of a Village Settlement Committee, and apportion amongst the land owners and inhabitants of the village the amount which they are required to contribute towards such remuneration. The amount so apportioned shall be recoverable in the manner prescribed for the time being for the recovery of taxes due to the Government. The remuneration shall be divided by the Settlement Officer among the members of the Village Settlement Committee in such proportion as he thinks fit.

14. (1) A Village Settlement Committee shall represent the village for which it is constituted in all matters of common interest, and shall for the purposes of the settlement be entitled *(Village Settlement Committee to represent village.)*

to bring and defend actions in its own name, and do any legal action in connection with the settlement. The Settlement Officer may award costs to or against the Committee in any action so instituted before him, and shall state by whom such costs shall be paid.

The Committee may with the approval of the Settlement Officer levy a contribution on the inhabitants of the village to cover any costs incurred by it. The District Commissioner shall apportion amongst the land owners and inhabitants of the village the amounts which they are required to contribute. Such amounts shall be recoverable in the manner prescribed for the recovery of taxes due to the Government.

(2) The Settlement Officer, in consultation with the District Commissioner, may appoint two or more members of the Village Settlement Committee to represent the interests of any section of the village for which the Committee is constituted, and such members shall have the powers and functions of the Village Settlement Committee in connection with the interests of that section.

(3) The Village Settlement Committee may, with the approval of the Settlement Officer, at any time delegate two or more of its members to act on behalf of the Committee.

Further duties of Settlement Committee.

15. (1) The Village Settlement Committee shall bring to the attention of the Settlement Officer or of any person who may be charged with the duty of protecting the interests of absentees, minors or persons under incapacity, the names of any such persons whose claims to rights to land in the village have not been presented; and where no person has been appointed to represent an absentee owner, the Committee may represent his interests before the Settlement Officer.

(2) The Village Settlement Committee shall attend and assist in the execution of settlement within the village area whenever required to do so by the Settlement Officer.

INVESTIGATION OF CLAIMS AND SETTLEMENT.

Claimants.

16. (1) After publication of the settlement notice in any village, all claimants to land in the village shall appear at such time and in such place as the Settlement Officer may direct.

(2) Claimants may appear in person or by an agent authorised in writing or appointed before the Settlement Officer, and shall produce to the Settlement Officer any instruments affecting the land which they claim. A claimant who fails to appear in person or by an agent may submit to the Settlement Officer a statement of his claim in writing. Where an agent so

— 31 —

Palestine No. 9 of 1928.

appointed is a member of the family of the person appointing him and is not an advocate, Stamp Duty shall not be payable on the document authorising him to appear before the Settlement Officer.

(3) If any claimant fails to attend in person or by authorised agent, the demarcation, registration or any other operation of settlement may proceed in his absence.

(4) Where one or more of several heirs of a deceased claimant or owner, or one or more of a group of heirs which has a separate interest from another group, appear, his or their appearance shall be deemed to be the appearance of all the heirs or of the group, as the case may be, unless the Settlement Officer otherwise directs.

17. (1) Claims to any right by a Moslem Wakf, whether to Mulk or Miri, shall be presented by the Mutawalli of the Wakf, or by such person as may be duly authorised by the Supreme Moslem Council. Representation of Wakf interest.

(2) Claims to any right by a Wakf of which the beneficiaries belong to a non-Moslem Community shall be presented either by the guardian of such Wakf or by such other person as the competent authority of the Community shall appoint.

18. Any religious or local authority, or any association, company or charitable institution which claims any right to land in a settlement area may appoint an agent to present and defend its claim during the settlement. Representation of religious authority, local authority or corporation.

19. The claims of the Government to land shall be presented by an officer appointed by the Attorney General. Government claims.

20. Claimants other than the Government shall demarcate or otherwise indicate on the ground the limits of the parcel to which their claims relate, in such manner as the Settlement Officer may direct. Demarcation of parcels on presentation of claims.

21. The Settlement Officer shall draw up for each block a list of claims hereinafter called the Schedule of Claims which shall contain the particulars prescribed by Regulation hereunder. Entry of claims on the claims schedule.

22. (1) The Settlement Officer in the course of demarcation, may - Power of Settlement Officer as to boundaries, rights of way and grouping of areas.

(a) when the boundary between separate parcels of land is a curved or irregular line or in the opinion of the Settlement Officer is inconvenient for the use of the land, lay out a fresh boundary in place of the original boundary and may adjust the rights of the owners of the land adjoining such boundary by exchange of land of equal value; or as provided in subsection (2) hereof;

— 32 —

Palestine No. 9 of 1928.

(b) make such alignment of property abutting on the public road or a right of way as may be required in the public interest; provided that he shall not make any such alignment of property abutting on any road to which the Width and Alignment of Roads Ordinance, 1926, has been applied by order of the High Commissioner;

(c) demarcate any existing road and right of way and any new right of way to a public road in favour of any owner whose land is surrounded by land of another owner or owners.

(2) If the Settlement Officer thinks that compensation should be paid to any person in respect of any alteration of boundary, alignment of property or right of way made by him under this Section, he shall make an Order for compensation and direct in such Order by whom such compensation is to be paid.

(3) The Settlement Officer may, on the application of two or more owners, group together, in one or more parcels, the areas of land owned by the applicants provided that such grouping shall not adversely affect the parcels of any other persons.

No parcellation after publication of notice.
23. No parcellation of land purporting to be either a subdivision of land held in individual shares or a permanent division of land held in common and periodically distributed among the inhabitants of the village shall have effect after the publication of the settlement notice, save as provided in Section 36 hereof. Provided that any parcellation which was effected prior to the publication of such notice may be approved and accepted by the Settlement Officer.

Adoption of Schedule.
24. The Schedule of Claims to land in any block as finally determined shall be signed by the Settlement Officer, and shall be posted at his office or camp, and a copy thereof shall be posted in the office of the Sub-District in which the village is situate.

Investigation and settlement of rights.
25. Not less than 15 days after the date of the posting of the Schedule of Claims the Settlement Officer shall commence the investigation and settlement of claims.

Addition of new claims prior to settlement.
26. (1) Subject to any Regulations under the Ordinance, a Settlement Officer may add any new claim to the Schedule of Claims at any time before the claims to rights in the block have been settled, if he is satisfied that there were reasonable

Palestine No. 9 of 1928.

grounds for failure to present the claim in due time, and that opposition to such claim and the investigation of other claims will not be adversely affected by such addition.

(2) Notice of such addition to the Schedule of Claims shall be published in such manner as the Settlement Officer shall think fit.

27. (1) The Settlement Officer shall investigate publicly all claims included in the Schedule of Claims, and the claimants to any parcel whose names appear on the Schedule shall be notified by notice published in the village to appear when the claims are investigated. Settlement of claims.

(2) If there are conflicting claims between two or more claimants, the dispute shall be heard and determined by the Settlement Officer, or, with the consent of all the parties, may be referred to arbitration. The Settlement Officer shall follow any Rules of procedure which may be issued by the Chief Justice under Section 10 hereof.

(3) If in a dispute no party applies as plaintiff, the Settlement Officer may designate one party to the dispute as plaintiff and the other as defendant, and may state which persons are represented by either party.

(4) If the Settlement Officer is satisfied that any person who has not presented a claim is entitled to any right to land, he may proceed as if such person had made a claim within the time prescribed.

(5) The Settlement Officer may, with the consent of the parties, refer to arbitration any dispute arising out of a claim and subject to the powers set out in the following sub-sections shall authenticate the award within 15 days of its issue. The award when so authenticated shall have the effect of a decision of the Settlement Officer; and for the purpose of the Stamp Duty Ordinance, 1927 shall be deemed to be an award of arbitrators appointed by a Court.

(6) The Settlement Officer may remit an award to the arbitrators for reconsideration :-

(a) If there is some discrepancy patent on the face of the award;

(b) If the arbitrators admit that they have made some mistake and desire the award to be remitted;

(c) If material evidence which could not with reasonable diligence have been discovered before the award was made has since been obtained.

— 34 —

Palestine No. 9 of 1928.

(7) The Settlement Officer may set aside the award:

(a) If the award has been procured by fraud or by the concealment of material documents;

(b) If there has been misconduct on the part of the arbitrators.

Rights of the Government to land.

28. (1) The rights of the Government to land of the category of Miri or Mulk which are required by law to be registered shall be investigated and settled. The rights of the Government to land of any other category shall be investigated and settled only if any claimant puts forward a claim which is in conflict with such right.

(2) Land used for general public purposes that falls within the category of Metrukeh shall be registered in the name of the Government; any land in the category of Metrukeh which is used for the public purposes of a village shall be settled and registered in the name of the village.

(3) All rights to land in any settlement area which are not established by any claimant and registered in accordance with the settlement shall belong absolutely to the Government.

Power of the Settlement Officer to refer question to Court.

29. (1) The Settlement Officer may refer to the Land Court or to the competent Religious Court any question which may arise with regard to—

(a) the true construction or validity or effect of any instrument;

(b) the category of any land;

(c) the extent or nature of any right;

(d) the constitution or internal administration of a Wakf affecting any land.

(2) The Court shall allow any party interested to appear before it, and may summon any other party and may order the production of any instrument.

(3) The Court may either give judgment on the question referred or may direct any proceedings to be instituted, or may issue any direction or instruction to the Settlement Officer relating to the matter.

— 35 —

Palestine No. 9 of 1928.

30. After the investigation of all claims, the Settlement Officer shall draw up a Schedule of Rights which shall show :- *Schedule of Rights.*

    (a) the District, Sub-District and village;

    (b) the name and number of the block;

    (c) the reference numbers of all parcels in the block;

    (d) the category of each parcel;

    (e) the area of the parcel;

    (f) any rights to the parcel, other than a lease for a period not exceeding three years; and any servitude affecting the parcel or enjoyed by the owner of the parcel over other land, including a right to water, and the name and address of the person entitled to such right or servitude;

    (g) any fixtures attaching to a parcel whether separately owned or not; and any subdivision of property in the parcel; and the name and address of the person recognised as entitled to such fixture or subdivision;

    (h) any survey fees and other fees or charges due from such persons on the registration of rights;

    (i) any other particulars which may be prescribed by Regulations.

31. Any transfer of land or of a charge made after the settlement of rights to a parcel has been effected, but before the Schedule of Rights for the village is posted, shall be entered separately in the Schedule. *Amendment of Schedule.*

32. (1) When any Schedule of Rights in any block or blocks is completed, the Settlement Officer shall, after giving such notice as may be prescribed by Regulation, read out the Schedule to the Village Settlement Committee and the claimants to rights in the block or blocks; provided that if any member of the Committee or any claimant is absent the Settlement Officer shall proceed in his absence. The Schedule shall be signed by the Settlement Officer and shall be posted at the office or camp of the Settlement Officer for a period of 15 days. One copy shall be posted for the like period at the office of the Sub-District in which the village is situate, and a notice of such posting shall be published in the Gazette. *Publication of Schedule of Rights.*

(2) After the posting of the Schedule, the Settlement Officer may correct clerical errors and introduce any clerical amendments or additions to the Schedule.

Palestine No. 9 of 1928.

Limitation as to subdivision of land.	33. The High Commissioner may from time to time issue an Order prescribing—

(a) that the shares in the ownership of undivided land, excluding sites of buildings, shall be expressed in integral square metres, and not in fractions of the area of the undivided land;

(b) the limitation to a minimum, or to different minima under conditions to be specified, of the area of any parcel or of the breadth of any parcel for which any person may be registered whether as a separate parcel or as a share of an undivided parcel;

(c) the adjustment with adjoining parcels of the boundaries of a parcel of which the breadth is below the specified minimum by the exchange of land of equal value;

(d) the method of adding any fragment of land which may not be registered in accordance with such order to the land of an adjoining owner, and of fixing the compensation to be paid by the adjoining owner who benefits by the addition.

REGISTRATION.

Closing of existing Land Registers.	34. After the publication of a settlement notice no fresh entry shall be made in the existing Land Registers relating to land in a village notified in accordance with Section 5 hereof.
Opening of new Registers.	35. A new Register, in a form to be prescribed by Regulation under this Ordinance, shall be opened for each village and notwithstanding any appeal which may be pending, the land shall be registered by the Registrar in such Register in accordance with the Schedule of Rights signed by the Settlement Officer.
Restriction on transfer pending registration.	36. (1) No voluntary transfer of rights to land in a notified village shall be made during the interval between the closing of the existing Registers and the posting of the Schedule of Rights, unless the Settlement Officer authorises such transfer to be effected immediately on grounds of urgency.

(2) Any involuntary transfer of rights which occurs by death or other cause during the said period shall be notified to the Settlement Officer by the person claiming such right.

(3) As soon as all the Schedules of Rights in respect of a village have been recorded in the Register of the village, the Schedule shall be in the custody of the Director of Lands.

— 37 —

Palestine No. 9 of 1928.

37. (1) Any person who is registered as having an interest in any parcel in accordance with the Schedule of Rights shall be entitled, after payment of any fees and charges due on account of the settlement, to receive without further charge a certified copy of the record of his interest in such parcel. Right to extract from the Register.

(2) If payment of any fees and charges is made in instalments in accordance with Regulations under this Ordinance, the person entitled to the interest shall receive a certified copy or extract as soon as he has paid the first instalment of such fees or charges.

38. Any disposition which occurs after the Schedule of Rights has been posted shall not be valid until it is duly registered in the Register of the village. Dispositions after postig of Schedule to be registered.

39. Where the death of any person recorded in the Schedule of Rights as the owner of any right occurs after the posting of the Schedule but before registration, any person to whom such right passes on the death shall apply to the Registrar to transfer the right to his name. He shall be liable to pay all fees and charges due on the initial registration, but shall be exempted from any additional payment on account of the registration of the transfer of the right. Rectification before registration.

40. Where any undivided parcel is periodically redistributed among co-owners, no transfer of any share shall be registered after the posting of the Schedule of Rights unless the undivided parcel has been partitioned. Restriction of transfer of undivided land.

41. No claim to compensation shall lie, and no action shall be maintainable against the Government - No claim to compensation on account of failure to locate parcel in existing Registers, etc.

(a) on account of any failure during the settlement to locate a parcel to which the record in any existing Registers or any existing title deed or judgment of the Court relates; or

(b) on account of any failure to establish any right to land which purports to be based on any record in an existing Register or an existing title deed; or

(c) on account of any error in the establishment of any boundaries, in the partition of any land or in the statement of any area.

42. Save as provided herein, the registration of land in the new Register shall invalidate any right conflicting with such registration. Registered right only to be valid.

— 38 —

Palestine No. 9 of 1928.

Prohibition of unregistered disposition.

43. No disposition of land registered in the new Register, other than a lease for a period of not more than three years, and no transmission of land on death shall be valid until it has been registered in the Register.

No action to lie in respect of unregistered disposition.

44. (1) No action shall be maintainable on the ground of any unregistered disposition against the owner of any registered right, provided that any person who has paid money in respect of any such invalid disposition shall be entitled to bring an action for the recovery of the sum.

(2) If any person is a party to a disposition, other than a lease for a period not exceeding 3 years, which has not been registered, and either enters into possession or permits the other party to enter into possession of the land, any Civil Court or Land Court in which an action concerning the land is pending may impose a fine upon him not exceeding one-fourth part of the value of the land.

Registers and plans to be in custody of Directors of Lands and Survey.

45. No Register and no original document or record on which the registration is based shall be taken out of the custody of the Director of Lands, and no original map, plan or other survey record shall be taken out of the custody of the Director of Surveys; provided always that any Court may order the Director of Lands or the Director of Surveys to produce in any Court at any appointed time any original register, document, map, plan or other survey record.

Right of Court to require duly authenticated copy.

46. (1) Any Land Court or Civil Court may require the Director of Lands or the Director of Surveys to produce or furnish a duly authenticated copy of:-

(a) any entry in the Registers;

(b) any instrument, document or record supporting such entry or relating thereto;

(c) any map, plan or other survey record relating to the position or extent of any parcel.

(2) Any such Court may at any time delegate an Officer to visit any Land Registry or Survey Office and verify such copy with the original preserved there.

(3) Any authenticated copy shall be accepted as proof of the contents of the document.

Palestine No. 9 of 1928.

47. An authenticated copy of any judgment of a Land Court or Civil Court concerning land registered under this Ordinance shall be sent to the Registrar of the District in which the land is situate; and, on payment of the fees due by the person in whose favour the judgment is given, the Registrar shall enter in the Register of the village any order affecting the land contained in the judgment.

<small>Entry on Register in virtue of judgment.</small>

48. (1) Upon the application of any interested party any Court may order the Registrar to record in the Register any caution with regard to the disposition of a parcel or any prohibition against the disposition of any parcel pending the decision of a case which has been entered before such Court.

<small>Entry of caution in Register.</small>

(2) Upon the application of the District Commissioner the Registrar shall record in the Register a note of any arrears of tithe or land tax due on any parcel, and no disposition of such parcel shall be entered unless it has been ascertained that such tithe or land tax has been paid.

<small>Entry in Register of arrears of tithes or land tax.</small>

PARTITION.

49. No partition in a settlement area of any parcel or parcels held in undivided shares by the inhabitants of a village or a section thereof shall be effected, save as provided in Sections 50-55 hereof. No partition shall be effected by the Settlement Officer until the period within which application may be made for leave of appeal from the decision of the Settlement Officer recorded in the Schedule of Rights has elapsed, or, if leave to appeal has been granted, until judgment in the appeal has been given in the Land Court.

<small>When partition may be effected</small>

50. Subject to the provisions of the previous Section and to any restriction with regard to the minimum area of land which may be registered, the Settlement Officer may-

<small>Conditions of partition.</small>

(a) upon the application of any person registered as the owner of a share in undivided land, divide such share from the remainder of the undivided land, and direct the divided share to be registered as a separate parcel or parcels, unless in the opinion of the Settlement Officer division would prejudice the use of the land;

(b) on the application of the registered owners of not less than two-thirds of the shares in the undivided land, partition the whole of the undivided land amongst all the registered owners, and order each divided share to be registered as a separate parcel or parcels.

Palestine No. 9 of 1928.

High Commissioner may order partition in public interest.

51. Notwithstanding any provision in the preceding sections, the High Commissioner may at any time direct a Settlement Officer to carry out the partition of any land held in divided ownership, if such partition is deemed to be in public interest.

System of partition.

52. (1) Partition shall be carried out in accordance with an agreement made between not less than two-thirds the owners of shares included in the Schedule of Rights approved by the Settlement Officer.

(2) In the absence of such agreement, partition shall be carried out by the Settlement Officer, in consultation with the Village Settlement Committee, by the drawing of lots, regard being had to the area and value of the lands to be partitioned, provided that on the application of the owners of not less than two-thirds of the shares of any undivided land, the Settlement Officer may group the land of each owner so as to provide one or more parcels for each owner.

(3) The Ottoman Provisional Law concerning partition, dated 1329 A.H., shall not apply to partitions carried out under this Ordinance.

Compensation to owner who establishes title to a share after partition.

53. Where a person establishes his right by action to a share in undivided land after the land has been partitioned in accordance with this Ordinance, or after a parcellation has been accepted by the Settlement Officer in accordance with Section 23 hereof and recorded in the Schedule of Rights, the persons between whom the land has been partitioned shall pay compensation to such person in such proportion as the Land Court thinks fit. The compensation shall be charged upon the land of the owners of the shares until it is fully paid.

Partition schedule.

54. The Settlement Officer shall prepare a Schedule of Partition of any land which has been partitioned in accordance with the provisions hereof. The Schedule shall include the particulars prescribed by Regulation under this Ordinance.

Notification of partition.

55. The Partition Schedule shall be notified to the owners affected and posted in the same way as the Schedule of Rights and a copy of such Schedule authenticated by the Settlement Officer and accompanied by a survey plan of the block comprised in it shall be transmitted to the Registrar to be recorded in the Registers of the village in which the block is situate. Partition shall be registered in accordance with the Partition Schedule notwithstanding any appeal from the Settlement Officer which may be pending.

— 41 —

Palestine No. 9 of 1928.

APPEAL - RECTIFICATION OF REGISTER.

56. (1) No appeal shall lie from the decision of a Settlement Officer as to any right to land, save with the leave of such Officer or of the President of a Land Court. Every application for leave to appeal shall be made by a petition in writing within one month from the date of the publication in the Gazette of the notice as to posting of the Schedule of Rights or the Partition Schedule containing the decision which is the subject of appeal, and shall be submitted to the Settlement Officer. If the Settlement Officer refuses the application, the applicant may, within 15 days of such refusal, refer it to the President of the Land Court stating the grounds for the appeal. *Appeal from Settlement Officer.*

(2) Where leave to appeal is granted, it shall be heard by the Land Court, and the Settlement Officer shall forward to the President of the Court all the documents relating to the case.

57. (1) The Land Court may either- *Powers of the Land Court on appeal.*

(a) decide the appeal on the evidence taken by the Settlement Officer; or

(b) rehear the evidence or hear fresh evidence and give judgment on the appeal; or

(c) remit the case to the Settlement Officer for retrial on the land.

(2) An appeal shall lie from the judgment of the Land Court to the Court of Appeal on a point of law. Notice of the appeal shall be lodged with the Court of Appeal within 30 days of the judgment if given in presence, or within 30 days of the notification of the judgment if it was given in absence.

(3) Where no appeal is brought from the judgment of the Land Court within the time prescribed, an authenticated copy of the judgment of the Land Court shall be communicated to the Registrar of the District in which the land is situate and to the Settlement Officer. The Registrar shall on payment of any fees due enter in the Register of the village any order affecting the land contained in the judgment.

58. After the expiration of the period prescribed in Section 56 no appeal shall lie from any decision recorded in the Schedule of Rights or the Partition Schedule unless in the opinion of the Settlement Officer or of the President of a Land Court to whom application is made:- *No appeal from Settlement Officer after period prescribed.*

Palestine No. 9 of 1928.

(a) any new fact is established which was unknown and could not have been within the knowledge of the interested party at an earlier date; or

(b) owing to sickness, minority, absence from Palestine or other similar incapacity, the claimant to a right has suffered prejudice which he was not able to bring to the attention of the Court previously.

Rectification of Register.

59. After the completion of the settlement, rectification of the Register may be ordered by the Land Court, subject to the law as to limitation of actions, either by annulling the registration, or in such other manner as the Court thinks fit, where the Court is satisfied that the registration of any person in respect of any right to land has been obtained by fraud; provided that, where a person has since the settlement acquired land in good faith and for value from a registered owner, the Court shall not order a rectification of the Register.

Remedy in case of fraud.

60. When any registration or any entry in the Register has been made or procured by or in pursuance of fraud and the entry cannot be rectified under this Ordinance, any person sustaining loss thereby shall be entitled to claim compensation against the person responsible for the fraud; provided that nothing herein shall involve either the Government or any officer of the Government in any liability for or in respect of any act or matter in good faith done or omitted to be done in the exercise or supposed exercise of the powers given by this Ordinance or by any Regulation made thereunder.

Correction of errors.

61. (1) A Settlement Officer may authorise a Registrar to correct any clerical errors in the Register, and to introduce clerical amendments or additions thereto, provided that all such changes are signed by the Registrar, and that a separate record is kept of corrections.

(2) Where a discrepancy is found after the registration of a settlement under this Ordinance:-

(a) between the boundaries or area of the parcels as appearing on the land and those shown on the survey plan; or

(b) between the area of any parcel as furnished by fresh survey, the area shown in the Register, and the area found by calculation from the survey plan;
the particulars which are recorded in the survey plan shall prevail; provided that if it is established that there was an error or omission in the original survey the Commissioner of Lands shall authorise the Director of Surveys to amend the

Palestine No. 9 of 1928.

survey plan and the Registrar to make the corresponding amendments in the Register; and provided further that, if the area shown in the Register was determined by a judgment of the Court, the amendement of the survey plan and of the Register shall be made only on an Order of the Court.

FEES AND MISCELLANEOUS.

62. (1) The High Commissioner by Order under this Ordinance may prescribe from time to time a scale of fees and other payments to be made on the hearing of actions before the Settlement Officer and on registration in the Registers of the rights to land which are recorded in a Schedule of Rights and a Schedule of Partition issued under this Ordinance. Payment of fees.

(2) The Commissioner of Lands shall cause a valuation of the land to be made in a manner to be prescribed by Regulation under the Ordinance for the purpose of assessing registration fees.

(3) A Settlement Officer shall decide in what cases a fee may be paid by instalments, and the number and period of instalments which will be paid. The fee or any instalments outstanding shall be a first charge on the land, subject to any charge existing at the date of registration. Payment of the balance outstanding at any time may be required by the Registrar if there is any disposition of the land other than a transfer on succession. Any fee and any instalment due may be recovered in accordance with the Law in force for recovering taxes of the Government.

63. Where application is made to the Settlement Officer for partion of a parcel owned in undivided shares within one monte of the date of the posting of the final Schedule of Rights in the village in which such parcel is situated, no fee shall be charged on account of the partition of such parcel, other than the fees due on survey and registration of the shares. Reduction of fees where partition applied for in prescribed time.

64. (1) Where any right to land registered in the existing Registers in the name of the claimant is recorded without modification in the Schedule of Rights, no fee shall be charged for the registration of such right in the new Registers. Fee where right recorded in existing Register.

(2) Where any right to land registered in existing Registers in the name of the claimant is recorded in the Schedule of Rights, subject to modification, the Settlement Officer may waive in whole or in part any fee which would otherwise be due upon the registration of such right; provided that in either case a fee shall be charged on account of survey.

— 44 —

Palestine No. 9 of 1928.

Regulations. 65. The High Commissioner in Executive Council may make, and when made, may vary or revoke Regulations for the purpose of carrying into effect the provisions of this Ordinance.

Offences and penalties. 66. (1) Any person who fails to obey or obstructs the carrying out of an order or instruction of a Settlement Officer in the execution of his duties, or obstructs the work of a Village Settlement Committee in the execution of their duties hereunder shall be liable on conviction to imprisonment for a period not exceeding six months or to a fine not exceeding £P. 50 or to both these penalties.

(2) Any person who removes or defaces any demarcation mark or survey mark, whether permanent or temporary, shall be liable on conviction to the same penalties.

Penalties for fraud. 67. (1) Any person who by any fraudulent means or by producing under a false name deeds or documents belonging to another person, causes any entry or registration to be made in the Schedule of Claims of the Schedule of Rights, or Partition Schedule either in his own name or the name of any other person shall be liable on conviction to imprisonment for a period not exceeding three years and to a fine not exceeding £P. 100.

(2) Any person who gives false evidence or makes a false statement before the Settlement Officer with a view to obtaining an entry in the Schedule of Claims or the Schedule of Rights or Partition Schedule, in his own name or in the name of any other person, shall be liable to the same penalties.

Ottoman Law not to apply. 68. The Ottoman Law of 1329 A. H. concerning Cadastral Survey shall not have effect in Palestine.

Application of Ordinance to demarcation of Ghor lands. 69. (1) The High Commissioner may, by order, confer all or any of the powers of a Settlement Officer under this Ordinance on an officer of the Government who is carrying out the demarcation of the State Domain in the Jordan Valley in accordance with the agreement published in the Gazette of the 15th of January, 1922.

(2) The High Commissioner may, in like manner, apply any provisions of this Ordinance in any area of the said lands demarcated or to be demarcated in accordance with such agreement, subject to any conditions that shall be stated in the Order.

PLUMER F. M.
High Commissioner

30th May, 1928.

SANCTIONED.

COMMUTATION OF TITHES AMENDMENT ORDINANCE, No. 27 OF 1928.

The thirtieth day of September, One thousand nine hundred and twenty-eight.

— 87 —

COMMUTATION OF TITHES AMENDMENT ORDINANCE

No. 27 of 1928.

An Ordinance to amend the Commutation of Tithes Ordinance, 1927.

BE IT ENACTED by the High Commissioner for Palestine with the advice of the Advisory Council thereof:

1. This Ordinance may be cited as the Commutation of Tithes Amendment Ordinance, 1928, and the Commutation of Tithes Ordinance, No. 49 of 1927 (hereinafter called the Principal Ordinance) and this Ordinance may together be cited as the Commutation of Tithes Ordinances, 1927-1928. *Short title.*

2. The definition of "fruit tree" in Section 2 of the Principal Ordinance is deleted and the following substituted therefor: *Definition.*

"Fruit tree' means a fruit producing tree the fruit of which was subject to tithe during the period over which the commuted tithe is calculated under this Ordinance, or is subject to tithe at the date on which this Ordinance becomes operative within the boundaries of the village.

3. Section 5 of the Principal Ordinance is deleted and the following substituted therefor: *Amendment of Section 5 of the Principal Ordinance.*

(1) The District Commissioner shall inform the Assessment Committee of:—

(a) The average aggregate amount of tithe assessed as payable during the period of years which shall be prescribed by the Order in respect of crops grown within the boundaries of the village, other than the produce of fruit trees; and

(b) The average aggregate amount of tithe assessed as payable during the like period on the produce of fruit trees within the boundaries of the village.

(2) The Assessment Committee shall thereupon prepare a list (hereinafter called the Assessment List) containing:—

(a) The names of the persons who are the reputed owners of land within the boundaries of the village, other than lands which are at the date of the Order or were during the last year in respect of which the average aggregate amount of tithe was assessed, planted with fruit trees, or which during the whole of the period of years in respect of which the average aggregate amount of tithe was assessed were planted with non-titheable crops;

Palestine No. 27 of 1928.

(b) The names of the persons who are the reputed owners of lands within the boundaries of the village planted with fruit trees at the date of the Order, or which were so planted during the last year of the period in respect of which the average aggregate amount of tithe is assessed.

(3) The Assessment Committee shall apportion:—

(a) The amount referred to in sub-clause 1 (a) hereof among the persons referred to in sub-clause 2 (a) hereof in the proportion of the potential productivity in terms of wheat of the lands respectively in the reputed ownership of such persons, if such lands are divided (Mafruz), and, if such lands are undivided (Musha'a), in the proportion of the respective shares in the reputed ownership of such persons: provided that, in a tribal area, such apportionment shall be made in accordance with tribal customs; and provided that, if it shall not be possible to make the apportionment in the proportion of the potential productivity in terms of wheat, the apportionment shall be made in the proportion of the potential productivity in terms of such other crop as the District Commissioner may determine;

(b) The amount referred to in sub-clause 1 (b) hereof among the persons referred to in sub-clause 2(b) hereof in the proportion of the actual average amount of tithe payable during the period of years prescribed by the Order in respect of the produce of the fruit trees respectively in the reputed ownership of such persons, provided that if it shall not be possible to determine accurately the actual average amount of tithe so payable by such persons, the apportionment shall be made on such other basis as may be proposed by the Village Assessment Committee and approved by the District Commissioner.

(4) If the lands planted with fruit trees and the lands cultivated with other titheable crops have been substantially changed during the period over which the average aggregate amount of tithe is assessed, or after that period but before the Ordinance becomes operative in a village, and it is impracticable for the Assessment Committee to apportion the tithe in the manner prescribed in the previous sub-clause, the Assessment Committee, with the approval of the District Commissioner, may distribute the average aggregate amount of tithe assessed as payable in respect both of crops and the produce of fruit trees together on such basis as may be approved by the District Commissioner.

— 89 —

Palestine No 27 of 1928.

4. The words "begin to" shall be inserted before the word "revise" in Section 9 of the Principal Ordinance. Amendment of Section 9 of the Principal Ordinance.

5. Where an Assessment Committee appointed by the District Commissioner under Section 4 or Section 14 of the Principal Ordinance fails, after notice from the District Commissioner, to carry out the assessment prescribed herein or the revision of the list of the reputed owners, the District Commissioner shall prepare or revise the assessment list, and apportion the tithes in accordance with the provisions of this Ordinance; and no appeal shall lie from his apportionment. District Commissioner may carry out assessment and apportionment in default by Committee.

6. (1) The High Commissioner may make, and when made may vary or revoke Regulations concerning the collection of tithes in any place in which an order is not made under the Principal Ordinance for the payment of commuted tithe. Regulations for the collection of tithe.

(2) Pending the making of any such Regulations, the assessment and collection of tithe shall be carried out in accordance with the Regulations dated the 5th June, 1923, and published in the Gazette of the 1st July, 1923, subject to the following modifications :—

(a) The word "Treasurer" shall be replaced by the words "Commissioner of Lands" wherever it occurs;

(b) The words "Treasury Inspector" shall be replaced by the words "Inspector appointed by the Commissioner of Lands".

(3) Any assessment or collection of tithe made prior to the date of this Ordinance in accordance with the Regulations dated the 5th June, 1923, shall be deemed to be and always to have been valid.

H. C. LUKE
Officer Administering the Government.

30th September, 1928.

Section 12: 1929

LAND COURTS AMENDMENT ORDINANCE, No. 7 OF 1929.

J.R. Chancellor.

— 17 —

LAND COURTS AMENDMENT ORDINANCE

No. 7 of 1929.

An Ordinance to amend the Land Courts Ordinance, 1921.

BE IT ENACTED by the High Commissioner for Palestine, with the advice of the Advisory Council thereof:-

1. This Ordinance may be cited as the Land Courts Amendment Ordinance, 1929; and the Land Courts Ordinance, 1921 (hereinafter called the Principal Ordinance) and this Ordinance may together be cited as the Land Courts Ordinances, 1921-1929. *Short title.*

2. Section 3 of the Principal Ordinance is repealed, and the following shall be substituted therefor:- *Amendment of Section 3 of Principal Ordinance.*

"No appeal shall lie from the judgment of the Land Court to the Court of Appeal, save on a question of Law.

The conditions of appeal shall be prescribed in Rules of Court to be made under this Ordinance".

15th February, 1929.

J. R. CHANCELLOR
High Commissioner.

EXEMPTION FROM TITHE ORDINANCE, No. 13 OF 1929.

J.R. Chancellor.

The thirtieth day of March, One thousand nine hundred and twenty-nine.

EXEMPTION FROM TITHE ORDINANCE

No. 13 of 1929.

An Ordinance to provide for the exemption from tithe of land used for the purpose of agricultural instruction or research.

BE IT ENACTED by the High Commissioner for Palestine, with the advice of the Advisory Council thereof:-

1. This Ordinance may be cited as the Exemption from Tithe Ordinance, 1929.   *Short title.*

2. No tithe shall be payable on the produce of any land utilised for the purpose of agricultural instruction or research and certified as such annually by the Director of Agriculture and Forests.   *Exemption from tithe of land of agricultural schools, etc.*

J. R. CHANCELLOR
High Commissioner.

30th March, 1929.

SANCTIONED.

PROTECTION OF CULTIVATORS ORDINANCE, No. 27 OF 1929.

thirty-first day of July, One thousand nine hundred and
twenty-nine.

PROTECTION OF CULTIVATORS ORDINANCE

No. 27 of 1920.

An Ordinance to provide for the protection of Agricultural Tenants.

BE IT ENACTED by the High Commissioner for Palestine, with the advice of the Advisory Council thereof :—

1. This Ordinance may be cited as the Protection of Cultivators Ordinance, 1920. Short title.

2. For the purposes of this Ordinance :— Definitions.

"Tenant" means a person who cultivates a holding under an agreement express or implied with a landlord, and pays the landlord a rent fixed either in money or in kind or a portion of the produce of the land. It includes a person who is hired by the landlord to do agricultural work and receives as his remuneration a portion of the produce of the holding which he cultivates, but not

(i) a person who is hired by the tenant to do agricultural work on those terms, or

(ii) a person hired to do agricultural work who receives as remuneration a money wage or a portion of the produce but does not cultivate a holding, or

(iii) a person who has been a tenant or has been hired by the landlord to do agricultural work for less than two years, or

(iv) a person who has obtained by auction a lease of State Domain for a period not exceeding two years.

It includes, also, the heirs of a tenant dying during the period of the tenancy; and where the tenant has acquired a holding by succession from his father or other ascendant or descendant, includes such ascendant or descendant.

"Landlord" means any person entitled for the time being to receive the rents and profits of any land.

"Holding" means a plot of Miri land cultivated by a tenant; and where the land of a village is held in undivided ownership or tenure, includes any portion of land so cultivated within the area of the village.

"Board" means a Board constituted under this Ordinance.

— 2 —

Palestine No. 27 of 1929.

"Rules of good husbandry" means, so far as is practicable, having regard to the character and position of the holding:—

(a) the maintenance of the land clean and in good condition; and

(b) such rules of good husbandry as are generally recognised as applying to holdings of the same character and in the same neighbourhood as the holding in respect of which the expression is to be applied.

"Miri" includes Miri Waqf land.

Termination of tenancy invalid without certain notice.

3. (1) Notwithstanding any provision in any contract to the contrary, a landlord of Miri land shall not be entitled to terminate the tenancy of a tenant who has been cultivating a holding for a period of two years or more, unless he shall have given to the tenant in writing notice to quit not less than one year from the 1st day of October following the date of the notice: Provided that nothing herein shall extend to the case where the tenant has failed to pay the rent at the rate payable during the year preceding the notice within a reasonable time from the due date of payment; or has failed to cultivate the land in accordance with the rules of good husbandry; or where under any Law of Bankruptcy in force an order of bankruptcy has been made against the tenant.

(2) In case of dispute, a Board appointed under this Ordinance shall determine, after consultation with the local Inspector of Agriculture, what, having regard to all the circumstances, is a reasonable period for the payment of rent due, and whether the tenant has failed to cultivate the land in accordance with the rules of good husbandry.

(3) If a landlord gives notice in writing to the tenant to terminate the tenancy on account of the failure of the tenant to pay the rent in due time, or to cultivate the land in accordance with the rules of good husbandry, the tenant shall be liable to eviction unless within 15 days of the receipt of such notice he applies in writing for reference of the question to the Board. If such application is made, the Board shall give its decision within 15 days of the receipt of the application. The landlord shall send a copy of the notice to the District Commissioner.

Provision as to increase of rent.

4. (1) The landlord shall not increase the rent of a holding unless he has given the tenant notice in writing of the proposed increase; and the increased rent shall not come into force before one year from the first day of October following the date of the notice.

— 3 —

Palestine No. 27 of 1929.

(2) If the tenant is not willing to pay the increased rent, he shall, within three months of the date of the notice, notify the landlord, who may thereupon give him notice to quit expiring on the date when the increased rent would come into force.

5. (1) Where a tenant has received a valid notice to quit, the landlord shall pay to the tenant compensation for disturbance in accordance with the provisions of this Section: Provided that he shall not be liable to pay compensation in any case where notice to quit is not required under Section 3 hereof. *Compensation for disturbance and improvements.*

(2) The compensation shall be a sum representing such loss or expense directly attributable to the quitting of the land as the tenant may unavoidably incur in connection with the sale or removal of his movable property: Provided that compensation shall not be payable in respect of the sale of any such property unless the tenant has before the sale given the landlord a reasonable opportunity of making a valuation thereof; and provided, also, that no compensation shall be payable under this Section :—

(a) where the landlord has made the tenant an offer in writing to withdraw a notice to quit, and the tenant has unreasonably refused or failed to accept the offer; or

(b) if the claim for compensation is not made within three months from the date at which the tenant quits the land.

(3) Where a tenant of a holding has made thereon any improvement comprised in the Schedule hereto, he shall, subject as hereinafter mentioned, be entitled on the termination of the tenancy, whether by a notice to quit or otherwise, to obtain from the landlord as compensation for the improvement such sum as represents the value of the improvement to an incoming tenant: Provided that in ascertaining the amount of compensation payable, there shall be taken into account any benefit which the landlord has given or allowed to the tenant executing the improvement, whether expressly stated in any contract of tenancy or not.

(4) Compensation under this Section shall not be payable in respect of any improvement comprised in Part I of the Schedule hereto unless the landlord has previously to the execution of the improvement consented in writing to the making thereof, and any such consent may be given by the landlord unconditionally, or upon such terms, as to compensation or otherwise, as may be agreed upon between the landlord and the tenant, and, if any such agreement is made, any compensation payable under the agreement shall be substituted for compensation under this Section. *Consent of landlord to improvements in Part I of Schedule.*

Palestine No. 27 of 1929.

Notice to landlord as to improvements in Part II of Schedule.

(5) Compensation shall not be payable in respect of any improvement comprised in Part II of the Schedule unless the tenant has given to the landlord not less than two months notice in writing of his intention to execute the improvement, and of the manner in which he proposes to do the work: Provided that—

    (a) if the improvement consists of application to the land of farmyard manure, it shall be sufficient for the tenant to give notice to the landlord once in each year; and

    (b) if the improvement consists of repairs to buildings which are necessary for the habitation of the tenant or the proper cultivation or working of the holding, the tenant shall not execute the repairs unless the landlord fails to execute them within a reasonable time after such notice.

Where notice is given under this subsection the landlord and tenant may agree on the terms of compensation or otherwise on which the improvement is to be executed; and if such agreement is made, compensation payable under the agreement shall be substituted for compensation under this Section.

Outgoing tenant to prepare or allow landlord to prepare land.

(6) If the landlord desires that a tenant who has received notice to quit in accordance with Section 3 hereof shall prepare the land for cultivation in the following year, he shall give notice to the tenant in writing to that effect, and if the tenant complies with the notice shall pay compensation to the tenant for the preparation of the land. If the tenant is unwilling to prepare the land he shall inform the landlord within one month of the receipt of the notice, and the landlord shall be entitled during the year of notice to prepare for cultivation in the following year any land of the tenant which is not under crop.

Board to decide disputes as to compensation.

(7) If any question arises whether compensation for disturbance or compensation for an improvement made by the tenant is payable, or as to the amount of any such compensation, the question shall be referred to a Board: Provided that no claim for compensation shall be heard by a Board unless particulars of the claim have been given by the landlord to the tenant or by the tenant to the landlord within three months from the termination of the tenancy by a notice to quit, or from the date at which the tenant quits the land where there has been no notice to quit.

(8) Where a tenancy is terminated by the landlord on account of the failure of the tenant to pay the rent due on the holding, such rent may be deducted from any compensation payable by the landlord to the tenant under this Section.

Palestine No. 27 of 1929.

6. (1) Where a tenant has cultivated a holding for a period of five years or more, the landlord terminating the tenancy, in addition to giving notice to quit and paying the compensation prescribed in the preceding Section, shall pay to the tenant a sum equal to one year's average annual rent paid by the tenant during the five years preceding the termination of the tenancy, whether such rent was paid in money or in kind, or a portion of the produce of the holding. Right of tenant of long standing to receive further compensation.

(2) The amount of compensation due under this Section shall, in default of agreement, be determined by a Board.

7. A Board shall consist of a District Officer, as President, nominated by the District Commissioner, and two members nominated, with the approval of the District Commissioner, by each of the landlord and the tenant. The two members shall be persons skilled in agriculture. The decisions of the Board in any matter referred to them under Section 3, 5 or 6 hereof shall be subject to the confirmation of a District Commissioner; and when confirmed by him shall be final. Constitution of Board.

8. (1) Where application is made to register a transfer of Miri land on which there are tenants who have received notice of termination of tenancy in accordance with this Ordinance, the Director of the Department of Lands shall not record the transfer in the Land Registers unless he is satisfied that security has been given by the landlord for carrying out any obligations to the tenants under this Ordinance, or unless the purchaser agrees that he will take over the obligations of the former landlord, and that any compensation that has been or shall be found due to the tenants shall be charged on the land. Land not to be transferred until provisions of Ordinance satisfied.

(2) Any compensation agreed to be due or found by a Board to be due to a tenant under this Ordinance shall be charged on the land until the whole of such compensation has been paid. Compensation charged on land.

9. The High Commissioner may make, and when made, may vary or revoke Regulations as to :— Regulations.

(a) the procedure of a Board;

(b) the fees payable to the members of a Board;

(c) any other matter herein requiring regulation.

10. Section 2 of the Transfer of Land Amendment Ordinance No. 2, 1921, is hereby repealed. Repeal.

— 6 —

Palestine No. 27 of 1929.

SCHEDULE.

Tenant's Improvements for which Compensation is payable.

PART I.

Improvements to which consent of landlord is required.

1. Erection, alteration or enlargement of buildings.

2. Making or improvement of roads or bridges.

3. Removal of tree-roots, boulders, stones, or other like obstructions to cultivation.

4. Making or improvement of works of irrigation, water courses, ponds, wells or reservoirs, or works for the application of water-power or for supply of water for agricultural or domestic purposes.

5. Making and renewal of permanent fences and walls.

6. Planting of orchards, vineyards, wind-breaks and hedges.

7. Erection and installation of prime-movers, steam, oil and gas engines, turbines, rams, and wind-mills and water-wheels.

8. Erection and installation of power-driven mills or machinery for the grinding, crushing or treatment of agricultural products.

PART II.

Improvements in respect of which notice to landlord is required.

9. Drainage.

10. Embankments and sluices against floods.

11. Application to land of farmyard manure.

12. Application to land of purchased artificial or other purchased manure.

— 7 —

Palestine No. 27 of 1929.

13. Repairs to buildings, being buildings necessary for the habitation of the tenant or the proper cultivation or working of the holding, other than repairs which the tenant is himself under obligation to execute:

Provided that the tenant before begining to execute any such repairs shall give to the landlord notice in writing of his intention, together with particulars of such repairs, and shall not execute the repairs unless the landlord fails to execute them within a reasonable time after receiving such notice.

31st July, 1929.

H. C. LUKE
Officer Administering the Government.

REGISTRATION OF LAND ORDINANCE, No. 28 OF 1929.

thirty-first day of July, One thousand nine hundred and twenty-nine.

REGISTRATION OF LAND ORDINANCE

No. 28 of 1929.

An Ordinance to provide for the registration in the Land Settlement of prescriptive title to land, and possessory title, and for similar purposes.

BE IT ENACTED by the High Commissioner for Palestine, with the advice of the Advisory Council thereof :-

1. (1) This Ordinance may be cited as the Registration of Land Ordinance, 1929. Short title and application.

(2) This Ordinance shall apply in any settlement area to which the Land Settlement Ordinance, 1928, has been applied, and shall be read together with the provisions of that Ordinance.

2. Where a Settlement Officer is satisfied that land is registered in the name of any person, and that another person has been in possession thereof for such period and under such conditions as will prevent any action for recovery of the land being heard, he shall enter the name of the person in possession in the Schedule of Rights as owner of the land in respect of the interest therein which was held by the person registered as owner : Provided that, where the person in whose name the land is registered opposes the application and the Settlement Officer is satisfied that the person making the application originally obtained possession from the registered owner as tenant or mortgagee, or otherwise than as owner, he shall not be bound to enter the name of the applicant in the Schedule of Rights as owner of the land, or he may enter it subject to such conditions as he thinks fit. Registration where prescriptive title to land is established.

3. Where a Settlement Officer is satisfied that land is registered in the name of any person; and- Registration of possessory title.

(a) that another person is in possession thereof in such circumstances that, if his possession continues for the period prescribed by law, any action for recovery thereof by the registered owner will not be heard thereafter;

(b) that the registered owner cannot be traced or makes no claim to the land;

he may enter the name of the person in possession in the Schedule of Rights as having a possessory title, and shall state the date on which his possession began.

— 2 —

Palestine No. 28 of 1929.

Effect of registration of possessory title.

4. The effect of registration with a possessory title shall be as follows :-

(a) The person previously registered as owner or his heirs shall thereafter be entitled to recover the land by action: Provided that such action is begun within the period prescribed by law.

(b) If action is brought within due time and judgment is given in favour of the registered owner or his heirs and is registered, the registration of any person with a possessory title shall be vacated, and the interest of any person claiming under him shall be deemed to be avoided from the date of registration of the judgment.

(c) The person registered with a possessory title and his successors shall be deemed to be owners of the land and entitled to the revenue thereof until the date of registration of judgment for recovery of the land by the registered owner.

(d) If no action for recovery of the land is brought by the registered owner or his heirs within the period prescribed by law, the Director of Lands, on being satisfied that the person registered with the possessory title, or his successors, are in possession, shall vacate the registration of the registered owner and enter the person registered with the possessory title as the owner of the land. And all rights and interests therein of the person previously registered as owner shall cease and determine.

(e) No disposition or transfer, otherwise than on the death of the registered owner or the person registered with a possessory title, shall operate to create any right to the land, and no entry thereof shall be made in the Land Registers.

Registration as owner of person in possession where no adverse registration of the land.

5. If a Settlement Officer is satisfied -

(a) that land has been in the possession of any person for such period and under such conditions as will prevent any action for recovery thereof being heard, and that no person is registered at the time of the settlement as owner; or

(b) that a person is in possession of land under an unregistered transfer to himself or his predecessor in title made by a person who was in possession at the date of the disposition but was not registered as owner, and that no other person has a registered interest in the land;

— 3 —

Palestine No. 28 of 1929.

he shall enter in the Schedule of Rights the name of the person in possession as owner of the land: Provided that nothing herein shall apply to Mahlul land or Mewat land, or shall derogate from the provisions of Article 78 of the Ottoman Land Code.

6. Nothing herein shall be deemed to affect the right of any person who has a lawful excuse, according to Article 1663 of the Civil Code. to claim any right to land which has been registered in the name of another person on account of possession for the period prescribed by law. Saving for rights of a person who has a lawful excuse.

31st July, 1929.

H. C. LUKE
Officer Administering the Government.

TRANSFER OF LAND AMENDMENT ORDINANCE, No. 30 OF 1929.

The fifteenth day of August, One thousand nine hundred and twenty-nine.

TRANSFER OF LAND AMENDMENT ORDINANCE

No. 30 of 1929.

An Ordinance to amend the Transfer of Land Ordinances.

BE IT ENACTED by the High Commissioner for Palestine, with the advice of the Advisory Council thereof:—

1. This Ordinance may be cited as the Transfer of Land Amendment Ordinance, 1929; and the Transfer of Land Ordinance, 1920 (hereinafter called the Principal Ordinance), the Transfer of Land Ordinance, 1921, the Transfer of Land Amendment Ordinance No. 2, 1921, and this Ordinance, may together be cited as the Transfer of Land Ordinances, 1920-1929. *Short title.*

2. In Section 16 of the Principal Ordinance, the words "The general superintendence and control over all Land Registry Offices in Palestine shall be vested in the Legal Secretary, who, with the sanction of the High Commissioner may from time to time make rules as to any of the following matters, subject to consultation with the Financial Secretary on the subject of fees as in subsection (f) below:" shall be cancelled; and the following words shall be substituted therefor: "The High Commissioner may make Rules as to any of the following matters:" *Amendment of Section 16 of Principal Ordinance.*

3. Any Rules made by the High Commissioner under the Principal Ordinance prior to the date hereof shall be deemed to have been validly made. *Validation of rules made prior to the date of Ordinance.*

15th August, 1929.

H. C. LUKE
Officer Administering the Government.

SURVEY ORDINANCE

No. 48 of 1929.

An Ordinance to regulate the survey of lands and the licensing of surveyors.

BE IT ENACTED by the High Commissioner for Palestine, with the advice of the Advisory Council thereof:-

1. This Ordinance may be cited as the Survey Ordinance, 1929. *Short title.*

2. In this Ordinance:- *Definitions.*

"Director" means the Director of the Department of Surveys.

"Land" includes houses, buildings, and anything fixed in the land.

"Licensed surveyor" means a surveyor licensed under this Ordinance or under any Ordinance repealed hereby.

"Public survey" means any survey directed by the High Commissioner.

"Surveyor" means a Government surveyor or a licensed surveyor.

"Survey mark" includes any trigonometrical station, survey beacon, mark or pole, whether above or below the surface of the ground.

PART I: Licensing of Surveyors.

3. (1) The High Commissioner may, on the advice of the Director, grant licences to persons desiring to practise the profession of surveying, and no person may practise that profession unless he is in possession of a licence. *Licensing of surveyors.*

(2) The grant, cancellation or suspension of any such licence shall be published in the Gazette.

4. (1) Any licensed surveyor who intentionally or through negligence, carelessness or culpable ignorance, makes an incorrect survey or delivers an incorrect plan or diagram of any land, or a plan which does not conform with the Regulations under this Ordinance, or makes an untrue report or memorandum of any survey, or fails to comply with the provisions of *Suspension or cancellation of licence.*

Palestine No. 48 of 1929.

any Regulations hereunder, or is convicted of any offence involving moral turpitude, shall be liable, on the report of the Director or on the complaint of any person aggrieved, to have his licence as a surveyor cancelled by Order of the High Commissioner, or suspended for such time as may be fixed by him; provided that no Order of cancellation or suspension shall be made unless the surveyor complained against has had an opportunity of being heard in his own defence.

(2) Such surveyor shall forthwith deliver the cancelled or suspended licence to the Director and shall be required to repay any fees which he may have received from any person in consideration of any such survey plan or diagram, if so ordered by the High Commissioner.

Plans made by unqualified persons not to be admitted in Land Registry or as evidence.

5. No map, plan, or diagram of land purporting to have been prepared after the date of the commencement of this Ordinance or of the Land Surveyors Ordinance repealed hereby shall be receivable at the Land Registry or admitted in evidence in any Court unless it has been prepared and signed by a surveyor or is a copy of such map, plan, or diagram certified as being a true copy by a surveyor; provided always that any Court for good cause shown may admit in evidence any map, plan, or diagram not made by a surveyor.

Penalties and disqualification.

6. (1) Any person who practises or professes to practise as a surveyor, not being the holder of a licence to practise, shall be punishable with a fine not exceeding £P. 50 in respect of each transaction in which he was engaged, and shall not be entitled to sue in any Court for remuneration in respect of a survey plan or map made by him.

(2) Any surveyor who fails to deliver up a licence which has been cancelled or suspended to the Director within 14 days of the Order of cancellation or suspension shall be liable on conviction to a fine not exceeding £P. 20.

Regulations.

7. The High Commissioner in Council may make Regulations:-

(a) Prescribing the conditions on which licences may be granted, the form of licences to be granted, and the fees payable in respect thereof;

(b) As to the method in which surveys shall be executed and plans shall be made for registration purposes.

(c) As to the filing by surveyors of plans for registration purposes.

— 3 —

Palestine No. 48 of 1929.

(d) As to any other matter requiring regulation under this part of the Ordinance.

PART II: Public Surveys.

8. (1) For the purposes of any public survey the Director or any surveyor authorised by him may enter upon any land with such assistants as may be required, and may affix or set up or place thereon or therein any survey mark and do all things necessary for such survey. Powers in relation to public surveys.

(2) The surveyor shall, when practicable, give reasonable notice to the owner or occupier of the land of his intention to enter thereon. A notice posted or circulated by a Mukhtar of a town or village not less than 24 hours prior to the entry shall be reasonable notice.

9. Any surveyor may, for the purpose of surveying any land which he is employed to survey, enter on and pass over any land, whether private or public, causing as little inconvenience to the owner or occupier of the land as possible. Power of surveyor to enter upon land.

10. (1) A District Commissioner, a Settlement Officer appointed under the Land Settlement Ordinance, 1928, or the Director or any surveyor authorised by the Director may by written Order require any person who owns, occupies, or is interested in any land or any land abutting thereon, or any person employed on or connected with the management or cultivation of such land, or any person in whose possession or power any documents relating to the boundaries of such land are alleged to be : — Powers of District Commissioner, Settlement Officer and surveyor with regard to demarcation of boundaries, etc.

(a) to attend personally or by agent before him at such time and place as may be stated in the notice for the purpose of pointing out the boundaries of such land, or of rendering such aid as may be necessary in setting up or repairing boundary marks or affording such assistance and information as may be needed for the purpose of demarcation;

(b) to produce any document in his possession or power relating to the boundaries of the land.

(2) Every such person upon whom such notice may be served shall be legally bound to attend as required by the notice and to do any of the things mentioned therein.

Palestine No. 48 of 1929.

(3) Any of the officers mentioned in subsection (1) hereof may by written Order require the owner or occupier of any land, within a reasonable time to be prescribed in the Order:-

(a) to demarcate the land, and for the purpose of demarcation to erect such boundary marks as the officer may direct;

(b) to clear any boundary or other line which it may be necessary to clear for the purpose of demarcation by cutting down or removing any trees, bush, fences, or growing crops.

(4) Compensation shall be paid by the Government to the owner of any trees cut or damaged in the exercise of the powers granted by this Section. The compensation shall be assessed by the District Commissioner, and in case of any dispute concerning the sufficiency of the amount tendered shall be finally determined by a Magistrate on application made to him by either of the disputing parties. No compensation, however, shall be payable for loss caused to the owner or occupier of land through the occupation of the land, or through clearance of boughs or hedges or of trees other than fruit trees.

(5) If it is necessary to provide labour or otherwise assist in the demarcation of the land, and if the owner or occupier fails to comply with the notice and it is necessary to employ hired labour for these objects, the officer may assess and recover from such owner or occupier the cost of the labour.

Penalty for removing survey marks.

11. Any unauthorised person who shall wilfully obliterate, remove, or injure any survey mark or any boundary mark affixed, set up, or placed for the purpose of any public survey shall, on conviction be liable to a fine not exceeding £P. 50 or imprisonment not exceeding three months or both penalties, and in addition may be ordered to pay the cost of the mark obliterated or removed, and the cost of the survey involved in establishing such mark, or the cost of repairing the mark damaged.

Duty of owner and occupier to maintain boundary and survey marks.

12. (1) The owner or occupier of any land, the boundaries of which have been defined by a public survey, shall maintain and repair all boundary marks erected.

(2) The owner and occupier of any land on or in which any survey mark has been affixed, set up, or placed shall preserve such survey mark, and shall forthwith report to the District Officer of the Sub-District if the mrrk shall be obliterated, removed, or injured, or shall require repair. If the mark is placed upon undivided village lands or public lands,

Section 13: 1930

COLLECTION OF TAXES (AMENDMENT) ORDINANCE, No. 7 OF 1930.

J.R. Chancellor.

The thirty-first day of March, One thousand nine hundred and thirty.

COLLECTION OF TAXES (AMENDMENT) ORDINANCE

No. 7 of 1930.

An Ordinance to amend the Collection of Taxes Ordinance, 1929.

No. 26 of 1929.

BE IT ENACTED by the High Commissioner for Palestine, with the advice of the Advisory Council thereof:-

1. This Ordinance may be cited as the Collection of Taxes (Amendment) Ordinance, 1930; and the Collection of Taxes Ordinance, No. 26 of 1929, (hereinafter called the Principal Ordinance) and this Ordinance may together be cited as the Collection of Taxes Ordinances, 1929-1930.

Short Title.

2. Section 5(1) of the Principal Ordinance shall be repealed, and the following shall be substituted therefor:

Amendment of Section 5 (1) of Principal Ordinance.

"5. (1) The tax collector shall demand immediate payment of the sum named therein from the person by whom it is payable, and, upon his refusal or neglect to pay, he shall enter the house or lands of the defaulter and seize such of his goods as he shall deem sufficient, and, subject to the provisions hereof, keep the goods so seized for the space of two days at the cost and charge of the person in default. If such person does not pay the sum due together with the costs and charges of seizure within the two days, the goods shall be sold by auction in accordance with an Order issued by the District Officer: provided that if the goods seized are perishable goods, they may be sold by auction forthwith by order of the District Officer. The proceeds of the sale shall be used for the payment of the sum due and the costs and expenses of execution, and the surplus, if any, shall be restored to the owner."

31st March, 1930.

J. R. CHANCELLOR
High Commissioner.

LAND SETTLEMENT (AMENDMENT) ORDINANCE, No. 18 OF 1930.

The thirty-first day of July, One thousand nine hundred and thirty.

LAND SETTLEMENT (AMENDMENT) ORDINANCE

No. 18 of 1930.

An Ordinance to amend the Land Settlement Ordinance, 1928.

No. 9 of 1928.

BE IT ENACTED by the High Commissioner for Palestine, with the advice of the Advisory Council thereof:—

1. This Ordinance may be cited as the Land Settlement (Amendment) Ordinance, 1930; and the Land Settlement Ordinance, No. 9 of 1928 (hereinafter referred to as the Principal Ordinance) and this Ordinance may together be cited as the Land Settlement Ordinances, 1928-1930.

Short Title.

2. In Section 2 of the Principal Ordinance —

Amendment of Section 2 of the Principal Ordinance.

(a) the definition of "Village" shall be deleted and the following shall be substituted therefor:—

" 'Village' includes a tribal area and any village lands within or abutting on a municipal area".

(b) The following definition shall be added:—

" 'Village Musha' means the lands of a village or of a section of a village held in undivided ownership and periodically distributed for cultivation among the inhabitants of the village or of a section thereof".

3. (1) The first sentence of Section 6 of the Principal Ordinance shall be amended as follows:—

Amendment of Section 6 of the Principal Ordinance.

"Save as provided herein, no action concerning rights to land in any village in which notification of settlement has been published shall be entered in any Land Court or Civil Court until the Schedule of Rights has been published in accordance with Section 32 hereof".

(2) The following subsection shall be added to Section 6 of the Principal Ordinance as subsection (2) thereof:—

(2) In any village in which notification of the settlement has been published, no application shall be entertained under the Correction of Land Registers Ordinance, 1926, for the correction of the existing registers. Any application entered before the notification is published may either be withdrawn, or, if not withdrawn, shall, if possible, be decided before the settlement is begun.

"Stay of applications under Correction of Land Registers Ordinance, 1926.

— 2 —

Palestine No. 18 of 1930.

Amendment of Section 9 of the Principal Ordinance.

4. (1) Paragraph (b) of Section 9 of the Principal Ordinance shall be deleted and the following shall be substituted therefor:-

"(b) order any claimant or any person whose name is included in the Schedule of Rights, or the Partition Schedule hereinafter mentioned, to mark out the boundaries of the land affected by his claim or specified in such Schedule in such manner and before such date as he may direct; and in default of compliance, may cause the boundaries to be marked at the expense of such person".

(2) The following words shall be added at the end of paragraph (c) of the said Section:-

"and may impose a fine of £P.2 in default of compliance with any summons or order".

Replacement of Section 16 of the Principal Ordinance.
Claims.

5. Section 16 of the Principal Ordinance shall be repealed, and the following shall be substituted therefor:-

"16. (1) After publication of the settlement notice in any village, every claimant to land in the village shall appear at such time and in such place as the Settlement Officer may direct, and shall submit a memorandum of his claim in the form prescribed by Regulation.

(2) The claimant may appear in person or by an agent authorised in writing or appointed before the Settlement Officer, and shall produce to the Settlement Officer any instruments affecting the land which he claims. When an agent so appointed is a member of the family of the person appointing him and is not an advocate, Stamp Duty shall not be payable on the document authorising him to appear before the Settlement Officer.

(3) If any claimant fails to attend in person or by an authorised agent, the demarcation, registration or any other operation of the settlement may proceed in his absence.

(4) Where one or more of the co-owners of a parcel, or one or more of the heirs of a deceased claimant or owner, or of a group of heirs which has a separate interest from another group, appear, his or their appearance shall be deemed to be the appearance of all the co-owners, or heirs or of the group, as the case may be, unless the Settlement Officer otherwise directs".

Amendment of Section 22 (1) (c) of the Principal Ordinance.

6. Section 22 (1) (c) of the Principal Ordinance shall be deleted, and the following shall be substituted therefor:-

Palestine No. 18 of 1930.

"(c) demarcate any existing road or path, and indicate any existing right of way or any new right of way to a public road in favour of any owner whose parcel is surrounded by other parcels".

7. (1) The following subsection shall be added to Section 27 as subsection (8) thereof:— *Addition to Section 27 of the Principal Ordinance.*

"(8) The Settlement Officer shall notify his decision in the case of any disputed claim to the parties at the hearing, or if a claimant is not present or represented at the hearing, shall send him written notification thereof".

(2) The following Section shall be inserted after Section 27 of the Principal Ordinance as Section 27A:—

"27A. (1) Notwithstanding anything in the preceding Sections, the Commissioner of Lands may by notice exclude from the Schedule of Claims the sites of houses of small value in a village and the buildings thereon. Where such notice is issued, the Settlement Officer shall draw up, in consultation with the Village Settlement Committee, a separate schedule of the sites and buildings, showing the reputed owners and such other particulars as he shall think fit. *Exclusion of sites of houses of small value from the Schedules of Claims.*

(2) Any person claiming to be the owner of a site and of a building thereon shall produce to the Settlement Officer any instrument showing the registration in his name of the parcel in the existing registers.

(3) The schedule of village sites and buildings shall be posted in the same way as the Schedule of Claims; but the Settlement Officer shall not investigate claims to parcels included in such Schedule, save that, where two or more persons claim that they are the owners of one parcel, he shall determine the claim".

8. In Section 28 (3) of the Principal Ordinance, the words "shall be registered in the name of the Government" shall be substituted for the words "shall belong absolutely to the Government". *Amendment of Section 28 (3) of the Principal Ordinance.*

9. The following shall be added to Section 30 of the Principal Ordinance:— *Addition to Section 30 of the Principal Ordinance.*

"Provided that, in the case of sites of houses of small value in a village and the buildings thereon, it shall not be necessary for the Settlement Officer to record in the Schedule of Rights all the particulars above mentioned, but he shall record the name of the reputed owner which appears in the

— 4 —

Palestine No. 18 of 1930.

schedule of sites and buildings referred to in Section 27A. hereof; and where he has investigated a disputed claim of ownership to a site or building thereon, or where a claimant has produced an instrument of registration of a site or building in the existing registers, he shall record the ownership of the parcel."

Addition to Section 32 of the Principal Ordinance.

10. The following subsection shall be added to Section 32 as subsection (3) thereof:—

"(3) During the period of 15 days in which the Schedule of Rights is posted, the Settlement Officer may, on application of any person claiming a right to land, revise his decision in the Schedule of Rights, provided that due notice is given to any person affected by the application for revision".

Amendment of Section 33 of the Principal Ordinance.

11. In Section 33 of the Principal Ordinance paragraph (a) shall be deleted.

Replacement of Section 34 of the Principal Ordinance.

12. Section 34 of the Principal Ordinance shall be repealed and the following shall be substituted therefor:—

"Closing of existing Land Registers.

34. No fresh entries relating to land in a village shall be made in the existing Land Registers after the publication of the Schedule of Claims as to the land of the village or any part of the village; provided that a Settlement Officer may at any time issue a notice under Section 8 hereof directing that no fresh entries shall be made in the existing Registers from the date prescribed in such notice."

Replacement of Sections 49 to 51 of the Principal Ordinance.

13. Sections 49 to 51 of the Principal Ordinance shall be repealed, and the following shall be substituted therefor:—

"When partition may be effected.

49. No partition in a settlement area of any parcel owned by two or more co-owners or of village musha' shall be effected save as provided in Section 50 to 55 hereof. No partition shall be effected by the Settlement Officer until the period within which application may be made for leave to appeal from the decision of the Settlement Officer recorded in the Schedule of Right has elapsed, or, if leave to appeal has been granted to a person whose claim to a share in the undivided parcel or village musha' has been rejected by the Settlement Officer, until judgment in the appeal has been given in the Land Court."

"Conditions of partition.

50. Subject to the provisions of the previous Section, the Settlement Officer may—

(a) upon the application of any person registered as the owner of a share in undivided land, divide such share from the remainder of the undivided land unless in his opinion division would prejudice the use of the land, and enter the

— 5 —

Palestine No. 18 of 1930.

divided parcels in the Schedule of Rights; provided that application for such partition shall be made on the submission of the claim to the share in accordance with Section 16 hereof;

(b) upon the application of the owners of not less than two thirds of the shares of the village musha' recorded in the Schedule of Rights, divide the musha' among the owners of the shares so recorded, and enter the parcels in the Schedule of Partition. Such Schedule shall be posted for a period of 15 days; and at the end of that period the Settlement Officer shall send it to the Registrar for entry of the parcels in the new Register."

"51. Notwithstanding any provision in the preceding Sections, the High Commissioner may at any time direct that the partition of any land held in undivided ownership shall be carried out, if such partition is deemed to be in the public interest." High Commissioner may order partition in public interest.

14. Section 52 (1) of the Principal Ordinance shall be repealed and the following be substituted therefor :- Replacement of Section 52(1) of the Principal Ordinance.

"(1) Partition shall be carried out in accordance with an agreement made between the owners of not less than two-thirds of the shares included in the Schedule of Rights, if approved by the Settlement Officer."

15. Section 53 of the Principal Ordinance shall be repealed, and the following shall be substituted therefor :- Replacement of Section 53 of the Principal Ordinance.

"53. (1) Where, after posting of the Schedule of Rights or the Schedule of Partition a person establishes his right by action to a share in a parcel of undivided land, the Land Court may order the rectification of the new register, or that compensation shall be paid to such person by the other co-owners in such manner as the Court may direct. Provided that in the case of village musha', if the right so established affects the total number of shares in the musha', the Land Court shall not order the rectification of the Schedule of Rights or the Schedule of Partition or of the new register, but shall order compensation to be paid. Rectification of Register or compensation to owner who establishes title to a share after posting of Schedule.

(2) Where the Settlement Officer has accepted the parcellation of village musha' in accordance with the proviso to Section 23 hereof, and prior to the posting of the Schedule of Rights or of the Schedule of Partition a person establishes his right to a share in the village musha', or where after the partition of village musha' has been carried out, but prior to the posting of the Schedule of Partition, a person establishes his right to a share in the musha', the Settlement Officer may award him compensation which shall be paid in such manner as he thinks fit.

— 6 —

Palestine No. 18 of 1930.

(3) Compensation in all cases shall be charged upon the land of the owners of the shares until it is fully paid."

Replacement of section 56(1) of the Principal Ordinance.

16. Section 56(1) of the Principal Ordinance shall be repealed, and the following shall be substituted therefor:—

Appeal from Settlement Officer.

"(1) No Appeal shall lie from the decision of a Settlement Officer as to any right to land save with the leave of such officer or of the President of a Land Court. An application for leave to appeal shall be made by a petition in writing within thirty days of the notification of the decision of the Settlement Officer in a disputed claim, and shall be submitted to the Settlement Officer. Application for leave to appeal may be made also by a claimant who is aggrieved by the decision of the Settlement Officer in an undisputed claim, within fifteen days from the date of the posting of the Schedule of Rights or the Partition Schedule containing the decision which is the subject of appeal. If the Settlement Officer refuses the application, the applicant may within fifteen days of such refusal refer it to the President of the Land Court stating the grounds for the appeal."

Amendment of Section 57(1)(c) of the Principal Ordinance.

17. In Section 57(1)(c), the words "on the land" shall be deleted.

Amendment of Section 59 of the Principal Ordinance.

18. In Section 59 of the Principal Ordinance, the following words shall be added after the words "obtained by fraud":—

"or that a right recorded in the existing Registers has been omitted or incorrectly set out in the Register."

Replacement of Section 61.

19. Section 61 of the Principal Ordinance shall be repealed, and the following shall be substituted therefor:—

"Correction of rerors.

61. (1) A Settlement Officer, or in his absence the Commissioner of Lands, may authorise a Registrar to correct any clerical errors in the Register, and to introduce clerical amendments or additions thereto, provided that all such changes are signed by the Registrar, and that a separate record is kept of corrections.

(2) Where after the publication of the Schedule of Rights it is established that a right recorded in the existing Registers has been omitted from the Schedule or incorrectly entered therein, the Settlement Officer may authorise the Registrar to make the corrections at any time before the completion of the registration of the land of the village in accordance with the Schedule. Notice of the correction shall be given by the Settlement Officer to the owner of the land and the holder of the right.

— 7 —

Palestine No. 18 of 1930.

(3) Where a discrepancy is found after the registration of a settlement under this Ordinance :-

(a) between the boundaries or area of the parcels as appearing on the land and those shown on the survey plan; or

(b) between the area of any parcel as furnished by fresh survey, the area shown in the Register, and the area found by calculation from the survey plan;

the particulars which are recorded in the survey plan shall prevail; provided that, if it is established by investigation of the Director of Surveys that there was an error or omission in the original survey, the Commissioner of Lands shall authorise the Director of Surveys to amend the survey plan and the Registrar to make the corresponding amendments in the Register; and provided further that, if the area shown in the Register was determined by a judgment of the Court, the amendment of the survey plan and of the Register shall be made only on an Order of the Court."

20. In Section 62 (3), the words "a District Commissioner" shall be substituted for the words "a Settlement Officer." *Amendment of Section 62(3) of the Principal Ordinance.*

21. Section 63 of the Principal Ordinance shall be repealed, and the following shall be substituted therefor :- *Replacement of Section 63.*

63. Where application is made to the Settlement Officer for partition of a share in accordance with the provisions of Section 50(a) hereof, or for partition of village musha' within one month of the date of the posting of the final Schedule of Rights in the village in which such musha' is situated, no fee shall be charged on account of the partition, other than the fees due on the survey and registration of the shares." *"Reduction of fees where partition applied for in prescribed time.*

22. Section 64(2) of the Principal Ordinance shall be repealed, and the following shall be substituted therefor :- *Replacement of Section 64(2) of the Principal Ordinance.*

"(2) Where any right to land registered in the existing Registers in the name of the claimant is recorded in the Schedule of Rights subject to modification, the Settlement Officer may waive in whole or in part any fee which would otherwise be due upon the registration of such right. A fee shall be charged on account of survey unless the land has been previously surveyed by the Director of Surveys, and a fee was paid therefor, and no fresh survey has been required in the settlement."

31st July, 1930.

S. S. DAVIS
Officer Administering the Government.

Section 14: 1931

PROTECTION OF CULTIVATORS (AMENDMENT) ORDINANCE, No. 3 OF 1931

J.R. Chancellor.

is twenty-ninth day of May, one thousand nine hundred and thirty

PROTECTION OF CULTIVATORS (AMENDMENT) ORDINANCE

No. 3 of 1931

An Ordinance to amend the Protection of Cultivators Ordinance, 1929, and to provide for the better protection of the tenants and occupants of agricultural land

---

BE IT ENACTED by the High Commissioner for Palestine, with the advice of the Advisory Council thereof:-

1. This Ordinance may be cited as the Protection of Cultivators (Amendment) Ordinance, 1931, and the Protection of Cultivators Ordinance, 1929, (hereinafter referred to as the Principal Ordinance) and this Ordinance may together be cited as the Protection of Cultivators Ordinances, 1929 and 1931. *Short Title.*

2. Section 2 of the Principal Ordinance is hereby amended by the deletion of the definition of the term "tenant" and by the substitution of the following:- *Amendment of Section 2 of the Principal Ordinance.*

" "Tenant" means a person who is cultivating and has cultivated a holding for a period of not less than two years under an agreement expressed or implied, with the landlord, and pays the landlord a rent fixed either in money or in kind, or in portion of the produce of the land, notwithstanding that he may have occupied the holding under successive agreements with different landlords and that the period of any one of such agreements may have been less than two years.

It includes a person who is hired by the landlord to do agricultural work and receives as his remuneration a portion of the produce of the holding which he cultivates, provided that he has been cultivating that holding continuously for a period of not less than two years.

It includes also the heirs of the tenant dying during the period of tenancy and, where the tenant has acquired a holding by succession, it includes his predecessor in title, provided that in each case the holding has been cultivated by the successive tenants continuously for a period of not less than two years.

It does not include a person who is hired to do agricultualr work and who receives as remuneration a money wage or portion of the produce but does not cultivate a holding."

3. Section 3 of the Principal Ordinance is hereby amended as follows:- *Amendment of Section 3 of the Principal Ordinance.*

Orders-in-Council, Ordinances and Public Notices

Palestine No. 3 of 1931

The words "The landlord shall send a copy of the notice to the District Commissioner" shall be deleted at the end of subsection (3); and the following subsection shall be added to the said Section:—

"Copy of notice of termination of tenancy to be given to District Commissioner.

(4) Every notice given under this Section shall be void and of no effect unless a copy thereof be served by the landlord on the District Commissioner of the District in which the land is situate within 30 days after the notice has been served on the tenant, and unless the notice contain a declaration by the landlord that its object is to terminate the tenancy in order that the land may be transferred with vacant possession if such be the object of the notice."

Addition of new Section.

4. The following Section shall be inserted in the Principal Ordinance as Section 3 (A).

"Order of Eviction not to be made unless Court satisfied as to provision for tenants and occupiers.

3 (A) (1) No Court or Judge shall make an Order for the eviction of a tenant pursuant to notice given under this Ordinance, unless the landlord satisfies the Court or Judge:—

(i) that the tenancy has been validly determined under this Ordinance, and,

(ii) unless the tenancy has been determined

(a) for failure to pay the rent within a reasonable time from the due date of payment, such time to be determined, in case of dispute, in accordance with the procedure laid down in Section 3 (2) of this Ordinance, or

(b) for failure to cultivate the land in accordance with the rules of good husbandry as defined in Section 2 of this Ordinance, or

(c) in virtue of an Order of Bankruptcy,

that the High Commissioner is satisfied that equivalent provision has been secured towards the livelihood of the tenant.

Provided that if an Eviction Order is made the tenant shall not be entitled to the compensation payable under Section 6 of this Ordinance.

Palestine No. 3 of 1931.

(2) No Court or Judge shall make an Order for the eviction of a person who is exercising and has exercised continuously for a period of 5 years a practice of grazing or watering animals or the cutting of wood or reeds or other beneficial occupation of similar character on the land whether by right, custom, usage or sufferance, unless the landlord satisfies the Court or Judge that the High Commissioner is satisfied that equivalent provision has been secured towards the livelihood of such person."

5. The following Section shall be inserted in the Principal Ordinance as Section 3 (B) :- _{Addition of new Section.}

"Payment of rent between termination of tenancy and eviction.

3 (B). If an order for eviction is made, rent shall be payable in respect of the period between the date of valid termination of the tenancy and the date of eviction at the rate payable at the former date as though the tenancy had continued until the date of eviction."

6. Section 4 of the Principal Ordinance is hereby repealed and the following substituted therefor:- _{Repeal of Section 4 of the Principal Ordinance.}

"No increase in rent without the sanction of the Board.

4. The landlord shall not increase the rent of a holding unless he shall first have obtained the sanction of the Board who shall have power, after hearing the landlord and the tenant and after taking such evidence and making such enquiries as they think fit, to decide by what amount, if any, the rent shall be increased. The increased rent shall not come into force before one year from the first day of October following the decision of the Board."

7. The amendments of the Principal Ordinance made by Sections 2, 3 and 6 of this Ordinance, and the Sections inserted in the Principal Ordinance as Sections 3 (A) and 3 (B) shall only remain in force until the twenty-eighth day of May, one thousand nine hundred and thirty two. _{Duration of the Ordinance.}

M. A. YOUNG
Officer Administering the Government

29th May, 1931.

Section 15: 1932

LAND DISPUTES (POSSESSION) ORDINANCE, No. 12 OF 1932

Arthur Wauchope

The seventeenth day of March, One thousand nine hundred and thirty-two.

LAND DISPUTES (POSSESSION) ORDINANCE

No. 12 of 1932

AN ORDINANCE TO ENABLE DISTRICT COMMISSIONERS TO MAKE ORDERS AS TO POSSESSION OF LAND CONCERNING WHICH A DISPUTE LIKELY TO CAUSE A BREACH OF THE PEACE EXISTS

BE IT ENACTED by the High Commissioner for Palestine, with the advice of the Advisory Council thereof:—

1. This Ordinance may be cited as the Land Disputes (Possession) Ordinance, 1932. *Short Title.*

2.—(1) Whenever a District Commissioner is satisfied from a police report or other information that a dispute likely to cause a breach of the peace exists concerning any land or water or the boundaries thereof within his District, he shall make an order in writing, stating the grounds of his being so satisfied, and requiring the parties concerned in such dispute to attend before him in person or by representative, within a time to be fixed by him and to put in written statements of their respective claims with regard to the fact of actual possession of the subject of dispute. *Procedure where dispute concerning land, etc., is likely to cause breach of peace.*

(2) For the purposes of this Section the expression "land or water" includes buildings, crops or other produce of land, and the rents or profits of any such property.

(3) A copy of the order shall be served in manner provided by Sub-section 10 upon such person or persons as the District Commissioner may direct, and at least one copy shall be published by being affixed to some conspicuous place at or near the subject of dispute.

(4) The District Commissioner shall then, without any reference to the merits or the claims of any such parties to a right to possess the subject of dispute, peruse the statements so put in, hear the parties, receive all such evidence as may be produced by them respectively, consider the effect of such evidence, take such further evidence (if any) and make such inspection (if any) as he thinks necessary, and, if possible, decide whether any and which of the parties was at the date of the order before mentioned in actual possession of the said subject of dispute: *Inquiry as to possession.*

Provided that, if it appears to the District Commissioner that any party has within two months next before the date of such order been forcibly dispossessed, he may treat the party so dispossessed as if he had been in possession at such date:

Provided also, that, if the District Commissioner considers the case one of emergency, he may at any time appoint a manager of the subject of dispute in the manner prescribed in Section 3 pending his decision under this Section.

Palestine No. 12 of 1932

(5) Nothing in this Section shall preclude any party so required to attend, or any other person interested, from showing that no such dispute as aforesaid exists or has existed; and in such case the District Commissioner shall cancel his said order, and all further proceedings thereon shall be stayed, but, subject to such cancellation, the order of the District Commissioner under Sub-section (1) shall be final.

Party in possession to retain possession until legally evicted.

(6) If the District Commissioner decides that one of the parties was or should under the first proviso to Sub-section (4) be treated as being in actual possession of the subject of dispute he shall issue an order declaring such party to be entitled to possession thereof until evicted therefrom in due course of law, and forbidding all disturbance of such possession until such eviction and when he proceeds under the first proviso to Sub-section (4) he may restore to possession the party forcibly dispossessed. Any order made under this Sub-section shall describe the boundaries of the subject of dispute either by a verbal description or by reference to a plan or to boundary marks affixed to the subject of dispute or in such other manner as the District Commissioner shall consider sufficient to enable the parties to the dispute to ascertain on the land the boundaries of the subject of dispute provided that a survey shall not be essential before an order under this Sub-section is made:

Provided that the District Commissioner may withdraw the said order at any time if he is satisfied that there is no longer any likelihood of a breach of the peace in regard to the subject of dispute.

(7) When any party to any such proceeding dies, the District Commissioner may cause any such one or more of the heirs of the deceased or such other persons as he shall appoint to represent the deceased to be made a party to the proceedings and shall thereupon continue the inquiry.

(8) If the District Commissioner is of opinion that any crop or other produce of the property, the subject of dispute in proceedings under this Section pending before him, is subject to speedy and natural decay, he may make an order for the proper custody or sale of such property, and, upon the completion of the inquiry, shall make such order for the disposal of such property or the sale proceeds thereof as he thinks fit.

(9) The District Commissioner may, if he thinks fit, at any stage of the proceedings under this Section, on the application of either party, issue a summons to any witness directing him to attend or to produce any document or thing.

(10) Proceedings under this Ordinance shall be deemed to be proceedings before a Magistrate as regards taking evidence on

— 3 —

Palestine No. 12 of 1933

oath, service of orders, summonses and other documents, enforcement of orders and other like matters but no appeal shall lie against any order by the District Commissioner under this Ordinance.

(11) An order made under Sub-section (6) shall prevent the alienation of the land which is the subject of dispute until a competent Court has determined the rights of the parties thereto or the order of the District Commissioner has been withdrawn and a copy of the order or of the judgment of the Court or notice of the withdrawal of the order shall be served on the Registrar of Lands who shall cause a note thereof respectively to be made in the land register.

3.—(1) If the District Commissioner decides that none of the parties was, at the date of the order referred to in Section 2 (1), in actual possession of the subject of dispute or is unable to satisfy himself as to which of them was, at such date, in actual possession of the subject of dispute, he may order that a person to be named in the order shall manage the subject of dispute until a competent Court has determined the rights of the parties thereto, or the person entitled to the possession thereof: *Power to appoint a manager of the subject of dispute.*

Provided that the District Commissioner may withdraw the said order at any time if he is satisfied that there is no longer any likelihood of a breach of the peace in regard to the subject of dispute.

(2) An order under Sub-section (1) shall prevent the alienation of the land which is the subject of dispute until a competent Court has determined the rights of the parties thereto or the order of the District Commissioner has been withdrawn and a copy of the order or of the judgment of the Court or notice of the withdrawal of the order shall be served on the Registrar of Lands who shall cause a note thereof respectively to be made in the land register.

(3) In the event of a receiver of the property, the subject of dispute, being subsequently appointed by any Court, possession shall be made over to him by the person appointed by the District Commissioner under Sub-section (1) who shall thereupon be discharged.

4.—(1) Whenever a District Commissioner is satisfied from a police report or other information that a dispute likely to cause a breach of the peace exists regarding any alleged right of user of any land or water for grazing, cutting wood or reeds, watering animals, irrigation, fishing or other like purposes *Disputes concerning user of immovable property for grazing, etc.*

Palestine No. 12 of 1932

(whether such right be claimed as a servitude or otherwise) within his District he may make an order in writing stating the grounds of his being so satisfied and requiring the parties concerned in such dispute to attend before him in person or by representative within a time to be fixed by him and to put in written statements of their respective claims, and shall there after inquire into the matter in the manner provided in Section 2, and the provisions of that Section shall, as far as may be, be applicable in the case of such inquiry.

(2) If it appears to the District Commissioner that such user is in fact practised he may make an order prohibiting any interference with the exercise of such practice until a competent Court has decided whether a right to such user exists:

Provided that no such order shall be made where the user is practised at all times of the year, unless such user has been practised within three months next before the institution of the inquiry, or where the user is practised only at particular seasons or on particular occasions, unless the user has been during the last of such seasons or on the last of such occasions practised before such institution.

(3) If it appears to the District Commissioner that such user has not been practised as aforesaid, he may make an order prohibiting any exercise of the alleged practice until a competent Court has decided whether a right to such user exists.

Local inquiry.
5.—(1) Whenever a local inquiry is necessary for the purpose of this Ordinance, the District Commissioner may depute any public officer to make the inquiry, and may furnish him with such written instructions as may seem necessary for his guidance, and may declare by whom the whole or any part of the necessary expenses of the inquiry shall be paid.

(2) The report of the person so deputed may be read is evidence in the case.

Order as to costs.
(3) When any costs have been incurred by any party to a proceeding under this Ordinance, the District Commissioner making an order under Section 2, Section 3 or Section 4 may direct by whom such costs shall be paid, whether by such party or by any other party to the proceeding, and whether in whole or in part or proportion. Such costs may include any expenses incurred in respect of witnesses, and of advocates' fees, which the District Commissioner may consider reasonable.

Palestine No. 12 of 1932

6. Nothing in this Ordinance shall enable a District Commissioner to override or vary an Order by a competent Court or a Chief Execution Officer in virtue of which one of the parties appearing before the District Commissioner in proceedings under this Ordinance shall be entitled to possession of the subject of dispute.

<small>District Commissioner not to have jurisdiction under the Ordinance if a Court or Chief Execution Officer has made an order.</small>

17th March, 1932.

A. G. WAUCHOPE
High Commissioner

PROTECTION OF CULTIVATORS (AMENDMENT) ORDINANCE (No.1), No. 16 OF 1932

The twenty-seventh day of May, One thousand nine hundred and thirty-two.

PROTECTION OF CULTIVATORS (AMENDMENT) ORDINANCE (No. 1),
No. 16 of 1932

AN ORDINANCE FURTHER TO AMEND THE PROTECTION OF CULTIVATORS ORDINANCE, 1929

BE IT ENACTED by the High Commissioner for Palestine with the advice of the Advisory Council thereof:—

1. This Ordinance may be cited as the Protection of Cultivators (Amendment) Ordinance (No. 1), 1932, and shall be read as one with the Protection of Cultivators Ordinance, 1929, (hereinafter called the Principal Ordinance), and the Protection of Cultivators (Amendment) Ordinance, 1931.

   Short Title.
   No. 27 of 1929.
   No. 3 of 1931.

2. Section 2 of the Principal Ordinance is hereby amended as follows:—

   Amendment of Section 2 of Principal Ordinance.

   (a) There shall be added in the first line thereof after the word "Ordinance" the words "unless the context otherwise requires".

   (b) The following proviso shall be added to the definition of "Holding" therein:— "provided that where a tenant has been moved by the landlord from one plot of land to another the tenant shall be deemed to remain in occupation of the same holding".

3. Section 2 of the Principal Ordinance is hereby amended by the addition of the following paragraph to the definition of "Tenant" (as set out in Section 2 of the Protection of Cultivators (Amendment) Ordinance, 1931) between the first and second paragraphs:—

   Amendment of Section 2 of Principal Ordinance.

   "It includes a sub-tenant".

4. Section 3(A) of the Principal Ordinance (as set out in Section 4 of the Protection of Cultivators (Amendment) Ordinance, 1931) is hereby amended as follows:—

   Amendment of Section 3(A) of Principal Ordinance.

   (a) by the substitution of the words "Court, Judge or Execution Officer" for the words "Court or Judge" wherever appearing therein.

   (b) The following paragraph shall be added to Sub-section (2),

   "Nothing in this Sub-section contained shall be deemed to authorise any person to enter upon any land save for the purpose of exercising the practice which he has exercised in the past".

— 2 —

Palestine No. 16 of 1932

Continuation of certain amendments of Principal Ordinance.

5. Notwithstanding anything contained in the Protection of Cultivators (Amendment) Ordinance, 1931, the amendments of and the additions to, the Principal Ordinance made by that Ordinance and the amendments of the Principal Ordinance made by this Ordinance shall remain in force until the twenty-eighth day of May, 1933.

A. G. WAUCHOPE
High Commissioner

27th May, 1932.

EXPROPRIATION OF LAND (AMENDMENT) ORDINANCE, No. 24 OF 1932

Arthur Wauchope

The thirtieth day of June, One thousand nine hundred and thirty-two.

EXPROPRIATION OF LAND (AMENDMENT) ORDINANCE

No. 24 of 1932

AN ORDINANCE TO AMEND THE EXPROPRIATION OF LAND ORDINANCE, 1926

BE IT ENACTED by the High Commissioner for Palestine, with the advice of the Advisory Council thereof.

Short Title.
1. This Ordinance may be cited as the Expropriation of Land (Amendment) Ordinance, 1932, and the Expropriation of Land Ordinance, 1926 (hereinafter referred to as the Principal Ordinance), and this Ordinance may together be cited as the Expropriation of Land Ordinances, 1926-1932.

Amendment of Section 2 of Principal Ordinance
2. The Principal Ordinance, Section 2, is hereby amended by the substitution of the following definition for the definition of "undertaking" appearing therein:—

"'Undertaking' means any undertaking certified by the High Commissioner to be of a public nature and any undertaking under a concession granted by the High Commissioner according to the terms of which land as herein defined may be expropriated for the purposes of the concession".

Substitution of new Section 3 in Principal Ordinance.
3. The following Section is hereby substituted for Section 3 in the Principal Ordinance:—

"3. Subject to the provisions of this Ordinance it shall be lawful for the promoters of any undertaking to treat and agree with the owner of any land required by them for the undertaking and with all persons having an interest in such land either for the absolute purchase thereof or for the possession or use thereof for a definite period, or for the acquisition of any easement required for the purpose of the undertaking".

30th June, 1932.

A. G. WAUCHOPE
High Commissioner

SANCTIONED.

LAND SETTLEMENT (AMENDMENT) ORDINANCE, No. 33 OF 1932

The second day of November, One thousand nine hundred and thirty-two.

LAND SETTLEMENT (AMENDMENT) ORDINANCE

No. 33 of 1932

AN ORDINANCE TO AMEND THE LAND SETTLEMENT ORDINANCE, 1928

BE IT ENACTED by the High Commissioner for Palestine with the advice of the Advisory Council thereof:—

1. This Ordinance may be cited as the Land Settlement (Amendment) Ordinance, 1932, and the Land Settlement Ordinance, 1928 (hereinafter called the principal Ordinance), the Land Settlement (Amendment) Ordinance, 1930, and this Ordinance may together be cited as the Land Settlement Ordinances, 1928-1932. {Short title. No. 9 of 1928. No. 18 of 1930.}

2. The following shall be added to section 56 of the principal Ordinance as sub-section (3) thereof:— {Addition to section 56 of the principal Ordinance.}

"(3) An appeal shall be decided in chambers unless the Court, of its own motion or on the application of any party, shall otherwise direct. At any such appeal in chambers no party shall be heard".

3. Any judgment given or order made by a Land Court in chambers in any appeal prior to the commencement of this Ordinance shall be deemed to be and always to have been validly given or made. {Validation.}

4. Section 30 of the principal Ordinance shall be repealed and the following shall be substituted therefor:— {Substitution of new section for section 30 of principal Ordinance.}

"(1) After the investigation of such claims to rights in a block as are undisputed, the Settlement Officer shall draw up a Schedule of Rights in such form and containing such particulars as may be prescribed by regulation under this Ordinance, and after dealing with such Schedule as hereinafter provided, shall transmit a signed copy thereof to the Registrar, together with a signed plan of the parcels comprised in the Schedule.

(2) Upon the determination by the Settlement Officer of any disputed claim, after the Schedule has been sent by him to the Registrar, the Settlement Officer shall inform the Registrar of his decision in such matter, and the Registrar shall thereupon enter particulars of the right which was in dispute in accordance with such decision in the appropriate page of the new register for which provision is made by section 35 of this Ordinance".

Palestine No. 33 of 1932

Substitution of new section for section 35 of principal Ordinance.

5. Section 35 of the principal Ordinance shall be deleted and the following shall be substituted therefor:—

"A new register in a form to be prescribed by regulation under this Ordinance shall be opened for each village and notwithstanding any appeal that may be pending the land shall be registered by the Registrar in such register in accordance with the Schedule of Rights and the plan transmitted as provided in sub-section (1) of section 30 of this Ordinance, and in accordance with the decisions of the Settlement Officer in the case of rights shown as disputed in the Schedule of Rights".

Addition to section 49 of principal Ordinance.

6. Section 49 of the principal Ordinance as enacted in section 13 of the Land Settlement (Amendment) Ordinance, 1930, shall be amended by the addition thereto of the following proviso:—

"Provided that where the subject matter of such appeal does not affect the total number of shares in which the parcel or village musha' is owned, the Settlement Officer may effect the partition notwithstanding that a judgment in the appeal has not been given by the Land Court".

2nd November, 1932.

M. A. YOUNG
Officer Administering the Government

Section 16: 1933

LAND SETTLEMENT (AMENDMENT) ORDINANCE, No. 22 OF 1933

The second day of June, One thousand nine hundred and thirty-three.

LAND SETTLEMENT (AMENDMENT) ORDINANCE,
No. 22 of 1933

An Ordinance to amend the Land Settlement Ordinance, 1928.

Be it enacted by the High Commissioner for Palestine with the advice of the Advisory Council thereof:—

Short title.
No. 9 of 1928.
No. 18 of 1930.
No. 33 of 1932.

1. This Ordinance may be cited as the Land Settlement (Amendment) Ordinance, 1933, and the Land Settlement Ordinance, 1928 (hereinafter referred to as the principal Ordinance), the Land Settlement (Amendment) Ordinance, 1930, the Land Settlement (Amendment) Ordinance, 1932, and this Ordinance may together be cited as the Land Settlement Ordinances, 1928-1933.

Amendment of section 2 of the principal Ordinance.

2. Section 2 of the principal Ordinance shall be amended by the substitution in the place of the definition of the word "village" appearing therein as enacted in paragraph (a) of section 2 of the Land Settlement (Amendment) Ordinance, 1930, of the following definition:—

> "'Village' includes any village lands within or abutting on a municipal area, a tribal area or any part thereof, and any area of land within a settlement area as may be prescribed by a Settlement Officer by notice under section 5 (1) of this Ordinance."

Amendment of section 3 of the principal Ordinance.

3. Section 3 of the principal Ordinance shall be amended by the deletion of the words "in any village" in sub-section (2) thereof.

2nd June, 1933.

H. H. TRUSTED
Officer Administering the Government

LAND LAW (AMENDMENT) ORDINANCE, No. 25 OF 1933

Arthur Wauchope

The Twenty-Third day of August, One Thousand Nine Hundred and Thirty-Three.

LAND LAW (AMENDMENT) ORDINANCE,
No. 25 of 1933.

AN ORDINANCE TO MAKE CERTAIN AMENDMENTS IN THE OTTOMAN LAND LAW.

BE IT ENACTED by the High Commissioner for Palestine, with the advice of the Advisory Council thereof:—

1. This Ordinance may be cited as the Land Law (Amendment) Ordinance, 1933. *Short title.*

2.—(1) The occupation of land by one or more co-heirs to the exclusion of the other co-heirs shall raise a presumption to the effect that the occupant holds the land on behalf or as agent of the co-heir or co-heirs not in occupation; but such presumption may be rebutted before a competent court by oral or written evidence that the occupation is adverse to the other co-heir or co-heirs. *Occupation of land by co-heirs.*

(2) No action between co-heirs for the recovery of land inherited from a common ancestor and in the possession of one or more co-heirs, to the exclusion of the others, shall be heard after the expiration of the period for bringing actions concerning land prescribed by law. Such period shall run from the beginning of the period of adverse occupation as determined under the preceding sub-section; or, if the claimant shall have been a minor or under any other disability at the beginning of the period of adverse occupation, from the date on which such claimant ceases to be a minor or to be under such disability.

(3) For the purposes of this section:

(a) the age of majority shall be taken to be eighteen years;

(b) persons under disability shall be deemed to include persons of unsound mind and persons interdicted by a competent court.

3. Notwithstanding any provision of the Ottoman Land Code or any other provision of the Land Law, any *miri* land which is or may become *mahlul* under the provisions of the Land Law, or any land reclaimed from the sea, a river, or a lake, may, subject to the rights of persons having a right of *tapu*, by notice in the Gazette under the hand of the High Commissioner, be declared by him to be public land within the meaning of paragraph (1) of article 12 of The Palestine Order-in-Council, 1922. *Disposal of mahlul land by Government.*

— 2 —

Palestine No. 25 of 1933

Determination of *tapu* value.

4.—(1) Notwithstanding any of the provisions of any Ottoman law relating to the grant of title deeds for State lands if land becomes subject to the right of *tapu* and there are persons entitled to a right of *tapu*, the value of the land shall be fixed by a Commission composed of the District Officer in charge of the Sub-District in which the land is situate and two unofficial members nominated by the District Commissioner.

For the purposes of this sub-section the definition of the term "District Commissioner" appearing in the Interpretation Ordinance, 1929, shall not apply.

Any valuation made by such Commission shall be subject to review by the Director of Lands whose decision shall be final. When the valuation of any land has been fixed, persons having a right of *tapu* in respect of such land shall be invited by the Director of Lands in order of the priority of their rights to accept within a period of thirty days from the date of such an invitation the grant of such land on payment of its value so fixed. If the offer is accepted by any such person the grant shall be made to him without any auction.

(2) Land which becomes *mahlul* in default of persons having a right of *tapu*, or in case of renunciation of the right by such persons and which is not declared to be public land as provided in section 3 of this Ordinance, shall be put to auction and shall subject to any reserve price which may be put upon such land by the Director of Lands (power in that behalf being hereby given him) be granted to the highest bidder. Notices of the auction shall be published in a newspaper circulating in the district in which the land is situate, and shall be posted in the town or village in which the land is situate.

(3) If no bid or no bid equal to the reserve price put upon the land by the Director of Lands is made at such auction for the land, it shall, at the expiration of a period of six months from the date of the auction become public land within the meaning of paragraph (1) of article 12 of The Palestine Order-in-Council, 1922.

Sale, etc., of land to include trees.

5. Notwithstanding anything in article 48 of the Ottoman Land Code, the sale or other disposition of *miri* land shall be deemed to include *mulk* trees planted thereon prior to the Ottoman Law concerning the right to dispose of immovable property dated the fifth day of Jumad-al-Awwal, 1331 (A.H.), although no mention of the trees is made in the deed of sale or other instrument, unless the ownership of the trees is registered separately from the land.

— 3 —

Palestine No. 25 of 1933

6. (1) Notwithstanding anything in articles 41 and 44 in the Ottoman Land Code contained:— [Limitation of exercise of rights of pre-emption.]

(a) no right to claim a transfer of land under any of the said articles shall be exerciseable on the part of any person more than one year after the right first accrued;

(b) where any period limited by the said articles is running at the commencement of this Ordinance, it shall expire at the termination of the period so limited, or on the expiration of one year from the commencement of this Ordinance, whichever first arrives.

(2) In any judgment awarding to a plaintiff the right to claim a transfer of land under articles 41, 44 and 45 of the Ottoman Land Code the court may order that such transfer shall be effected within such period not exceeding three months as the court may deem fit: and where any order has been so made for the transfer of any land and owing to any default of the person in whose favour such order has been made such transfer is not completed within the time specified therein the right to such transfer arising under judgment or otherwise, shall cease and determine.

7. In every provision of the Ottoman Land Code and any other Ottoman Law concerning immovable property in Palestine fixing the period within which any action may be heard or any right may be exercised, the terms 'month' and 'year' shall be deemed to refer to a calendar month or year respectively according to the Gregorian calendar. [Interpretation of 'month' and 'year' in Ottoman Land Law.]

8. Notwithstanding any provision in the Ottoman Law, absence from Palestine of a person claiming to be entitled to bring an action or exercise any right as to land, during the whole or any part of the period limited by law for the commencement of the action or the prescription of the right, shall not prevent the commencement or interrupt the running of the period, and if a person absent from Palestine has appointed an agent in Palestine, the absence of such an agent from Palestine during the whole or any part of the period shall not prevent the commencement or running of the period: [Absence from Palestine not to interrupt prescription.]

Provided that, where a person has been absent prior to the commencement of this Ordinance, the effect of such absence shall be interpreted in accordance with the law in force at the time of his absence.

9. To remove doubts it is hereby declared that the lessee of land who has registered a lease in the Land Registry may, save where the lease contains a condition to the contrary, mortgage [Right to mortgage a leasehold interest.]

— 4 —

Palestine No. 25 of 1933

his interest in accordance with the law of mortgage for the time being in force and such mortgage may be registered in the Land Registry by the mortgagee, either in addition to or instead of, the mortgagor.

Ottoman Law not to have effect. 10. Articles 109, 110, 111 and 126 of the Ottoman Land Law shall no longer have effect.

23rd August, 1933.

A. G. WAUCHOPE
High Commissioner.

WEIGHTS AND MEASURES (AMENDMENT) ORDINANCE, No. 36 OF 1933

Arthur Wauchope

The Twenty-Third day of August, One Thousand Nine Hundred and Thirty-Three.

WEIGHTS AND MEASURES (AMENDMENT) ORDINANCE, No. 36 of 1933

AN ORDINANCE TO AMEND THE WEIGHTS AND MEASURES ORDINANCE, 1928

BE IT ENACTED by the High Commissioner for Palestine, with the advice of the Advisory Council thereof:—

Short title.

No. 2 of 1928.

1. This Ordinance may be cited as the Weights and Measures (Amendment) Ordinance, 1933, and the Weights and Measures Ordinance, 1928 (hereinafter referred to as the principal Ordinance), and this Ordinance may together be cited as the Weights and Measures Ordinances, 1928-1933.

Substitution of new section in the place of section 12 of the principal Ordinance.

2. Section 12 of the principal Ordinance shall be deleted and the following section shall be substituted in the place thereof:—

"12. If, at any time, the High Commissioner-in-Council is of the opinion that it is desirable to prohibit the use of any weights and measures other than metric weights and measures, he may, by Order-in-Council, declare that, from a date to be specified in such order, and with such reservations from and exceptions to the application of the metric system of weights and measures as may be specified in such order, the use of any weight or measure other than a metric weight or measure shall be unlawful and thereupon any contract or dealing in any work or goods, disposition of land or other thing which is to be carried out, done or made by weight or measure shall be deemed to be carried out, done or made according to metric weights and measures, and otherwise shall be void."

A. G. WAUCHOPE
High Commissioner.

23rd August, 1933.

PROTECTION OF CULTIVATORS ORDINANCE, No. 37 OF 1933

OFFICER ADMINISTERING THE
GOVERNMENT

28th September, 1933.

The Thirty First of August, One Thousand Nine Hundred and Thirty Three.

PROTECTION OF CULTIVATORS ORDINANCE,
No. 37 of 1933

AN ORDINANCE TO PROVIDE FOR THE PROTECTION OF CERTAIN CULTIVATORS

BE IT ENACTED by the High Commissioner for Palestine, with the advice of the Advisory Council thereof:—

1. This Ordinance may be cited as the Protection of Cultivators Ordinance, 1933. — *Short title.*

2. In this Ordinance, unless the context otherwise requires, the following expressions have the meanings hereby assigned to them, that is to say:— — *Interpretation.*

"Board" means a Board constituted under this Ordinance.

"District Commissioner" means the Commissioner of the District in which a holding or subsistence area is situated. The definition of the District Commissioner in the Interpretation Ordinance, 1929, as enacted in the Interpretation (Amendment) Ordinance, 1933, shall not apply to the interpretation of this Ordinance. — *No. 34 of 1929. No. 4 of 1933.*

"Holding" means a plot of miri land occupied and cultivated by a tenant, and where the land of a village or any portion of such land is held in undivided ownership or tenure, includes such land or portion of land so occupied and cultivated within the area of the village:

Provided that where a tenant has been moved by a landlord from one or more plots of land to another plot or plots the plot or plots from which the tenant was moved and the plot or plots to which the tenant was moved shall together be deemed to be a holding.

"Landlord" means the person other than a rent collector or other agent to whom the tenant pays or is liable to pay rent directly or through an agent or where no rent is payable would be liable to pay rent if payable and includes the predecessors and successors in title of such person.

"Miri land" includes miri waqf land.

"Rent" means any payment in money or kind, and includes any share of the produce of a holding.

— 2 —

Palestine No. 37 of 1933

"Statutory tenant" means any person, family or tribe occupying and cultivating a holding otherwise than as the owner thereof. It includes any wife or relative of any person occupying and cultivating a holding who may have with the knowledge of the landlord cultivated such holding, and where the person occupying and cultivating a holding has acquired it by succession it includes the predecessors in title of the person so acquiring the holding. It includes the heirs of a statutory tenant. It includes a person who is hired by the landlord to do agricultural work and receives as remuneration a portion of the produce of the holding which he cultivates. It does not include a person who is hired to do agricultural work and who receives as remuneration a money wage or portion of the produce, but does not cultivate a holding.

Termination of tenancy by notice, etc.

3.—(1) Notwithstanding any provision of any contract to the contrary where any statutory tenant has occupied and cultivated a holding for a period of not less than one year, the landlord thereof shall not be entitled to terminate the tenancy unless he shall have given to the tenant in writing notice to quit not less than one year from the first day of October following the date of the notice:

Provided that nothing herein shall extend to the case where any agreement between the landlord and the statutory tenant provides for any longer notice than the notice provided for herein.

(2) Every notice to quit given under this section shall be void and of no effect unless a copy thereof is served by the landlord on the District Commissioner of the district in which the land is situated within thirty days after the notice has been served on the statutory tenant, and unless the notice contains a declaration by the landlord that its object is to terminate the tenancy in order that the land may be transferred with vacant possession, if such be the object of the notice.

Tenant neglecting a holding grossly.

4.—(1) Notwithstanding anything contained in section 3 of this Ordinance, if the landlord gives notice in writing to a statutory tenant who has occupied and cultivated a holding for a period of not less than one year to terminate the tenancy because such tenant has neglected his holding grossly and wilfully, the tenant shall be liable to eviction after the expiration of three months from the date of such notice unless within fifteen days of the receipt of such notice he applies to the District Officer and the landlord in writing for reference of the question whether he has so neglected his holding to a Board and the

Palestine No. 37 of 1933

Board decides that he has not so neglected it. If such application is made the Board shall give its decision within fifteen days of its constitution.

(2) If at the time of his eviction therefrom there is any crop ungathered upon the holding which has been planted by the tenant the landlord shall pay to the tenant compensation in respect thereof.

Such compensation shall be assessed by a Board, and in assessing such compensation the Board shall have regard to the state of such crop and to the amount of money and labour which the tenant has expended upon such crop.

5.—(1) In case of a dispute a Board shall determine after consultation with the local Inspector of Agriculture what having regard to all the circumstances is a reasonable period for the payment of rent due.

Certain disputes to be determined by a Board.

(2) Either party to the dispute may give notice thereof to the District Officer and shall give a copy of such notice to the other party.

6.—(1) No court or judge or execution officer shall give any judgment or make any order for the eviction of a statutory tenant who has occupied and cultivated a holding for a period of not less than one year save in accordance with the following provisions:—

Order for eviction only to be granted in certain cases.

   (a) Where the tenant has paid when due or has paid within a reasonable time in accordance with the decision of a Board all rent due in respect of the holding, no such judgment shall be given or order made,

      1. unless a notice to quit has been given by the landlord in accordance with the provisions of section 3 of this Ordinance, and

      2. urless it is made to appear to the court or judge or execution officer that the tenant

         (a) has been provided with a subsistence area approved by the High Commissioner, or

         (b) the High Commissioner is satisfied that the tenant has other land sufficient to enable him to maintain his customary means of livelihood in an occupation with which he is familiar, and

Palestine No. 37 of 1933

3. unless the questions whether the statutory tenant is entitled to compensation for disturbance and for improvements made by such tenant to the holding have been referred to a Board, and if such questions have been so referred unless those questions have been decided by the Board and any amount of compensation in respect thereof assessed by the Board, shall have been deposited with a Notary Public, and

4. if the statutory tenant has cultivated the holding under the landlord for a period of not less than five years consecutively preceding the date when the notice to quit expired, unless in addition to any compensation fixed under the preceding paragraph a sum equivalent to one year's average rent of the holding has been assessed by a Board and deposited with a Notary Public, and

5. if any compensation is payable under the provisions of section 17 of this Ordinance unless such compensation has been assessed by the Board and deposited with a Notary Public.

(b) Where the tenant has not paid all rent due in respect of the holding within a reasonable time in accordance with the decision of a Board no such judgment shall be given or order made,

(i) unless the question whether the statutory tenant is entitled to compensation for improvements made by such tenant to the holding has been referred to a Board and if such question has been so referred and any amount of compensation in respect thereof assessed by the Board, unless such amount shall have been deposited with a Notary Public, and

(ii) if any compensation is payable under the provisions of section 17 of this Ordinance unless such compensation has been assessed by the Board and deposited with a Notary Public, and

(iii) unless a notice to quit has been given by the landlord in accordance with the provision of section 3 of this Ordinance:

Provided that nothing herein shall be deemed to affect the provision for eviction in section 4 of this Ordinance contained.

Palestine No. 37 of 1933

(2) Subject to the provisions of section 12 of this Ordinance any sum deposited with a Notary Public in accordance with the provisions of sub-section (1) hereof shall, if a judgment is given or order made for eviction, be paid to the statutory tenant against whom such judgment or order is given or made on the Notary Public being satisfied that the tenant has complied with the terms of such judgment or order, or if no such judgment or order is given or made any such sum shall be returned to the person who made the deposit.

(3) If a judgment is given or order made for eviction rent shall be payable in respect of the period between the date when the notice to quit expired and the date of eviction at the rate payable prior to the termination of the tenancy as though the tenancy had continued until the date of eviction.

7. The rights under this Ordinance of, Effect of sale or transfer.

(a) any statutory tenant who has occupied and cultivated a holding for not less than one year, or

(b) any person lawfully occupying any subsistence area,

shall not be affected by any sale or transfer of such holding or area or of any immovable property of which such holding or area forms part including any sale effected under the Ottoman Provisional Law for the Mortgage of Immovable Property dated the 25th February, 1326, or the Mortgage Law Amendment Ordinances 1920-1929 or under any law relating to Execution for the time being in force.

8.—(1) A Board shall consist of a District Officer as President nominated by the District Commissioner and two members nominated with the approval of the District Commissioner, one by the landlord and the other by the tenant. Constitution of Board, etc.

(2) The decisions of the Board in any matter referred to them under this Ordinance shall be subject to confirmation by the District Commissioner, and when confirmed by him shall be final.

(3) If within one month of the nomination of the President of a Board either the landlord or the tenant shall fail to submit the name of the member of the Board who will represent him to the District Commissioner for his approval, the District Commissioner shall nominate some person to represent the party so failing, and such person so nominated shall be deemed to have been nominated by such party.

Palestine No. 37 of 1933

Subsistence area.

9.—(1) A subsistence area shall be determined by a Board. Such area shall as nearly as circumstances permit be in the same Sub-District and in the vicinity of the holding from which the statutory tenant is being ejected, and shall be such land as will enable the statutory tenant to maintain his customary means of livelihood in an occupation with which he is familiar:

Provided that the High Commissioner may from time to time declare the minimum amount of land which shall be a subsistence area in any locality or of any category of land.

(2) The Board shall determine the rent payable by the statutory tenant in respect of a subsistence area.

(3) The landlord or tenant may apply to a Board not less than five years from the last decision of a Board in respect thereof to vary a subsistence area or the rent thereof.

(4) No person lawfully occupying a subsistence area shall be evicted therefrom save upon the recommendation of a Board with the approval of the High Commissioner.

(5) Where it appears that any tenant of a subsistence area is grossly and wilfully neglecting the area the landlord of such area may apply in writing to a District Officer for reference of the question whether the tenant of such area has grossly and wilfully neglected the area to a Board and if the Board is satisfied that he has so neglected the area it may recommend his eviction therefrom.

(6) If at the time of his eviction therefrom there is any crop ungathered upon a subsistence area which has been planted by the tenant the landlord shall pay to the tenant compensation in respect thereof.

Such compensation shall be assessed by a Board and in assessing such compensation the Board shall have regard to the state of such crop and to the amount to money and labour which the tenant has expended upon such crop.

(7) The tenant of a subsistence area shall not sell or mortgage his tenancy right:

— 7 —

Palestine No. 37 of 1933

Provided that, upon the recommendation of a Board, with the approval of the High Commissioner, he may be allowed to sell his tenancy right to the landlord if the Board is satisfied —

    (a) that the tenant occupies or will without delay occupy other land not less than the subsistence area, and in the vicinity thereof sufficient to enable him to maintain for himself and his dependants, if any, a standard of living not less than that yielded by his subsistence area, in an occupation with which he is familiar, or

    (b) has obtained other permanent occupation which will enable him to maintain such standard of living as aforesaid.

In such a case the amount to be paid by a landlord to the tenant by way of purchase price shall be determined by the Board.

(8) The heirs of a tenant of a subsistence area shall have the same rights and liabilities in respect of such area as the tenant had.

10.—(1) Where any statutory tenant who has been in occupation of a holding for not less than one year,   *Compensation for disturbance.*

    (a) vacates his holding in consequence of a notice to quit, or

    (b) is evicted from his holding by reason of any judgment given or order made under the provision of section 6 (1)(a) of this Ordinance,

the landlord shall pay to such statutory tenant compensation for disturbance to be assessed by a Board in accordance with the provisions of this section.

(2) The compensation shall be a sum representing such loss or expense directly attributable to the quitting of the land as the tenant may unavoidably incur in connection with the sale or removal of his movable property:

Provided that compensation shall not be payable in respect of the sale of any such movable property unless the statutory tenant has before the sale given the landlord a reasonable opportunity of making a valuation thereof, and

Provided also that no compensation shall be payable under this section

Palestine No. 37 of 1933

(a) where the landlord has made the tenant an offer in writing to withdraw the notice to quit and the tenant has unreasonably refused or failed to accept the offer, or

(b) if the claim for compensation is not made within three months from the date at which the statutory tenant quits the land.

Compensation for improvements.

11.—(1) Where a statutory tenant of a holding has made thereon any improvements comprised in the first schedule to this Ordinance, he shall, subject to the provisions of this Ordinance, be entitled on the termination of the tenancy whether by notice to quit or otherwise to obtain from the landlord as compensation for the improvements such sum as represents the value of the improvements to an incoming tenant:

Provided that in ascertaining the amount of compensation payable there shall be taken into account any benefit which the landlord has given or allowed to the tenant executing the improvements whether expressly stated in any contract of tenancy or not.

(2) Compensation under this section shall not be payable in respect of any improvement comprised in Part I of the first schedule to this Ordinance unless the landlord has previously to the execution of the improvement consented in writing to the making thereof, and any such consent may be given by the landlord unconditionally, or upon such terms, as to compensation or otherwise, as may be agreed upon between the the landlord and the statutory tenant, and, if any such agreement is made, the question whether the statutory tenant is entitled to compensation under this section shall be deemed to have been referred to and decided by a Board and any compensation payable under the agreement shall be deemed to be compensation payable under this section and to have been assessed by the Board.

(3) Compensation shall not be payable in respect of any improvement comprised in Part II of the first schedule to this Ordinance unless the statutory tenant has given to the landlord not less than two months' notice in writing of his intention to execute the improvement, and of the manner in which he proposes to do the work:

Provided that:

(a) if the improvement consists of application to the land of farmyard manure, it shall be sufficient for the statutory tenant to give notice to the landlord once in each year; and

Palestine No. 37 of 1933

(b) if the improvement consists of repairs to buildings which are necessary for the habitation of the statutory tenant or the proper cultivation or working of the holding, the statutory tenant shall not execute the repairs unless the landlord fails to execute them within a reasonable time after such notice.

Where notice is given under this sub-section the landlord and statutory tenant may agree on the terms of compensation or otherwise on which the improvement is to be executed; and, if any such agreement is made, the question whether the statutory tenant is entitled to compensation under this section shall be deemed to have been referred to and decided by a Board and any compensation payable under the agreement shall be deemed to be compensation payable under this section and to have been assessed by the Board.

(4) The amount of compensation payable for improvement made by the statutory tenant under the provisions hereof shall be assessed by a Board:

Provided that no claim for compensation shall be heard by a Board unless particulars of the claim have been given by the landlord to the statutory tenant or by the statutory tenant to the landlord within three months of the termination of the tenancy by a notice to quit, or within three months from the date at which the statutory tenant quits the holding where there has been no notice to quit.

12. Where a tenancy of a holding is terminated and any rent is due from the statutory tenant to the landlord in respect thereof such rent may be deducted from any compensation payable by the landlord to the statutory tenant in respect of the disturbance or improvements or otherwise. *Arrears of rent may be set off against compensation.*

13. The landlord shall not increase the rent of a holding unless he shall have first obtained the sanction of the District Officer who shall have power after hearing the landlord and the statutory tenant and after taking such evidence and making such enquiries as he thinks fit to decide by what amount, if any, the rent shall be increased. The increased rent shall not come into force before one year from the first day of October following the decision of the District Officer. *Rent not to be increased without sanction of a Board.*

14.—(1) Where a superior landlord recovers against the landlord of a statutory tenant (in this section hereinafter referred to as the immediate landlord), a judgment for possession or order of eviction for nonpayment of rent or otherwise in respect of any land comprised in a holding the estate of the *Provision where statutory tenant is a sub-tenant.*

— 10 —

Palestine No. 37 of 1933

immediate landlord shall be deemed to be determined as if the judgment for possession or order of eviction had been executed.

(2) No such judgment or order shall be executed against a statutory tenant, and his tenancy of the holding shall not be affected except that the superior landlord shall become the landlord of the statutory tenant and may proceed for the recovery of all rent due from the statutory tenant to the immediate landlord as if it had always been due to the superior landlord, and shall from the date of such judgment or order be entitled to recover the rent of the holding from the statutory tenant.

(3) If the superior landlord recovers from the statutory tenant any rent in respect of any period prior to his becoming the landlord of the statutory tenant he shall be liable to account to the immediate landlord therefor.

<small>Special powers to District Commissioners.</small>
15. Notwithstanding anything contained in this Ordinance the District Commissioner may on the application of the landlord authorize the resumption by him of a holding or part thereof on being satisfied,

(a) that such resumption is required for some reasonable and sufficient purpose having relation to the good of the holding or of the adjoining land, including development by drainage or irrigation or by closer settlement or colonization or disposal for building purposes, and

(b) (i) that the statutory tenant will retain sufficient land of such nature as to enable him to maintain his customary means of livelihood in occupations with which he is familiar, such land being as far as possible in the vicinity of the home from which the transfer may cause his displacement, or

(ii) that the purpose for which the resumption of the holding is sought comprises the provision for the statutory tenant of developed land sufficient for the maintenance of himself and his family, together with adequate subsistence for them, pending the development of such land.

<small>Land not to be transferred until the provisions of this Ordinance satisfied.</small>
16.—(1) Where application is made to register a transfer of any miri land in which there is a statutory tenant who has received notice of termination of tenancy in accordance with this Ordinance, the Director of the Department of Lands shall not record the transfer in the Land Registers unless he is satisfied that security has been given by the landlord for carrying out any obligations to the statutory tenant under this Ordinance, or unless the purchaser agrees that he will take over the

Palestine No. 37 of 1933

obligations of the former landlord, and that any compensation that has been or shall be found due to the statutory tenant shall be charged on the land.

(2) Any compensation agreed to be due or found by a Board to be due to a statutory tenant under this Ordinance shall be charged on the land until the whole of such compensation has been paid.

(3) The provisions of this section shall not apply to any holding when the Director of the Department of Lands is satisfied that all compensation for disturbance or improvements or otherwise payable in respect of such holding has been assessed by a Board and deposited with a Notary Public.

17.—(1) If the landlord desires that a tenant who has received notice to quit or a statutory tenant who has received notice to quit in accordance with section 3 hereof shall prepare the land for cultivation in the following year, he shall give notice to the tenant in writing to that effect. A copy of such notice shall be served by the landlord on the District Commissioner. If the tenant complies with the notice the landlord shall pay compensation to the tenant for the preparation of the land. If the tenant is unwilling to prepare the land he shall inform the landlord within one month of the receipt of the notice, and the landlord shall be entitled during the year of notice to prepare for cultivation in the following year any land of the tenant which is not under crop.

Outgoing tenant to prepare or allow landlord to prepare land.

(2) The amount of any compensation payable hereunder shall in case of dispute be assessed by a Board.

18.—(1) No court or judge or execution officer shall make an order for the eviction of a person who has exercised by himself or his agent habitually at the appropriate seasons for not less than five consecutive years within a period of not more than seven years prior to the date when application is made for any such order a practice of grazing or watering animals or the cutting of wood or reeds or other beneficial occupation of similar character on the land whether by right, custom, usage or sufferance, unless the landlord satisfies the court or judge or execution officer that the High Commissioner is satisfied that provision of equal value has been secured towards the livelihood of such person.

Protection of certain practices.

(2) Nothing in this section contained shall be deemed to authorise any person to enter upon any land save for the purpose of exercising the practice which he has exercised in the past.

Palestine No. 37 of 1933

Certain matters to be decided by a Commission.

19.—(1) Any dispute,

(a) as to whether any person is a statutory tenant of a holding, or

(b) as to the length of time that any statutory tenant has occupied and cultivated a holding, or

(c) as to whether any person is the landlord of a holding, or

(d) as to whether any person has exercised continuously any practice of grazing or watering animals or cutting wood or reeds or other beneficial occupation of a similar character by right, custom, usage or sufferance,

shall be referred to a special Commission to be appointed by the High Commissioner.

(2) Any person aggrieved by the decision of any such Commission may appeal to the High Commissioner-in-Council whose decision shall be final and no appeal shall lie therefrom to any court.

(3) Where in any proceedings between any parties before any court it appears that any question material in such proceedings has been decided as between such parties or between parties through whom such parties respectively claim by a Commission under the provisions of this section such question shall be deemed to be res judicata, and such court shall be bound by the decision of the Commission, or if there has been any appeal therefrom by the decision of the High Commissioner-in-Council.

(4) For the purposes of this section the High Commissioner may appoint a Commission consisting of not less than three persons, one of whom shall be a British judicial officer who shall act as chairman of such Commission.

Regulations.

20. The High Commissioner may make, and when made, may vary or revoke regulations as to:—

(a) the procedure of a Board,

(b) the fees payable to the members of a Board,

(c) the practice and procedure to be followed in any enquiry before any Commission appointed under the provisions of section 19 of this Ordinance, including the taking of evidence and the right of audience of any persons before any such Commission,

— 13 —

Palestine No. 37 of 1933

(d) any other matter herein requiring regulation.

21. Nothing in this Ordinance shall apply to any person who at the commencement thereof is occupying and cultivating any holding of which the Government of Palestine is the landlord.

Saving.

22. Any notice to quit served on a tenant after the twenty-third day of July, 1933, which would not have been a valid notice if this Ordinance had been in operation at the date of the service thereof shall be null and void.

Notice to quit served prior to the commencement of this Ordinance.

Any notice to quit served on a tenant after the twenty-third day of July, 1933, which would have been a valid notice if this Ordinance had been in operation at the date of the service thereof shall be deemed to have been given and served under the provisions of this Ordinance.

23. The Ordinances set out in the second schedule to this Ordinance are hereby repealed.

Repeal.

FIRST SCHEDULE.

TENANT'S IMPROVEMENTS FOR WHICH COMPENSATION IS PAYABLE.

PART I.

IMPROVEMENTS TO WHICH CONSENT OF LANDLORD IS REQUIRED.

1. Erection, alteration or enlargement of buildings.

2. Making or improvement of roads or bridges.

3. Removal of tree-roots, boulders, stones, or other like obstructions to cultivation.

4. Making or improvement of works of irrigation, water courses, ponds, wells or reservoirs, or works for the application of water-power or for supply of water for agricultural or domestic purposes.

5. Making and renewal of permanent fences and walls.

6. Planting of orchards, vineyards, wind-breaks and hedges.

— 14 —

Palestine No. 37 of 1933

7. Erection and installation of prime-movers, steam, oil and gas engines, turbines, rams, and wind-mills and water-wheels.

8. Erection and installation of power-driven mills or machinery for the grinding, crushing or treatment of agricultural products.

PART II.

Improvements in respect of which notice to landlord is required

1. Drainage.

2. Embankments and sluices against floods.

3. Application to land of farmyard manure.

4. Application to land of purchased artificial or other purchased manure.

5. Repairs to buildings, being buildings necessary for the habitation of the tenant or the proper cultivation or working of the holding, other than repairs which the tenant is himself under obligation to execute:

SECOND SCHEDULE

No. 27 of 1929.	Protection of Cultivators Ordinance, 1929.
No. 3 of 1931.	Protection of Cultivators (Amendment) Ordinance, 1931.
No. 16 of 1932.	Protection of Cultivators (Amendment) Ordinance (No. 1), 1932.
No. 30 of 1932.	Protection of Cultivators (Amendment) Ordinance (No. 2), 1932.
No. 17 of 1933.	Protection of Cultivators (Extension) Ordinance, 1933.

31st August, 1933.

A. G. WAUCHOPE
High Commissioner.

CO-OPERATIVE SOCIETIES ORDINANCE, No. 50 OF 1933

Arthur Wauchope

This twenty seventh day of December, one thousand nine hundred and **thirty-three.**

CO-OPERATIVE SOCIETIES ORDINANCE,
No. 50 of 1933

AN ORDINANCE TO CONSOLIDATE AND AMEND THE LAW RELATING TO CO-OPERATIVE SOCIETIES

BE IT ENACTED by the High Commissioner for Palestine, with the advice of the Advisory Council thereof:—

1. This Ordinance may be cited as the Co-operative Societies Ordinance, 1933. *Short title.*

2. In this Ordinance, unless the context otherwise requires:— *Definitions.*

   (a) "Audit union" means a registered association of societies, of which the principal object is to arrange for the audit of the registered societies which are its members in addition to supervision and co-operative education;

   (b) "Central society" means a registered society established to facilitate the operations of registered societies in accordance with co-operative principles and includes an audit union and a central financing society;

   (c) "Central financing society" means a registered society of which the principal object is to make loans to other registered societies;

   (d) "Committee" means the governing body of a registered society to whom the management of its affairs is entrusted;

   (e) "Member" includes a person joining in the application for the registration of a society and a person admitted to membership after registration in accordance with the rules and this Ordinance and the regulations made thereunder;

   (f) "Officer" includes a president, chairman, secretary, treasurer, director, manager, member of committee, or other person empowered under the rules to give directions in regard to the business;

   (g) "Registered society" means a society registered or deemed to be registered under this Ordinance;

   (h) "Registrar" means a person appointed to perform the duties of a Registrar of Co-operative Societies under this Ordinance;

   (i) "Regulations" means regulations made under this Ordinance;

— 2 —

Palestine No. 50 of 1933

(j) "Rules" means the registered rules of a society for the time being in force and includes a registered amendment of the rules.

Registrar.

3. The High Commissioner may appoint a person to be Registrar of Co-operative Societies for Palestine or any portion of it, and may appoint persons to assist such Registrar, and may, by general or special order, confer on any such person all or any of the powers of a Registrar under this Ordinance.

Objects of societies.

4. Subject to the provisions hereinafter contained, a society which has as its objects the promotion of thrift, self help and mutual aid among persons with common economic needs so as to bring about better living, better business and better methods of production, or a society established for the purpose of facilitating the operations of such societies, may if not already registered under the Co-operative Societies Ordinance, 1920, be registered under this Ordinance with or without limited liability.

Provided that unless the High Commissioner by general or special order otherwise directs, the liability of a society of which a member is a registered society shall be limited.

Restriction on interest of member.

5.—(1) Where a society has a share capital, no member, other than a registered society or a body corporate admitted to membership under section 6 (1), shall hold more than one-fifth of the capital.

(2) Where a society has no share capital, no member, other than a registered society or a body corporate admitted to membership under section 6 (1), shall have or claim any interest in the capital of the society exceeding one-fifth of the capital.

Qualifications for membership.

6.—(1) The members of a registered society may be:—

(a) individual persons who have completed their eighteenth year; and

(b) other registered societies.

Provided that in the case of societies other than those whose principal object is the making of loans to members, the Registrar may approve the admission as members of bodies corporate other than registered societies.

(2) No society, other than a society of which a member is a registered society, shall be registered under this Ordinance which does not consist of at least seven persons who have completed their eighteenth year and, where the object of the society is the creation of funds to be lent to its members, unless such persons:—

Palestine No. 50 of 1933

(a) reside in the same town or its immediate vicinity or reside or intend to reside in the same village or group of villages in Palestine, or

(b) save where the Registrar otherwise directs are members of the same class or occupation.

(3) In the case of registered societies, whose principal object is the making of loans to members, the High Commissioner may by regulation prescribe that no person may be a member of more than one such society.

(4) No audit union shall be registered which does not consist of at least twenty registered societies.

7. When any question arises whether for the purposes of this Ordinance a person resides in a town or its immediate vicinity or resides or intends to reside in the same village or in the same group of villages in Palestine or as to the class to which a society belongs, or as to its sphere of operations, or whether a person belongs to a particular class or occupation, the question shall be decided by the Registrar, whose decision shall be final. *Determination of residence.*

8.—(1) For purposes of registration an application to register shall be made to the Registrar. *Application for registration.*

(2) The application shall be signed:—

(a) in the case of a society of which no member is a registered society, by at least seven persons qualified in accordance with the requirements of sub-section (1) of section 6; and

(b) in the case of a society of which a member is a registered society, by a duly authorised person on behalf of every such registered society, and where not all the members of the society are registered societies, by seven other members or, when there are less than seven other members, by all of them.

(3) The application shall be accompanied by two copies of the proposed rules of the society and by the name or names of some person or persons who will negotiate with the Registrar about the settlement of the rules.

9. (1) If the Registrar is satisfied that a society has complied with the provisions of this Ordinance and the regulations and that its proposed rules are not contrary to the Ordinance or to the regulations, he may either register the society or refuse registration without assigning any reason for such refusal. *Registration of Society.*

Palestine No. 50 of 1933

(2) Notwithstanding anything hereinafter contained, the provisions of section 22 (2) and section 24 of the Companies Ordinances, 1929-1932, shall apply to a society applying for registration under this Ordinance as if the word "Company" included a co-operative society and the words "Registrar of Companies" included the Registrar of Co-operative Societies.

Registration fees.
10.—(1) A society which adopts without substantial amendment the model rules approved by the Registrar for a society of that class, shall pay no fee for registration and a notice of its registration shall be published without charge in the Gazette.

(2) Every other society shall on registration pay a fee of four pounds and shall also pay such charge for the notice of registration in the Gazette as the High Commissioner may by general or special order prescribe.

(3) The decision of the Registrar, as to the class to which a society belongs, and as to whether the model rules have been adopted without substantial amendment, shall be final.

(4) A certificate of registration, and a copy of the rules as approved, stamped with the official seal of the Registrar, shall be delivered to every society without charge on its registration.

Certificate of registration conclusive evidence.
11. A certificate of registration signed by the Registrar shall be conclusive evidence that the society is duly registered unless it is proved that the registration of the society has been cancelled.

Amendment of rules.
12.—(1) No amendment of the rules of a registered society shall be valid until the same has been registered under the Ordinance, for which purpose two copies of the amendment shall be forwarded to the Registrar.

(2) If the Registrar is satisfied that the amendment of the rules is not contrary to this Ordinance or to the regulations, he may either register the amendment or refuse registration, without assigning any reason for such refusal.

(3) When the Registrar registers an amendment of the rules of a registered society he shall issue to the society on payment of the prescribed fee a copy of the amendment certified and sealed by him which shall be conclusive evidence that the same is duly registered.

Amalgamation of societies.
13.—(1) Any two or more societies may, with the approval of the Registrar, by a resolution passed at a special general

— 5 —

Palestine No. 50 of 1933

meeting of each society held for the purpose, by a three-fourths majority of the members, amalgamate as a single society: provided that each member has had clear thirty days' written notice of the proposed amalgamation and the date of the meeting. Such an amalgamation may be effected without a dissolution, or a division of the funds, of the amalgamating societies. The resolution of the societies concerned shall on such amalgamation be a sufficient conveyance to vest the assets and liabilities of the amalgamating societies in the amalgamated society; provided that any dissenting member may withdraw from the society subject to the provisions of its rules.

(2) Any society may by a resolution passed in accordance with the procedure laid down in sub-section (1) transfer its assets and liabilities to any other society which is prepared to accept them:

Provided that when any such amalgamation or transfer of assets and liabilities involves the transfer of its liabilities by any society to any other society, it shall not be made without giving three months' notice to the creditors of both or all such societies.

Provided further that if a creditor or creditors of any of the societies concerned objects or object to such amalgamation or transfer of assets and liabilities and gives or give written notice to that effect to the society or societies concerned one month before the date fixed for such amalgamation or transfer, the amalgamation or transfer shall not be made until the dues of such creditor or creditors have been satisfied.

(3) A previous notice of the intended amalgamation and a subsequent notice of the completed amalgamation and of the Registrar's approval shall be published in the Gazette on the payment of such charge as the High Commissioner may by general or special order prescribe.

14.—(1) The committee may at any time call a general meeting of the society and shall call such meeting within one month after receipt of a requisition in writing from the Registrar or from a central society to which the society is affiliated or from some other body specified in the rules of the society or from such number of members or proportion of the total number of members as may be similarly specified.

General meetings.

(2) If a general meeting is not called in accordance with such requisition, the Registrar shall have power to call a general meeting of the society himself. The costs, if any, incurred by the Registrar, shall be recovered from the society under section 58 of this Ordinance as a sum due to the Government.

Palestine No. 50 of 1933

Rights and duties of members.

15.—(1) No member of a registered society shall exercise the rights of a member unless or until he has made such payment to the society in respect of membership or acquired such interest in the society as may be prescribed by the rules.

(2) A member on admission to a society shall become liable for the obligations of the society which have been incurred previous to his membership.

Voting.

16.—(1) Every member of a society shall have at least one vote in its affairs, but no member shall have more than one vote.

Provided that:—

(a) in the case of an equality of votes the chairman shall also have a casting vote.

(b) in a consumers' distributive society or a society of agricultural purchase or service or sale additional votes may be allotted as the rules may provide on the basis of each member's patronage of the society during the past financial year. But no member may have more than one-twentieth of the total votes.

(c) a society which has invested any part of its funds in shares of, or is affiliated to, another society, may appoint one of its members to vote in the affairs of such other registered society and may have as many votes as may be prescribed by the rules of the latter society, but no member may have more than one-twentieth of the total votes.

(d) a society which operates in a town or in more than one village may in its rules provide for local meetings or for a meeting of representatives locally elected. Such representatives may have as many votes as may be prescribed by the rules.

(e) a member not residing in Palestine may appoint another member as his proxy but no member shall act as proxy for more than two other members.

(2) Save as provided in clauses (c), (d) and (e) no proxies shall be allowed.

Redemption of shares.

17. The shares or interest of a member in the capital of a registered society shall not be transferable but shall be redeemed by the society subject to the provisions of its rules and any regulation issued hereunder.

Registered address of societies.

18. Every registered society shall have an address in Palestine, registered in accordance with the regulations, to which all notices and communications may be sent, and shall send to the Registrar notice of any change thereof.

— 7 —

Palestine No. 50 of 1933

19. Every registered society shall keep a copy of this Ordinance and of the regulations and of its rules and a list of its members, open to inspection free of charge at the registered address of the society during such hours as the office of the society is open for business.

Right of inspection of rules etc.

20.—(1) The books of every registered society shall be audited at least once in each year. When a society is affiliated to an audit union, the audit shall be carried out by an officer of that union appointed by the union, who shall be registered in the manner prescribed by regulation under this Ordinance, or licensed as a public auditor by Government; and when it is not so affiliated, the annual general meeting of the society shall appoint an auditor licensed as a public auditor by Government and in both cases the appointment shall be subject to the veto of the Registrar; provided that the Registrar may, at his discretion, sanction the audit of the books of any registered society by an officer of his Department.

Audit.

(2) The audit under subsection (1) hereof shall include *inter alia* an examination of over-due debts, if any, the verification of the cash balance and securities, and a valuation of the assets and liabilities of the society.

(3) The audit union or auditor appointed under sub-section (1) hereof shall have free access to the books, accounts, vouchers and all other papers of a society and shall be allowed to verify its cash balance and securities.

The directors, managers and other officers of the society shall furnish to the audit union or other person appointed to audit the accounts of a society all such information as to its transactions and working as the audit union or such person may require.

(4) The audit union or auditor appointed under sub-section (1) hereof to audit the accounts of a society shall have power, when necessary:—

(i) to summon any officer, agent, servant or member of the society who there is reason to believe can give valuable information in regard to any transaction of the society or the management of its affairs,

(ii) to require the production of any book or document relating to the affairs of or any cash or securities belonging to the society by the officer, agent, servant or member in possession of such book, document, cash or securities.

(5) If the Registrar is not satisfied with the audit reports of any union, he may:—

Palestine No. 50 of 1933

(a) appoint an auditor or auditors to audit on his behalf the societies affiliated to the union, and charge to the societies such fee as he thinks fit;

(b) suspend the power of the union to audit the societies affiliated to it. The power of suspension shall be exercised subject to the sanction of the High Commissioner. Provided that no order of suspension shall be made until the union has been given an opportunity of making an explanation in writing.

Incorporation of societies.

21. The registration of a society shall render it a body corporate by the name under which it is registered, with perpetual succession and a common seal, and with power to hold movable and immovable property, to enter into contracts, to institute and defend suits and other legal proceedings and to do all things necessary for the purposes of its constitution.

Power of fining members.

22. A registered society may by its rules take power to impose fines upon members by the authority of the general meeting or of the committee or in such other manner as the rules may provide. Such fines shall be debts due to the society.

Debts of members to society.

23.—(1) All monies payable or due by a member to a registered society under this Ordinance, or the rules of such society or in connection with its business shall be a debt due from such member to the society and shall be recoverable as such.

(2) For the purpose of provisional execution on debts due by members of a society to a society a certificate signed and sealed by the officer or officers for the time being entrusted with the management of the affairs of the society shall be held to be an authenticated document within the meaning of article 130 of the Code of Civil Procedure.

Society to have charge on shares of members in respect of debts due to Society.

24.—(1) A registered society shall, in respect of any debt due from a member or past member to the society, have a charge upon the share or interest in the capital and on the deposits of such member or past member and upon any dividend, bonus or other portion of the surplus payable to such member or past member, and may set off any sum credited or payable to a member or past member in or towards payment of any such debt.

(2) The shares of a registered society shall not be pledged to the society by any of its members as security for a loan.

Exemption of shares from attachment.

25. Subject to the provisions of section 24, the share or interest of a member in the capital of a registered society shall

Palestine No. 50 of 1933

not be liable to attachment or sale under any decree or order of a Court of Justice in respect of any debt or liability incurred by such member, nor shall a receiver in insolvency be entitled to or have any claim on such share or interest.

26.—(1) (a) It shall be lawful for any registered society to make advances by way of loan in accordance with its registered rules to a member of such society. *Charges in favour of societies.*

(b) A registered society may when making a loan to a member or when a member is indebted to such society require the member to create a charge in favour of the society in such form as may be prescribed on all crops or other agricultural produce, felled timber, animals, fodder, agricultural or industrial implements, machinery, raw materials and stock-in-trade, whether at the date when such charge is created the property comprised in the charge is or is not in existence or is or is not acquired by the person giving the charge.

(2) (a) A charge created under sub-section (1) hereof shall be deemed to be duly executed if signed in duplicate by the member executing the same in the presence of the officer or officers for the time being entrusted with the management of the affairs of the society. *Execution and registration of charges.*

(b) It shall be the duty of such officer or officers for the time being entrusted with the management of the affairs of the society forthwith to file one copy of the charge in the office of the society, and to lodge the other copy within twenty-one days with the District Officer of the sub-district in which the property comprised in the charge is situated.

(c) The District Officer upon receiving a copy of a charge together with the prescribed fee shall forthwith file the same and shall keep a book called the Register Book of Co-operative Societies Charges in the prescribed form in which particulars of all such charges received by him shall be entered forwarding to the society an acknowlegment of registration.

(d) Any person shall be entitled to inspect the file of charges in the office of a society and upon payment of the prescribed fee the Register Book of Co-operative Societies Charges and take extracts therefrom.

(3) The Registrar on being satisfied that an omission to register a charge within the time hereinbefore required was accidental or due to inadvertence or to some other sufficient cause or is not of a nature to prejudice the position of creditors or members of the society or that on other grounds it is just

Palestine No. 50 of 1933

and equitable to grant relief, may, on the application of the society or any person interested and on such terms and conditions as seems to the Registrar just and expedient, order that the time for registration be extended.

Effect of registration of charge.

(4) (a) The registration of a charge in accordance with the provisions of sub-section (2) hereof shall constitute a first charge and security in favour of the society making the loan or otherwise:

Provided that nothing contained herein shall affect:—

(i) any claim of the Government in respect of taxes or money recoverable as such or of a landlord in respect of rent or money recoverable as rent, or

(ii) the rights of any *bona fide* purchaser for value without notice, or

(iii) the rights of any prior mortgagee or encumbrancer.

(b) The registration of a charge by the District Officer shall be deemed to affect with notice of the charge any person dealing with any property comprised in the charge.

Notification of repayment of loan to be given.

(5) As soon as the loan or debt in respect of which a charge under this Ordinance has been given has been repaid, the officer or officers for the time being entrusted with the management of the affairs of the society shall forthwith record the same in the copy filed in the office of the society and shall within twenty-one days from the date of payment notify the District Officer, and upon receipt of such notice the District Officer shall forthwith make an entry of satisfaction in the Register Book of Co-operative Societies Charges.

Assignment of charges.

27. A registered society may borrow money on the security of any charge which it holds under section 26 (1) hereof if such charge is executed and registered in accordance with the provisions of this Ordinance, and may for this purpose assign any such charge and such assignment when registered as aforesaid shall operate as a first charge in favour of the assignee subject to the provisions of section 26 (4) hereof.

Charges created by societies on their own property.

28. Subject to registration in compliance with section 59 hereof, a registered society may create a charge on any of its own property of the nature described in section 26 (1) (b) hereof which may be charged in security of any loan in the manner described in section 26 hereof and it shall not be an objection to any right of the society or of the person from

— 11 —

Palestine No. 50 of 1933

whom the society borrows money that the subject matter of the charge which is given as security is not in existence, is not acquired, or is not capable of delivery at the time the security is given. The provisions of this section shall apply to any charge which has been executed and registered by a registered society under Part V of the Companies Ordinances, 1929-1932, prior to the commencement of this Ordinance if such charge would be valid under this Ordinance.

29.—(1) Any member or past member of a society who disposes of or deals with or attempts to dispose of or deal with any property comprised in any charge registered under this Ordinance, without first obtaining the leave in writing of the committee shall be liable on conviction to a fine not exceeding fifty pounds. Penalty for dealing with property charged.

(2) Nothing in this section shall relieve any member or past member of any penalties, or bar the society from seeking any other remedies which may be otherwise provided under this Ordinance or under any other law for the time being in force.

30. A registered society, having as one of its objects the disposal of any produce of agricultural or animal husbandry or handicrafts of its members, may either in its rules or in a separate document contract with its members that they shall dispose of all their produce, or of such amounts or descriptions as may be stated therein, to or through the society for a stated period, and may in any such contract provide for payment of a specific sum per unit of weight or other measure as liquidated damages for infringement of the contract, and such sum shall be a debt due to the society. Contracts for disposal of produce to or through a society.

31.—(1) On the death of a member of the society such society may within a period of one year from the death of such member transfer the share or interest of the deceased member to a person nominated in accordance with the rules of the society, if duly admitted a member of the society in accordance with the regulations and the rules of the society, or, if there is no person so nominated, to such person as may appear to the committee to be the heir or legal representative, as the case may be, a sum representing the value of such member's share or interest as ascertained in accordance with the regulations and rules: Deceased members.

Provided that such nominee, heir or legal representative, as the case may be, may require that payment shall be made by the society within one year from the death of the member of the value of the share or interest of such member ascertained as aforesaid.

(2) A society shall subject to the provisions of sections 24 and 26 and unless prevented by an order of a competent Court pay to such nominee, heir or legal representative, as the case may be, all other monies due to the deceased member from the society.

(3) All transfers and payments made by a society in accordance with the provisions of this section shall be valid and effectual against any demand made upon the society by any other person.

Liability of estates of deceased members.

32. The estate of a deceased member shall be liable for a period of one year from the end of the financial year of the society following his decease for the debts of a registered society as they existed at the time of his decease.

Liability of past members.

33. The liability of a past member for the debts of a registered society as they existed at the time when he ceased to be a member shall continue for a period of two years from the end of the financial year of the society following the date of his ceasing to be a member.

Register of members.

34. Any register or list of members or shares kept by any registered society shall be *prima facie* evidence of any of the following particulars entered therein:—

(a) the date at which the name of any person was entered in such register or list as a member;

(b) the date at which any such person ceased to be a member.

Certification of copies of entries.

35.—(1) A copy of any entry in any book, register or list regularly kept in the course of business and in the possession of the society shall, if duly certified in such manner as may be prescribed by the regulations, be admissible in evidence of the existence of the entry and shall be admitted as evidence in the matters and transactions therein recorded in every case where, and to the same extent to which, the original entry would, if produced, have been admissible to prove such matters.

(2) No officer of a society shall in any legal proceedings to which the society is not a party be compelled to produce any of the society's books, the contents of which can be proved under subsection (1), or to appear as a witness to prove the matters, transactions and accounts therein recorded, unless by order of the Court or a Judge made for special cause.

Transactions with non-members.

36.—(1) A registered society shall not make a loan to any person other than a member:

— 13 —

Palestine No. 50 of 1933

Provided that, with the general or special sanction of the Registrar, a registered society may make loans to another registered society,

Provided further that a registered society may employ the services of another registered society as its agent for collection of bills and other business purposes and may maintain a current account with such registered society for this purpose.

Provided also that a society may, with the sanction of the Registrar, make loans to persons other than members out of funds provided for that specific purpose by any person or group of persons not being themselves the persons to whom such loans are to be made.

(2) The High Commissioner may, by general or special order, prohibit or restrict the lending of money on mortgage of immovable property by any registered society or class of registered societies.

37. A registered society shall receive deposits and loans from persons who are not members only to such extent and under such conditions as may be prescribed by the rules.   *Deposits and loans from non-members.*

38. The transactions of a registered society with persons other than members shall be subject to the provisions of its registered rules.   *Transactions with non-members.*

39.—(1) No part of the funds of a registered society shall be divided by way of bonus or dividend or otherwise among its members at a rate exceeding that prescribed in the regulations.   *Disposal of the surplus.*

(2) Every society which does or can derive a surplus from its transactions shall maintain a reserve fund.

(3) In the case of a credit or producers' society at least one-fourth of the surplus of the society each year shall be carried to the reserve fund and in the case of any other society at least one-tenth of the surplus of the society each year shall be carried to the reserve fund, and such reserve fund may be used in the business of the society or may be invested, as required by the regulations.

(4) The reserve fund shall be indivisible and no member shall be entitled to a specific share in such fund, save in the case where a registered society is in liquidation or is being wound up. In such case that portion of the reserve fund left over after all liabilities have been met shall, except where the rules of the society otherwise provide, be divided among the members in such proportion as the share capital or interest of each member bears to the capital of the registered society.

Palestine No. 50 of 1933

(5) The surplus in each year shall be calculated before the payment of any dividend or bonus or rebate to members or non-members.

(6) When a dividend is paid on shares, all shares shall rank equally for dividend, and no class of shares shall have a preference over others.

Distribution of surplus.	40. Subject to the provisions of section 39 the balance of the surplus of a society in any year after making the prescribed provision for the reserve fund may, together with any available surplus of past years, be distributed amongst its members, and in the case of consumers' and of producers' societies, also among persons who are not members, to the extent and under the conditions prescribed by the regulations or by the rules of such societies.
Provident fund.	41. Any society may establish a provident fund for its members out of contributions from such members in accordance with the rules made by the society in this behalf and may contribute to such provident fund from its surplus, after the prescribed payments have been made to the reserve fund, provided that such provident fund shall not be used in the business of the society; and provided further, that no part of such provident fund shall be considered as an asset of the society.
Contributions to charities.	42. Any registered society may, after such allocation has been made to the reserve fund as is required by section 39, contribute an amount not exceeding 50% of the remaining surplus to any charitable purpose or purpose of public utility recognised as such by the Registrar, and when the paid-up share capital and the reserve fund are not less than the amount held in the form of loans and deposits from non-members, may contribute an amount exceeding 50% of the said remaining surplus.
Inquiry into the affairs of societies.	43.—(1) The Registrar may of his own motion and shall on the application of a majority of the committee, or of any other body constituted by the rules of the society or of not less than one-third of the members or of the audit union to which the society is affiliated, hold an inquiry or direct some person authorised by him by order in writing in this behalf to hold an inquiry into the constitution, working and financial condition of a registered society:

Provided that when an inquiry is made other than on the Registrar's own motion, he may require the applicant or applicants to deposit a sum sufficient to cover the estimated expenses involved by such inquiry.

(2) All officers and members of the society shall furnish such information in regard to the affairs of the society as the Registrar or the person authorised by the Registrar may require.

— 15 —

Palestine No. 50 of 1933

44.—(1) The Registrar may, on the application of a creditor of a registered society, inspect or direct some person authorised by him in writing in this behalf to inspect the books of the society: *Inspection of books of society.*

Provided that:—

(a) the applicant satisfies the Registrar that the debt is a sum then due, and that he has demanded payment thereof and has not received satisfaction within a reasonable time, and

(b) the applicant deposits with the Registrar such sum as security for the costs of the proposed inspection as the Registrar may require.

(2) The Registrar shall communicate the result of any such inspection to the creditor.

45. Where an inquiry is held under section 43 or an inspection is made under section 44 the Registrar may, after giving the parties an opportunity to be heard, apportion the costs, or such part of the costs as he may think right, between the society, the members or creditor demanding the inquiry or inspection, the officers or former officers, and the members or past members of the society. *Apportionment of costs of enquiry.*

46.—(1) If the Registrar, after an inquiry has been held under section 43 or after an inspection has been made under section 44 or on receipt of an application made by three-fourths of the members of a co-operative society, is of opinion that the society ought to be dissolved, he may order the society to be wound up, and shall publish his order in the Gazette. *Winding-up of societies.*

(2) Any member of a co-operative society may, within two months from the date of the publication of an order made under subsection (1), appeal from such order as provided in section 51.

(3) Where no appeal is presented within two months from the publication of an order for the winding-up of a co-operative society, the order shall take effect on the expiry of that period.

(4) Where an appeal is presented within two months, the order shall not take effect until it is confirmed by the appellate authority.

(5) No society shall be wound up or liquidated save by the order of the Registrar.

Palestine No. 50 of 1933

Power of Registrar to order society to be wound up when number of members less prescribed minimum.

47. If it is proved to the Registrar's satisfaction that the number of members of any society has been reduced to less than the number which would be required for the registration of such a society under section 6, he shall order the society to be wound up.

Powers of liquidator.

48.—(1) Where the Registrar has made an order under section 46 or section 47 hereof for the winding-up of a society, the Official Receiver shall, by virtue of his office, become the provisional liquidator and shall continue to act as such until he or any person becomes liquidator and is capable of acting as such, provided, nevertheless, that the Registrar may by order published in the Gazette appoint some person other than the Official Receiver as liquidator.

(2) If the Registrar appoints a person other than the Official Receiver to act as liquidator in accordance with the preceding sub-section, the procedure to be applied to the winding-up shall be that prescribed by Regulations under this Ordinance and the provisions of Part VI of the Companies Ordinances, 1929-1932, shall not be applicable. The winding-up shall be conducted under the sole control of the Registrar, and the liquidator, notwithstanding anything contained in section 46 hereof relating to the time when the order for winding-up shall take effect, shall have power to take immediate possession of all assets belonging to the society, and of all books, records and other documents pertaining to the business thereof, and to carry on the business of the society as far as may be necessary for the beneficial winding-up of the same.

(3) A liquidator appointed by the Registrar under subsection (2) shall, as soon as the order of winding-up takes effect, have power:—

(a) to institute and defend suits and other proceedings on behalf of the society by his name or office;

(b) from time to time to determine by order the debts payable and the contribution to be made or remaining to be made by the members or past members or by the estates or nominees, heirs or legal representatives of deceased members or by any officer, to the assets of the society, such contribution including debts due from such members or persons. In the case of a society the liability of which is not limited such contributions shall be determined at the discretion and order of the liquidator both as to the persons who shall be called upon to pay and the amounts which they shall pay, but without prejudice to any right of contribution amongst themselves;

— 17 —

Palestine No. 50 of 1933

(c) to investigate all claims against the society, and, subject to the provisions of this Ordinance, to decide by order questions of priority arising between claimants;

Provided that the following debts as they existed at the date of the order for winding-up shall have priority over all other debts:—

(i) All taxes, customs and excise dues and all other monies due from the society to Government;

(ii) All local rates due from the society to a Municipality or Local Council.

(d) to pay claims against the society (including interest up to the date of the order for winding-up) according to their respective priorities, if any, in full or rateably, as the assets of the society permit; the surplus, if any, remaining after payment of the claims being applied in payment of interest from the date of such order at a rate fixed by him but not exceeding the contract rate in any case;

(e) to determine by order by what persons and in what proportions the costs of the liquidation are to be borne.

(4) Subject to any regulations, a liquidator appointed under sub-section (2) shall, in so far as such powers are necessary for carrying out the purposes of this section, have power to summon and enforce the attendance of witnesses and to compel the production of documents by the same means and (so far as may be) in the same manner as is provided in the case of a Civil Court under the Code of Civil Procedure.

(5) Any person aggrieved by any order of the liquidator may appeal to the Registrar against such order within two months from the date of the issue of the order.

(6) Orders of a liquidator under sub-sections (3) (b), (c) and (e) of this section shall, save as provided in section 58, be enforced on application to the Chief Execution Officer in the same manner as a decree of the District Court.

49.—(1) Where, in the course of the winding-up of a society it appears that any person who has taken part in the organization or management of the society or any past or present president, chairman, secretary, member of the managing committee or officer or employee of the society has misapplied or retained or become liable or accountable for any money or property of the society or has been guilty of dishonesty or breach of trust with regard to the money or property of the society, the Registrar may, on the application of the liquidator or of any creditor contributory,

Responsibility of officers, etc.

Palestine No. 50 of 1933

examine into the conduct of such person and make an order requiring him to repay or restore the money or property or any part thereof respectively with interest at such rate as the Registrar thinks just or to contribute such sum to the assets of the society by way of compensation in regard to the misapplication, retainer, dishonesty or breach of trust as the Registrar thinks fit.

(2) This section shall not operate as a bar to the prosecution of the offender for any act for which he may be criminally responsible.

Cancellation of registration.

50.—(1) The liquidator shall, in addition to his report to the Court, inform the Registrar when the winding-up has been completed, and the Registrar shall, on receiving such intimation or after receiving the final report of the liquidator, if any, appointed under section 48 (2), cancel the registration of the society, and the society shall thereupon cease to exist as a corporate body.

(2) A notice of the cancellation shall be published by the Registrar in the Gazette at the cost of the funds of the society.

Appeals.

51. An appeal may be made to the High Commissioner by any party affected by an order of the Registrar under sections 9, 12, and 49 within two months from the date of the order and under section 46 within two months from the publication of the order, and no appeal shall lie to any Land or Civil Court.

Arbitration in disputes.

52.—(1) A registered society may by its rules provide for the settlement of disputes touching the business of the society by reference to the Registrar or otherwise. A claim by a registered society for any debt or demand due to it from a member, past member, or the nominee, heir or legal representative of a deceased member, including a fine imposed in accordance with the rules, whether such debt or demand be admitted or not, is a dispute touching the business of the society within the meaning of this sub-section.

(2) If the rules provide that all disputes or any class or classes of dispute touching the business of the society which may arise:—

(a) among members, past members, and persons claiming through members, past members and deceased members, or

(b) between a member, past member or person claiming through a member, past member or deceased member and the society, its committee or any officer, agent or servant of the society, or

— 19 —

Palestine No. 50 of 1933

 (c) between the society or its committee and any officer, agent or servant of the society, or

 (d) between the society and any other registered society,

shall be referred to the Registrar for decision, then the Registrar may, on the receipt of such reference,

 (aa) decide the dispute himself, or

 (bb) subject to such regulations as may be prescribed, refer it for disposal to an arbitrator or arbitrators.

(3) Subject to such regulations as may be prescribed the Registrar may withdraw any reference referred under sub-section (2) (bb) and deal with it in the manner provided in the said sub-section.

(4) Where the Registrar has referred a dispute to an arbitrator or arbitrators as provided in sub-section (2) (bb), the Registrar may

 (a) approve the award, or

 (b) on his own motion or on an application made to him within ten days of the date of the award by a party to the dispute, revise the award or remit any matter or matters referred to in the award to the arbitrator or arbitrators for reconsideration by them.

(5) Any decision of the Registrar given under sub-section (2) (aa) and any decision by the arbitrator or arbitrators under sub-section (2) (bb), which has been approved by the Registrar under the preceding sub-section, shall have the force of a judgment of a District Court which is not subject to appeal, and shall be executed in like manner.

53. Where the Registrar is satisfied that any person with intent to defeat or delay the execution of any order that may be passed against him under section 48 (3) or section 49, or of any decision that may be given in a dispute under section 52:— *Provisional attachment of property.*

 (a) is about to dispose of the whole or any part of his property, or

 (b) is about to remove the whole or any part of his property from the local limits of the jurisdiction of the Registrar,

the Registrar may, unless adequate security is furnished, direct the provisional attachment of the said property or such part

Palestine No. 50 of 1933

thereof as he thinks necessary and such attachment shall have the same effect as if it had been made by a competent Civil Court.

Exemption from provisions of Ordinance regarding registration.

54. Notwithstanding anything contained in this Ordinance, the High Commissioner may by special order in each case and subject to such conditions, if any, as he may impose, exempt any society from any of the requirements of this Ordinance as to its registration.

Exemption from general provisions of Ordinance.

55.—(1) The High Commissioner may, by general or special order, exempt any registered society from any of the provisions of this Ordinance and may direct that such provisions shall apply to such society with such modifications as may be specified in the order.

(2) The Registrar may, with the general sanction of the High Commissioner, temporarily exempt any society registered prior to the date of this Ordinance from any of the provisions of the Ordinance provided that the total period of such temporary exemption shall not exceed three years.

Use of word "co-operative".

56.—(1) Every registered society shall have the word "co-operative" or its Arabic or Hebrew equivalent as part of its name and no society or body other than a society registered under this Ordinance shall have the word "co-operative" or its Arabic or Hebrew equivalent or any word derived from the same root as part of its name.

"Limited".

(2) Every registered society of which the liability of members is limited shall have the word "limited" or its Arabic or Hebrew equivalent as the last word of its name.

"Bank".

(3) No society shall have the word "bank" or "banking" as part of its name unless it is registered in accordance with the provisions of sub-section (4).

Application for use of the words "bank" or "banking".

(4) A registered society which incorporates or is desirous of incorporating in its name the word "bank" or "banking" shall file with the Registrar of Companies a copy of its rules together with a copy of its certificate of registration by the Registrar of Co-operative Societies certified as required by section 35 of this Ordinance. The Registrar of Companies shall thereupon submit the rules to the High Commissioner, who may at his absolute discretion either authorise or refuse the registration of the society. If the High Commissioner authorises the registration, the Registrar of Companies shall upon payment of the prescribed fees enter such society upon his Register.

— 21 —

Palestine No. 50 of 1933

(5) Any society or body which contravenes the provisions of this section shall be liable to a fine not exceeding ten pounds and such offence if continued shall constitute a new offence in every week during which the offence continues. *Penalty for contravention of section 56.*

57. Where any society : — *Penalties for offences.*

   (1) fails to give any notice, send any return or document or to do or allow to be done any act or thing which is required by this Ordinance or the regulations made thereunder or by the Companies Ordinances as applied by sections 59 and 60,

   (2) wilfully refuses or omits to do any act or to furnish any information required for the purpose of this Ordinance or of the said regulations by the Registrar or other authorised person or of the Companies Ordinances as applied by sections 59 and 60,

   (3) does anything forbidden by this Ordinance or by the regulations, or by the Companies Ordinances as applied by sections 59 and 60,

   (4) wilfully furnishes false or insufficient returns or information,

the society and every officer who is bound by the rules or otherwise to fulfil the duty whereof the breach is an offence, and, where there is no such officer, every member of the committee or other body corresponding thereto, unless such member is proved to have been ignorant of or to have attempted to prevent the commission of the offence, shall be guilty of an offence under this Ordinance and shall be liable to a fine not exceeding five pounds and every such offence if continued shall constitute a new offence in every week during which the default continues.

58.—(1) All sums due from a co-operative society or from an officer or member or past member of a society as such to the Government, and all sums awarded as costs under section 45, shall be recovered in the same manner as arrears of taxes under the Collection of Taxes Ordinances, 1929-1932, as though the same had been declared to be subject to the law for the collection of taxes, on a requisition being made by the Registrar to the District Commissioner. *Recovery of sums due to Government.*

(2) Sums due from a co-operative society and recoverable under sub-section (1) may be recovered firstly, from the property of the society and secondly, in the case of a society of which the liability of the members is limited, from the members subject to the limit of their liability and, in the case of other societies, from the members.

Palestine No. 50 of 1933

Application of Companies Ordinance.

59.—(1) The provisions of the Companies Ordinances, 1929-1932, shall not, save as provided in sections 9 (2) and 60 (1) hereof, apply to registered societies except so far as relates to:—

(a) the registration of debentures, mortgages and charges;

(b) the winding-up of societies where the Official Receiver by virtue of his office acts as provisional liquidator;

(c) an application to a Court under section 117 of the Companies Ordinances, 1929-1932, for the sanction of a compromise; provided that, except in winding-up proceedings through the Official Receiver, no such application shall be entertained by any Court save on the certificate of the Registrar.

(d) The removal of defunct societies from the register in accordance with the provisions of section 242 of the Companies Ordinances, 1929-1932.

(2) The provisions of the Companies Ordinances, 1929-1932, referred to in sub-section (1) hereof shall apply to a co-operative society as if the word "company" included a co-operative society and the words "Registrar of Companies" included the Registrar of Co-operative Societies.

Societies carrying on insurance business.

60.—(1) A registered society which is carrying on or desires to commence to carry on insurance business shall file with the Registrar of Companies a copy of its rules, together with a copy of its certificate of registration by the Registrar of Co-operative Societies, certified as required by section 35 of this Ordinance. The Registrar of Companies shall thereupon submit the rules to the High Commissioner who may in his absolute discretion either authorise or refuse the registration of the society. If the High Commissioner authorises the registration, the Registrar of Companies shall, upon payment of the prescribed fees, enter such society upon his register as a society entitled to transact insurance business and such society shall as from the date of such entry be subject to the obligations imposed upon insurance companies as though such society was a company registered under the Companies Ordinances, 1929-1932, and sections 100 (1) to (4) and 101 shall be deemed to apply *mutatis mutandis* to any such society.

(2) A society which commences to carry on insurance business before it is entered by the Registrar of Companies as a society entitled to carry on insurance business, or a society already carrying on insurance business, which fails to comply with subsection (1) within three months from the date on which this Ordinance comes into force, shall be guilty of an offence under section 57.

Arbitration Ordinance.

61. The Arbitration Ordinance, 1926, shall not apply to proceedings under section 52 (2) of this Ordinance.

— 23 —

Palestine No. 50 of 1933

62.—(1) The Banking Ordinance, 1921, shall not apply to registered societies, which do not undertake the business of receiving deposits in current account from others than their own members. **Banking Ordinance.**

(2) A society which undertakes the business of receiving deposits in current account from other than its own members, shall comply with the provisions of the Banking Ordinance, 1921, and shall be subject to registration as provided in section 56 (4) hereof. The society shall further comply with all the provisions of this Ordinance and of the regulations under this Ordinance with regard to audit.

63.—(1) Every society existing immediately prior to the commencement of this Ordinance which has been registered under the Co-operative Societies Ordinance, 1920, shall be deemed to be registered under this Ordinance and, notwithstanding anything in this Ordinance contained, the rules of any such society shall continue in force, unless altered or rescinded in accordance with the provisions of section 12 hereof, until the thirty-first day of December, 1934, and so far as such rules are not inconsistent with the express provisions of this Ordinance or of any regulations made thereunder, they shall continue in force after such date until so altered or rescinded. **Societies and rules already registered.**

(2) All appointments, regulations and orders made, notifications and notices issued and suits and other proceedings instituted under the said Ordinance shall, so far as may be, be deemed to have been respectively made, issued and instituted under this Ordinance.

64.—(1) The Registrar may make regulations with regard to:— **Regulations by the Registrar.**

(a) the model rules, forms of accounts, and balance sheets, including forms to be used and returns to be made by auditors;

(b) the books and registers to be maintained by societies;

(c) the returns and reports to be made to him annually or otherwise by societies;

(d) the returns and reports to be made to him by liquidators, and the disposal of the books and papers of societies on the completion of liquidation;

(e) the form of the certificate required under section 35, and the person by whom such certificate shall be signed.

(2) Such regulations shall have effect when sanctioned by the High Commissioner.

Palestine No. 50 of 1923

Regulations by the High Commissioner.

65.—(1) The High Commissioner may, for the whole or any part of Palestine and for any society or class of societies, make regulations to carry out the purposes of this Ordinance.

(2) In particular and without prejudice to the generality of the foregoing power such regulations may:—

(a) subject to the provisions of section 5, prescribe the maximum number of shares or portion of the capital of a society which may be held by a member;

(b) prescribe the forms to be used and the conditions to be complied with in the making of applications for the registration of a society and the procedure in the matter of such applications;

(c) prescribe the matters in respect of which a society may or shall make rules and the procedure to be followed in making, altering or abrogating rules and the conditions to be satisfied prior to such making, alteration or abrogation;

(d) prescribe the conditions to be complied with by persons applying for admission or admitted as members and provide for the election and admission of members and the payment to be made and the interests to be acquired before the exercise of the right of membership;

(e) provide for ascertaining the value of a member's share or interest on termination of membership;

(f) provide for general meetings of the members and for the procedure at such meetings and the powers to be exercised by such meetings;

(g) provide for the appointment, suspension and removal of the members of the committee and other officers and for the procedure at meetings of the committee and for the powers to be exercised and the duties to be performed by the committee and other officers;

(h) provide for the audit of the accounts and the charges, if any, to be made for such audit, and for the periodical publication of a balance sheet showing the assets and liabilities of a society;

(i) provide for the formation and maintenance of a register of members and where the society has a share capital, of a register of shares;

Palestine No. 50 of 1933

(j) prescribe the persons who, not being licensed auditors, may audit the accounts of registered societies on behalf of audit unions and provide for the registration of such persons;

(k) prescribe the prohibitions and restrictions subject to which the societies may trade with persons who are not members;

(l) provide for the formation and maintenance of reserve funds, and the objects to which such funds may be applied and for the investment of any funds under the control of a society;

(m) prescribe the extent to which a society may limit the number of its members;

(n) prescribe the conditions under which the surplus may be distributed to the members of a society and the maximum rate of dividend on share capital which may be paid by societies;

(o) prescribe the procedure to be followed in presenting and disposing of appeals;

(p) provide for securing that the share capital of any society shall be variable in such a way as may be necessary to secure that shares shall not appreciate in value and that necessary capital shall be available for the society as required;

(q) provide that persons qualified under the rules of the society shall not be excluded from membership without due cause;

(r) prescribe the procedure to be followed by a liquidator appointed by the Registrar under section 48, and the disposal of the surplus assets of the society;

(s) prescribe the mode of appointing an arbitrator or arbitrators and the procedure to be followed in proceedings before the Registrar or such arbitrator or arbitrators and for fixing and levying the expenses of determining the dispute;

(t) provide for the issue and service of processes and for proof of service thereof;

(u) provide for the writing-off of bad debts;

Palestine No. 50 of 1933

(v) regulate the manner in which funds may be raised by means of shares or debentures or otherwise;

(w) provide for the withdrawal and expulsion of members and for the payments to be made to them and for the liabilities of past members;

(x) provide for the nomination of a person to whom the interest of a deceased member may be paid or transferred;

(y) provide for the inspection of documents in the Registrar's office and the levy of fees for granting certified copies of the same.

Repeal. 66.—(1) The Co-operative Societies Ordinances, 1920-1933, are hereby repealed.

(2) Section 230 (3) of the Companies Ordinance, 1929, is hereby repealed.

A. G. WAUCHOPE
High Commissioner.

27th December, 1933.

Section 17: 1934

PROTECTION OF CULTIVATORS (AMENDMENT) ORDINANCE, No. 7 OF 1934

Arthur Wauchope

his third day of February One Thousand Nine Hundred and Thirty-Four.

PROTECTION OF CULTIVATORS (AMENDMENT) ORDINANCE, No. 7 of 1934.

An Ordinance to amend the Protection of Cultivators Ordinance, 1933.

Be it enacted by the High Commissioner for Palestine with the advice of the Advisory Council thereof:—

1. This Ordinance may be cited as the Protection of Cultivators (Amendment) Ordinance, 1934, and the Protection of Cultivators Ordinance, 1933 (hereinafter referred to as the principal Ordinance) and this Ordinance may together be cited as the Protection of Cultivators Ordinances, 1933-1934. *Short title.*

2. Section 9 (1) of the principal Ordinance shall be amended by the deletion of the words "A subsistence area shall be determined by a Board", and the following words shall be substituted therefor: "A subsistence area shall be determined by a Board and shall be subject to the approval of the High Commissioner." *Amendment of section 9 of the principal Ordinance.*

3. Section 19 of the principal Ordinance shall be amended as follows:— *Amendment of section 19 of the principal Ordinance.*

(a) Sub-section (2) thereof shall be deleted and the following sub-section substituted therefor:—

"(2) The decision of such Commission shall be by vote of the members thereof, and if there be an equality of votes the chairman shall have an additional or casting vote.

The decision of such Commission shall be final and no appeal shall lie therefrom:

Provided that an appeal therefrom on a point of law shall lie to the Land Court by leave of that Court by case stated.

The Chief Justice may with the concurrence of the High Commissioner make rules of Court regulating the practice and procedure in appeals under this section."

(b) Sub-section (3) thereof shall be deleted and the following sub-section substituted therefor:—

"(3) Where in any proceedings between any parties before any court it appears that any question material in such proceedings has been decided as between such parties or between parties through whom such parties respectively claim under the provisions of this section such question shall be deemed to be *res judicata*, and such court shall be bound by the decision given in accordance with the provisions of this section."

(c) Sub-section (4) thereof shall be deleted and the following sub-section shall be be substituted therefor:

"(4) For the purposes of this section the High Commissioner may appoint one or more Commissions consisting respectively of not less than two persons one of whom he shall appoint to be chairman of the Commission".

A. G. WAUCHOPE
High Commissioner.

3rd February, 1934.

COLLECTION OF TAXES (AMENDMENT) ORDINANCE, No. 16 OF 1934.

Arthur Wauchope

COLLECTION OF TAXES (AMENDMENT) ORDINANCE, No. 16 of 1934.

An Ordinance to amend the Collection of Taxes Ordinance, 1929.

BE IT ENACTED by the High Commissioner for Palestine with the advice of the Advisory Council thereof:—

1. This Ordinance may be cited as the Collection of Taxes (Amendment) Ordinance, 1934, and the Collection of Taxes Ordinance, 1929 (hereinafter called the principal Ordinance), the Collection of Taxes (Amendment) Ordinance, 1932, and this Ordinance may together be cited as the Collection of Taxes Ordinances, 1929-1934. *Short title. No. 26 of 1929. No. 34 of 1932.*

2. Section 8 of the principal Ordinance shall be deleted and the following section shall be inserted in the place thereof:— *Substitution of new section in place of section 8 of the principal Ordinance.*

"8.—(1) If no sufficient goods of the defaulter are found in his house or upon his lands, and if, on inquiry, it shall appear that the defaulter owns immovable property, whether registered in his name or not, capable of being sold for the payment of the sum due, the District Commissioner, upon proof of such insufficiency, may issue a warrant for the sale of such immovable property or sufficient part thereof in like manner as if it were sold by order of the competent court for payment of a judgment debt:

Provided that:—

(a) where such immovable property consists in whole or in part of a house in the occupation of the defaulter, there shall be left to or provided for the defaulter, such house accommodation as shall in the opinion of the District Commissioner be necessary for him and his family,

(b) if the defaulter is a farmer, there shall be exempted from the sale so much land as shall in the opinion of the District Commissioner be necessary for the support of himself and his family.

(2) The proceeds of such sale shall be applied in payment of the sum due; and the surplus thereof, after deducting the sum due and the cost and charges of the sale and all proceedings in connection therewith, shall be paid to the defaulter.

— 2 —

(3) If the defaulter owns more than one immovable property, he may select which of his properties shall be sold:

Provided that the value is, in the opinion of the District Commissioner, adequate to cover the sum due; and provided, further, that if the proceeds of the sale of the property so selected are not sufficient for the payment of the sum due, another property may be selected for sale by the District Commissioner.

A. G. WAUCHOPE
High Commissioner.

31st May, 1934.

LAND DISPUTES (POSSESSION) (AMENDMENT) ORDINANCE, No. 19 OF 1934.

OFFICER ADMINISTERING THE
GOVERNMENT.

~ September, 1934.

LAND DISPUTES (POSSESSION) (AMENDMENT) ORDINANCE, No. 19 of 1934.

An Ordinance to amend the Land Disputes (Possession) Ordinance, 1932.

Be it enacted by the High Commissioner for Palestine with the advice of the Advisory Council thereof:—

1. This Ordinance may be cited as the Land Disputes (Possession) (Amendment) Ordinance, 1934, and the Land Disputes (Possession) Ordinance, 1932, (hereinafter referred to as the principal Ordinance) and this Ordinance, may together be cited as the Land Disputes (Possession) Ordinances, 1932-1934. *Short title. No. 12 of 1932.*

2. Section 2, sub-section (6) of the principal Ordinance, shall be amended by the addition thereto of the following further proviso:— *Amendment of section 2 of the principal Ordinance.*

"Provided also that such withdrawal shall not be deemed to deprive of possession the party declared to be entitled to possession of the subject of the dispute".

3. Section 6 of the principal Ordinance shall be deleted and the following section shall be substituted in the place thereof:— *Substitution of new section in place of section 6 of the principal Ordinance.*

"6. Nothing in this Ordinance shall enable a District Commissioner to override or vary an order made by a competent court, a Settlement Officer in accordance with the provisions of the Land Settlement Ordinance, 1928, or by a Chief Execution Officer in virtue of which one of the parties appearing before the District Commissioner in proceedings under this Ordinance shall be entitled to possession of the subject of dispute".

A. G. WAUCHOPE
High Commissioner.

17th August, 1934.

Section 18: 1935

RURAL PROPERTY TAX ORDINANCE, No. 1 OF 1935.

Supplement No. 1.

to the

Palestine Gazette Extraordinary No. 486 of 16th January, 1935.

RURAL PROPERTY TAX ORDINANCE,
No. 1 of 1935.

AN ORDINANCE TO PROVIDE FOR THE TAXATION OF CERTAIN LANDS AND BUILDINGS.

BE IT ENACTED by the High Commissioner for Palestine with the advice of the Advisory Council thereof:—

1. This Ordinance may be cited as the Rural Property Tax Ordinance, 1935. *Short title.*

2. In this Ordinance, unless the context otherwise requires, the following words shall have the meanings hereby respectively assigned to them, that is to say:— *Interpretation.*

"Completion" of an industrial building shall be deemed to be when such building is occupied in whole or in part or is roofed whichever shall first occur.

"District Officer" includes any person duly authorised to act for a district officer.

"House and land tax" includes the Ottoman house and land (werko) tax, werko meqtu', the Ottoman tax on buildings (musaqqafat), the mukata' tax, the badl ushr tax, and the meqtu' Izara Zamin.

"Industrial building" means any building, structure or erection of which the net annual value is in the opinion of an official valuer more than twenty pounds, constructed and used

— 2 —

or intended to be used solely for the purpose of an industrial undertaking in which mechanically driven machinery is used or in connection therewith together with the land on which such building, structure or erection stands and any yard or any land adjacent to such building, structure or erection and used or intended to be used in connection with such building, structure or erection whether such building, structure or erection be inhabited or not or used or not:

Provided that any addition to any industrial building of which the net annual value is in the opinion of an official valuer more than twenty pounds shall itself be deemed to be a separate industrial building.

"Land" includes buildings other than industrial buildings and anything fixed in the land.

"Owner" means the owner of property within an area specified in an Order made by the High Commissioner under section 3 of this Ordinance, and:—

(a) where the property in question has been settled means the registered owner of such property;

(b) where the property in question has not been settled means the person who is in receipt of the rents and profits of the property in such circumstances that he is the reputed owner thereof whether or not he is in possession or is the registered owner:

Provided that in case of a dispute the registered owner shall be deemed to be the owner,

and includes every occupant of Government owned land by virtue of a lease, express or implied.

"Prescribed" means prescribed by rules made by the High Commissioner under section 41 of this Ordinance.

No. 9 of 1928.
"Settled" used with reference to land means any land included in a schedule of rights or schedule of partition posted in accordance with the provisions of the Land Settlement Ordinance, 1928.

No. 49 of 1927.
"Tithe" includes the tithe payable under the Ottoman law prior to the introduction of the commuted tithe and the commuted tithe payable under the Commutation of Tithes Ordinance, 1927.

"Uncultivable land" means land which cannot be cultivated except by recourse to methods other than and additional to the normal methods of sound husbandry and which entail the disbursement of extraordinary expense.

— 3 —

"Urban area" means any area described in an Order made by the High Commissioner under section 3 of the Urban Property Tax Ordinance, 1928. No. 23 of 1928.

"Year" means, notwithstanding anything contained in the Interpretation Ordinance, 1929, the period from the first day of April to the thirty-first day of March following, both days inclusive. No. 34 of 1929.

3.—(1) The High Commissioner may by Order declare that a tax (to be known and hereinafter referred to as the rural property tax), which shall be assessed, levied, collected and paid in accordance with the provisions of this Ordinance, shall be payable annually to the High Commissioner as from the first day of April next following the date of such Order, for the use of the territory of Palestine, on all lands and industrial buildings within such area, not being an urban area, as may be described in such Order. Power of High Commissioner to apply Ordinance.

(2) As from the date upon which the rural property tax becomes payable in any area by reason of an Order made by the High Commissioner under sub-section (1) hereof, the house and land tax and tithe shall cease to be leviable in such area:

Provided that nothing in this sub-section contained shall be deemed to affect the collection of any house and land tax or tithe due in respect of any period prior to the date upon which the rural property tax became payable and proceedings for the recovery of any such tax or tithe so due may be taken as if no Order under sub-section (1) hereof had been made.

4.—(1) The rural property tax shall be payable by the owner:— By whom rural property tax payable.

    (a) upon land, at the rate set out in the schedule to this Ordinance in respect of the category to which such land belongs:

    Provided that the High Commissioner-in-Council, with the approval of the Secretary of State may, by Order:—

        (i) postpone payment of any rural property tax due or about to fall due, in respect of any land until such date as may be set out in such Order or until further Order, or

        (ii) reduce, until such date as may be mentioned in such Order, or until further Order, the rates set out in the schedule to this Ordinance, either generally or in any area or in any part of any area to which this Ordinance has been applied and in each of the foregoing cases, either in respect of all lands or any stated category of land, or

— 4 —

(iii) both postpone payment of rural property tax under sub-paragraph (i) hereof and reduce the rates set out in the schedule to this Ordinance under sub-paragraph (ii) hereof,

if the High Commissioner-in-Council is satisfied that it is proper so to do, having regard to any emergency affecting Palestine or any area or any part of an area, which is:—

(I) due to unavoidable natural causes, or

(II) due to such a fall in the value of crops as in the opinion of the High Commissioner-in-Council makes the granting of the relief which may be effected under this proviso expedient;

(b) upon any industrial building, at such rate not exceeding fifteen per centum of the net annual value of such industrial building as computed in accordance with section 9 of this Ordinance, as shall be prescribed annually by Order of the High Commissioner-in-Council.

(2) The High Commissioner-in-Council may on or after the thirty-first day of March, 1938, by Order vary the categories or rates or both set out in the schedule to this Ordinance:

[Provided that each time the High Commissioner-in-Council shall vary the schedule under this sub-section the schedule as so varied shall remain unaltered for a period of not less than five years from the date from which any such variation shall take effect.]

Development of land and completion of buildings to be notified to District Officers.

5.—(1) The owner of any land which on or after the first day of April next following the date of any Order made by the High Commissioner under section 3 of this Ordinance relating to the area in which such land is situated shall:—

(a) be brought under cultivation, having previously been uncultivable land, or

(b) be planted with bananas or citrus trees or other fruit trees, or

(c) be planted as a forest, or

(d) be brought under irrigation by any system of irrigation other than a system involving for its upkeep and continuity the continuous use of mechanical aid and regular expenditure on the part of such owner,

shall, within three months from the commencement of such cultivation, plantation or bringing of such irrigation, give notice of such fact to the District Officer of the sub-district in which the land is situated, in a form to be prescribed.

(2) Where the completion of any industrial building takes place on or after the first day of April next following the date of any Order made by the High Commissioner under section 3 of this Ordinance relating to the area in which such industrial building is situated, the owner of such industrial building shall, within three months from such completion, give notice of such fact to the District Officer of the sub-district in which such industrial building is situated, in a form to be prescribed.

6.—(1) The owner of any land who is lawfully enjoying exemption from either house and land tax or tithe or both house and land tax and tithe on the thirty-first day of March next following the date of the Order made by the High Commissioner under section 3 of this Ordinance relating to an area in which the land of such owner is situated shall enjoy such exemption from the rural property tax as may be prescribed: Exemption, etc.

Provided that:—

(a) such owner shall within three months from the first day of April next following the date of the Order made by the High Commissioner under section 3 of this Ordinance relating to the area in which such land is situated give notice to the District Officer of the sub-district in which the land is situated in a form to be prescribed, of particulars of such exemption from house and land tax or tithe, and

(b) the owner shall satisfy the District Commissioner that he enjoyed such exemption and that such exemption is applicable to the rural property tax, and

(c) if such owner shall dispose of any land in respect of which he is enjoying such exemption the person in whose favour he has disposed of the land shall not be entitled to such exemption unless such person shall satisfy the District Commissioner that the exemption is applicable to him.

(2) The owner of any land who is enjoying exemption from tithes in accordance with the Decree dated the twenty-fifth day of September, 1920, and published in the Gazette dated the fifteenth day of November, 1920, in respect of vineyards planted with American stock on the thirty-first day of March next following the date of the Order made by the High Commissioner under section 3 of this Ordinance relating to the area in which the vineyards are situated, shall enjoy exemption from the rural property tax for the remainder of the period to which he is entitled under such Decree. No. 31

(3) The owner of any land:—

— 6 —

(a) which having previously been uncultivable land has been brought under cultivation within six calendar years immediately preceding the first day of April next following the date of the Order made by the High Commissioner under section 3 of this Ordinance relating to the area in which such land is situated, or

(b) which has been planted with bananas within two calendar years immediately preceding such first day of April, or

(c) which has been planted with citrus trees within six calendar years immediately preceding such first day of April, or

(d) which has been planted with any fruit trees other than bananas or citrus trees within ten calendar years immediately preceding such first day of April, or

(e) which having previously been uncultivable land shall be brought under cultivation or be planted with bananas or citrus trees or any fruit trees other than bananas or citrus trees subsequently to such first day of April,

shall not be liable to any increase of the rural property tax by reason of such cultivation or plantation:—

(i) in the case of land which having previously been uncultivable land was brought under cultivation prior to such first day of April, for a period equal to six calendar years less a period commencing from the date of the commencement of such cultivation and ending on such first day of April, and

(ii) in the case of land which was planted with bananas, prior to such first day of April for a period equal to two calendar years less a period commencing on the date of the commencement of such plantation and ending on such first day of April, and

(iii) in the case of land which was planted with citrus trees prior to such first day of April for a period equal to six calendar years less a period commencing on the date of the commencement of such plantation and ending on such first day of April, and

(iv) in the case of land which was planted with any fruit trees other than bananas or citrus trees prior to such first day of April for a period equal to ten calendar years less a period commencing on the date of the commencement of such plantation and ending on such first day of April, and

— 7 —

(v) in the case of land which, subsequently to such first day of April, shall be brought under cultivation having previously been uncultivable land or be planted with bananas or citrus trees or any fruit trees other than bananas or citrus trees, for periods of six, two, six and ten years respectively, each such period running from the commencement of the year next following the year during which such cultivation or plantation took place;

provided that:—

(I) in the case of land which having previously been uncultivable land was brought under cultivation or was planted with bananas or citrus trees or any fruit trees other than bananas or citrus trees prior to such first day of April, the owner shall have given notice of such fact to the District Officer of the sub-district within which such land is situated within three months from such first day of April on a form to be prescribed, or

(II) in the case of land which having previously been uncultivable land shall be brought under cultivation or be planted with bananas or citrus trees or any fruit trees other than bananas or citrus trees subsequently to such first day of April, the owner shall have complied with sub-section (1) of section 5 of this Ordinance:

Provided that where any owner in any notice given to the District Officer under paragraph (I) hereof or under sub-section (1) of section 5 of this Ordinance shall state as the area of his land in which cultivation or plantation has taken place, any area other than the true area, then when such true area is ascertained, such owner shall, without prejudice to any penalty which may be incurred by him under sub-section (1) of section 36 of this Ordinance, be liable to pay the rural property tax on such true area at the rate set out in the schedule to this Ordinance in respect of the category within which such area after such cultivation or plantation falls as from the commencement of such cultivation or plantation.

(4) The owner of any industrial building, the completion of which:—

(a) took place within three calendar years immediately preceding the first day of April next following the date of the Order made by the High Commissioner under section 3 of this Ordinance, relating to the area in which such industrial building is situated, or

(b) shall take place subsequently to such first day of April,

shall be exempt from the rural property tax:—

(i) in the case of an industrial building the completion of which took place prior to such first day of April, for a period equal to three calendar years less a period commencing on the date of the completion of such industrial building and ending on such first day of April, and

(ii) in the case of an industrial building the completion of which shall take place subsequently to such first day of April, for a period of three years from the commencement of the year next following the year during which the completion of such industrial building took place,

provided that:—

(I) in the case of an industrial building the completion of which took place prior to such first day of April, the owner shall have given notice of such fact to the District Officer of the sub-district in which such industrial building is situated within three months of such first day of April on a form to be prescribed, or

(II) in the case of an industrial building the completion of which takes place subsequently to such first day of April, the owner shall have complied with sub-section (2) of section 5 of this Ordinance:

Provided that the rural property tax shall be payable on the site of any industrial building exempted hereunder.

(5) The owner of any industrial building who carries out any reconstruction work within such industrial building, whereby the net annual value of such industrial building is in the opinion of the official valuer increased by more than twenty pounds shall not be liable to the rural property tax in respect of the amount by which such net annual value is so increased for a period of three years commencing from the beginning of the year next following the year during which such reconstruction work is completed:

Provided that such owner shall within three months from the commencement of such reconstruction work have given notice of that fact to the District Officer of the sub-district within which such industrial building is situated.

(6) The High Commissioner may, as in his discretion he shall think fit, on the recommendation of the District Commissioner, remit the rural property tax either wholly or in part on any land being land used as a threshing-floor or cemetery.

No. 10 of 1924. (7) If a plantation or crop on land is totally destroyed either in pursuance of an Order under section 6 of the Plant Protection Ordinance, 1924, or by a Plant Inspector in exercise of the powers in him vested by section 7 of that Ordinance or is

— 9 —

otherwise in the opinion of the District Commissioner totally destroyed the owner shall be exempt from the rural property tax on such land for the year in which such plantation [or crop] was destroyed:

Provided that:—

(a) if the rural property tax for such land in respect of such year has already been paid it shall be refunded, and

(b) the rural property tax shall be payable on such land as from the commencement of the year next following the year in respect of which exemption is granted by this sub-section at the rate set out in the schedule to this Ordinance in respect of the category within which such land, after such destruction, may fall.

(8) When the aggregate amount of the rural property tax payable by any owner is ascertained such amount shall be increased or decreased as the case may be to the nearest five mils.

7. The High Commissioner may, by Order, appoint such persons as he may consider necessary to be official valuers for the purpose of this Ordinance.

<small>Appointment of official valuers.</small>

8.—(1) An official valuer shall, as soon as may be possible after his appointment, from information to be obtained by him, prepare:—

<small>Official valuer to prepare rural property tax rolls and valuation lists.</small>

(a) rolls in a form to be prescribed (each one of which is in this Ordinance referred to as a rural property tax roll) showing in respect of the area to which each such rural property tax roll refers (such area for the purposes of this Ordinance being deemed to be a village) within which of the categories set out in the schedule to this Ordinance the lands in each sub-division (such sub-division for the purposes of this Ordinance being deemed to be a block) of such area fall:

Provided that the site of a building (other than an industrial building) not being a building the site of which falls within category 4 of the schedule to this Ordinance, shall be deemed for the purpose of the preparation of the rural property tax roll to be of the same category as the land surrounding such site, and where such site is surrounded in part by land of one category and in part by land of another category or other categories, the site shall be deemed to be of the category of such land in respect of which the highest rate of tax is in the schedule to this Ordinance set out, and

— 10 —

(b) lists in a form to be prescribed (each one of which is in this Ordinance referred to as a valuation list) showing in respect of each village in which any industrial buildings are situated the net annual value [and the names of the owners] of all such industrial buildings.

(2) As soon as the rural property tax roll and valuation list (if any) in respect of any village shall have been prepared in accordance with sub-section (1) hereof, such rural property tax roll and valuation list shall be signed by an official valuer who shall forthwith send two copies of each to the District Officer of the sub-district in which such village is situated, together with two copies of a map of such village stamped by the Director of Surveys and the official valuer showing the lands of the village divided into blocks and the District Officer shall thereupon post one copy of such rural property tax roll and valuation list and map at the District Office and the other in some conspicuous position in the village and the date of posting shall be certified on each copy by him.

(3) The posting of the rural property tax roll and of the valuation list and of the map in accordance with sub-section (2) hereof, shall be deemed to be sufficient notice for all purposes of all the particulars contained therein respectively.

Assessment of industrial buildings.

9.—(1) The net annual value of an industrial building shall for the purposes of this Ordinance be the rent for which such industrial building might be expected to let from year to year after deducting one third on account of cost of repairs and other charges.

(2) If an industrial building is not leased or if in the opinion of the official valuer the rent of an industrial building appears to the official valuer not to represent the true rental value he shall assess the annual value thereof having regard to the following considerations:—

   (a) the size, materials and state of repair of the property and the amenities and value of the site;

   (b) the use to which the property is put;

   (c) the rent paid for or the income produced by similar properties in the same or similar localities:

Provided that no account shall be taken of any plant or machinery in or on the property.

Official valuer's power of entry, etc.

10. The owners and tenants of land and industrial buildings within any area specified in any Order made by the High Commissioner under section 3 of this Ordinance, shall admit an official valuer to any and every part of such land and industrial buildings and it shall be lawful for an official valuer:—

— 11 —

(a) at any reasonable time to enter, survey and examine all or any part of the property, and

(b) to do or cause to be done anything reasonably necessary to draw up the rural property tax roll or valuation list and in particular and without prejudice to the generality of the powers hereby conferred, an official valuer may require any person to produce for inspection any book or account or document of title, contract of lease, plan, specification or building contract and may take any copy of or extract from any such book, account or document, and

(c) administer oaths for the purpose of any enquiry or proceedings which he is required or empowered to carry out under this Ordinance.

11.—(1) Within fourteen days from the date of posting of the rural property tax roll in the village as certified on such roll by the District Officer any person may submit to an official valuer, through the District Officer, an objection to such rural property tax roll on any one or more of the following grounds, that is to say:— Objections to rural property tax roll and valuation list.

(a) that the area of any category of land in any block is wrongly set out:

Provided that nothing in this paragraph contained shall enable any person to object to any area set out in the rural property tax roll as being of category 4 (built-on area) or the position and limits of such area as shown on the map referred to in sub-section (2) of section 8 of this Ordinance;

(b) that the area of any block has been wrongly set out in the rural property tax roll.

(2) Within fourteen days from the date of posting of the valuation list in the village as certified on such list by the District Officer any person may submit to an official valuer, through the District Officer an objection to such valuation list on any one or more of the following grounds, that is to say:—

(a) that the objector has been wrongly included in or excluded from the list;

(b) that some other person has been wrongly included in or excluded from the list; or

(c) that the net annual value of any industrial building is too high or too low.

— 12 —

(3) Every objection under the provisions of this section shall be in writing and in a form to be prescribed and shall state the ground of the objection and shall give such particulars as may be necessary in support of such grounds.

Power of official valuer to amend roll and/or list.

12.—(1) On receipt of any objection to the rural property tax roll or valuation list duly made in accordance with the provisions of section 11 of this Ordinance the official valuer shall consider each such objection and after making such enquiries as he may deem necessary shall have power to amend the rural property tax roll or the valuation list or both the rural property tax roll and the valuation list:

Provided that:—

(a) if the official valuer shall consider any objection to the rural property tax roll to be without foundation and shall decide to make no amendment thereto in pursuance thereof, he shall give notice of such fact to the objector on a form to be prescribed, and the date appearing upon such form shall be deemed to be the date of the decision of the official valuer in respect of such objection, and

(b) if the official valuer shall consider any objection to the valuation list:—

(i) to be without foundation and decide to make no amendment thereto in pursuance thereof, he shall give notice of such fact to the objector on a form to be prescribed and the date appearing upon such form shall be deemed to be the date of the decision of the official valuer in respect of such objection, or

(ii) to be sufficiently well founded to warrant further consideration, he shall give notice of such fact on a form to be prescribed to the objector and to any other person whom he may think may be affected by such objection and shall in such form state the time and place fixed for the hearing of the objection;

(c) if the objector or any other person informed of the proceedings is not present at the time and place stated in such form for the hearing of the objection, the official valuer may, notwithstanding such absence, make such decision on the objection as he may deem right.

(2) Any amendment to the rural property tax roll or valuation list made by an official valuer in accordance with the provisions of sub-section (1) hereof shall be endorsed by him upon the rural property tax roll or valuation list as the case may be and on any copies thereof which have been posted in accordance

with the provisions of sub-section (2) of section 8 of this Ordinance. Each such endorsement shall be initialled and dated by such official valuer and the date of any such endorsement made on the copy of the rural property tax roll or the valuation list posted at the District Office shall be deemed to be the date of the decision of the official valuer in respect of the objection as a result of which it was made.

13.—(1) The High Commissioner may by Order appoint such number of committees as he may consider necessary, to be appeal committees for the purposes of hearing appeals from the decisions of official valuers and may in any such Order or by a subsequent Order under this sub-section allocate regions to each such appeal committee: Appointment of appeal committees.

Provided that each such appeal committee shall consist of three members as under:—

(a) An Assistant District Commissioner or a District Officer (other than a District Officer who has appeared as a party in any proceedings under section 12 of this Ordinance) who shall be chairman of the appeal committee;

(b) Another officer of the Government of Palestine;

(c) A person other than an officer of the Government of Palestine.

(2) An appeal committee and any member thereof shall have the powers of an official valuer as set out in section 10 of this Ordinance.

(3) All acts, orders, matters and things directed to be done or made by an appeal committee shall be lawfully done or made if done or made by or with the consent of a majority of the members of such committee.

14. Any person:— Appeals to appeal committees from the decisions of official valuers.

(a) whose objection to the rural property tax roll has been rejected by an official valuer under section 12 of this Ordinance, or

(b) whose objection to the valuation list has been rejected by an official valuer under section 12 of this Ordinance, or

(c) whose assessment has been altered or who has been included in the valuation list as the result of any objection made by any other person,

— 14 —

may, within fourteen days of the date of the decision by the official valuer, appeal, in a form to be prescribed, to the chairman of the appeal committee appointed under section 13 of this Ordinance in respect of the region in which the property affected by such decision is situated.

Powers and duties of appeal committee to decide appeals, etc.

15.—(1) The appeal committee shall upon receipt of any appeal duly made in accordance with the provisions of section 14 of this Ordinance, give notice, in a form to be prescribed, to the appellant and to the official valuer (who shall be respondent) of the time and place fixed for the hearing of the appeal.

(2) At the time and place so fixed the appeal committee shall hear and determine the appeal:

Provided that:—

(a) no appeal shall be heard by an appeal committee unless the appellant has paid any deposit prescribed on account of costs, and

(b) if any party to the appeal is not present at the time and place fixed for the hearing of the appeal, the appeal committee may, notwithstanding such absence, make such decision as they may deem right.

(3) Upon the determination of any appeal, the appeal committee may make such order as to costs as they may think proper.

(4) Any amendment to the rural property tax roll or valuation list made by the appeal committee in accordance with the provisions of sub-section (2) hereof shall be endorsed by the chairman of such committee upon the rural property tax roll or valuation list as the case may be and on any copies thereof which have been posted in accordance with the provisions of sub-section (2) of section 8 of this Ordinance and each such endorsement shall be initialled and dated by the chairman of the appeal committee and the date of any such endorsement made on the copy of the rural property tax roll or valuation list posted at the District Office shall be deemed to be the date of the decision of the appeal committee in respect of the appeal as a result of which it was made and shall further be deemed to be notice of the decision to all persons interested.

(5) A decision of an appeal committee so endorsed shall be final and no appeal shall lie therefrom:

Provided that any party to any proceedings before an appeal committee may ask the committee to state a case upon a point of law material to the issue arising out of the proceedings for the opinion of the District Court, and the appeal committee shall thereupon state such case.

— 15 —

16.—(1) The areas of the categories of the lands of any village and such categories as shown on the rural property tax roll as finally amended (if there have been any objections) or if there have been no objections, then as shown on the rural property tax roll as posted in the village under sub-section (2) of section 8 of this Ordinance, shall be the areas and categories of the lands of such village for the purposes of this Ordinance until amended as in this Ordinance provided.

Determination of roll and list.

(2) The net annual value of the industrial buildings within any village as shown on the valuation list as finally amended (if there have been any objections) or, if there have been no objections, then as shown on the valuation list as posted in the village under sub-section (2) of section 8 of this Ordinance, shall be the net annual value of the industrial buildings within such village for the purposes of this Ordinance until amended as in this Ordinance provided.

17. The rural property tax payable in respect of the lands of the area described in an Order made by the High Commissioner under section 3 of this Ordinance shall be distributed amongst the owners of such lands as at the thirty first day of March next following the date of such order in the manner hereinafter provided.

Tax in respect of lands to be distributed amongst owners.

18.—(1) (a) At any time prior to the first day of April next following the date of the Order made by the High Commissioner under section 3 of this Ordinance relating to the area within which any village of which the lands or some of the lands have not been settled is situated, the District Commissioner of the district within which such village is situated shall appoint a tax distribution committee consisting of such number of inhabitants of the village as he may think fit:

Distribution of tax in respect of unsettled land.

Provided that the District Commissioner may appoint any person to be a member of a tax distribution committee notwithstanding that such person is not an inhabitant of the village if such person is an owner of land within the village, or the representative of such person whether such representative be an inhabitant of the village or not.

(b) All acts, orders, matters and things directed to be done or made by a tax distribution committee shall be lawfully done or made if done or made by or with the consent of the majority of the members of such committee. In the case of an equal division of opinion the question shall be referred by the committee or by any member thereof to the District Commissioner whose decision shall be final.

(2) On or as soon as may be possible after the first day of April next following the date of the Order made by the High Commissioner under section 3 of this Ordinance relating to the area in which any village in respect of which a tax distribution

— 16 —

committee has been appointed is situated the District Officer of the sub-district in which such village is situated shall give notice to the tax distribution committee on a form to be prescribed:

   (a) if the village for which such committee has been appointed is one of which the lands have not been settled :—

      (i) of the amount of the rural property tax payable in respect of the lands of such village, and

      (ii) of the date prior to which the list referred to in sub-section (3) hereof shall be prepared, or

   (b) if the village for which such committee has been appointed is one of which some of the lands have not been settled :—

      (i) of the date prior to which the list referred to in sub-section (3) hereof shall be prepared, and

      (ii) of the lands of the village which were not settled on the thirty-first day of March next following the date of the Order made by the High Commissioner under section 3 of this Ordinance, and

      (iii) of the amount of the rural property tax payable in respect of such lands.

(3) The tax distribution committee shall thereupon commence to prepare under the general supervision of the District Officer a list hereinafter referred to as a distribution list in a form to be prescribed showing the amount of the rural property tax payable by each owner of lands in the village or in that part of the village referred to in paragraph (b) (ii) of sub-section (2) hereof, having regard to the area and category of land owned by such owner in the village or part of the village as the case may be as at the day mentioned in paragraph (b) (ii) of sub-section (2) hereof:

Provided that :—

   (a) the preparation by a tax distribution committee of any distribution list shall be carried out by such committee only at such time and in such place in the village as may be specified in a notice to be posted by the District Officer at the District Office and in some conspicuous place in the village and any person who may desire to be present at such preparation may attend, and

— 17 —

(b) if a tax distribution committee fails to prepare a distribution list prior to the date specified by the District Officer the District Commissioner may prepare such list and no objection shall be heard to any such list.

19. On the first day of April next following the date of the Order made by the High Commissioner under section 3 of this Ordinance relating to the area in which any village of which the lands or some of the lands have been settled is situated, the District Officer of the sub-district in which such village is situated shall, if the village is one of which the lands have been settled, commence to prepare a distribution list in respect of the lands of such village or if the village is one of which some of the lands have been settled, commence to prepare a distribution list in respect of such lands, showing the amount of the rural property tax payable by each owner of land in such village or such part of the village having regard to the area and category of land owned by such owner in the village or part of the village as the case may be as at the day prior to the day upon which such District Officer commences to prepare any distribution list under this section.

<small>Distribution of tax in respect of settled land.</small>

20. A distribution list prepared in accordance with sections 18 and 19 of this Ordinance shall be in such form and shall be made available for inspection in such manner as may be prescribed.

<small>Distribution list to be open to inspection.</small>

21. Any person whose name appears in a distribution list (other than a distribution list prepared by the District Commissioner) who is aggrieved by reason of the unfairness or incorrectness of the apportionment made by such list or by reason of the insertion or incorrectness of any matter in such list or by reason of the omission of any matter therefrom, may object:—

<small>Objections to distribution lists.</small>

(a) if the distribution list was prepared by a tax distribution committee to the tax distribution committee through the District Officer of the sub-district within which the village is situated, and

(b) if the distribution list was prepared by a District Officer, to the District Officer:

Provided that:—

(i) nothing herein contained shall be deemed to enable any person to object to the category of any land as appearing on any rural property tax roll finally determined as provided in sub-section (1) of section 16 of this Ordinance, and

(ii) every such objection shall be made:—

(I) within fourteen days of the day upon which the distribution list is made available for inspection in accordance with section 20 of this Ordinance, and

— 18 —

(II) in such manner and in such form as may be prescribed.

<small>Power of tax distribution committee and/or District Officer to amend distribution list.</small>

22.—(1) On receipt of any objection to a distribution list duly made in accordance with the provisions of section 21 of this Ordinance, the tax distribution committee or the District Officer as the case may be, shall consider each such objection and after making such enquiries as they or he may deem necessary shall have power to amend the distribution list:

Provided that:—

(a) if the tax distribution committee or the District Officer shall consider any objection to the distribution list to be without foundation and shall decide to make no amendment thereto in pursuance thereof they or he shall give notice of such fact to the objector on a form to be prescribed and the date appearing upon such form shall be deemed to be the date of the decision of the tax distribution committee or the District Officer as the case may be in respect of such objection, and

(b) if the tax distribution committee or the District Officer shall consider any objection to the distribution list to be sufficiently well founded to warrant further consideration, they or he shall give notice of such fact on a form to be prescribed to the objector and to any other person whom they or he may think may be affected by such objection and they or he shall in such form state the time and place fixed for the hearing of the objection, and

(c) if the objector or any other person informed of the proceedings is not present at the time and place stated in such form for the hearing of the objection, the tax distribution committee or the District Officer as the case may be, may, notwithstanding such absence, make such decision on the objection as they or he may deem right.

(2) Any amendment to a distribution list made by a tax distribution committee or District Officer in accordance with the provisions of sub-section (1) hereof shall be endorsed in the case of an amendment made by a tax distribution committee, by the District Officer at the request of such committee, and in the case of an amendment made by a District Officer, by the District Officer upon the distribution list made available for inspection in accordance with the provisions of section 20 of this Ordinance. Each such endorsement shall be initialled and dated by the District Officer and the date of any such endorsement shall be deemed to be the date of the decision of the tax distribution committee or District Officer as the case may be in respect of the objection as a result of which it was made.

— 19 —

23. Any person whose name appears in the tax distribution list may, if he feels aggrieved by any decision made under section 22 of this Ordinance, within fourteen days of the date of such decision appeal in a form to be prescribed to the District Commissioner of the District in which the property affected by such decision is situated.

Appeals to District Commissioner from the decisions of tax distribution committees and/or District Officer.

24.—(1) The District Commissioner shall upon receipt of any appeal duly made in accordance with the provisions of section 23 of this Ordinance, give notice in a form to be prescribed to the appellant and to the tax distribution committee or District Officer as the case may be, (who shall be the respondent or respondents) of the time and place fixed for the hearing of the appeal.

Powers and duties of District Commissioner to decide appeals, etc.

(2) At the time and place so fixed the District Commissioner shall hear and determine the appeal:

Provided that:—

(a) no appeal shall be heard by a District Commissioner unless the appellant has paid any deposit prescribed on account of costs, and

(b) if any party to the appeal is not present at the time and place fixed for the hearing of the appeal the District Commissioner may, notwithstanding such absence, make such decision as he may deem right, and

(c) it shall be lawful, for the purpose of any appeal hereunder, for the District Commissioner to administer oaths.

(3) Upon the determination of any appeal, the District Commissioner may make such order as to costs as he may think proper.

(4) The District Commissioner shall cause any amendment to the distribution list made by him in accordance with the provisions of sub-section (2) hereof to be endorsed upon the distribution list made available for inspection in accordance with the provisions of section 20 of this Ordinance and each such endorsement shall be initialled and dated by the person making it and the date of any such endorsement shall be deemed to be the date of the decision of the District Commissioner in respect of the appeal as a result of which it was made and shall further be deemed to be notice of the decision to all persons interested

(5) A decision of the District Commissioner so endorsed shall be final and no appeal shall lie therefrom:

— 20 —

Provided that any party to any proceedings before a District Commissioner may ask the District Commissioner to state a case upon a point of law material to the issue arising out of the proceedings for the opinion of the District Court and the District Commissioner shall thereupon state such case.

Determination of distribution lists.

25. The amount of the rural property tax payable by each owner of land within any village as shown on the distribution list or lists in respect of such village as finally amended (if there have been any objections) or, if there have been no objections, as shown on the distribution list or lists as made available for inspection in accordance with the provisions of section 20 of this Ordinance shall be the amount of the rural property tax payable by such owner in respect of the lands to which such distribution list or lists refer until amended as in this Ordinance.

Official valuer to prepare annually supplementary rural property tax rolls and supplementary valuation lists.

26.—(1) An official valuer shall on or before a date in each year to be specified by Order of the High Commissioner, the first such year being the year in respect of which the rural property tax is first levied under this Ordinance, prepare:—

(a) a supplementary rural property tax roll in a form to be prescribed in respect of each village in which changes in the categories of land have taken place:—

  (i) in the case of the first supplementary rural property tax roll, since the rural property tax roll was determined as provided in sub-section (1) of section 16 of this Ordinance, and

  (ii) in the case of any supplementary rural property tax roll subsequent to the first supplementary rural property tax roll, since the previous supplementary rural property tax roll was determined as provided in sub-section (1) of section 27 of this Ordinance,

showing such changes:

Provided that any land which has been brought under irrigation by any system of irrigation involving for its upkeep and continuity the continuous use of mechanical aid and regular expenditure on the part of the owner shall not thereby be deemed to have changed in category;

(b) a supplementary valuation list in a form to be prescribed in respect of each village in which any of the undermentioned industrial buildings are situated, that is to say:—

— 21 —

(i) any industrial building :—

(I) in the case of the first supplementary valuation list, not included in the valuation list as determined under sub-section (2) of section 16 of this Ordinance, and

(II) in the case of any supplementary valuation list subsequent to the first supplementary valuation list, not included in the previous supplementary valuation list as determined under sub-section (2) of section 27 of this Ordinance,

either because the completion of such industrial building was not effected or it was a building which was not an industrial building within the meaning of this Ordinance or it was omitted, and

(ii) any industrial building of which the net annual value has increased or decreased by twenty per centum or more :—

(I) in the case of the first supplementary valuation list, since the valuation list was determined as provided in sub-section (2) of section 16 of this Ordinance, and

(II) in the case of any supplementary valuation list subsequent to the first supplementary valuation list, since the previous supplementary valuation list was determined as provided in sub-section (2) of section 27 of this Ordinance,

showing the net annual value of such industrial buildings.

(2) For the purpose of enabling the official valuer to prepare a supplementary valuation list, any owner or District Officer may give notice on a form to be prescribed to the official valuer of any industrial building which in the opinion of such owner or District Officer should be included in a supplementary valuation list.

(3) All the provisions of this Ordinance relating to the posting of the rural property tax rolls and valuation lists, objections thereto, amendment thereof as the result of such objections and appeals against the decisions of official valuers in respect of such objections shall apply mutatis mutandis to supplementary rural property tax rolls and supplementary valuation lists respectively prepared in accordance with the provisions of sub-section (1) hereof.

— 22 —

Determination of supplementary rural property tax rolls and supplementary valuation lists.	27.—(1) The areas of the categories of the lands of any village and such categories as shown on the supplementary rural property tax roll as finally amended (if there have been any objections) or if there have been no objections then as shown on the supplementary rural property tax roll as posted in the village shall be the areas and categories of such lands for the purposes of this Ordinance as from the commencement of the year next following the year in which such supplementary rural property tax roll was prepared until amended as in this Ordinance provided. (2) The net annual value of the industrial buildings within any village as shown on the supplementary valuation list as finally amended (if there have been any objections) or if there have been no objections then as shown on the supplementary valuation list as posted in the village shall be the net annual value of such industrial buildings for the purposes of this Ordinance as from the commencement of the year next following the year in which such supplementary valuation list was prepared until amended as in this Ordinance provided.
Re-distribution of tax.	28. Upon the first day of April next following the determination of any supplementary rural property tax roll as provided in sub-section (1) of section 27 of this Ordinance, the rural property tax payable in respect of the lands to which it refers shall be distributed amongst the owners of such land in the manner provided in sections 18 to 24, both inclusive, of this Ordinance, such sections for this purpose being applied mutatis mutandis: Provided that the list prepared by the tax distribution committee or by the District Officer or by the District Commissioner shall be called a supplementary distribution list.
Determination of supplementary distribution lists.	29. The amount of the rural property tax payable by each owner of land as shown on the supplementary distribution list or lists as finally amended (if there have been any objections) or if there have been no objections, then as shown on the supplementary distribution list or lists as made available for inspection shall be the amount of the rural property tax payable by such owner in respect of the lands to which such supplementary distribution list or lists refer, as from the commencement of the year in which such supplementary distribution list or lists were prepared until amended as in this Ordinance provided.
When tax shall be due.	30. The rural property tax shall be due:— (a) in respect of the year commencing on the first day of April next following the date of an Order made by the High Commissioner under section 3 of this Ordinance relating to any area, as under:— (i) on all industrial buildings within such area, on the first day of April;

— 23 —

(ii) on any land within such area, on the day the distribution list in respect of such land is made available for inspection in accordance with the provisions of section 20 of this Ordinance, notwithstanding the right to object to such list conferred upon owners by section 21 of this Ordinance, or any objection actually made thereunder:

Provided that upon the determination of such distribution list as provided in section 25 of this Ordinance hen if any owner has paid any sum in excess of the sum payable by him as shown on the distribution list so determined such sum shall be refunded to him, or if any owner has paid any sum less than the sum payable by him as shown on the distribution list so determined, such sum shall be payable by such person and may be recovered as an arrear of the rural property tax:

(b) in respect of any year subsequent to the year commencing on the first day of April next following the date of an Order made by the High Commissioner under section 3 of this Ordinance relating to any area, as under:—

(i) on all industrial buildings within such area, on the first day of April;

(ii) on any land within such area other than land appearing on the supplementary rural property tax roll prepared in the preceding year, on the first day of April;

(iii) on any land appearing on the supplementary rural property tax roll prepared in the preceding year, on the day the supplementary distribution list in respect of such land is posted, notwithstanding the right to object to such supplementary distribution list conferred upon owners by section 28 of this Ordinance or any objections actually made thereunder:

Provided that upon the determination of such supplementary distribution list as provided in section 29 of this Ordinance then if any owner has paid any sum in excess of the sum payable by him as shown on the supplementary distribution list so determined such sum shall be refunded to him or if any owner has paid any sum less than the sum payable by him as shown on the supplementary distribution list so determined such sum shall be payable by such person and may be recovered as an arrear of the rural property tax:

— 24 —

Provided that the District Commissioner may direct that any owner liable for an amount of the rural property tax exceeding two pounds may pay such tax by such instalments and subject to such conditions as the District Commissioner may in such direction set out.

Provisions relating to change of ownership.

31.—(1) Any owner of any land or of any industrial building who on or after the first day of April next following the date of any Order made by the High Commissioner under section 3 of this Ordinance relating to the area in which such land or industrial building is situated shall sell or exchange such land or industrial building or otherwise dispose thereof in any other manner, and any person who on or after such first day of April shall become owner of any land or industrial building within such area by way of succession shall forthwith give notice to the District Officer of the sub-district in which such land or industrial building is situated of such fact in a form to be prescribed.

(2) On receipt of any notice duly made in accordance with the provisions of sub-section (1) hereof, the District Officer shall, after making such enquiries as he may deem necessary, have power to substitute the name of any person in the place of the name of any owner of any property appearing in any distribution list, supplementary distribution list, valuation list or supplementary valuation list which has been posted in accordance with the provisions of this Ordinance.

Each amendment made hereunder shall be initialled and dated by the District Officer and any person whose name is substituted for the name of any owner of any property under this sub-section, shall be deemed to be the owner of such property for the purposes of this Ordinance as from the first day of April next following the date of such amendment.

(3) Nothing in this section shall be deemed to alter, determine or render void any liability of any person whose name is substituted for that of any owner under the provisions of sub-section (2) hereof by contract, agreement or otherwise concerning the liability of such person to pay to such owner any tax due in respect of any property, provided always that such owner shall remain liable to Government for the payment of the rural property tax due in respect of any period prior to the date when such person is deemed to be the owner of such property for the purposes of this Ordinance under sub-section (2) hereof.

Collection of arrears of tax. No. 26 of 1929.

32. Any rural property tax which shall be in arrear may be recovered in accordance with the provisions of the Collection of Taxes Ordinance, 1929, and the rural property tax shall be deemed to be a tax to which that Ordinance applies:

Provided that the posting of the distribution list, supplementary distribution list, valuation list and supplementary valuation list shall be deemed to be good and sufficient demand to all owners.

— 25 —

appearing thereon respectively to pay the rural property tax appearing against their names and no demand notes shall be required.

33. Where the name of any person liable to pay the rural property tax is not known, it shall be sufficient for any of the purposes of this Ordinance to designate him as "the owner" without any further description.   *Owner need not be named.*

34. Whenever it is provided in this Ordinance that notice shall be given to any owner or person for any of the purposes of this Ordinance, such notice shall be deemed to have been so given if forwarded by post to the last known address of such owner or person or if such address is not known then by affixing the notice in some conspicuous part of the property of such owner or person: *Provisions relating to notices under this Ordinance.*

Provided that notice given in accordance with the provisions of this section to any owner being a co-owner of any property held in joint ownership shall be deemed to be notice to all the other co-owners of such property.

35. The District Officer may at any time cause to be corrected any clerical errors in the rural property tax roll or supplementary rural property tax roll or valuation list or supplementary valuation list or distribution list or supplementary distribution list and may introduce clerical amendments or additions thereto respectively provided that all such corrections, amendments or additions are signed by the District Officer and that a separate record is kept by him of such errors, amendments or additions.   *Power of District Officer to correct errors.*

36.—(1) Any person who in any form prescribed wilfully makes any false statement and any person who refuses to answer any question or wilfully makes a false answer to any question put to him by any person in order to obtain information which will enable such person to carry out any duties imposed upon or exercise any powers conferred upon him by this Ordinance, shall be guilty of an offence and shall on conviction be liable to imprisonment for a term not exceeding one year or to a fine not exceeding one hundred pounds or to both such penalties.   *Offences and penalties.*

(2) Any person who shall in any way obstruct any other person in the carrying out of any duties imposed upon or in the exercise of any powers conferred upon such other person by this Ordinance, shall be guilty of an offence and shall on conviction be liable to imprisonment for a term not exceeding one year or to a fine not exceeding one hundred pounds or to both such penalties.

(3) Any owner or person who shall fail to comply with the provisions of section 5 or section 31 of this Ordinance, shall be guilty of an offence and shall on conviction be liable to impri-

— 26 —

sonment for a term not exceeding three months or to a fine not exceeding twenty pounds or to both such penalties.

Provisions relating to occupants of Government lands.

37. Every occupant of Government owned land in virtue of an implied lease shall pay an amount equal to the amount of the rural property tax due on such land as rental in respect thereof.

Tax to be first charge on property, etc.

38.—(1) The rural property tax shall be a first charge on the property in respect of which it is payable and no transaction relating to such property shall be entered in any Government register until the rural property tax thereon has been paid.

(2) Without prejudice to the provisions of section 32 of this Ordinance, if the owner of any property in respect of which the rural property tax is payable is absent from Palestine the said tax shall be payable by and may be recovered from the agent, if any, of any such owner to the extent of the amount of any moneys collected by the agent on behalf of such owner provided always the owner shall remain liable to the Government for the payment of the rural property tax.

(3) Where any land or any industrial building is held in joint ownership, the rural property tax may be collected from any one or more of the co-owners and the co-owner or co-owners from whom the rural property tax is collected shall have a right of contribution from the other co-owner or co-owners in the proportion of the respective shares of such other co-owner or co-owners.

(4) Nothing in this Ordinance shall be deemed to alter, determine or render void any liability of a tenant to his landlord by contract, agreement or otherwise, concerning the liability of the tenant to pay to the landlord any tax due in respect of the property provided always that the owner shall remain liable to Government for the payment of the rural property tax.

The Commissioner of Lands to supervise this Ordinance.

39. The Commissioner of Lands shall exercise general supervision and control over the carrying out of this Ordinance.

Power of Chief Justice to make certain rules.

40. The Chief Justice may with the approval of the High Commissioner make rules regulating the practice and procedure in applications to a District Court upon a case stated under the provisions of this Ordinance.

Power of High Commissioner to make rules.

41. The High Commissioner may make rules for the carrying out of this Ordinance.

Revocation.

42. The Commutation of Tithes Ordinance, 1927, and the Decree dated the twenty-fifth day of September and published in the Gazette dated the fifteenth day of November, 1920, relating to the exemption from tithes of vineyards planted with American stock shall cease to have effect in any area described in any Order made by the High Commissioner under section 3 of this Ordinance as from the first day of April next following the date of such Order.

— 27 —

SCHEDULE

Category	Description	Rate of Tax per dunum Mils
1	Citrus (excluding Acre Sub-District)	825
2	Citrus (Acre Sub-District)	410
3	Bananas	560
4	Village built-on area or reserved therefor	160
5	1st Grade Irrigated Land and ø 1st Grade Fruit Plantation	40
6	2nd Grade Irrigated Land and ø 2nd Grade Fruit Plantation	35
7	3rd Grade Irrigated Land and ø 3rd Grade Fruit Plantation	30
8	1st Grade Ground Crop Land 4th Grade Irrigated Land and ø 4th Grade Fruit Plantation	25
9	2nd Grade Ground Crop Land 5th Grade Irrigated Land and ø 5th Grade Fruit Plantation	20
10	3rd Grade Ground Crop Land 6th Grade Irrigated Land and ø 6th Grade Fruit Plantation	18
11	4th Grade Ground Crop Land 7th Grade Irrigated Land and ø 7th Grade Fruit Plantation	15
12	5th Grade Ground Crop Land 8th Grade Irrigated Land and ø 8th Grade Fruit Plantation	12
13	6th Grade Ground Crop Land 9th Grade Irrigated Land and ø 9th Grade Fruit Plantation	8
14	7th Grade Ground Crop Land and 10th Grade Irrigated Land	nil
15	8th Grade Ground Crop Land	nil
16	Forests planted and indigenous and uncultivable land	nil

ø Other than Citrus and Bananas.

15th January, 1935.

A. G. WAUCHOPE
High Commissioner.

LAND SETTLEMENT (AMENDMENT) ORDINANCE, No. 25 OF 1935.

Arthur Wauchope

High Commissioner

LAND SETTLEMENT (AMENDMENT) ORDINANCE,
No. 25 of 1935.

AN ORDINANCE TO AMEND THE LAND SETTLEMENT ORDINANCE, 1928.

BE IT ENACTED by the High Commissioner for Palestine with the advice and consent of the Advisory Council thereof:—

Short title.

1. This Ordinance may be cited as the Land Settlement (Amendment) Ordinance, 1935, and the Land Settlement Ordinance, 1928 (hereinafter referred to as the principal Ordinance) the Land Settlement (Amendment) Ordinance, 1930, the Land Settlement (Amendment) Ordinance, 1932, the Land Settlement (Amendment) Ordinance, 1933 and this Ordinance may together be cited as the Land Settlement Ordinances, 1928-1935.

Amendment of section 10 of the principal Ordinance.

2. Section 10 of the principal Ordinance shall be amended by the addition thereto of the following sub-section:—

"(4) At any time after the publication of the settlement notice, or at any stage in any proceedings before the Settlement Officer relating to the ownership of land in a settlement area, the Settlement Officer shall have power and shall be deemed always to have had power to make, vary or rescind an interim order for possession of any land affected by such notice or any land to which such proceedings relate, in favour of any person claiming or counterclaiming possession, and any such order as aforesaid may be made by the Settlement Officer of his own motion, or on the application of any person claiming or counterclaiming possession".

24th May, 1935.

A. G. WAUCHOPE
High Commissioner.

RURAL PROPERTY TAX (AMENDMENT) ORDINANCE, No. 26 OF 1935.

Arthur Wauchope

RURAL PROPERTY TAX (AMENDMENT) ORDINANCE, No. 26 of 1935.

AN ORDINANCE TO AMEND THE RURAL PROPERTY TAX ORDINANCE, 1935.

BE IT ENACTED by the High Commissioner in Council with the advice of the Advisory Council thereof:—

1. This Ordinance may be cited as the Rural Property Tax (Amendment) Ordinance, 1935.
Short title.

2. The Rural Property Tax Ordinance, 1935, is hereby amended by the insertion of the following section as section 43:
Amendment of the Rural Property Tax Ordinance, 1935.

"Exemption from tax not to affect certain rights. 43. Where no Rural Property Tax is payable upon any land by reason of its being of a category upon which no such tax is payable under the provisions of the schedule to this Ordinance, the non payment of such tax in respect of such land shall not be deemed to affect, or to be evidence of, the rights of any person in respect of such land".

20th June, 1935.

A. G. WAUCHOPE
High Commissioner.

EXPROPRIATION OF LAND (AMENDMENT) ORDINANCE, No. 30 OF 1935.

Officer Administering the Government

EXPROPRIATION OF LAND (AMENDMENT) ORDINANCE,
No. 30 of 1935.

AN ORDINANCE TO AMEND THE EXPROPRIATION OF LAND ORDINANCE, 1926.

BE IT ENACTED by the High Commissioner for Palestine with the advice of the Advisory Council thereof:—

1. This Ordinance may be cited as the Expropriation of Land (Amendment) Ordinance, 1935, and the Expropriation of Land Ordinance, 1926 (hereinafter referred to as the principal Ordinance), the Expropriation of Land (Amendment) Ordinance, 1932, and this Ordinance may together be cited as the Expropriation of Land Ordinances, 1926-1935. *Short title.*

2. Section 22 of the principal Ordinance shall be deleted and the following section shall be substituted therefor:— *Substitution of new section in the place of section 22 of the principal Ordinance.*

"Where any land is taken under this Ordinance by the promoters for the purpose of widening any existing road or part of it, or for the construction of a new road, the owner of the land expropriated shall not be entitled to compensation unless the area taken exceeds one quarter part of the total area of the plot which he owns. Provided that, if it is established that hardship would be caused if no compensation were paid, the High Commissioner may in his discretion grant such compensation as, having regard to all the circumstances of the case, he shall think fit. If the area taken from any owner exceeds one quarter part of the total area of the plot owned by him, compensation shall be paid to the owner for the land taken in excess of such one quarter part in accordance with the provisions of this Ordinance".

8th August, 1935.

A. G. WAUCHOPE
High Commissioner.

Section 19: 1937

LAND TRANSFER (AMENDMENT) ORDINANCE, No. 20 OF 1937.

Officer Administering the Government
~~High Commissioner~~

LAND TRANSFER (AMENDMENT) ORDINANCE,
No. 20 of 1937.

An Ordinance to amend the Land Transfer Ordinance.

Be it enacted by the High Commissioner for Palestine, with the advice of the Advisory Council thereof :—

1. This Ordinance may be cited as the Land Transfer (Amendment) Ordinance, 1937, and shall be read as one with the Land Transfer Ordinance, hereinafter referred to as the principal Ordinance. *Short title.* *Cap. 81.*

2. Section 7 of the principal Ordinance shall be amended by the addition of the following proviso at the end thereof :— *Amendment of section 7 of the principal Ordinance.*

"Provided that where a registered mortgage contains a covenant by the mortgagor not to lease the mortgaged property without the consent of the mortgagee the Director shall refuse to register any lease by the mortgagor of the mortgaged property unless the written consent of the mortgagee is first lodged with the Director of Lands."

19th August, 1937.

A. G. WAUCHOPE
High Commissioner.

LAND LAW (AMENDMENT) ORDINANCE, No. 34 OF 1937.

Arthur Wauchope
High Commissioner

LAND LAW (AMENDMENT) ORDINANCE,
No. 34 of 1937.

AN ORDINANCE TO AMEND THE LAND LAW (AMENDMENT) ORDINANCE.

BE IT ENACTED by the High Commissioner for Palestine, with the advice of the Advisory Council thereof :—

1. This Ordinance may be cited as the Land Law (Amendment) Ordinance, 1937, and shall be read as one with the Land Law (Amendment) Ordinance, hereinafter referred to as the principal Ordinance. *(Short title. Cap. 78.)*

2. The principal Ordinance shall be amended by the addition of the following section thereto, as section 10 :— *(Addition of new section in principal Ordinance, as section 10.)*

"10. As from the commencement of the Land Law (Amendment) Ordinance, 1937, no registration shall be made or document of title issued in respect of :— *(No registration or document of title for building, trees, etc.)*

(a) the ownership of trees, or

(b) the ownership of buildings, or

(c) any right to build, or to add to buildings already erected, upon land :

Provided that the provisions of this section shall not apply to any tree, building or right already registered in the Land Registry at the commencement of the Land Law (Amendment) Ordinance, 1937, or which forms the subject matter of a judgment of a competent court or a decision of a Land Settlement Officer given prior to that date."

24th November, 1937.

W. D. BATTERSHILL
Officer Administering the Government.

Section 20: 1938

LAND TRANSFER (AMENDMENT) ORDINANCE, No. 16 OF 1938.

[signature]
High Commissioner

LAND TRANSFER (AMENDMENT) ORDINANCE,
No. 16 of 1938.

AN ORDINANCE TO AMEND THE LAND TRANSFER ORDINANCE.

BE IT ENACTED by the High Commissioner for Palestine, with the advice of the Advisory Council thereof :—

1. This Ordinance may be cited as the Land Transfer (Amendment) Ordinance, 1938, and shall be read as one with the Land Transfer Ordinance, hereinafter referred to as the principal Ordinance. *Short title.* *Cap. 61.*

2. Section 14 of the principal Ordinance shall be repealed and the following section substituted therefor :— *Substitution of new section for section 14 of the principal Ordinance.*

"Sale of land in satisfaction of judgment debts and mortgages.

14.—(1) Application for the sale of immovable property in execution of a judgment or in satisfaction of a mortgage shall be made to the President of the District Court who, upon such application, —

(a) shall have power, and shall be deemed always to have had power, to order the sale of such immovable property;

(b) shall have power to order postponement of the sale if he is satisfied that the debtor has reasonable prospects of payment if given time, or that, having regard to all the circumstances of the case, including the needs of the creditor, it would involve undue hardship to sell the property of the debtor.

(2) Where any sale is ordered under this section in satisfaction of a mortgage, it shall be conducted in the Execution Office of the District Court as if the sale were a sale in execution of a judgment.

(3) Where, prior to the commencement of the Land Transfer (Amendment) Ordinance, 1938, any sale in satisfaction of a mortgage has been carried out in the Execution Office of any Court, such sale shall not be deemed to be invalid by reason only that it has not been carried out in the Tapou registry office."

5th May, 1938.

HAROLD MACMICHAEL
High Commissioner.

Section 21: 1939

LAND TRANSFER (AMENDMENT) ORDINANCE, No. 1 OF 1939.

LAND TRANSFER (AMENDMENT) ORDINANCE,
No. 1 of 1939.

AN ORDINANCE TO AMEND THE LAND TRANSFER ORDINANCE.

BE IT ENACTED by the High Commissioner for Palestine, with the advice of the Advisory Council thereof :—

1. This Ordinance may be cited as the Land Transfer (Amendment) Ordinance, 1939, and shall be read as one with the Land Transfer Ordinance, hereinafter referred to as the principal Ordinance. *Short title.*

2. The principal Ordinance shall be amended by the insertion, after section 9 thereof, of the following section as section 9A :— *Insertion of new section in the principal Ordinance as section 9A.*

"Dispositions entailing subdivision to conform to prescribed town planning and land settlement minima.

9A. The Director shall not give the consent required by section 4 to any disposition of immovable property which entails the division or parcellation thereof, unless he has satisfied himself that such division or parcellation —

  (a) conforms with the provisions prescribing minimum areas of parcels in respect of such immovable property, contained in any approved outline, detailed or parcellation town planning scheme, copies of which have been deposited at the office of the local town planning commission in accordance with the provisions of the Town Planning Ordinance, 1936; and

  (b) conforms with all other provisions of any such town planning scheme as aforesaid affecting such immovable property : provided that where in the opinion of the Director the urgency of any particular case necessitates that the requirements of this paragraph should be dispensed with, he may dispense with the same accordingly; and

  (c) in the case of immovable property which is or has been the subject of land settlement operations, also conforms with the conditions as to minimum area and shape of parcels prescribed in respect thereof under section 34 of the Land (Settlement of Title) Ordinance :

Cap. 80.

— 2 —

Provided that nothing in this section shall be deemed to prohibit the Director from giving his consent to the disposition, in favour of an owner of adjoining immovable property, of any immovable property the area or shape of which does not conform with such of the provisions or conditions referred to in paragraphs (a) and (c) hereof as may be applicable thereto, if the combined area and shape of the property so disposed of and such adjoining property conforms with the said provisions or conditions."

HAROLD MACMICHAEL
High Commissioner.

30th January, 1939.

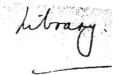

LAND TRANSFER (AMENDMENT) ORDINANCE, No. 39 OF 1939.

High Commissioner

LAND TRANSFER (AMENDMENT) ORDINANCE, No. 39 of 1939.

An Ordinance to amend the Land Transfer Ordinance.

Be it enacted by the High Commissioner for Palestine, with the advice of the Advisory Council thereof:—

1. This Ordinance may be cited as the Land Transfer (Amendment) Ordinance, 1939, and shall be read as one with the Land Transfer Ordinance, hereinafter referred to as the principal Ordinance. *(Short title. Cap. 81.)*

2. Section 14 of the principal Ordinance shall be amended by the addition of the following subsections at the end thereof:— *(Amendment of section 14 of the principal Ordinance.)*

"(4) Where an application for the sale of immovable property is made under this section the President of the District Court shall have power at any time, whether before or after the making of an order for the sale of such immovable property, to appoint a Receiver of such property wherever it appears to him just and convenient so to do.

(5) The President of the District Court shall have all such powers incidental to the making of such appointment as are for the time being vested in, or exercisable by, a District Court with respect to the appointment of a Receiver in connection with any action brought therein, and the provisions of any rules of court in force from time to time governing or prescribing the manner of appointment by a District Court of Receivers, their duties, liabilities and remuneration shall apply *mutatis mutandis* to any case where a Receiver is appointed by the President of a District Court as aforesaid.

(6) Where, prior to the commencement of the Land Transfer (Amendment) Ordinance, 1939, the President of a District Court has appointed a Receiver of any immovable property in connection with an application under this section for the sale of such property, and at the commencement of that Ordinance such receivership was still subsisting, the appointment of such Receiver shall be deemed to have been validly made as though it had been made after the commencement of the said Ordinance.

(7) In any application under this section the President of the District Court shall have all the powers of a District Court with regard to the awarding of costs."

HAROLD MACMICHAEL
High Commissioner.

22nd September, 1939.

LAND COURTS (AMENDMENT) ORDINANCE, No. 46 OF 1939.

High Commissioner

LAND COURTS (AMENDMENT) ORDINANCE, No. 46 of 1939.

An Ordinance to amend the Land Courts Ordinance.

BE IT ENACTED by the High Commissioner for Palestine, with the advice of the Advisory Council thereof:—

1. This Ordinance may be cited as the Land Courts (Amendment) Ordinance, 1939, and shall be read as one with the Land Courts Ordinance, hereinafter referred to as the principal Ordinance, and shall come into force on the first day of January, 1940.

Short title and commencement. Cap. 75.

2. Section 3 of the principal Ordinance shall be amended by the substitution of the following paragraph for paragraph (d) thereof:—

"(d) where there is a dispute as to the ownership of the land, or any rights in or over the land, to hear the case and give a judgment:

Provided that nothing in the Magistrates' Courts Jurisdiction Ordinance, 1939, shall be deemed to prevent a Land Court from making an order for the possession of any land in respect of the ownership of which it gives a judgment;".

Amendment of section 3 of the principal Ordinance.

3. Section 6 of the principal Ordinance shall be amended by the substitution of the words "on the application of a party with notice to all other parties" for the words "within six months of its issue" appearing in subsection (2) thereof.

Amendment of section 6 of the principal Ordinance.

4. The principal Ordinance shall be amended by the deletion of the words "and District" from the heading appearing above section 10 thereof.

Amendment of heading in the principal Ordinance.

5. The following heading and section shall be added at the end of the principal Ordinance:—

Insertion of new heading and sections in the principal Ordinance.

"*Constitution of Land Courts.*

Constitution of Land Courts.

11.—(1) Land Courts shall be constituted as follows:—

(a) where the value of the land or the subject matter of the dispute exceeds two hundred and fifty pounds, of a president or relieving president of a district court;

(b) where the value of the land or the subject matter of the dispute does not exceed two hundred and fifty pounds, of a British magistrate's court;

— 2 —

(c) where the value of the land or the subject matter of the dispute does not exceed one hundred and fifty pounds, of a magistrate's court, other than a British magistrate's court.

(2) The registry of the court in which any proceedings under this Ordinance are brought under the provisions of this section shall be deemed to be the registry of a land court.

(3) The practice and procedure applicable to Magistrates' Courts shall apply to proceedings in Land Courts constituted of a Magistrate's Court :

Provided that the provisions of the Civil Procedure Rules, 1938, regulating appeals shall apply to appeals from Land Courts to the Supreme Court sitting as a Court of Appeal."

Saving

6. Nothing in this Ordinance shall be deemed to affect the jurisdiction of any court to try any action commenced before the coming into force of this Ordinance, and such action shall be tried as though this Ordinance had not come into operation.

Provided that in any such case if the trial thereof has not, on the coming into force of this Ordinance, actually commenced before the Land Court, and all the parties concerned agree thereto, application may be made to the Registrar to transfer such case to a Land Court constituted in accordance with the provisions of this Ordinance, and such case shall thereupon be transferred accordingly and the provisions of the principal Ordinance, as amended by this Ordinance, shall apply to the trial of any such case.

22nd November, 1939.

HAROLD MACMICHAEL
High Commissioner.

LAND (SETTLEMENT OF TITLE) (AMENDMENT) ORDINANCE, No. 48 OF 1939.

High Commissioner

LAND (SETTLEMENT OF TITLE) (AMENDMENT) ORDINANCE, No. 48 of 1939.

AN ORDINANCE TO AMEND THE LAND (SETTLEMENT OF TITLE) ORDINANCE.

BE IT ENACTED by the High Commissioner for Palestine, with the advice of the Advisory Council thereof :—

1. This Ordinance may be cited as the Land (Settlement of Title) (Amendment) Ordinance, 1939, and shall be read as one with the Land (Settlement of Title) Ordinance, hereinafter referred to as the principal Ordinance, and shall come into operation on the first day of January, 1940.
Short title and commencement. Cap. 80.

2. Section 6 of the principal Ordinance shall be amended by the addition of the following words after the words "any such action may be withdrawn :" appearing in subsection (1) thereof :—
"and, if such action cannot be decided before the settlement is begun, the court on its own motion may order it to be stayed and defer judgment therein until the publication of the schedule of rights under section 33, or may order that it shall be determined by the settlement officer."
Amendment of section 6 of the principal Ordinance.

3. Section 19 of the principal Ordinance shall be amended by the substitution of the word "may" for the word "shall" appearing therein.
Amendment of section 19 of the principal Ordinance.

4. Section 28 of the principal Ordinance shall be repealed, and the following section substituted therefor :—
Substitution of new section for section 28 of the principal Ordinance.

"*Exclusion of area from settlement area.*" 28. Notwithstanding anything contained in the preceding sections, the High Commissioner may, by notice, exclude any area from a settlement area, and thereafter the settlement officer shall not perform any act of settlement within the area so excluded, except such act as may be necessary for the purpose of demarcating the boundary between the settlement area and the area so excluded."

5. Section 29 of the principal Ordinance shall be repealed, and the following sections shall be substituted therefor :—
Substitution of new sections for section 29 of the principal Ordinance.

"*Rights of Government to land.*" 29. The rights of the Government in land shall be investigated and settled whether they are formally claimed or not. All rights to land which are not established by any claimant shall be registered in the name of the High Commissioner in trust for the Government of Palestine.

— 2 —

Registration of certain metrukeh and lands assigned for public purposes.

29A. Land which is proved to be of the metrukeh category and which has been used *ab antiquo* for public purposes, or land which has been legally assigned for public purposes, shall be registered in the name of the High Commissioner in trust for the Government of Palestine; provided that where the land is assigned for the uses of a town or village, and there has been constituted a legal body having power to hold and dispose of immovable property on behalf of that town or village, it shall be registered in the name of such legal body."

Amendment of section 31 of the principal Ordinance.

6. Section 31 of the principal Ordinance shall be amended by the repeal of subsection (1) thereof and the substitution of the following subsection therefor :—

"(1) After the investigation of rights the settlement officer shall divide the block into parcels or units of registration so that each different category is shown in a separate parcel and he shall thereupon draw up a schedule of rights in such form and containing such details as may be prescribed. After dealing with such schedule as hereinafter provided he shall transmit a signed copy thereof to the registrar, together with a signed plan of the parcels comprised in the schedule."

Amendment of section 33 of the principal Ordinance.

7. Section 33 of the principal Ordinance shall be amended —

(a) by the substitution of the word "thirty" for the word "fifteen" appearing in subsection (2) thereof; and

(b) by the repeal of subsection (4) thereof and the substitution of the following subsection therefor :—

"(4) During the period of thirty days in which the schedule of rights is posted, any person claiming a right to land may apply to the settlement officer, and thereupon the settlement officer may revise his decision in the schedule of rights if due notice is given to any person affected by the application for revision".

Amendment of section 53 of the principal Ordinance.

8. Section 53 of the principal Ordinance shall be amended as follows :—

(a) paragraph (a) thereof shall be renumbered as paragraph (a)(i) and shall be amended by the addition of the following sub-paragraph thereto as sub-paragraph (ii) :—

"(ii) The chief clerk of the court before which any action under sub-paragraph (i) hereof has begun shall forthwith notify the Director of Land Registration accordingly.";

— 3 —

(b) paragraph (d) thereof shall be amended by the deletion of the words "the Director of Lands" appearing therein and the substitution of the following words therefor :—

"or if during such period the registered owner or his heirs shall signify in writing to the Director of Land Registration his or their consent to the registration of the person registered with the possessory title as the owner of the land, the Director of Land Registration,".

9. Section 56 of the principal Ordinance shall be amended by the substitution of the words "by the Supreme Court sitting as a Court of Civil Appeal" for the words "the land court" wherever they appear therein.

Amendment of section 56 of the principal Ordinance.

10. Section 63 of the principal Ordinance shall be amended as follows :—

Amendment of section 63 of the principal Ordinance.

(a) by the substitution of the words "the Chief Justice" for the words "the president of a land court" appearing in line 3 of subsection (1) thereof;

(b) by the substitution of the word "thirty" for the word "fifteen" appearing in the tenth and fourteenth lines respectively of subsection (1) thereof;

(c) by the substitution of the words "the Chief Justice through the Chief Registrar" for the words "the president of the land court" appearing in lines 14 and 15 of subsection (1) thereof;

(d) by the repeal of subsection (2) thereof and the substitution of the following subsection therefor :—

"(2) Where leave to appeal is granted it shall be heard by the Supreme Court sitting as a Court of Civil Appeal and such appeal shall be entered within thirty days of the date of the order granting leave if made in the presence of the applicant, or within thirty days from the notification to him if made in his absence, and grounds of appeal shall be filed and fees paid and security furnished, in accordance with the Civil Procedure Rules, 1938 : Provided that an appellant may enter an appeal before the service upon him of such notification.

The settlement officer shall forward to the Chief Registrar all the documents relating to the case.";

(e) by the repeal of subsection (3) thereof.

Amendment of section 64 of the principal Ordinance.

11. Section 64 of the principal Ordinance shall be amended as follows:—

(a) by the substitution of the following marginal note for the marginal note thereto:—

"Procedure on appeal.";

(b) by the substitution of the following subsection for subsection (1) thereof:—

"(1) The Civil Procedure Rules, 1938, shall apply to the hearing and determination of the appeal.";

(c) by the repeal of subsection (2) thereof;

(d) by the deletion of the words from "where" to "prescribed" inclusive, appearing in lines 1 and 2 of subsection (3) thereof;

(e) by the substitution of the words "Supreme Court" for the words "land court" appearing in line 3 of subsection (3) thereof.

Saving.

12. All appeals from the decisions of Land Settlement Officers in respect of which applications for leave to appeal have been made to the Land Court prior to the coming into operation of this Ordinance shall be heard and determined as though this Ordinance had not been passed:

Provided that in any such case if the hearing of the appeal has not, on the coming into operation of this Ordinance, commenced before the Land Court, and all the parties concerned agree thereto, application may be made to the Registrar to transfer such appeal to the Supreme Court sitting as a Court of Civil Appeal, and such case shall thereupon be transferred accordingly, and the provisions of the principal Ordinance, as amended by this Ordinance, shall apply to the hearing and determination of any such appeal.

22nd November, 1939.

HAROLD MACMICHAEL
High Commissioner.

Section 22: 1940

Supplement No. 2
to the
Palestine Gazette Extraordinary No. 988 of 28th February, 1940.

PALESTINE ORDERS IN COUNCIL, 1922 TO 1939.
REGULATIONS BY THE HIGH COMMISSIONER UNDER ARTICLE 16D.

IN EXERCISE of the powers vested in me by Article 16D of the Palestine Orders in Council, 1922 to 1939, I, SIR HAROLD ALFRED MACMICHAEL, K.C.M.G., D.S.O., High Commissioner for Palestine, do hereby make the following regulations:—

1. These regulations may be cited as the Land Transfers Regulations, 1940, and shall be deemed to have come into force on the eighteenth day of May, 1939. *Citation and commencement.*

2. For the purpose of these regulations there shall be two zones in Palestine which shall be demarcated as set out in the Schedule hereto. *Definitions of Zone A and Zone B.*

The boundaries of Zone A and Zone B are indicated on the Palestine Index to Villages and Settlements Map signed by the High Commissioner which is deposited in the office of the Director of Land Registration and is available for inspection during office hours.

3. The transfer of land situated within Zone A save to a Palestinian Arab shall be prohibited: *Transfer of land within Zone A.*

Provided that the High Commissioner may, if he considers it desirable so to do —

(a) permit of the mortgage of such land to such companies or societies as he may approve;

(b) permit the transfer of such land by Palestinian Arabs to religious or charitable institutions;

(c) permit the transfer of such land to persons not being Palestinian Arabs if in his opinion such transfer is necessary

— 328 —

for the purpose of consolidating existing holdings, or of effecting the parcellation of village musha' within the meaning of the Land (Settlement of Title) Ordinance;

Cap. 80.

(d) in the case of land within the said Zone owned by persons not being Palestinian Arabs, by general or special order, permit the transfer of such land to persons not being Palestinian Arabs;

Provided further that the High Commissioner may, if he considers it desirable so to do, authorize the transfer of any land situated within the said Zone to persons not being Palestinian Arabs, if application for the registration of such transfer was lodged in the Land Registry before the date of publication of these regulations in the *Gazette*;

Provided further that this regulation shall not apply to any transfer of land made in the execution of any judgment or order of a Court, Chief Execution Officer or Land Settlement Officer —

(a) in satisfaction of a mortgage executed and registered before the date of the coming into force of these regulations, or

(b) delivered or made before the date of publication of these regulations in the *Gazette*.

Transfer of land within Zone B.

4. The transfer of land situated within Zone B, by a Palestinian Arab save to a Palestinian Arab, shall be prohibited unless the person to whom such transfer is intended to be made has received the approval in writing of the High Commissioner which he may in his unfettered discretion grant or refuse:

Provided that this regulation shall not apply to any transfer of land made in the execution of any judgment or order of a Court, Chief Execution Officer or Land Settlement Officer —

(a) in satisfaction of a mortgage executed and registered before the date of the coming into force of these regulations, or

(b) delivered or made before the date of publication of these regulations in the *Gazette*.

Effect of transfer of land in contravention of these regulations.

5. Any transfer of land made in contravention of the provisions of these regulations shall be null and void.

Provisions with regard to affidavits.

6.—(1) The High Commissioner may require any person making application for the High Commissioner's approval to the transfer of any land under these regulations, to support such application by affidavits by himself or any other person.

(2) Any person —

(a) who knowingly makes any false statement in any affidavit made for the purpose of these regulations, or

(b) who knowingly uses for the purposes of these regulations any affidavit containing any false statement,

is guilty of an offence and is liable to imprisonment for seven years.

7. The provisions of these regulations shall be in addition to, and not in derogation of, the provisions of the Land Transfer Ordinance. Provisions of these regulations to be in addition to those of Land Transfer Ordinance.
Cap. 81.

8. Nothing in these regulations shall be deemed — Saving.

(a) to apply to the transfer of any land situated within the area of any municipal corporation established from time to time under the provisions of the Municipal Corporations Ordinance, 1934; or

(b) to apply to the transfer of any public lands by or on behalf of the High Commissioner or to the transfer of any land to the High Commissioner in accordance with any law or Ordinance or otherwise; or

(c) to affect the power to expropriate land under the provisions of any law or Ordinance for the time being in force.

9. For the purposes of these regulations :— Definitions.

"Palestinian Arab" shall be deemed to be an Arab who is ordinarily resident in Palestine. In case of any dispute as to whether a person is an Arab or whether he is ordinarily resident in Palestine, the question shall be referred to the High Commissioner whose decision thereon shall be final;

"land" includes water, buildings, trees and any interest in, or right in, to or over, land, water, buildings or trees;

"transfer" includes leases, mortgages, charges and any other dispositions.

HAROLD MACMICHAEL
High Commissioner.

20th February, 1940.

— 390 —

SCHEDULE.
ZONE A.

The area comprising :—   ACRE SUB-DISTRICT.

The whole, with the exception of Blocks 18025, 18039, 18040 and 18041 of the village of Manshiya.

SAFAD SUB-DISTRICT.

(a) The following villages in whole :—

'Alma	Jish	Rihaniya
'Ammuqa	Kafr Bir'im	Sabalan
Dallata	Malikiya, El	Safsaf
Deishum	Marun er Ras	Saliha
'Eitarun	Marus	Sammu'i
Fara	Meirun	Sa'sa'
Farradiya	Mughr ed Duruz	Teitaba
Ghabbatiya	Qabba'a	Yarun
Hurfeish	Qaddita	
Jazair el Hindaj	Ras el Ahmar, Er	

(b) The portions of the following villages lying to the west of the road from Rosh Pinna to Metulla :—

Hatsor   Yesud ham Ma'ala

TIBERIAS SUB-DISTRICT.

(a) The following villages in whole :—

'Eilabun	Khirbat el Wa'ra es Sauda	Mansura, El
Hittin	Maghar	Nimrin

(b) The portion of the following village lying to the north of the road from Nazareth to Tiberias :—

Lubiya

NAZARETH SUB-DISTRICT.

(a) The following villages in whole :—

Bu'eina	Mash-had	Tur'an
Kafr Kanna	Nazareth	Umm Qubei
Kafr Manda	Reina, Er	'Uzeir
Kaukab	Rummana	
Kefar ha Horesh	Saffuriya	

(b) The portions of the following villages lying to the north of the road from Haifa to Nazareth :—

'Ilut	Mujeidil	Yafa
Ma'lul	Nahalal	

— 331 —

HAIFA SUB-DISTRICT.

(a) The following villages in whole :—

Abu Shusha	Ijzim	Naghnaghiya, En
Abu Zureiq	'Isfiya	Qannir
'Ar'ara	Ji'ara	Qira Wa Qamun
'Arab Baniha	Kafrin, El	Rihaniya, Er
Beit Lahm	Kafr Qari'	Sabbarin
Buteimat, El	Khureiba, El	Shafa 'Amr
Daliyat el Karmil	Khirbat ed Damun	Sindyana, Es
Daliyat er Ruha	Khirbat Lidd	Umm esh Shauf
Ghubaiya el Fauqa, El	Khirbat Shallala	Umm ez Zinat
Ghubaiya et Tahta, El	Khubbeiza	Wadi 'Ara
I'billin	Mishmar ha'Emeq	

(b) The portions of the following villages lying to the north of the road from Haifa to Nazareth :—

Jeida	Waldheim	Qusqus-Tab'un

(c) The portions of the following villages lying to the east of the road from Jaffa to Haifa :—

'Ein Ghazal	Jaba'
'Ein Haud	Mazar, El

(d) The portion of Et Tira lying east of the Jaffa—Haifa Road and south of the Wadi Kafr Samir.

JENIN SUB-DISTRICT.

The whole.

BEISAN SUB-DISTRICT.

The following villages in whole :—

'Arida, El	Ghazzawiya, El	Samiriya, Es
Ashrafiya, El	Hamra, El	Tell esh Shauk
Beisan	Khuneizir, El	Umm 'Ajra
Farwana	Masil el Jizl	Zarra'a, Ez
Fatur, El	Safa, Es	

TULKARM SUB-DISTRICT.

(a) The following villages in whole :—

'Anabta	Beit Lid	'Illar
'Attara, El	Dannaba	Irtah
'Attil	Deir el Ghusun	Jaiyus
'Azzun	Falama	Jatt
Bal'a	Fardisiya	Kafr 'Abbush
Baqa el Gharbiya	Far'un	Kafr el Labad
Baqa esh Sharqiya	Habla	Kafr Rumman

— 332 —

TULKARM SUB-DISTRICT (Continued).

Kafr Sur	Nazla el Wusta, En	Saffarin
Kafr Zibad	Nazlat Abu Nar	Seida
Kur	Nazlat 'Isa	Shufa
Nazla el Gharbiya, En	Qaffin	Shuweika
Nazla esh Sharqiya, En	Ramin	Zeita
	Ras, Er	

(b) The portions of the following villages lying to the east of the railway from Lydda to Haifa :—

'Attil Detached	Kafr Jammal	Tira, Et
Jaljuliya	Qalqiliya	Raml Zeita

(c) The following villages in part :—

Blocks 7974 7975 7976 7977 7978 8076 8077 8103 8104 8105 8106 8107 8108 8109 8110 8111 and the village built-on area of Qaqun.

Blocks 8157 8158 8159 8160 8165 8166 8167 8168 8169 8170 8171 8172 8173 8174 8175 8176 8177 8178 8179 8180 8181 8182 8183 and 8184 of Tulkarm.

Blocks 7858 7859 7860 7861 7862 7863 7869 7870 and 7887 of Qalansuwa.

The portion of Et Taiyiba lying to the east of the railway from Lydda to Haifa and Blocks 7825 and 7828 of that village.

NABLUS SUB-DISTRICT.

The whole with the exception of the portion of the following village lying to the west of the railway from Lydda to Haifa :—

Kafr Qasim

RAMALLAH SUB-DISTRICT.

The whole.

RAMLE SUB-DISTRICT.

(a) The following villages in whole :—

Abu el Fadl (Es Sautariya)	Ben Shemen	Deir el Hawa
Barfiliya	Bil'in	Deir Muheisin
Barriya, El	Bir Imma'in	Deir Qaddis
Beit 'Itab	Bir Salim	Deir Tarif
Beit Jimal	Budrus	Haditha, El
Beit Jiz	Bureij	Idhnibba
Beit Nabala	Burj, El	'Innaba
Beit Nuba	Danyal	Jarash
Beit Susin	Deiraban	Jilya
	Deir Abu Salama	Jimzu

Ramle Sub-District (Continued).

Jindas	Khirbat Zakariya	Qula
Kefar Uriya	Khulda	Rafat
Khalayil, El	Kunnisa, El	Ramle, Er
Kharbata	Latrun	Rantis
Kharruba	Lubban, El	Sajad
Kheima, El	Lydda	Sarafand el 'Amar
Khirbat Beit Far	Midya, El	Shabtin
Khirbat el Buweiriya	Mughallis	Shilta
Khirbat el Qubeiba	Mukheizin, El	Shuqba
Khirbat edh Dhuheiriya	Ni'lin	Sufla
	Qazaza	Tina, Et
Khirbat Ismallah	Qibya	Tira, Et
Khirbat Musmar	Qubab, El	

(b) The portions of the following villages lying to the east of the railway from Lydda to Haifa :—

Majdal Yaba   Muzeiri'a, El

Jaffa Sub-District.

(a) The following villages in whole :—

Miqve Yisrael   Safiriya, Es

(b) The portion of the following village lying to the east of the railway from Lydda to Haifa :—

Muweilih, El

(c) The portion of the following villages lying to the south of the road from Tel Aviv to Wilhelma :—

Kafr 'Ana	Yahudiya, El	Saqiya
Kheiriya, El	Salama	

(d) Blocks 6296 6297 6298 6299 6300 6301 6302 6303 6304 6305 6306 6307 6308 6309 and 6310 of Wilhelma.

Blocks 7050 7055 7056 7057 7058 7059 7063 7064 7065 7066 7069 7152 7153 7160 and 7161 of Jaffa.

The village of Beit Dajan excluding Blocks 6095 6096 and 6097.

Blocks 6001 6002 6003 6004 6005 6006 6007 6008 6009 6010 6011 6015 6016 6017 6018 6019 6023 6024 6025 6026 6027 6028 6029 6030 6031 6032 6033 6034 6035 6036 6037 6038 6039 6040 6041 and 6042 of Yazur.

Jericho Sub-District.

The whole.

Jerusalem Sub-District.

The whole, with the exception of the town-planning area of Jerusalem.

— 334 —

BETHLEHEM SUB-DISTRICT.

The whole.

HEBRON SUB-DISTRICT.

The whole.

GAZA SUB-DISTRICT.

The following villages in whole :—

'Abasan	Hamama	Khirbat Khisas
Abu Middein	Hatta	Kaufakha
Ard el Ishra	Hirbiya	Kaukaba
Bani Suheila	Huj	Majdal, El
Barbara	Huleiqat	Muharraqa, El
Beit 'Affa	'Ibdis	Najd
Beit Hanun	'Iraq el Manshiya	Nazla
Beit Jirja	'Iraq Suweidan	Ni'ilya
Beit Lahiya	Jabaliya	Nuseirat
Beit Tima	Jaladiya	Rafah
Bi'lin	Jiya, El	Sawafir el Gharbiya, Es
Bureir	Julis	
Deir el Balah	Jura, El	Sawafir esh Sharqiya, Es
Deir Suneid	Juseir	
Dimra	Karatiya	Summeil
Faluja, El	Khan Yunis	Sumeiri
Gaza	Khirbat Ikhza'	Sumsum

BEERSHEBA SUB-DISTRICT.

The area north of a line passing from a point on the Palestine—Trans-Jordan boundary where the Wadi running north-east from 'Ain Hosb joins the Wadi Jeeb, thence in a south-westerly direction along the Wadi to 'Ain Hosb, thence along the 'Ain Hosb-Kurnub road to Rujm al Balawi, Rujm al Kanasiya, Naqb Ras um-Julaid, Ras Ghwairib, Ras Naqb Gharib, 'Ain al Murra, Wadi Irmeileh, Wadi Abdo, to Bir al Hafir, and thence due west till it meets the frontier between Palestine and Egypt.

ZONE B.

The area comprising :—

SAFAD SUB-DISTRICT.

(a) The following villages in whole :—

Abil el Qamh	Aiyelet hash Shahar	'Arab esh Shamalina
Abisiya, El	'Akbara	'Azaziyat and 'Ein Fit

SAFAD SUB-DISTRICT (Continued).

Banyas
Barjiyat, El
Beisamun
Biriya
Buleida
Buteiha, El
Buweiziya, El
Dafna
Darbashiya, Ed
Dardara
Dawwara
Deir Mamas
Dhahiriya el Fauqa, Edh
Dhahiriya et Tahta, Edh
Dureijat
'Ein et Tina
'Ein Zeitim
'Ein ez Zeitun
Fir'im
Ghuraba
Hula
Hula Concession Area
Hunin
Hura
Juhula
Jalabina
Ja'una
Jubb Yusuf
Kafr Qila
Khalisa, El
Khan ed Duweir
Kharrar, El
Kefar Gil'adi
Khirbat el Hiqab
Khirbat es Summan
Khirbat Yarda
Khisas
Khiyam el Walid
Kirad el Baqqara
Kirad el Ghannama
Lazzaza
Mahanayim
Mallaha
Manara, El
Mansura, El
Mansurat el Kheit
Meis
Metulla
Mishmar hay Yarden
Muftakhira, El
Mughr esh Shab'an
Mughr el Kheit
Nabi Yusha'
Na'ima, En
Qadas
Qeitiya
Qudeiriya, El
Rosh Pinna
Safad
Salihiya, Es
Sanbariya
Shuna, Esh
Shauqa et Tahta
Tuba
Tuleil
Udeisa
Ulmaniya, El
Weiziya ('Almin)
Weiziya
Zanghariya
Zawiya, Ez
Zuq el Fauqani, Ez
Zuq et Tahtani, Ez

(b) The portions of the following villages lying to the east of the road from Rosh Pinna to Metulla :—

Hatsor
Yesud ham Ma'ala

TIBERIAS SUB-DISTRICT.

(a) The following villages in whole :—

Afiqim
Beit Gan
Bitanya
Dalhamiya
Deganiya 'A'
Deganiya 'B'
Ghuweir Abu Shusha
Hadatha
Hamma, El
Kafr Harib
Kafr Kama
Kafr Sabt
Kefar Hittim
Kefar Gun
Khan el Minya
Kinneret Group
Kinneret
Ma'dhar
Majdal
Manara, El
Menahamiya
Migdal
Mitspa
Nuqeib
Poriya
Sejera
Samakh
Samakiya, Es
Samra, Es
Sharona
Sha'ara
Shajara, Esh
Tabigha, Et
Tell el Hunud
Tiberias
'Ubeidiya, El
'Ulam
Yaquq
Yavneel

— 336 —

(b) The portion of the following village lying to the south of the road from Nazareth to Tiberias :—

Lubiya

NAZARETH SUB-DISTRICT.

(a) The following villages in whole :—

'Afula	Indur	Mount Tabor
'Arab es Subeih	Kefar Barukh	Na'ura
Balfourya	Kefar Gid'on	Nein
Dabburiya	Kefar Tavor	Ramat David
Dahi, Ed	Kefar Yeladim	Sarid
'Ein Mahil	Mahane Yisrael	Sulam
Gevat	Merhavya Settlement	Tamra
Ginneigar	Merhavya Group	Tel 'Adashim
Iksal	Mizra'	Umm el Ghanam

(b) The portions of the following villages lying to the south of the road from Haifa to Nazareth :—

'Ilut	Mujeidil	Yafa
Ma'lul	Nahalal	

HAIFA SUB-DISTRICT.

(a) The following villages in whole :—

Atlit	Kafr Lam	Sarafand, Es
Beit She'arim	Kefar Yehoshu'a	Sheikh Bureik, Esh

(b) The portions of the following villages lying to the south of the road from Haifa to Nazareth :—

Jeida	Waldheim	Qusqus-Tab'un

(c) The portions of the following villages lying to the west of the road from Jaffa to Haifa :—

'Ein Ghazal	Jaba'
'Ein Haud	Mazar, El

(d) The portion of Et Tira lying west of the Jaffa—Haifa road but excluding Blocks 10740 and 10743.

BEISAN SUB-DISTRICT.

The following villages in whole :—

Bashatiwa, El	Gesher	Kafra
Bawati, El	Hamidiya, El	Kaukab el Hawa
Beit Alfa	Heftsi-Bah	Kefar Yehezqel
Bira, El	Jabbul	Murassas, El
Danna	Jisr el Majami'	Qevutsat hag Giv'a
'Ein Harod	Kafr Misr	Qumiya

— 337 —

BEISAN SUB-DISTRICT (Continued).

Sakhina, Es	Taiyiba, Et	Wadi el Bira
Shatta	Tel Yosef	Yubla
Sirin	Tira, Et	Zab'a

GAZA SUB-DISTRICT.

The following villages in whole :—

'Arab Sukreir	Beit Daras	Qastina
'Arqubiya	Gan Yavne	Sawafir esh Shama-
Barqa	Isdud	liya, Es
Batani Gharbi	Masmiya el Kabira, El	Tell et Turmus
Batani Sharqi	Masmiya es Saghira, El	Yasur
Beer Tuviya		

BEERSHEBA SUB-DISTRICT.

The area south of a line passing from a point on the Palestine—Trans-Jordan boundary where the Wadi running north-east from 'Ain Hosb joins the Wadi Jeeb, thence in a south-westerly direction along the Wadi to 'Ain Hosb, thence along the 'Ain Hosb-Kurnub road to Rujm al Balawi, Rujm al Kanasiya, Naqb Ras um-Julaid, Ras Ghwairib, Ras Naqb Gharib, 'Ain al Murra, Wadi Irmeileh, Wadi Abdo, to Bir al Hafir, and thence due west till it meets the frontier between Palestine and Egypt.

STATEMENT EXPLANATORY OF THE LAND TRANSFERS REGULATIONS.

Article 6 of the Mandate, which requires the Administration of Palestine to encourage close settlement by Jews on the land, also requires it to ensure that the rights and position of other sections of the population are not prejudiced.

Paragraph 16 of the Statement of Policy of His Majesty's Government regarding Palestine, dated the 17th May, 1939, drew attention to the fact that the Reports of several expert Commissions had indicated that, owing to the natural growth of the Arab population and the steady sale in recent years of Arab land to Jews, there was now in certain areas no room for further transfers of Arab land, whilst in some other areas such transfers of land must be restricted if Arab cultivators were to maintain their existing standard of life and a considerable landless Arab population was not soon to be created. It was therefore announced that the High Commissioner would be given general powers to prohibit and regulate transfers of land. The accompanying regulations have been made in order to give effect to this announcement. As stated in paragraph 17 of the Statement of Policy of May, 1939, the policy of Government will be directed towards the development of the land and the improvement, where possible, of methods of cultivation. In the

— 338 —

light of such development it will be open to the High Commissioner, should he be satisfied that the "rights and position" of the Arab population will be duly preserved, to review and modify any orders passed relating to the prohibition or restriction of the transfer of land.

2. Two zones, Zone A and Zone B, have been demarcated in Palestine within which transfers of land will be controlled. In determining the boundaries of these zones, Government has had special regard to the provisions of Article 6 of the Mandate. Zone A includes the hill country as a whole together with certain areas in the Gaza and Beersheba Sub-Districts where the land available is already insufficient for the support of the existing population; in this zone the transfer of land to a person other than a Palestinian Arab will be prohibited save in exceptional cases for which special provision is made in the regulations. The sanction of the High Commissioner required by the regulations to transfers of land in this zone between persons not being Palestinian Arabs may be accorded by general order, thus dispensing with the necessity for a special order in each individual case of this description.

3. In Zone B such transfers may be permitted in accordance with certain conditions set forth in paragraph 5 of this explanatory statement. This zone includes the Plains of Esdraelon and Jezreel, Eastern Galilee, the maritime plains between Haifa and Tantura and between the southern boundary of the Ramle Sub-District and Beer Tuviya, and the southern portion of the Beersheba Sub-District (the Negeb).

4. There will be no restrictions on transfers in those parts of Palestine not included in Zone A or Zone B. These parts include all municipal areas, the Haifa Industrial Zone described in Appendix 8 of the Report of the Palestine Partition Commission and roughly speaking the maritime plain between Tantura and the southern boundary of the Ramle Sub-District.

5. Transfers of land in Zone B by a Palestinian Arab to any person other than a Palestinian Arab will be null and void unless the sanction of the High Commissioner to the transfer has previously been sought and obtained. In this regard it is the desire of His Majesty's Government that the recommendations of recent Commissions should generally be followed and in pursuance of this policy the Secretary of State has accepted the recommendation of the High Commissioner that, while his final discretion shall be left unfettered, his powers will be exercised generally on the following lines.

Sanction to a transfer of land within Zone B by a Palestinian Arab to a person other than a Palestinian Arab will not ordinarily be granted unless the transfer can be shown to be either :—

(i) for the purpose of consolidating, extending, or facilitating the irrigation of holdings already in the possession of the transferee or of his community, the land to be transferred being contiguous to such holdings; or

(ii) for the purpose of enabling land held in undivided shares by the transferor and the transferee to be parcellated; or

(iii) in furtherance of some special scheme of development in the joint interests of both Arabs and Jews to which Government may have signified its approval.

6. The regulations have effect from the 18th May, 1939, but the High Commissioner is empowered, at his discretion, to sanction retrospectively any transfer of land in either Zone A or Zone B, which would be unlawful under the terms of the regulations, provided that application for the registration of such transfer was lodged in the Land Registry prior to the date of their publication. Generally speaking, he will require to be satisfied that the transaction was initiated *bona fide* before the 18th May, the onus of proof being on the transferee. In the absence of such sanction the transaction in question will be null and void.

7. Application for sanction to transfers of land, where required by the regulations, should be addressed to the District Commissioner of the District in which the land is situated who will forward it to the High Commissioner for his orders.

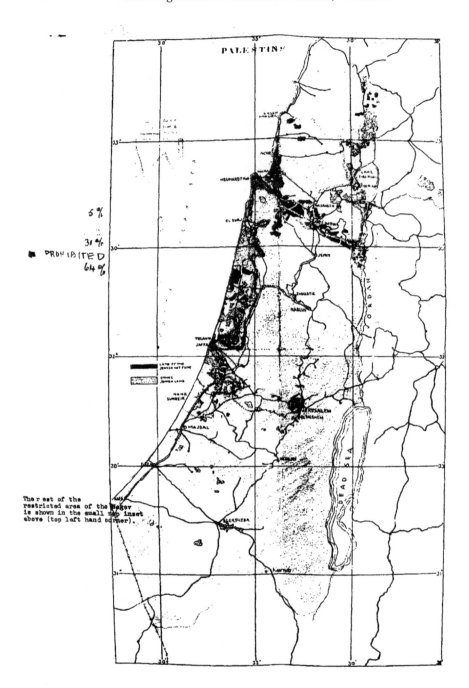

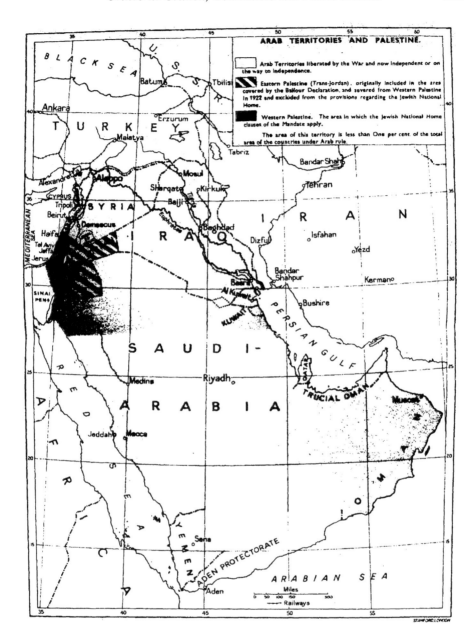

Section 23: 1941

LAND TRANSFER (FEES) RULES (AMENDMENT) ORDINANCE, No. 11 OF 1941.

High Commissioner

LAND TRANSFER (FEES) RULES (AMENDMENT) ORDINANCE, No. 11 of 1941.

LAND TRANSFER (FEES) RULES (AMENDMENT) ORDINANCE, 1941.

BE IT ENACTED by the High Commissioner for Palestine, with the advice of the Advisory Council thereof :—

1. This Ordinance may be cited as the Land Transfer (Fees) Rules (Amendment) Ordinance, 1941.   *Short title.*

2. Paragraph (7) of rule 3 of the Land Transfer (Fees) Rules, 1939, shall be revoked and the following paragraph substituted therefor :—   *Amendment of Land Transfer (Fees) Rules, 1939.*

"(7) *Sale of mortgaged properties at the request of the mortgagee.*

(a) 3% on the purchase price realised on sale by auction— Registration Fees.

(b) 2½% on the purchase price realised on sale by auction— Execution Fees.

The above fees shall be payable on the sale and provisional registration of property under section 10(2) of the Credit Banks Ordinance, or section 3 of the Mortgage Law (Amendment) Ordinance : provided that if the former owner redeems the land, and the bank or company in whose name such provisional registration is made shall not become the definite owner of the property, the registration fee of 3% shall be refunded, but any other Land Registry fees shall be retained."   *Cap. 29. Cap. 95.*

3. This Ordinance shall be deemed to have come into force at the date of the coming into force of the Land Transfer (Fees) Rules, 1939.   *Commencement.*

10th May, 1941.

HAROLD MACMICHAEL
High Commissioner.

LAND LAW (AMENDMENT) ORDINANCE, No. 39 OF 1941.

Officer Administering the Government.

LAND LAW (AMENDMENT) ORDINANCE,
No. 39 of 1941.

An Ordinance to amend the Land Law (Amendment) Ordinance.

Be it enacted by the High Commissioner for Palestine, with the advice of the Advisory Council thereof :—

1. This Ordinance may be cited as the Land Law (Amendment) Ordinance, 1941, and shall be read as one with the Land Law (Amendment) Ordinance, hereinafter referred to as the principal Ordinance.   *Short title.*   *Cap. 78.*

2. Section 6 of the principal Ordinance shall be amended by the insertion of the words "may require the plaintiff to pay into court security for costs and, upon such payment being made," between the words "the court" and "may order" appearing in subsection (2) thereof.   *Amendment of section 6 of the principal Ordinance.*

HAROLD MACMICHAEL
High Commissioner.

16th December, 1941.

Section 24: 1942

RURAL PROPERTY TAX ORDINANCE, No. 5 OF 1942.

High Commissioner

GOVERNMENT OF PALESTINE.

RURAL PROPERTY TAX ORDINANCE,
No. 5 of 1942.

AN ORDINANCE TO CONSOLIDATE AND AMEND THE LAW PROVIDING FOR THE IMPOSITION OF RURAL PROPERTY TAX.

BE IT ENACTED by the High Commissioner for Palestine, with the advice of the Advisory Council thereof :—

1. This Ordinance may be cited as the Rural Property Tax Ordinance, 1942, and shall come into force on the first day of April, 1942. *Short title and commencement.*

2. In this Ordinance, unless the context otherwise requires :— *Interpretation.*

"Completion" of an industrial building shall be deemed to be when such building is occupied in whole or in part or is roofed whichever shall first occur.

"Disposition" includes a sale, partition, mortgage, lease, gift, devise by will, dedication of waqf of every description, and constitution of a charitable trust; but it does not include a parcellation, combination, transfer or discharge of a mortgage, correction of the terms of a mortgage, or a transfer by succession.

"District Officer" includes any person duly authorised to act for a district officer.

"House and land tax" includes the Ottoman house and land (werko) tax, werko meqtu', the Ottoman tax on buildings (musaqqafat), the muqata'a tax, the badl ushr tax, and the meqtu' Ijara Zamin and urban property tax.

— 2 —

"Industrial building" means any building, structure or erection of which the net annual value is in the opinion of an official valuer more than twenty pounds, constructed and used or intended to be used solely for the purpose of an industrial undertaking in which mechanically driven machinery is used or in connection therewith together with the land on which such building, structure or erection stands and any yard or any land adjacent to such building, structure or erection and used or intended to be used in connection with such building, structure or erection whether such building, structure or erection be inhabited or not or used or not:

Provided that all buildings and land adjacent thereto which form indispensible units of a single industrial undertaking shall, save for the purpose of exemption under section 6(3), be deemed to form one industrial building :

"Land" includes buildings other than industrial buildings and anything fixed in the land.

"Owner" means the owner of property within an area specified in an Order made by the High Commissioner under section 3 of this Ordinance, and where there is a registered owner of such property it means the registered owner, and where there is no registered owner it means the person who is in receipt of the rents and profits of the property in such circumstances that he is the reputed owner thereof, and in the case of Government owned land it includes every occupant thereof by virtue of a lease, express or implied.

"Prescribed" means prescribed by rules made by the High Commissioner under section 41 of this Ordinance.

Cap. 80.

"Settled" used with reference to land means any land included in a schedule of rights or schedule of partition posted in accordance with the provisions of the Land (Settlement of Title) Ordinance.

Cap. 140.

"Tithe" includes the tithe payable under the Ottoman law prior to the introduction of the commuted tithe and the commuted tithe payable under the Tithe (Commutation) Ordinance.

"Top-worked" in reference to citrus trees means subjected to the operation of changing the variety or kind of budded or grafted citrus trees by cutting the trees back and budding or grafting with other varieties or kinds of citrus fruit.

— 3 —

"Uncultivable land" means land which cannot be cultivated except by recourse to methods other than and additional to the normal methods of sound husbandry and which entail the disbursement of extraordinary expense.

"Urban area" means any area described in an order made by the High Commissioner under section 3 of the Urban Property Tax Ordinance, 1940.

"Year" means, notwithstanding anything contained in the Interpretation Ordinance, the period from the first day of April to the thirty-first day of March following, both days inclusive.

No. 42 of 1940.

Cap. 69.

3.—(1) The High Commissioner may by order declare that a tax (to be known and hereinafter referred to as the rural property tax), which shall be assessed, levied, collected and paid in accordance with the provisions of this Ordinance, shall be payable annually to the High Commissioner as from the first day of April next following the date of such order, for the use of the territory of Palestine, on all lands and industrial buildings within such area, not being an urban area, as may be described in such order.

Power of High Commissioner to apply Ordinance.

(2) As from the date upon which the rural property tax becomes payable in any area by reason of an order made by the High Commissioner under subsection (1) hereof, the house and land tax and tithe shall cease to be leviable in such area :

Provided that nothing in this subsection contained shall be deemed to affect the collection of any house and land tax or tithe due in respect of any period prior to the date upon which the rural property tax became payable and proceedings for the recovery of any such tax or tithe so due may be taken as if no order under subsection (1) hereof had been made.

4.—(1) The rural property tax shall be payable by the owner :—

(a) upon land, at the rate set out in the schedule to this Ordinance in respect of the category to which such land belongs :

Provided that the High Commissioner in Council may, by order :—

(i) postpone payment of any rural property tax due or about to fall due, in respect of any land until such date as may be set out in such order or until further order, or

(ii) reduce, until such date as may be mentioned in such order, or until further order, the rates set out in the schedule to this Ordinance, either generally or in any area or in any part of any area to which this Ordinance has been applied and in each of the foregoing cases, either in respect of all lands or any stated category of land, or

By whom rural property tax payable.

— 4 —

 (iii) both postpone payment of rural property tax under sub-paragraph (i) hereof and reduce the rates set out in the schedule to this Ordinance under sub-paragraph (ii) hereof,

if the High Commissioner in Council is satisfied that it is proper so to do, having regard to any emergency affecting Palestine or any area or any part of an area, which is:—

 (I) due to unavoidable natural causes, or

 (II) due to such a fall in the value of crops as in the opinion of the High Commissioner in Council makes the granting of the relief which may be effected under this proviso expedient;

(b) upon any industrial building, at such rate not exceeding fifteen per centum of the net annual value of such industrial building as computed in accordance with section 9 of this Ordinance, as shall be prescribed annually by order of the High Commissioner in Council.

(2) The High Commissioner in Council may by order vary the categories or rates or both set out in the schedule to this Ordinance:

Provided that each time the High Commissioner in Council shall vary under this subsection any category or rate set out in the schedule, the category or rate so varied shall remain unaltered for a period of not less than five years from the date from which such variation shall take effect.

Change of categories etc. to be notified to District Officers.

5.—(1) Where, on or after the first day of April next following the date of any order made by the High Commissioner under section 3 of this Ordinance relating to the area in which any land is situated,

(a) the land is brought under cultivation, having previously been uncultivable land, or

(b) the land is planted with bananas or citrus trees or other fruit trees, or

(c) the land is planted as a forest, or

(d) the land is brought under irrigation by any system of irrigation other than a system involving for its upkeep and continuity the continuous use of mechanical aid and regular expenditure on the part of such owner, or

(e) a plantation on the land is uprooted, or

(f) a building on the land becomes or ceases to be an industrial building,

the owner of such land shall, within three months from the commencement of such cultivation, plantation, bringing of such irrigation or uprooting, or within three months from the date when such building became or ceased to be an industrial building, give notice

— 5 —

of such fact to the District Officer administering the area in which the land is situated, in a form to be prescribed, and the official valuer shall, on verification, to his satisfaction, change the category of the land as in his discretion he shall think proper, with effect from the first day of April next following such notification.

(2) Where the completion of any industrial building takes place on or after the first day of April next following the date of any order made by the High Commissioner under section 3 of this Ordinance relating to the area in which such industrial building is situated, the owner of such industrial building shall, within three months from such completion, give notice of such fact to the District Officer administering the area in which such industrial building is situated, in a form to be prescribed.

6.—(1) The owner of any land who is enjoying exemption from tithes in accordance with the Decree dated the twenty-fifth day of September, 1920, and published in the *Gazette* dated the fifteenth day of November, 1920, in respect of vineyards planted with American stock on the thirty-first day of March next following the date of the order made by the High Commissioner under section 3 of this Ordinance relating to the area in which the vineyards are situated, shall enjoy exemption from the rural property tax for the remainder of the period to which he is entitled under such Decree. *Exemptions and remissions. No. 31.*

(2) The owner of any land :—

(a) which having previously been uncultivable land has been brought under cultivation within six calendar years immediately preceding the first day of April next following the date of the order made by the High Commissioner under section 3 of this Ordinance relating to the area in which such land is situated, or

(b) which has been planted with bananas within one calendar year immediately preceding such first day of April, or

(c) which has been planted with citrus trees within six calendar years immediately preceding such first day of April, or

(d) which has been planted with any fruit trees other than bananas or citrus trees within ten calendar years immediately preceding such first day of April, or

(e) which having previously been uncultivable land shall be brought under cultivation or be planted with bananas or citrus trees or any fruit trees other than bananas or citrus trees subsequently to such first day of April,

shall not be liable to any increase of the rural property tax by reason of such cultivation or plantation :—

(i) in the case of land which having previously been uncultivable land was brought under cultivation prior to such first

— 6 —

day of April, for a period equal to six calendar years less a period commencing from the date of the commencement of such cultivation and ending on such first day of April, and

(ii) in the case of land which was planted with bananas, prior to such first day of April for a period equal to one calendar year less a period commencing on the date of the commencement of such plantation and ending on such first day of April, and

(iii) in the case of land which was planted with citrus trees prior to such first day of April for a period equal to six calendar years less a period commencing on the date of the commencement of such plantation and ending on such first day of April, and

(iv) in the case of land which was planted with any fruit trees other than bananas or citrus trees prior to such first day of April for a period equal to ten calendar years less a period commencing on the date of the commencement of such plantation and ending on such first day of April, and

(v) in the case of land which, subsequently to such first day of April, shall be brought under cultivation having previously been uncultivable land or be planted with bananas or citrus trees or any fruit trees other than bananas or citrus trees, for periods of six, one, six and ten years respectively, each such period running from the commencement of the year next following the year during which such cultivation or plantation took place;

provided that :—

(I) in the case of land which having previously been uncultivable land was brought under cultivation or was planted with bananas or citrus trees or any fruit trees other than bananas or citrus trees prior to such first day of April, the owner shall have given notice of such fact to the District Officer administering the area in which such land is situated within three months from such first day of April on a form to be prescribed, or

(II) in the case of land which having previously been uncultivable land shall be brought under cultivation or be planted with bananas or citrus trees or any fruit trees other than bananas or citrus trees subsequently to such first day of April, the owner shall have complied with subsection (1) of section 5 of this Ordinance :

Provided that where any owner in any notice given to the District Officer under paragraph (I) hereof or under subsection (1) of section 5 of this Ordinance shall state as the area of his land in which cultivation or plantation has taken place, any area other than the true area, then when such true area is ascertained, such owner shall, without prejudice to any penalty which may be incurred by him under subsection (1) of section 36 of this Ordinance, be liable to pay the rural property tax on such true area at the rate set out in the schedule to this Ordinance in respect of the category within which such area after such cultivation or plantation falls as from the first day of April next following the commencement of such cultivation or plantation.

(3) The owner of any industrial building, the completion of which :—

(a) took place within three calendar years immediately preceding the first day of April next following the date of the Order made by the High Commissioner under section 3 of this Ordinance, relating to the area in which such industrial building is situated, or

(b) shall take place subsequently to such first day of April, shall be exempt from the rural property tax :—

(i) in the case of an industrial building the completion of which took place prior to such first day of April, for a period equal to three calendar years less a period commencing on the date of the completion of such industrial building and ending on such first day of April, and

(ii) in the case of an industrial building the completion of which shall take place subsequently to such first day of April, for a period of three years from the commencement of the year next following the year during which the completion of such industrial building took place,

provided that :—

(1) in the case of an industrial building the completion of which took place prior to such first day of April, the owner shall have given notice of such fact to the District Officer of the sub-district in which such industrial building is situated within three months of such first day of April on a form to be prescribed, or

(II) in the case of an industrial building the completion of which takes place subsequently to such first day of April, the owner shall have complied with subsection (2) of section 5 of this Ordinance :

Provided that the rural property tax shall be payable on the site of any industrial building exempted hereunder.

For the purposes of this subsection "industrial building" includes any addition to an industrial building where the net annual value of the addition is in the opinion of an official valuer more than twenty pounds.

(4) The owner of any industrial building who carries out any reconstruction work within such industrial building, whereby the

— 8 —

net annual value of such industrial building is in the opinion of the official valuer increased by more than twenty pounds, shall not be liable to the rural property tax in respect of the amount by which such net annual value is so increased for a period of three years commencing from the beginning of the year next following the year during which such reconstruction work is completed:

Provided that such owner shall within three months from the completion of such reconstruction work have given notice of that fact to the District Officer administering the area in which such industrial building is situated.

(5) The District Commissioner may, as in his discretion he shall think fit, remit the rural property tax either wholly or in part on

<ul><li>(a) any land being used as a threshing floor set aside for the use of the village, or as a cemetery not exempt under the Rates and Taxes (Exemption) Ordinance, 1938: provided that in the case of a threshing floor application for remission shall be made prior to the thirty-first day of July of each year;</li></ul>

No. 18 of 1938.

<ul><li>(b) any land on which a plantation or crop has been destroyed, either in execution of an order under section 8 of the Plant Protection Ordinance, or inadvertently;</li></ul>

Cap. 111.

<ul><li>(c) any land, for any year during which a plantation or crop thereon has been unlawfully destroyed or damaged;</li><li>(d) any industrial building, for any year during any part of which the building has in his opinion been rendered unusable or uninhabitable by reason of its having been destroyed or damaged: provided that no remission or refund under this paragraph shall have the effect of exempting the site upon which the industrial building stands or stood from payment of the rural property tax:</li></ul>

Provided that —

<ul><li>(i) if the rural property tax for such land or building in respect of such year has already been paid, the whole or so much thereof as would have been remitted if not already paid, shall be refunded; and</li><li>(ii) the rural property tax shall be payable on such land or building or site, as from the commencement of the year next following the year in respect of which remission is granted by this subsection, at the rate set out in the schedule to this Ordinance in respect of the category within which the land or building or site may then fall.</li></ul>

(6) Where any citrus grove having an area of not less than one dunum has been top-worked, the rural property tax in respect of the land on which such grove is situated shall for a period equal to four calendar years, or, if the top-working was commenced

— 9 —

before the first day of April, 1942, then for a period equal to four calendar years less the period between the date on which the top-working was commenced and the first day of April, 1942, be payable at the rate set out in the schedule to this Ordinance for the ground crop category or irrigated land category to which such land would belong if it were not planted with citrus.

Provided that the owner of such grove shall have given notice in writing of such top-working to the District Officer administering the area in which such grove is situated, —

(a) within three months of the commencement of the top-working, or

(b) if the top-working was commenced before the first day of April, 1942, then before the first day of July, 1942.

(7) The provisions of section 11 shall not apply to applications for exemption under this section.

7. The High Commissioner may, by order, appoint such persons as he may consider necessary to be official valuers for the purpose of this Ordinance. *Appointment of official valuers.*

8.—(1) An official valuer shall, as soon as may be possible after his appointment, from information to be obtained by him, prepare :— *Official valuer to prepare rural property tax rolls and valuation lists.*

(a) rolls in a form to be prescribed (each one of which is in this Ordinance referred to as a rural property tax roll) showing in respect of the area to which each such rural property tax roll refers (such area for the purposes of this Ordinance being deemed to be a village) within which of the categories set out in the schedule to this Ordinance the lands in each subdivision (such sub-division for the purposes of this Ordinance being deemed to be a block) of such area fall :

Provided that the site of a building (other than an industrial building) not being a building the site of which falls within category 4 of the schedule to this Ordinance, shall be deemed for the purpose of the preparation of the rural property tax roll to be of the same category as the land surrounding such site, and where such site is surrounded in part by land of one category and in part by land of another category or other categories, the site shall be deemed to be of the category of such land in respect of which the highest rate of tax is in the schedule to this Ordinance set out, and

(b) lists in a form to be prescribed (each one of which is in this Ordinance referred to as a valuation list) showing in respect of each village in which any industrial buildings are situated the net annual value and the names of the owners of all such industrial buildings.

(2) As soon as the rural property tax roll and valuation list (if any) in respect of any village shall have been prepared in accordance

with subsection (1) hereof, such rural property tax roll and valuation list shall be signed by an official valuer who shall forthwith send two copies of each to the District Officer administering the area in which such village is situated, together with two copies of a map of such village stamped by the Director of Surveys and the official valuer showing the lands of the village divided into blocks and the District Officer shall thereupon deposit one copy of such rural property tax roll and valuation list and map at the District Office and the other copy shall be handed to the Mukhtar for posting in the village, and the date of posting shall be certified on each copy by the District Officer.

(3) The posting of the rural property tax roll and of the valuation list and of the map in accordance with subsection (2) hereof, shall be deemed to be sufficient notice for all purposes of all the particulars contained therein respectively.

Assessment of industrial buildings.

9.—(1) The net annual value of an industrial building shall for the purposes of this Ordinance be the rent for which such industrial building might be expected to let from year to year after deducting one-third on account of cost of repairs and other charges.

(2) If an industrial building is not leased or if in the opinion of the official valuer the rent of an industrial building appears to the official valuer not to represent the true rental value he shall assess the annual value thereof having regard to the following considerations :—

(a) the size, materials and state of repair of the property and the amenities and value of the site;

(b) the use to which the property is put;

(c) the rent paid for or the income produced by similar properties in the same or similar localities :

Provided that no account shall be taken of any plant or machinery in or on the property.

District Officer's and official valuer's power of entry, etc.

10. The owners and tenants of land and industrial buildings within any area specified in any order made by the High Commissioner under section 3 of this Ordinance, shall admit a District Officer or an official valuer to any and every part of such land and industrial buildings and it shall be lawful for a District Officer or an official valuer :—

(a) at any reasonable time to enter, survey and examine all or any part of the property, and

(b) to do or cause to be done anything reasonably necessary to draw up the rural property tax roll or valuation list, and in particular and without prejudice to the generality of the powers hereby conferred, a District Officer or an official valuer

— 11 —

may require any person to produce for inspection any book or account or document of title, contract of lease, plan, specification or building contract and may take any copy of or extract from any such book, account or document, and

(c) to administer oaths for the purpose of any enquiry or proceedings which he is required or empowered to carry out under this Ordinance.

11.—(1) Within fourteen days from the date of posting of the rural property tax roll in the village as certified on such roll by the District Officer any person may submit to an official valuer, through the District Officer, an objection to such rural property tax roll on any one or more of the following grounds, that is to say:— Objections to rural property tax roll and valuation list.

(a) that the area of any category of land in any block is wrongly set out:

Provided that nothing in this paragraph contained shall enable any person to object to any area set out in the rural property tax roll as being of category 4 (built-on area) or the position and limits of such area as shown on the map referred to in subsection (2) of section 8 of this Ordinance;

(b) that the area of any block has been wrongly set out in the rural property tax roll.

(2) Within fourteen days from the date of posting of the valuation list in the village as certified on such list by the District Officer any person may submit to an official valuer, through the District Officer, an objection to such valuation list on any one or more of the following grounds, that is to say:—

(a) that the objector has been wrongly included in or excluded from the list;

(b) that some other person has been wrongly included in or excluded from the list;

(c) that the net annual value of any industrial building is too high or too low;

(d) that a building has been wrongly included in the list as an industrial building.

(3) Every objection under the provisions of this section shall be in writing and in a form to be prescribed and shall state the ground of the objection and shall give such particulars as may be necessary in support of such grounds.

12.—(1) On receipt of any objection to the rural property tax roll or valuation list duly made in accordance with the provisions of section 11 of this Ordinance the official valuer shall consider each such objection and after making such enquiries as he may deem necessary shall have power to amend the rural property tax Power of official valuer to amend roll and/or list.

roll or the valuation list or both the rural property tax roll and the valuation list:

Provided that:—

(a) if the official valuer shall consider any objection to the rural property tax roll to be without foundation and shall decide to make no amendment thereto in pursuance thereof, he shall give notice of such fact to the objector on a form to be prescribed, and the date appearing upon such form shall be deemed to be the date of the decision of the official valuer in respect of such objection, and

(b) if the official valuer shall consider any objection to the valuation list:—

   (i) to be without foundation and decide to make no amendment thereto in pursuance thereof, he shall give notice of such fact to the objector on a form to be prescribed and the date appearing upon such form shall be deemed to be the date of the decision of the official valuer in respect of such objection, or

   (ii) to be sufficiently well founded to warrant further consideration, he shall give notice of such fact on a form to be prescribed to the objector and to any other person whom he may think may be affected by such objection and shall in such form state the time and place fixed for the hearing of the objection;

(c) if the objector or any other person informed of the proceedings is not present at the time and place stated in such form for the hearing of the objection, the official valuer may, notwithstanding such absence, make such decision on the objection as he may deem right.

(2) Any amendment to the rural property tax roll or valuation list made by an official valuer in accordance with the provisions of subsection (1) hereof shall be endorsed by him upon the rural property tax roll or valuation list as the case may be and on any copies thereof which have been posted in accordance with the provisions of subsection (2) of section 8 of this Ordinance. Each such endorsement shall be initialled and dated by such official valuer and the date of any such endorsement made on the copy of the rural property tax roll or the valuation list deposited at the District Office shall be deemed to be the date of the decision of the official valuer in respect of the objection as a result of which it was made.

Appointment of appeal committees.

13.—(1) The District Commissioner may appoint such number of committees as he may consider necessary, to be appeal committees for the purposes of hearing appeals from the decisions of official valuers and may in making such appointment or at any time thereafter allocate regions to each such appeal committee:

— 18 —

Provided that each such appeal committee shall consist of three members as under :—

  (a) An Assistant District Commissioner or a District Officer (other than a District Officer who has appeared as a party in any proceedings under section 12 of this Ordinance) who shall be chairman of the appeal committee;

  (b) Another officer of the Government of Palestine;

  (c) A person other than an officer of the Government of Palestine.

(2) An appeal committee and any member thereof shall have the powers of an official valuer as set out in section 10 of this Ordinance.

(3) All acts, orders, matters and things directed to be done or made by an appeal committee shall be lawfully done or made if done or made by or with the consent of a majority of the members of such committee.

14. Any person :—   *Appeals to appeal committees from the decisions of official valuers.*

  (a) whose objection to the rural property tax roll has been rejected by an official valuer under section 12 of this Ordinance, or

  (b) whose objection to the valuation list has been rejected by an official valuer under section 12 of this Ordinance, or

  (c) whose assessment has been altered or who has been included in the valuation list as the result of any objection made by any other person,

may, within fourteen days of the posting or affixing of the official valuer's decision in a public place or of its transmission to such person through the post (whichever date first occurs), appeal, in a form to be prescribed, to the chairman of the appeal committee appointed under section 13 of this Ordinance in respect of the region in which the property affected by such decision is situated.

15.—(1) The appeal committee shall upon receipt of any appeal duly made in accordance with the provisions of section 14 of this Ordinance, give notice, in a form to be prescribed, to the appellant and to the official valuer (who shall be respondent) of the time and place fixed for the hearing of the appeal   *Powers and duties of appeal committee to decide appeals, etc.*

(2) At the time and place so fixed the appeal committee shall hear and determine the appeal :

Provided that :—

  (a) no appeal shall be heard by an appeal committee unless the appellant has paid any deposit prescribed on account of costs, and

— 14 —

(b) if any party to the appeal is not present at the time and place fixed for the hearing of the appeal, the appeal committee may, notwithstanding such absence, make such decision as they may deem right.

(3) Upon the determination of any appeal, the appeal committee may make such order as to costs as they may think proper.

(4) Any amendment to the rural property tax roll or valuation list made by the appeal committee in accordance with the provisions of subsection (2) hereof shall be endorsed by the chairman of such committee upon the rural property tax roll or valuation list as the case may be and on any copies thereof which have been posted and deposited in accordance with the provisions of subsection (2) of section 8 of this Ordinance and each such endorsement shall be initialled and dated by the chairman of the appeal committee and the date of any such endorsement made on the copy of the rural property tax roll or valuation list deposited at the District Office shall be deemed to be the date of the decision of the appeal committee in respect of the appeal as a result of which it was made and shall further be deemed to be notice of the decision to all persons interested.

(5) A decision of an appeal committee so endorsed shall be final and no appeal shall lie therefrom :

Provided that any party to any proceedings before an appeal committee may ask the committee to state a case upon a point of law material to the issue arising out of the proceedings for the opinion of the District Court, and the appeal committee shall thereupon state such case.

Determination of roll and list.

16.—(1) The areas of the categories of the lands of any village and such categories as shown on the rural property tax roll as finally amended (if there have been any objections) or if there have been no objections, then as shown on the rural property tax roll as posted in the village under subsection (2) of section 8 of this Ordinance, shall be the areas and categories of the lands of such village for the purposes of this Ordinance until amended as in this Ordinance provided.

(2) The net annual value of the industrial buildings within any village as shown on the valuation list as finally amended (if there have been any objections) or, if there have been no objections, then as shown on the valuation list as posted in the village under subsection (2) of section 8 of this Ordinance, shall be the net annual value of the industrial buildings within such village for the purposes of this Ordinance until amended as in this Ordinance provided.

17. The rural property tax payable in respect of the lands of the area described in an order made by the High Commissioner under section 3 of this Ordinance shall be distributed amongst the owners of such lands as at the thirty-first day of March next following the date of such order in the manner hereinafter provided.

Tax in respect of lands to be distributed amongst owners.

18.—(1) (a) At any time prior to the first day of April next following the date of the order made by the High Commissioner under section 3 of this Ordinance relating to the area within which any village of which the lands or some of the lands have not been settled is situated, the District Commissioner of the district within which such village is situated shall appoint a tax distribution committee consisting of such number of inhabitants of the village as he may think fit:

Distribution of tax in respect of land not settled.

Provided that the District Commissioner may appoint any person to be a member of a tax distribution committee notwithstanding that such person is not an inhabitant of the village if such person is an owner of land within the village, or the representative of such person whether such representative be an inhabitant of the village or not.

(b) All acts, orders, matters and things directed to be done or made by a tax distribution committee shall be lawfully done or made if done or made by or with the consent of the majority of the members of such committee. In the case of an equal division of opinion the question shall be referred by the committee or by any member thereof to the District Commissioner whose decision shall be final.

(2) On or as soon as may be possible after the first day of April next following the date of the order made by the High Commissioner under section 3 of this Ordinance relating to the area in which any village in respect of which a tax distribution committee has been appointed is situated, the District Officer administering the area in which such village is situated shall give notice to the tax distribution committee on a form to be prescribed:

(a) if the village for which such committee has been appointed is one of which the lands have not been settled:—

(i) of the amount of the rural property tax payable in respect of the lands of such village, and

(ii) of the date prior to which the list referred to in subsection (3) hereof shall be prepared, or

(b) if the village for which such committee has been appointed is one of which some of the lands have not been settled:—

(i) of the date prior to which the list referred to in subsection (3) hereof shall be prepared, and

(ii) of the lands of the village which were not settled on the thirty-first day of March next following the date of the order made by the High Commissioner under section 3 of this Ordinance, and

(iii) of the amount of the rural property tax payable in respect of such lands.

(3) The tax distribution committee shall thereupon commence to prepare under the general supervision of the District Officer a list hereinafter referred to as a distribution list in a form to be prescribed showing the amount of the rural property tax payable by each owner of lands in the village or in that part of the village referred to in paragraph (b)(ii) of subsection (2) hereof, having regard to the area and category of land owned by such owner in the village or part of the village as the case may be as at the day mentioned in paragraph (b)(ii) of subsection (2) hereof:

Provided that :—

(a) the preparation by a tax distribution committee of any distribution list shall be carried out by such committee only at such time and in such place in the village as may be specified in a notice to be posted by the District Officer at the District Office and in some conspicuous place in the village and any person who may desire to be present at such preparation may attend, and

(b) if a tax distribution committee fails to prepare a distribution list prior to the date specified by the District Officer, the District Commissioner may prepare such list and no objection shall be heard to any such list.

<small>Distribution of tax in respect of settled land.</small>

19. On the first day of April next following the date of the order made by the High Commissioner under section 3 of this Ordinance relating to the area in which any village of which the lands or some of the lands have been settled is situated, the official valuer shall, if the village is one of which the lands have been settled, commence to prepare a distribution list in respect of the lands of such village or if the village is one of which some of the lands have been settled, commence to prepare a distribution list in respect of such lands, showing the amount of the rural property tax payable by each owner of land in such village or such part of the village having regard to the area and category of land owned by such owner in the village or part of the village as the case may be as at the day prior to the day upon which such official valuer commences to prepare any distribution list under this section.

<small>Distribution list to be open to inspection.</small>

20. A distribution list prepared in accordance with sections 18 and 19 of this Ordinance shall be in such form and shall be made available for inspection in such manner as may be prescribed.

21. Any person whose name appears in a distribution list (other than a distribution list prepared by the District Commissioner), or any other person, who is aggrieved by reason of the unfairness or incorrectness of the apportionment made by such list or by reason of the insertion or incorrectness of any matter in such list or by reason of the omission of any matter therefrom, may object :— _{Objections to distribution lists.}

    (a) if the distribution list was prepared by a tax distribution committee to the tax distribution committee through the District Officer administering the area in which the village is situated, and

    (b) if the distribution list was prepared by an official valuer, to the official valuer through the District Officer administering the area in which the village is situated :

Provided that :—

    (i) nothing herein contained shall be deemed to enable any person to object to the category of any land as appearing on any rural property tax roll finally determined as provided in subsection (1) of section 16 of this Ordinance, and

    (ii) every such objection shall be made :—

        (I) within fourteen days of the day upon which the distribution list is made available for inspection in accordance with section 20 of this Ordinance, and

        (II) in such manner and in such form as may be prescribed.

22.—(1) On receipt of any objection to a distribution list duly made in accordance with the provisions of section 21 of this Ordinance, the tax distribution committee or the official valuer, as the case may be, shall consider each such objection and after making such enquiries as they or he may deem necessary shall have power to amend the distribution list : _{Power of tax distribution committee and/or official valuer to amend distribution list.}

Provided that :—

    (a) if the tax distribution committee or the official valuer shall consider any objection to the distribution list to be without foundation and shall decide to make no amendment thereto in pursuance thereof they or he shall give notice of such fact to the objector on a form to be prescribed and the date appearing upon such form shall be deemed to be the date of the decision of the tax distribution committee or the official valuer as the case may be in respect of such objection, and

    (b) if the tax distribution committee or the official valuer shall consider any objection to the distribution list to be sufficiently well founded to warrant further consideration, they or he shall give notice of such fact on a form to be

— 18 —

prescribed to the objector and to any other person whom they or he may think may be affected by such objection and they or he shall in such form state the time and place fixed for the hearing of the objection, and

(c) if the objector or any other person informed of the proceedings is not present at the time and place stated in such form for the hearing of the objection, the tax distribution committee or the official valuer as the case may be, may, notwithstanding such absence, make such decision on the objection as they or he may deem right.

(2) Any amendment to a distribution list made by a tax distribution committee or official valuer in accordance with the provisions of subsection (1) hereof shall be endorsed by the District Officer at the request of the tax distribution committee or the official valuer before the distribution list is made available for inspection in accordance with the provisions of section 20 of this Ordinance. Each such endorsement shall be initialled and dated by the District Officer and the date of any such endorsement shall be deemed to be the date of the decision of the tax distribution committee or official valuer as the case may be in respect of the objection as a result of which it was made.

Appeals to District Commissioner from the decisions of tax distribution committees and/or District Officer.

23. Any person may if he feels aggrieved by any decision made under section 22 of this Ordinance, within fourteen days of the date of such decision, appeal in a form to be prescribed to the District Commissioner of the District in which the property affected by such decision is situated.

Powers and duties of District Commissioner to decide appeals, etc.

24.—(1) The District Commissioner shall upon receipt of any appeal duly made in accordance with the provisions of section 23 of this Ordinance, give notice in a form to be prescribed to the appellant, and to the tax distribution committee or official valuer as the case may be (who shall be the respondents or respondent), of the time and place fixed for the hearing of the appeal.

(2) At the time and place so fixed the District Commissioner shall hear and determine the appeal:

Provided that:—

(a) no appeal shall be heard by a District Commissioner unless the appellant has paid any deposit prescribed on account of costs, and

(b) if any party to the appeal is not present at the time and place fixed for the hearing of the appeal the District Commissioner may, notwithstanding such absence, make such decision as he may deem right, and

(c) it shall be lawful, for the purpose of any appeal hereunder, for the District Commissioner to administer oaths.

(3) Upon the determination of any appeal, the District Commissioner may make such order as to costs as he may think proper.

(4) The District Commissioner shall cause any amendment to the distribution list made by him in accordance with the provisions of subsection (2) hereof to be endorsed upon the distribution list made available for inspection in accordance with the provisions of section 20 of this Ordinance and each such endorsement shall be initialled and dated by the person making it and the date of any such endorsement shall be deemed to be the date of the decision of the District Commissioner in respect of the appeal as a result of which it was made and shall further be deemed to be notice of the decision to all persons interested.

(5) A decision of the District Commissioner so endorsed shall be final and no appeal shall lie therefrom :

Provided that any party to any proceedings before a District Commissioner may ask the District Commissioner to state a case upon a point of law material to the issue arising out of the proceedings for the opinion of the District Court and the District Commissioner shall thereupon state such case.

25. The amount of the rural property tax payable by each owner of land within any village, as shown on the distribution list or lists in respect of such village as finally amended (if there have been any objections) or, if there have been no objections, as shown on the distribution list or lists as made available for inspection in accordance with the provisions of section 20 of this Ordinance, shall be the amount of the rural property tax payable by such owner in respect of the lands to which such distribution list or lists refer until amended as in this Ordinance. *Determination of distribution lists.*

26.—(1) An official valuer shall in each year, the first such year being the year in respect of which the rural property tax is first levied under this Ordinance, prepare :— *Official valuer to prepare annually supplementary rural property tax rolls and supplementary valuation lists.*

  (a) a supplementary rural property tax roll in a form to be prescribed in respect of each village in which changes in the categories of land have been made by him :—

  (i) in the case of the first supplementary rural property tax roll, since the rural property tax roll was determined as provided in subsection (1) of section 16 of this Ordinance, and

  (ii) in the case of any supplementary rural property tax roll subsequent to the first supplementary rural property tax roll, since the previous supplementary rural property tax roll was determined as provided in subsection (1) of section 27 of this Ordinance, showing such changes:

Provided that any land which has been brought under irrigation by any system of irrigation involving for its upkeep and continuity the continuous use of mechanical aid and regular expenditure on the part of the owner shall not thereby be deemed to have changed in category;

(b) a supplementary valuation list in a form to be prescribed in respect of each village in which any of the undermentioned industrial buildings are situated, that is to say:—

(i) any industrial building:—

(I) in the case of the first supplementary valuation list, not included in the valuation list as determined under subsection (2) of section 16 of this Ordinance, and

(II) in the case of any supplementary valuation list subsequent to the first supplementary valuation list, not included in the previous supplementary valuation list as determined under subsection (2) of section 27 of this Ordinance,

either because the completion of such industrial building was not effected or it was a building which was not an industrial building within the meaning of this Ordinance or it was omitted, and

(ii) any industrial building of which the net annual value has increased or decreased by twenty per centum or more:—

(I) in the case of the first supplementary valuation list, since the valuation list was determined as provided in subsection (2) of section 16 of this Ordinance, and

(II) in the case of any supplementary valuation list subsequent to the first supplementary valuation list, since the previous supplementary valuation list was determined as provided in subsection (2) of section 27 of this Ordinance,

showing the net annual value of such industrial buildings.

(2) For the purpose of enabling the official valuer to prepare a supplementary valuation list, owners shall, and any District Officer may, give notice, on a form to be prescribed, to the official valuer of any industrial building which should in accordance with the provisions of this section be included in a supplementary valuation list.

— 21 —

(3) All the provisions of this Ordinance relating to the posting of the rural property tax rolls and valuation lists, objections thereto, amendment thereof as the result of such objections and appeals against the decisions of official valuers in respect of such objections shall apply *mutatis mutandis* to supplementary rural property tax rolls and supplementary valuation lists respectively prepared in accordance with the provisions of subsection (1) hereof.

27.—(1) The categories of the lands of any village and the areas thereof, as shown on the supplementary rural property tax roll as finally amended (if there have been any objections) or if there have been no objections then as shown on the supplementary rural property tax roll as posted in the village, shall be the categories and areas of such lands for the purposes of this Ordinance as from the commencement of the year next following the year in which such supplementary rural property tax roll was prepared until amended as in this Ordinance provided : _{Determination of supplementary rural property tax rolls and supplementary valuation lists.}

Provided that the official valuer may at any time after the first day of April alter such rolls to include any change of categories which in his opinion have become necessary by reason of parcellations or any other changes which may have occurred through the medium of the Land Registry between the date of the preparation of the supplementary roll by the official valuer and the following thirty-first day of March, inclusive.

(2) The net annual value of the industrial buildings within any village as shown on the supplementary valuation list as finally amended (if there have been any objections) or if there have been no objections then as shown on the supplementary valuation list as posted in the village shall be the net annual value of such industrial buildings for the purposes of this Ordinance as from the commencement of the year next following the year in which such supplementary valuation list was prepared until amended as in this Ordinance provided.

28.—(1) On or as soon as possible after the first day of April next following the determination of any supplementary rural property tax roll as provided in subsection (1) of section 27 of this Ordinance, the District Officer administering the area in which the land is situated shall prepare a supplementary distribution list in the form to be prescribed showing all changes which have occurred since the preparation of the last distribution list or supplementary distribution list and shall post the list in the village. _{Supplementary distribution lists.}

(2) Any person may object to any entry in the supplementary distribution list within fourteen days from the day upon which it was made available for inspection and if any person is not satisfied with the decision of the District Officer on his objection

he may appeal under section 23 of this Ordinance and the appeal shall be dealt with under the provisions of section 24 of this Ordinance.

<small>Determination of supplementary distribution lists.</small>

29. The amount of the rural property tax payable by each owner of land, as shown on the supplementary distribution list or lists as finally amended (if there have been any objections) or if there have been no objections, then as shown on the supplementary distribution list or lists as made available for inspection, shall be the amount of the rural property tax payable by such owner in respect of the lands to which such supplementary distribution list or lists refer, as from the commencement of the year in which such supplementary distribution list or lists were prepared until amended as in this Ordinance provided.

<small>When tax shall be due.</small>

30. The rural property tax shall be due :—

   (a) in respect of the year commencing on the first day of April next following the date of an Order made by the High Commissioner under section 3 of this Ordinance relating to any area, as under :—

   (i) on all industrial buildings within such area, on the first day of April;

   (ii) on any land within such area, on the day the distribution list in respect of such land is made available for inspection in accordance with the provisions of section 20 of this Ordinance, notwithstanding the right to object to such list conferred upon owners by section 21 of this Ordinance, or any objection actually made thereunder :

   Provided that upon the determination of such distribution list as provided in section 25 of this Ordinance then if any owner has paid any sum in excess of the sum payable by him as shown on the distribution list so determined such sum shall be refunded to him, or if any owner has paid any sum less than the sum payable by him as shown on the distribution list so determined, such sum shall be payable by such person and may be recovered as an arrear of the rural property tax;

   (b) in respect of any year subsequent to the year commencing on the first day of April next following the date of an order made by the High Commissioner under section 3 of this Ordinance relating to any area, as under :—

   (i) on all industrial buildings within such area, on the first day of April;

(ii) on any land within such area other than land appearing on the supplementary rural property tax roll prepared in the preceding year, on the first day of April;

(iii) on any land appearing on the supplementary rural property tax roll prepared in the preceding year, on the day the supplementary distribution list in respect of such land is posted, notwithstanding the right to object to such supplementary distribution list conferred upon owners by section 28 of this Ordinance or any objections actually made thereunder:

Provided that upon the determination of such supplementary distribution list as provided in section 29 of this Ordinance then if any owner has paid any sum in excess of the sum payable by him as shown on the supplementary distribution list so determined such sum shall be refunded to him or if any owner has paid any sum less than the sum payable by him as shown on the supplementary distribution list so determined such sum shall be payable by such person and may be recovered as an arrear of the rural property tax:

Provided that the District Commissioner may direct that any owner liable for an amount of the rural property tax exceeding two pounds may pay such tax by such instalments and subject to such conditions as the District Commissioner may in such direction set out.

31.—(1) Any owner of any land or of any industrial building who on or after the first day of April next following the date of any order made by the High Commissioner under section 3 of this Ordinance relating to the area in which such land or industrial building is situated shall sell or exchange such land or industrial building or otherwise dispose thereof in any other manner, and any person who on or after such first day of April shall become owner of any land or industrial building within such area by way of succession shall forthwith give notice to the District Officer administering the area in which such land or industrial building is situated of such fact in a form to be prescribed. *[Provisions relating to change of ownership.]*

(2) On receipt of any notice duly made in accordance with the provisions of subsection (1) hereof, or in the event of any fact of which notice is required to be given by that subsection coming otherwise to his knowledge, the District Officer shall, after making such enquiries as he may deem necessary, have power to substitute the name of any person in the place of the name of any owner of any property appearing in any distribution list, supplementary distribution list, valuation list or supplementary valuation list which has been posted in accordance with the provisions of this Ordinance.

— 24 —

Any person whose name is substituted for the name of any owner of any property under this subsection shall be deemed to be the owner of such property for the purposes of this Ordinance as from the first day of April next following the date of such substitution.

(3) Nothing in this section shall be deemed to alter, determine or render void any liability of any person whose name is substituted for that of any owner under the provisions of subsection (2) hereof by contract, agreement or otherwise concerning the liability of such person to pay to such owner any tax due in respect of any property, provided always that such owner shall remain liable to Government for the payment of the rural property tax due in respect of any period prior to the date when such person is deemed to be the owner of such property for the purposes of this Ordinance under subsection (2) hereof.

Collection of rural property tax.
Cap. 137.

32. Any rural property tax may be recovered in accordance with the provisions of the Taxes (Collection) Ordinance, and the rural property tax shall be deemed to be a tax to which that Ordinance applies :

Provided that the posting of the distribution list, supplementary distribution list, valuation list and supplementary valuation list shall be deemed to be good and sufficient demand to all owners appearing thereon respectively to pay the rural property tax appearing against their names and no demand notes shall be required.

Owner need not be named.

33. Where the name of any person liable to pay the rural property tax is not known, it shall be sufficient for any of the purposes of this Ordinance to designate him as "the owner" without any further description.

Service of notice.

34. Wherever it is provided in this Ordinance that notice shall be given or sent for any purpose to any person, the notice shall be deemed to be sufficiently served if it is delivered, or transmitted through the post, to his known address. Where property is owned in undivided shares, the notice shall be deemed to be served on the owner of the property if it is delivered or transmitted through the post to the known address of any one of the co-owners.

Errors and omissions in rolls or lists.

35.—(1) The official valuer or the District Officer may at any time cause to be corrected any errors in the rural property tax roll or supplementary rural property tax roll or valuation list or supplementary valuation list or distribution list or supplementary distribution list and may introduce clerical amendments or additions thereto respectively, provided that all such corrections, amendments or additions are signed by the official valuer or the District Officer and that a separate record is kept by him of such errors, amendments or additions.

— 25 —

(2) Any property liable to rural property tax which is omitted from any of the rolls or list mentioned in subsection (1) hereof shall not, by reason of such omission, be relieved of its liability : such property may be added to the roll or list by the District Officer at any time while the roll or list is in operation, and the owner thereof shall thereupon become liable to payment of the tax for the year in which such addition is made and for the payment of any tax for the preceding year or years during which the roll or list has been in operation : notice in writing shall be given to the owner of such property of the tax assessed thereon, and the tax so assessed shall become payable, subject to the provisions for objection and appeal in this Ordinance, on the expiration of thirty days from the date of the notice.

(3) The omission from a roll or list of any matters required by this Ordinance to be included therein shall not of itself render the list invalid.

(4) The entry of the name of any person on a distribution list or supplementary distribution list as owner of any land shall not in itself be deemed to constitute such person owner of such land for the purpose of this Ordinance, or to render him liable to pay rural property tax thereon, if he is not in fact the owner thereof as defined in section 2.

36.—(1) Any person who omits to fill in or submit as required by this Ordinance any particulars or information in any form prescribed, or who in any form prescribed wilfully makes any false statement and any person who refuses to answer any question or wilfully makes a false answer to any question put to him by any person in order to obtain information which will enable such person to carry out any duties imposed upon or exercise any powers conferred upon him by this Ordinance, shall be guilty of an offence and shall on conviction be liable to imprisonment for a term not exceeding one year or to a fine not exceeding one hundred pounds or to both such penalties.

_{Offences and penalties.}

(2) Any person who shall in any way obstruct any other person in the carrying out of any duties imposed upon or in the exercise of any powers conferred upon such other person by this Ordinance, shall be guilty of an offence and shall on conviction be liable to imprisonment for a term not exceeding one year or to a fine not exceeding one hundred pounds or to both such penalties.

(3) Any owner or person who shall fail to comply with the provisions of section 5 or section 31 of this Ordinance, shall be guilty of an offence and shall on conviction be liable to imprisonment for a term not exceeding three months or to a fine not exceeding twenty pounds or to both such penalties, and in addition he shall pay any amount of tax which would have been payable by him if he had given notice in accordance with those sections or either of them.

Occupants of Government owned land under implied lease.	37. Every occupant of Government owned land in virtue of an implied lease shall pay rent in respect of such land at the rate prescribed in the schedule to this Ordinance for rural property tax on such land : provided that in the case of land planted with citrus, bananas or as a fruit plantation, the rent payable shall be at the rate of tax prescribed in the said schedule for the ground crop category or irrigated land category to which the land would belong if not so planted.
Tax to be first charge on property, etc.	38.—(1) The rural property tax shall be a first charge on the property in respect of which it is payable and no disposition relating to such property shall be entered in any Government register until the rural property tax thereon has been paid. (2) Without prejudice to the provisions of section 32 of this Ordinance, if the owner of any property in respect of which the rural property tax is payable is absent from Palestine the said tax shall be payable by and may be recovered from the agent, if any, of any such owner to the extent of the amount of any moneys collected by the agent on behalf of such owner, provided always that the owner shall remain liable to the Government for the payment of the rural property tax. (3) Where any land or any industrial building is held in joint ownership, the rural property tax may be collected from any one or more of the co-owners, and the co-owner or co-owners from whom the rural property tax is collected shall have a right of contribution from the other co-owner or co-owners in the proportion of the respective shares of such other co-owner or co-owners and may attach the land or building and/or the revenue therefrom until he has recovered the amount due from the other co-owner or co-owners. (4) Nothing in this Ordinance shall be deemed to alter, determine or render void any liability of a tenant to his landlord by contract, agreement or otherwise, concerning the liability of the tenant to pay to the landlord any tax due in respect of the property, provided always that the owner shall remain liable to Government for the payment of the rural property tax.
District Officer's copies of documents to be deemed correct record.	39. The figures and particulars in the copies of the rural property tax rolls, supplementary rural property tax rolls, valuation lists, supplementary valuation lists, tax distribution lists and supplementary tax distribution lists deposited with the District Officer, shall be deemed to be the correct figures and particulars, provided that any amendments which may have been decided upon under section 12(2), 16(1) or 27(1) have been inserted therein.
The Director of Land Settlement to supervise this Ordinance.	40. The Director of Land Settlement shall exercise general supervision and control over the carrying out of this Ordinance.

— 27 —

41. The Chief Justice may with the approval of the High Commissioner make rules regulating the practice and procedure in applications to a District Court upon a case stated under the provisions of this Ordinance. Power of Chief Justice to make certain rules.

42. The High Commissioner may make rules for the carrying out of this Ordinance. Power of High Commissioner to make rules.

43. Where rural property tax is payable upon any land, or where it is not payable upon any land by reason of the land being of a category upon which no such tax is payable under the provisions of the schedule to this Ordinance, the payment or non-payment (as the case may be) of such tax in respect of such land shall not be deemed to affect, or to be evidence of, the rights of the Government of Palestine, or of any person as against the Government of Palestine, in respect of the land; but such payment or non-payment may be produced as evidence of possession of the land as against any person other than the Government of Palestine. Payment or non-payment of tax not to affect or determine rights in land.

44.—(1) The Tithes (Commutation) Ordinance, and the Decree dated the twenty-fifth day of September and published in the *Gazette* dated the fifteenth day of November, 1920, relating to the exemption from tithes of vineyards planted with American stock shall cease to have effect in any area described in any order made by the High Commissioner under section 3 of this Ordinance as from the first day of April next following the date of such order. Repeal, etc.

(2) The Rural Property Tax Ordinance is hereby repealed: No. 1 of 1935.

Provided that all rules, orders, notices, directions, appointments or instruments made, given or executed under the Ordinance hereby repealed and in force at the date of the commencement of this Ordinance shall continue in force as if they had been made, given or executed under this Ordinance, until revoked or varied under this Ordinance.

SCHEDULE

Category	Description	Rate of Tax (Mils)
1	Citrus (excluding Acre Sub-District)	400 per dunum or part thereof.
2	Citrus (Acre Sub-District)	40 per dunum or part thereof.
3	Bananas	560 per dunum or part thereof.

— 28 —

Category	Description	Rate of Tax Mils
4	Village built-on area or land reserved therefor and any area which in the opinion of the official valuer is reserved for the erection of buildings	160 per dunum or part thereof
5	1st Grade Irrigated Land and ø 1st Grade Fruit Plantation	40 per dunum or part thereof
6	2nd Grade Irrigated Land ø 2nd Grade Fruit Plantation	35 per dunum or part thereof
7	3rd Grade Irrigated Land and ø 3rd Grade Fruit Plantation	30 per dunum or part thereof
8	1st Grade Ground Crop Land 4th Grade Irrigated Land and ø 4th Grade Fruit Plantation	25 per dunum or part thereof
9	2nd Grade Ground Crop Land 5th Grade Irrigated Land and ø 5th Grade Fruit Plantation	20 per dunum or part thereof
10	3rd Grade Ground Crop Land 6th Grade Irrigated Land and ø 6th Grade Fruit Plantation	18 per dunum or part thereof
11	4th Grade Ground Crop Land 7th Grade Irrigated Land and ø 7th Grade Fruit Plantation	15 per dunum or part thereof
12	5th Grade Ground Crop Land 8th Grade Irrigated Land and ø 8th Grade Fruit Plantation	12 per dunum or part thereof
13	6th Grade Ground Crop Land 9th Grade Irrigated Land and ø 9th Grade Fruit Plantation	8 per dunum or part thereof
14	7th Grade Ground Crop Land and 10th Grade Irrigated Land	nil per dunum or part thereof
15	8th Grade Ground Crop Land	nil per dunum or part thereof
16	Forests planted and indigenous and uncultivable land	nil per dunum or part thereof

ø Other than Citrus and Bananas.

30th March, 1942.

HAROLD MACMICHAEL
High Commissioner.

PUBLIC LANDS ORDINANCE, No. 6 OF 1942.

Macpherson
Officer Administering the Government.

PUBLIC LANDS ORDINANCE,
No. 6 of 1942.

AN ORDINANCE TO DELEGATE TO THE DIRECTOR OF LAND SETTLEMENT THE POWER TO SIGN LEASES OF STATE DOMAIN, AND TO THE DIRECTOR OF LAND REGISTRATION THE POWER TO SIGN DEEDS FOR THE PURCHASE OF PROPERTY BY GOVERNMENT.

WHEREAS Articles 12 and 13 respectively of the Palestine Order in Council, 1922, vest all rights in or in relation to any public lands in the High Commissioner, and empower him to make grants or leases or to permit such lands to be temporarily occupied on such terms or conditions as he may think fit subject to the provisions of any Ordinance; *Preamble.*

AND WHEREAS it is expedient to make provision for the delegation of certain of these powers :

BE IT ENACTED by the High Commissioner for Palestine, with the advice of the Advisory Council thereof :

1. This Ordinance may be cited as the Public Lands Ordinance, 1942. *Short title.*

2. The Director of Land Settlement may, subject to any general or special direction of the High Commissioner, execute for and on behalf of the High Commissioner any lease of public lands or any licence for the occupation of public lands. *Power of Director of Land Settlement to execute leases and licences of public lands.*

3. The Director of Land Registration may, subject to any general or special direction of the High Commissioner, execute for and on behalf of the High Commissioner any deed of sale whereby property is purchased by or on behalf of the Government of Palestine or by or on behalf of His Majesty's Forces. *Power of Director of Land Registration to execute deeds of sale of land purchased by or for Government or His Majesty's Forces.*

4. The Public Lands Ordinance is hereby repealed. *Repeal. Cap. 122.*

30th March, 1942.

HAROLD MACMICHAEL
High Commissioner.

FORESTS (AMENDMENT) ORDINANCE, No. 7 OF 1942.

Officer Administering the Government.

FORESTS (AMENDMENT) ORDINANCE,
No. 7 of 1942.

AN ORDINANCE TO AMEND THE FORESTS ORDINANCE.

BE IT ENACTED by the High Commissioner for Palestine, with the advice of the Advisory Council thereof :—

1. This Ordinance may be cited as the Forests (Amendment) Ordinance, 1942, and shall be read as one with the Forests Ordinance, hereinafter referred to as the principal Ordinance. *Short title. Cap. 61.*

2. The principal Ordinance is hereby amended by the addition thereto of the following section as section 27 :— *Addition of section 27 to the principal Ordinance.*

"Provision regarding validity of proclamations under section 3 and orders under section 13.

27. Any proclamation proclaiming any land to be a forest reserve, made under section 3 whether before or after the date of the coming into force of this section, and any order declaring any forest reserve to be a closed forest area, made under section 13 whether before or after the said date, shall be deemed to have been and to be properly and validly made and all conditions precedent to such proclamation or order shall be deemed to have been complied with until the contrary is proved by any person alleging it."

HAROLD MACMICHAEL
High Commissioner.

30th March, 1942.

LAND (SETTLEMENT OF TITLE) (AMENDMENT) ORDINANCE.
No. 12 of 1942.

High Commissioner

LAND (SETTLEMENT OF TITLE) (AMENDMENT) ORDINANCE,

No. 12 of 1942.

AN ORDINANCE TO AMEND THE LAND (SETTLEMENT OF TITLE) ORDINANCE.

BE IT ENACTED by the High Commissioner for Palestine, with the advice of the Advisory Council thereof :—

1. This Ordinance may be cited as the Land (Settlement of Title) (Amendment) Ordinance, 1942, and shall be read as one with the Land (Settlement of Title) Ordinance, hereinafter referred to as the principal Ordinance. *[Short title. Cap. 80.]*

2. Section 13 of the principal Ordinance, as amended by the Public Officers (Change of Title) Ordinance, 1940, shall be further amended by the deletion of the words "Director of Land Settlement" appearing in subsection (1) thereof and by the substitution of the words "settlement officer" therefor. *[Amendment of section 13 of the principal Ordinance. No. 12 of 1940.]*

3. Section 31 of the principal Ordinance, as amended by the Land (Settlement of Title) (Amendment) Ordinance, 1939, shall be further amended by the repeal of subsection (2) thereof and by the substitution of the following subsection therefor :— *[Amendment of section 31 of the principal Ordinance. No. 48 of 1939.]*

> "(2) Upon the determination by the settlement officer of any right which was not settled before the transmission of the schedule to the registrar as aforesaid, the settlement officer shall inform the registrar of his decision in the matter, and the registrar shall thereupon enter particulars of such right in accordance with such decision in the appropriate page of the new register for which provision is made by section 36."

4. Section 65 of the principal Ordinance shall be amended by the deletion of the words from "unless" to "is made" inclusive and the substitution of the following words therefor :— *[Amendment of section 65 of the principal Ordinance.]*

> "unless the settlement officer or the Chief Justice, upon application being made to him, is of the opinion that—".

24th June, 1942.

HAROLD MACMICHAEL
High Commissioner.

LAND COURTS (AMENDMENT) ORDINANCE, No. 14 OF 1942.

High Commissioner

LAND COURTS (AMENDMENT) ORDINANCE,
No. 14 of 1942.

AN ORDINANCE TO AMEND THE LAND COURTS ORDINANCE.

BE IT ENACTED by the High Commissioner for Palestine, with the advice of the Advisory Council thereof :—

1. This Ordinance may be cited as the Land Courts (Amendment) Ordinance, 1942, and shall be read as one with the Land Courts Ordinance, hereinafter referred to as the principal Ordinance. <small>Short title.
Cap. 75.</small>

2. Section 11 of the principal Ordinance, as enacted in section 5 of the Land Courts (Amendment) Ordinance, 1939, shall be amended by the substitution of the following paragraph for paragraph (a) of subsection (1) thereof :— <small>Amendment of section 11 of the principal Ordinance.
No. 46 of 1939.</small>

> "(a) where the value of the land or the subject matter of the dispute exceeds two hundred and fifty pounds, of a Court consisting of a president or a relieving president, or two judges of a District Court;".

24th June, 1942.

HAROLD MACMICHAEL
High Commissioner.

ately I have heard is that his
Section 25: 1943

LAND TRANSFER (AMENDMENT) ORDINANCE,
No. 13 OF 1943.

High Commissioner

LAND TRANSFER (AMENDMENT) ORDINANCE,
No. 13 of 1943.

AN ORDINANCE TO AMEND THE LAND TRANSFER ORDINANCE.

BE IT ENACTED by the High Commissioner for Palestine, with the advice of the Advisory Council thereof:—

1. This Ordinance may be cited as the Land Transfer (Amendment) Ordinance, 1943, and shall be read as one with the Land Transfer Ordinance, hereinafter referred to as "the principal Ordinance". — Short title. Cap. 81.

2. Subsection (4) of section 4 of the principal Ordinance shall be repealed and the following substituted therefor:— — Amendment of section 4 of the principal Ordinance.

"(4) The petition shall be accompanied by proof of the title of the transferor or applicant and, if so required by the Director, a plan prepared for registration purposes of the immovable property concerned. The petition shall also contain an application for registration of a deed to be executed for the purpose of carrying into effect the terms of the disposition".

HAROLD MACMICHAEL
High Commissioner.

6th August, 1943.

LAND (ACQUISITION FOR PUBLIC PURPOSES) ORDINANCE,
No. 24 OF 1943.

High Commissioner

LAND (ACQUISITION FOR PUBLIC PURPOSES) ORDINANCE, No. 24 of 1943.

An Ordinance to provide for the Acquisition of Land or any Interest therein for Public Purposes, and for the Payment of Compensation therefor.

Be it enacted by the High Commissioner for Palestine, with the advice of the Advisory Council thereof:—

1. This Ordinance may be cited as the Land (Acquisition for Public Purposes) Ordinance, 1943.   *Short title.*

2.—(1) In this Ordinance, unless the context otherwise requires—   *Interpretation.*
"Court" means the Land Court in whose jurisdiction the land in question is situated;
"Land" includes land of any category or tenure and any building, tree or other thing fixed on the land and any portion of the sea, or shore or a river and any right, interest or easement in or over land or water;
"Public purpose" includes any purpose of a public nature certified by the High Commissioner to be a public purpose.

(2) For the purposes of this Ordinance, the court shall consist of president or a relieving president of a district court sitting alone.   *Constitution of court.*

3. Where the High Commissioner is satisfied that it is necessary or expedient for any public purpose so to do he may —   *Powers of High Commissioner.*

(a) acquire the ownership of any land;

(b) acquire the possession or use of any land for a definite period;

(c) acquire any easement on any land or any other right thereon or thereover;

(d) impose any easement on any land or any other restraint on the exercise of any right incidental to ownership thereof,

paying such compensation or consideration as may be agreed upon or determined under the provisions of this Ordinance.

4.—(1) Whenever land in any locality is required for any public purpose it shall be lawful for the High Commissioner and his servants and workmen to do all or any of the following things:—   *Preliminary investigation.*

(a) to enter upon and survey and take levels of any land in such locality;

(b) to dig or bore into the subsoil;

(c) to do all other acts necessary to ascertain whether the land is suitable for such purpose and the value of the land and of the buildings, trees and crops thereon;

(d) to clear the land proposed to be acquired and to set out and mark the boundaries of such land and the work (if any) proposed to be made thereon:

— 2 —

Provided that no person shall enter into any building or upon enclosed court or garden attached to a dwelling house (except with the consent of the occupier thereof) without previously giving the occupier at least seven days' notice of his intention to do so.

(2) As soon as conveniently may be after any entry made under section (1) the High Commissioner shall pay for all damage done and in case of dispute as to the amount to be paid either the High Commissioner or the person claiming compensation may refer the dispute to the court whose decision shall be final.

Notices.

5. The High Commissioner shall cause public notice (which notice shall be in the form set out in the Schedule or to the like effect to be posted at convenient places or near the land to be acquired stating that he intends to acquire the land. He shall also cause such notice to be published in the *Gazette*, and, in addition, if any person is registered as owner of the land, he shall cause such notice to be served on such person either personally or by leaving it for him at his last known place of abode or by sending it through the post by registered letter addressed to him there.

Power of disposal of land.

6. It shall be lawful for all persons entitled to any land —

(a) to sell it or otherwise dispose of the ownership thereof to the High Commissioner;

(b) to permit the possession or use thereof for a definite period by the High Commissioner;

(c) to create any easement thereon or any other right thereon or thereover in favour of the High Commissioner;

(d) to create or acquiesce in, in favour of the High Commissioner any restraint on the exercise of any right incidental to ownership thereof,

and to enter into all necessary agreements for all or any of the purposes; and, in particular, any company, or trustee, guardian curator or other person representing any person under disability may, by force of this Ordinance and notwithstanding anything to the contrary in any law, memorandum or articles of association or other document, do in relation to such land all or any of the aforesaid acts and enter into all necessary agreements for any purpose.

Notice of intention to acquire and power to take possession

7. The High Commissioner may, by such notice as aforesaid or any subsequent notice published in like manner, direct that persons claiming to have any right or interest in the land to be acquired yield up possession of the land after the expiration of the period specified in the notice, which period shall not be less than six weeks from the posting of such notice, unless the land is urgently required for the public purpose.

At the expiration of such period the High Commissioner shall be entitled to enter into and take possession of the land accordingly.

Provided that a notice under section 5 hereof or under this section shall not be construed as an admission on the part of the High Commissioner that the land is held by anybody in private ownership or in private lawful possession, and the publication of such notice or notices shall not be deemed to operate as an estoppel against the Government of Palestine to claim the land as vacant State land.

— 3 —

If the owners or occupiers of the land to be acquired refuse to let the High Commissioner to enter into possession, the High Commissioner may apply to the court which, if satisfied that the High Commissioner is entitled to possession under the last preceding section, shall issue an order commanding possession to be delivered.

Procedure on failure to give possession.

If at or after the expiration of six weeks after the posting of notice no claim shall be lodged with the High Commissioner in respect of such land, or if the person who may have lodged any claim and the High Commissioner shall not agree as to the amount of the compensation to be paid for the right or interest in such land belonging to such person, or if such person has not given satisfactory evidence in support of his claim or if separate and conflicting claims are made in respect of the said land, or if the Government claims that the land is vacant State land, the amount of compensation due, if any, in every such case of disputed interest or title shall be settled by the court which shall have jurisdiction to hear and determine in all cases mentioned in this section upon a summons taken out by the High Commissioner or any person holding or claiming any right or interest in any land named in any notice aforesaid.

Disputes as to compensation and title to be settled by court.

Where any person upon whom a summons has been served shall appear at the time appointed, a decision may be given *ex parte* upon hearing the evidence adduced; and such decision shall be as final as if given after hearing in the presence of such person.

Decision in absence of parties.

No person shall at any time be required to sell or dispose of any right or interest in a part only of any house or other building to the High Commissioner if such person be willing and able to sell or convey the whole thereof.

Party not to be compelled to sell or convey part of a house.

In estimating the compensation to be awarded for any land or any interest therein, the court shall act in accordance with the following rules :—

Rules for assessment of compensation.

(a) No allowance shall be made on account of the acquisition being compulsory :

(b) The value of the land shall, subject as hereinafter provided, be taken to be the amount which the land, if sold in the open market by a willing seller, might be expected to realise :

Provided that the court in estimating such compensation shall assess the same according to what it shall find, to have been the value of such land right or interest on the said basis at the time when the High Commissioner published the notice to acquire the same, and without regard to any improvements or works made or constructed thereafter to be made or constructed thereafter on the said land :

Provided further that where the Army, Navy, Air Force or any other Government Department has been in possession of the land, by virtue of a title less than absolute ownership, compensation shall be assessed without regard to any increase in value on account of works constructed on the said land by the Army, Navy, Air Force or other Government Department. :

Provided further that the court, in estimating such compensation, shall give consideration to all returns and assessments of capital or rental value for taxation made by or acquiesced in by the claimant;

(c) the special suitability or adaptability of the land for any purpose shall not be taken into account if it is a purpose to which it

— 4 —

could be applied only in pursuance of powers derived from legislation or for which there is no market apart from the special needs of a particular purchaser or the requirements of the High Commissioner;

(d) where the land is and but for the compulsory acquisition would continue to be devoted to a purpose of such a nature that there is no general demand or market for land for that purpose, the compensation may, if the court is satisfied that re-instatement in some other place is *bona fide* intended, be assessed on the basis of the reasonable cost of such equivalent re-instatement;

(e) in assessing the rent to be paid for the lease of land, the court shall assess such rent on the basis that it shall be such annual amount as will be reasonable compensation to the owner for the actual loss which he is likely to sustain by reason of the acquisition, or a reasonable return to the owner on the capital value of the land not exceeding six per centum of that value as assessed in accordance with the provisions of the preceding paragraphs, whichever amount shall be the less;

(f) the court shall assess the compensation to be paid by way of damage for the imposition of any easement or other restraint on the exercise of any rights incidental to ownership on the basis of the amount by which the value of the land assessed in accordance with the preceding paragraphs shall have been diminished by reason of the imposition of such easement or restraint;

(g) where part only of the land belonging to any person is acquired under this Ordinance the court shall take into consideration any enhancement of the value of the residue of the land by reason of the proximity of any improvements or works made or constructed or to be made or constructed by the High Commissioner;

(h) the court shall also have regard to the damage, if any, to be sustained by the owner by reason of the severance of the land acquired for public purposes from other land belonging to such owner or other injurious effect on such other land by the exercise of the powers conferred by this Ordinance.

Compensation for loss of rents.

13. Where the High Commissioner has in pursuance of a notice under section 5 entered into possession of any land, the court may award compensation to the owner of such land and to all parties entitled to any right or interest therein for loss of rents for the period between the time the High Commissioner so entered into possession, and the time when the consideration due under an agreement has been paid to the person entitled thereto, or compensation has been paid into court under the provisions of this Ordinance.

When the High Commissioner may withdraw from the acquisition of land.

14. Nothing in this Ordinance shall be taken to compel the High Commissioner to complete the acquisition of any land unless he shall have entered into possession of the land or has failed within one month of the decision of the court to intimate to the court that he does not intend to proceed with the acquisition:

Provided that the owner of the land and all persons entitled to any right or interest in the land shall be entitled to receive from the High Commissioner all such costs as may have been incurred by them by reason or in consequence of the proceedings for acquisition, and com-

— 5 —

pensation for the damage (if any) which they may have sustained by reason or in consequence of the notice of intended acquisition.

The amount of such costs and compensation, if not agreed upon, shall be determined by the court.

15.—(1) Where the High Commissioner has made an unconditional offer in writing of any sum as compensation to any claimant and the sum awarded by the court to that claimant does not exceed the sum offered, the court shall, unless for special reasons it thinks proper not to do so, order the claimant to bear his own costs and to pay the costs of the High Commissioner so far as they were incurred after the offer was made. *Provision as to costs.*

(2) If the court is satisfied that a claimant has failed to comply with any demands of the High Commissioner as set forth in the notice given under section 5 in sufficient time to enable the High Commissioner to make a proper offer, the foregoing provisions of this section shall apply as if an unconditional offer had been made by the High Commissioner at the time when, in the opinion of the court, sufficient particulars should have been furnished and the claimant had been awarded a sum not exceeding the amount of such offer.

(3) Where a claimant has made an unconditional offer in writing to accept any sum as compensation and has complied with the demands of the High Commissioner set out as aforesaid and the sum awarded is equal to or exceeds that sum the court shall, unless for special reasons it may think proper not to do so, order the High Commissioner to bear his own costs and to pay the costs of the claimant, so far as they were incurred after the offer was made.

(4) Subject as aforesaid, the costs of any proceedings shall be in the discretion of the court who may direct to and by whom and in what manner those costs shall be paid:

Provided that such costs shall be in accordance with the prescribed scale.

(5) Where the court orders the claimant to pay the costs or any part of the costs of the High Commissioner, the High Commissioner may deduct the amount so payable by the claimant from the amount of compensation due to him.

16. The decision of the court respecting any compensation or any question of disputed interest or title shall be final and conclusive in regard to all parties upon whom summonses have been served as aforesaid, or who have appeared and claimed or on whose behalf any person, having authority to that effect, has claimed any land or any right or interest therein, but it shall be lawful for persons upon whom summonses have not been served, or who have not appeared or claimed, or on whose behalf no claim has been made, to make a claim at any time within one year after the date of the final decision; and in all cases where any compensation has been awarded, whether the same be in the form of a sum of money or an annual rent, the amount thereof or such part thereof as shall be payable within the said period of one year shall be paid into court (except where a valid written title to the land shall be delivered or where the court shall otherwise direct) and shall not be paid out of court until the said period of one year shall have elapsed from the date of such final decision, after which *Postponement of payment of compensation.*

— 6 —

upon application to the court by any person claiming as aforesaid to be interested therein it may be paid to whomsoever the court may direct. The payment into court of the compensation or where the compensation is in the form of rent, the payment of such rent as it accrues due to the parties shall operate as a complete discharge and acquittance to the High Commissioner of all claims in respect of such lands but shall not hinder any subsequent proceedings by any person claiming to have a better right thereto against the person to whom such payment has been made:

<small>Payment by High Commissioner to operate as complete discharge of compensation.</small>

Provided always that any person claiming to be interested in any compensation paid into court (such compensation or some part thereof not having been paid out of court) may within thirty days from the date of the final decision and not after claim that such compensation or any part thereof be paid to him. All claims for compensation to be paid out of court, made after twelve months shall have elapsed after the final decision of the court, shall be made by notice of motion in the manner provided by the rules of court for the time being in force regulating the service of motions, and supported by an affidavit stating the grounds on which the claim is based.

<small>Registered owners or parties in possession as owners to be deemed entitled to land.</small>

17. If any question arises in respect of the title to any land to be acquired under this Ordinance, the registered owners or if the land is not registered then the persons in possession as being the owners thereof at the time of the acquisition of such land shall be deemed to have been lawfully entitled to such land, unless the contrary be shown to the satisfaction of the court; and they and all parties claiming under them or consistently with their possession shall be deemed entitled to the consideration or compensation money, but without prejudice to any subsequent proceedings against such parties at the instance of any person claiming to have a better right thereto:

Provided that when the Government of Palestine claims that the land is vacant State land, the onus of proof that the land is held in absolute private ownership or in lawful possession by any person shall be with any person making such allegation.

<small>High Commissioner exonerated upon payment.</small>

18. The payment to any person to whom any consideration or compensation shall be paid or the payment into court of any compensation upon a decision of the court shall effectually discharge the High Commissioner from responsibility for the application or being answerable for the misapplication thereof:

Provided that where any person other than the owner is in possession, or where any person is in possession in any representative character, the High Commissioner may pay such consideration or compensation to such persons and in such proportions and instalments and after such notice as the court may direct.

<small>Certificate of title.</small>

19. The High Commissioner may apply *ex parte* by summons at any time to the court for a certificate of title, and the court shall upon proof of the posting of the notice in accordance with the provisions of section 5, grant a certificate of title in the prescribed form to the land described in such notice which certificate shall not be questioned or defeasible by reason of any irregularity or error or defect in the notice or want of notice or of any other irregularity, error or defect in the proceedings previous to the obtaining of such certificate and such certificate shall be sufficient authority to the Director of Land

— 7 —

1. Registration to cause the necessary entries to be made in the land registers.

2. Where any land is acquired under this Ordinance for the purpose of widening any existing road or part of it, or for the construction of a new road, playground or recreation ground the owner of the land so acquired shall not be entitled to compensation unless the area taken exceeds one quarter part of the total area of the plot which he owns:

Provided that, if it is established that hardship would be caused if no compensation were paid, the High Commissioner may in his discretion grant such compensation as, having regard to all the circumstances of the case, he shall think fit. If the area taken from any owner exceeds one quarter part of the total area of the plot owned by him, compensation shall be paid to the owner for the land taken in excess of such one quarter part in accordance with the provisions of this Ordinance.

Gratuitous expropriation for widening roads.

2.—(1) Where, by the acquisition of any land under this Ordinance for the purpose of making a new road or of widening an existing road, any land is increased in value, the High Commissioner shall, if he make a claim for that purpose within one year of the execution of the work, be entitled to recover from any person whose property is so increased in value a contribution towards the cost of the work, not exceeding one fourth of the amount of that increase :

Provided that, where a contribution is imposed under this section, compensation shall be paid for any land taken for the purpose of widening a road; and the amount of compensation may be set off against the contribution due under this section.

(2) Any question whether any land is increased in value within the meaning of this section and as to the amount of such increase shall, in default of agreement, be determined by the court.

(3) In default of agreement, the contribution due from the owner towards the cost of the work shall be payable in not less than four equal annual instalments and shall be recoverable as a civil debt by the High Commissioner from the owner of the land for the time being.

Betterment charge where land taken for making or widening of roads.

3.—(1) Any person may apply to the High Commissioner requesting him to acquire any land on behalf and for the use of such person and if, in the opinion of the High Commissioner, the acquisition thereof is likely to prove useful to the public, he may proceed to acquire it under the provisions of this Ordinance.

(2) Where the person applying to the High Commissioner under the provisions of subsection (1) is a municipal corporation or a local council or any other local authority or any person who is the holder of a concession whereunder he is entitled to require the High Commissioner to acquire any land on its behalf, the High Commissioner may, by notice published in the *Gazette*, authorise such person to exercise all the powers and perform all the obligations conferred or imposed on the High Commissioner under the provisions of this Ordinance, and such person shall thereupon be vested with all the powers and obligations of the High Commissioner under this Ordinance.

Acquisition by persons other than the High Commissioner.

— 8 —

(3) If the High Commissioner acquires any land on behalf and the use of any person, other than a person within the meaning of section (2), he shall require such person to enter into an agreement with him providing to his satisfaction for the following matters namely:—

(a) the payment to him of the cost of the acquisition;
(b) the transfer, on such payment, of the land to the person;
(c) the terms on which the land shall be held by such person; and
(d) where the acquisition is for the construction of any work or works, the time within which and the conditions on which the work or works shall be executed and maintained, and the terms (if any) on which the public shall be entitled to use the work or works.

Penalty for hindering the taking of possession of land.

23. Any person who shall—

(a) wilfully hinder or obstruct the High Commissioner, or any person acting on his behalf or under his authority, from entering upon or using any land in pursuance of the provisions of this Ordinance; or
(b) molest, hinder or obstruct such person when in possession of such land,

shall be guilty of an offence and liable on conviction to a fine of twenty-five pounds or to imprisonment for three months or to both such penalties.

Application of Ordinance to waqf lands and other like lands.

24.—(1) In the application of this Ordinance to land dedicated as waqf, the trustee (mutawalli) of any waqf, or in the absence of a trustee the Administration of Awqaf, shall have all the powers of, and be subject to all the obligations imposed by this Ordinance upon the owner of the land, and the compensation for the land shall be paid to the trustee (mutawalli) of the waqf, or, in the absence of any such trustee, to the Treasury of the Awqaf in the name of the waqf property concerned.

(2) In the application of this Ordinance to land subject to other religious, charitable or the like trusts, the person or authority responsible for the administration of such land shall have all the powers of and be subject to all the obligations imposed by this Ordinance upon the owner of the land, and the compensation for the land shall be paid to him.

Rules.

25. The High Commissioner may make rules prescribing —

(a) the forms to be used under this Ordinance;
(b) the scale of costs in respect of the award of compensation under this Ordinance;
(c) the means by which claims for several interests in the same land shall be heard at the same time;
(d) generally, for the application of this Ordinance.

Repeal.
Cap. 77.
Cap. 74.

26. The Land (Expropriation) Ordinance and the Land (Acquisition for the Army and Air Force) Ordinance are hereby repealed:

Provided that all rules, notices and certificates made or issued under the Ordinances hereby repealed and in force at the date of the co mencement of this Ordinance shall remain in force until revoked or varied under this Ordinance:

Provided further that any proceedings commenced before the date of commencement of this Ordinance under any of the Ordinances hereby repealed may be continued and enforced under the respective Ordinances hereby repealed as if this Ordinance had not been passed.

SCHEDULE.
FORM.
THE LAND (ACQUISITION FOR PUBLIC PURPOSES) ORDINANCE, 1943.

Notice is hereby given that the following lands (describe lands, giving measurements and showing boundaries whenever practicable) are required by the High Commissioner for public purposes absolutely or for a term of years, or for so long as the same may be used for public purposes.

Any person claiming to have any right or interest in the said lands is required within six weeks from the date of this notice to send to the Director, Department of Land Settlement, a statement of his right and interest and of the evidence thereof, and of any claim made by him in respect of such right or interest.

The High Commissioner is willing to treat for the acquisition of the said lands.

And notice is also hereby given that the High Commissioner intends to enter into possession of the said lands at the expiration of   days from the date of this notice.

The   day of

Chief Secretary.

10th November, 1943.

HAROLD MACMICHAEL,
High Commissioner.

Section 26: 1944

RURAL PROPERTY TAX (AMENDMENT) ORDINANCE,
No. 11 OF 1944.

High Commissioner

RURAL PROPERTY TAX (AMENDMENT) ORDINANCE, No. 11 of 1944.

An Ordinance to amend the Rural Property Tax Ordinance, 1942.

Be it enacted by the High Commissioner for Palestine, with the advice of the Advisory Council thereof:—

1. This Ordinance may be cited as the Rural Property Tax (Amendment) Ordinance, 1944, and shall be read as one with the Rural Property Tax Ordinance, 1942, hereinafter referred to as "the principal Ordinance". *(Short title. No. 5 of 1942.)*

2. Section 2 of the principal Ordinance shall be amended — *(Amendment of section 2 of the principal Ordinance.)*

(a) by the insertion therein immediately after the definition of "District Officer" of the following definition:—

"'Fish pond' means any pond utilised for the cultivation of fish therein.";

(b) by the deletion of the definition of "Land" appearing therein and the substitution therefor of the following definition:—

"'Land' includes buildings other than industrial buildings, fish ponds and anything fixed in the land.";

(c) by the deletion of the expression "section 41" occurring in the definition of "Prescribed" appearing therein and the substitution therefor of the expression "section 42".

3. The principal Ordinance shall be amended by the insertion thereof immediately after section 5 thereof, of the following section, as section 5A:— *(Insertion of new section, as section 5A, in the principal Ordinance.)*

Fish ponds.

5A.—(1) Where, before the first day of April, 1944, the utilisation of any fish pond on any land situated in any area described in an order made by the High Commissioner under section 3 of this Ordinance has been commenced, the owner of such fish pond shall, within three months from the first day of April, 1944, give notice to the District Officer administering the area in which the land is situated, in a form to be prescribed, and the official valuer shall, on verification to his satisfaction, change the category of the land as in his discretion he shall think proper, with effect from the first day of April, 1944,

and rural property tax shall be payable on such fish pond as from that date.

(2) Where, on or after the first day of April, 1944, the utilisation of any fish pond on any land situated in any area described in an order made by the High Commissioner under section 3 of this Ordinance is commenced, or any such fish pond ceases to be on such land, the owner of such fish pond shall, within three months from the date of such commencement or cessation, as the case may be, give notice of such fact to the District Officer administering the area in which the land is situated, in a form to be

— 2 —

prescribed, and the official valuer shall, on verification to his satisfaction, change the category of the land as in his discretion he shall think proper, with effect from the first day of April next following such notification."

Insertion of new section, as section 30A, in the principal Ordinance.

4. The principal Ordinance shall be amended by the insertion therein, immediately after section 30 thereof, of the following section, as section 30A:—

"Penalty for non-payment of tax.

30A. If the rural property tax is not paid within six months from the date or dates on which it is due a sum equal to twenty per centum of the amount of the tax payable shall be added thereto, and the provisions of this Ordinance relating to the collection and recovery of rural property tax shall apply to the collection and recovery of such sum, provided that the District Commissioner may for any good cause shown direct the recovery of any sum less than the full penalty and may enhance the sum so directed to be recovered from time to time in the case of a continuing default, so however that the total sum so directed to be recovered shall not exceed twenty per centum of the amount of the tax payable."

Amendment of section 36 of the principal Ordinance.

5. Section 36 of the principal Ordinance shall be amended by the deletion of the words and figures "section 5 or section 31" appearing in subsection (3) thereof, and the substitution therefor of the following words and figures:—

"section 5, 5A or 31".

Insertion of new section, as section 39A, in the principal Ordinance.

6. The principal Ordinance shall be amended by the insertion therein, immediately after section 39 thereof, of the following section, as section 39A:—

"Certified copies and extracts.

39A.—(1) Any person may at any reasonable time require a copy of, or an extract from, any list, roll or other record made or kept for the purposes of this Ordinance, to be certified by the District Officer, and there shall be paid for such certified copy or extract such fees as may be prescribed.

(2) Any such copy or extract, if duly certified under the hand of the District Officer to be a true copy of, or extract from, such list, roll or other record, shall be admissible in evidence in all legal proceedings as of equal validity with such list, roll or other record, and any document purporting to be a copy of, or an extract from, any list, roll or other record certified as aforesaid, shall be deemed to be such copy or extract unless and until the contrary is proved."

Amendment of Schedule to the principal Ordinance.

7. The Schedule to the principal Ordinance shall be amended by the deletion of categories 14, 15 and 16 and all particulars relating thereto appearing therein and the substitution therefor of the following categories and particulars relating thereto:—

— 3 —

"Category	Description	Rate of Tax Mils
14	7th Grade Ground Crop Land and 10th Grade Irrigated Land	4 per dunum or part thereof.
15	8th Grade Ground Crop Land	2 per dunum or part thereof.
16	Forests planted and indigenous and uncultivable land	nil per dunum or part thereof.
17	Fish ponds	560 per dunum or part thereof."

8. This Ordinance shall come into force on the 1st day of April, 1944.   Commencement.

HAROLD MACMICHAEL
High Commissioner.

10th March, 1944.

LAND (SETTLEMENT OF TITLE) (AMENDMENT) ORDINANCE, No. 18 OF 1944.

High Commissioner

LAND (SETTLEMENT OF TITLE) (AMENDMENT) ORDINANCE,
No. 18 OF 1944.
AN ORDINANCE TO AMEND THE LAND (SETTLEMENT OF TITLE) ORDINANCE.

BE IT ENACTED by the High Commissioner for Palestine, with the advice of the Advisory Council thereof:—

1. This Ordinance may be cited as the Land (Settlement of Title) Amendment) Ordinance, 1944, and shall be read as one with the Land (Settlement of Title) Ordinance, hereinafter referred to as "the principal Ordinance". *Short title.* *Cap. 80.*

2. Subsection (1) of section 69 of the principal Ordinance shall be amended by the addition of the following words at the end thereof:— *Amendment of section 69 of the principal Ordinance.*

", and also in regard to any other matter necessary to give effect to the provisions of this Ordinance."

HAROLD MACMICHAEL
High Commissioner,

March, 1944.

VILLAGE ADMINISTRATION ORDINANCE, No. 23 OF 1944.

Officer Administering Government

VILLAGE ADMINISTRATION ORDINANCE, No. 23 OF 1944.

AN ORDINANCE TO PROVIDE FOR THE ADMINISTRATION OF VILLAGES.

PART I—PRELIMINARY.

BE IT ENACTED by the High Commissioner for Palestine, with the advice of the Advisory Council thereof:—

1. This Ordinance may be cited as the Village Administration Ordinance, 1944.   *Short title.*

2. In this Ordinance, unless the context otherwise requires —   *Interpretation.*

"Administrative Officer" means the District Commissioner or the officer of the District Administration appointed by the District Commissioner to be in charge of the sub-district or administrative sub-division in which the village is situated.

"District Commissioner" means the District Commissioner (as defined in the Interpretation Ordinance) of the district in which the village or village area in question is situated.   *Cap. 69.*

"Mukhtar", except in subsection (1) of section 36 of this Ordinance, means a Mukhtar or Assistant Mukhtar holding office as such in accordance with the provisions of Part V of this Ordinance.

"President of the District Court" means the President or Relieving President of the District Court having jurisdiction in the area in question.

"Village" means an area which has been or which may hereafter be declared to be a village or tribal unit under Article 11 of the Palestine Orders in Council, 1922 to 1940:

Provided that any such area which is within the jurisdiction of a Municipal or Local Council shall not be a village for the purposes of this Ordinance:

Provided further that, where a part of any such area is within the jurisdiction of a Municipal or Local Council, that part of the area shall not form part of the village for the purposes of this Ordinance.

"Village Area" means an area in respect of which an order under section 3 of this Ordinance is in force.

"Village Council" means a Council established in accordance with the provisions of section 4 of this Ordinance.

"Village Court" means a court established in accordance with the provisions of section 17 of this Ordinance.

Part II—Village Councils.

Application of Part II of Ordinance to villages.

3. It shall be lawful for the High Commissioner by order to declare from time to time that any village or part thereof shall be brought within the operation of this Part of this Ordinance. Upon such order being made this Part of this Ordinance shall extend accordingly to any such village or part thereof.

Establishment of Village Council.

4. In every village area there shall be established a Village Council.

Constitution of Village Council.

5.—(1) A Village Council shall consist of —

(a) the mukhtar or mukhtars of the village ex officio:

(b) not less than three and not more than twelve persons (the number to be determined from time to time by the District Commissioner) chosen by such categories of persons ordinarily resident in the village area and in such manner as may from time to time be approved by the District Commissioner:

Provided that a person shall not be a member of a Village Council by virtue of the preceding provisions of this paragraph unless he is a Palestinian citizen of not less than twenty one years of age who is ordinarily resident in the village area and unless his appointment has been approved by the District Commissioner:

Provided further that the membership of any such person may be terminated by the District Commissioner if, in the opinion of the District Commissioner, such person is no longer a Palestinian citizen, or is no longer ordinarily resident in the village area, or is no longer a fit and proper person to hold office or has become incapable of carrying out the duties of his office.

In approving the manner of choosing members of a Village Council under this paragraph the District Commissioner may give directions, inter alia, as to the number of persons to be chosen as representatives of any particular quarter or community.

(2) If any member of a Village Council, other than a Mukhtar of the village, shall die or resign or otherwise cease to hold office, the vacancy shall be filled in accordance with the provisions of paragraph (b) of subsection (1) unless the District Commissioner otherwise directs:

Provided that no proceeding or action of the Village Council shall be invalidated by any vacancy in the membership thereof.

(3) A person shall not preside over a Village Council or act as a member thereof when any matter is under consideration in which he is interested otherwise than as a member of the Council, and an Administrative Officer may give general or special directions for the enforcement of this provision.

(4) The District Commissioner shall appoint one of the members of the Village Council to be Chairman and one to be Deputy Chairman thereof. If the Chairman is absent or is precluded from interest from presiding, the Deputy Chairman shall preside unless he is absent or is so precluded. If both the Chairman and Deputy Chairman are absent or are so precluded, the Administrative Officer shall appoint a member to act temporarily as Chairman.

(5) A Village Council may, as to the chairmanship or deputy-chairmanship or as to the membership thereof, be reconstituted from time

— 3 —

time by the District Commissioner whenever in his opinion such constitution is desirable, and subsections (1) and (4) of this section, as the case may be, shall apply in relation to such reconstitution.

(5) The quorum of a Village Council for the purpose of meetings shall be such as is determined from time to time by the District Commissioner.

6.—(1) A Village Council shall be vested with juristic personality and shall have a corporate seal and shall be entitled to make contracts and may sue and be sued in its own name.

(2) A Village Council shall be entitled to acquire, hold and dispose of property, moveable and immoveable:

Provided that, except in the cases provided for by subsection (4) of this section and by section 7 of this Ordinance, a Village Council shall not acquire, sell, mortgage, lease, exchange or otherwise dispose of immoveable property or any interest therein without the approval of the District Commissioner.

(3) The Corporate seal shall be in the custody of the Chairman of the Village Council and shall not be affixed to any document save in the presence of the Chairman and not less than two other members of the Village Council who shall respectively sign their names to such document in token of their presence.

(4) Upon the establishment of a Village Council, the High Commissioner may give directions for vesting in the Village Council all or any lands in the village area which are then owned by the Government of Palestine or are the property of the village or are held in trust for the village and thereupon the lands to which the directions relate shall vest in the Village Council and shall be registered accordingly in the Land Registry free of charge.

A Village Council to have juristic personality.

7.—(1) An order under section 3 of this Ordinance may at any time be varied or revoked by further order of the High Commissioner.

(2) Where an order is varied by the addition of a new area, subsection (4) of section 6 shall apply in relation to lands in the new area as it does to lands included in an original order.

(3) Where an order is revoked, or varied by excluding an area, the High Commissioner may give such directions as he may deem appropriate as to the disposal or vesting and as to the registration of the lands of the Village Council in the area, or the excluded area, as the case may be, and thereupon such lands shall be disposed of or shall vest and shall be registered in accordance with the directions. The High Commissioner may also give any other directions which he may deem appropriate consequential on the revocation or variation of the order, including directions as to the disposal or vesting of property other than land or otherwise as to the liquidation or partial liquidation, as the case may be, of the affairs of the Village Council, and all such directions shall have effect according to the tenor thereof.

Variation and revocation of orders under section 3.

8. The jurisdiction of a Village Council shall extend over the whole of the lands in the village area:

Provided that, as regards lands owned by the Government of Palestine, this section shall have effect subject to such general or special restrictions or exclusions as are provided for by order of the High Commissioner.

Jurisdiction of Village Council.

— 4 —

Power of Village Council to carry out works, etc.

9. It shall be lawful for every Village Council:—
   (1) to establish schools and school gardens;
   (2) to establish dispensaries;
   (3) to provide and regulate public markets and places of public auction;
   (4) to provide slaughter-houses, and to regulate the slaughter of animals;
   (5) to undertake the construction, paving, lighting or improving of any street or public place;
   (6) to undertake the provision and regulation of public water supplies;
   (7) to undertake works of afforestation and terracing;
   (8) to require the execution of works in accordance with the provisions of the Village Roads and Works Ordinance;

Cap. 149.

   (9) to appoint or dismiss clerks and other officials and employees of the Council;
   (10) generally to perform any public work which may tend to promote the sanitation and cleanliness of the village area and the health, security or well-being of the inhabitants thereof.

Village Council to comply with directions of District Commissioner.

10. Every Village Council shall, with regard to any of the matters enumerated in the preceding section and such powers as may be exercised by them under section 11 of this Ordinance, comply with such directions as the District Commissioner may deem it necessary or expedient to give in the interests of the health, security or well-being of the inhabitants of the village area.

Power of Village Council to make by-laws.

11.—(1) Every Village Council shall have power to make by-laws for the carrying out of all or any of the objects hereinbefore mentioned and also for:—
   (a) requiring the streets and other public places to be kept clear of refuse or obstructions;
   (b) prohibiting the accumulation on private property of filth or refuse dangerous to the public health and requiring the abatement of any nuisance arising from private cesspits, or drains or otherwise;
   (c) requiring the cleaning, maintenance and protection from contamination of fountains, drains, aqueducts, tanks, reservoirs and other water supplies;
   (d) controlling the width of streets and building operations;
   (e) preventing the spread of infectious or contagious diseases;
   (f) requiring the reporting of births and deaths to such authorities as may be designated;
   (g) regulating the burial of the dead;
   (h) prohibiting or regulating the cutting and destruction of trees, shrubs, grass or other forest produce;
   (i) requiring measures for the destruction of weeds and control of agricultural diseases and pests;
   (j) requiring measures for the preservation of soil from erosion;
   (k) fixing the date and time of harvests;
   (l) regulating the grazing and watering of livestock;
   (m) prohibiting or regulating the movement of livestock;

— 5 —

(n) providing for the control of dogs and for other anti-rabic measures;

(o) preventing the spread of diseases of livestock including poultry and bees;

(p) regulating the procedure for the distribution and the cultivation of village masha'a lands;

(q) protecting Government, village or other public property lying within the village lands;

(r) regulating and maintaining property boundary marks;

(s) any other purpose which may be approved by the District Commissioner as being conducive to the health, security or well-being of the inhabitants of the village area.

(2) All such by-laws shall be subject to the approval of the District Commissioner and shall not come into force until they have been so approved.

(3) Any such by-laws may provide for the payment of fees and charges in connection with matters with which a Village Council is required or empowered to deal under this or any other Ordinance.

(4) All by-laws made and approved under this section shall be published by posting them in some conspicuous place in the village and shall thereupon come into force. A certificate as to such publication by a District Commissioner or an Administrative Officer shall be conclusive proof of the due enactment and publication of the by-laws specified in such certificate:

Provided that such publication may, in addition to posting as aforesaid, be made by village crier.

(5) Every person who, by any act or omission, shall contravene any by-law made under this section shall be guilty of an offence and shall be liable for such offence to such penalty, not exceeding a fine of five pounds or fifteen days imprisonment, as shall be specified in the by-law. Any such fine shall be paid to the Village Fund established in accordance with section 14 of this Ordinance.

(6) Any such by-law may provide that, in addition to any penalty imposed by a by-law, any expenses incurred by a Village Council in consequence of the breach of such by-law, or in the execution of any work directed by any by-law to be executed by any person and not executed by him, shall be paid by the person committing such breach or failing to execute such work, and the amount of any such expenses shall be recoverable as a debt due from such person to the Village Council.

(7) It shall be the duty of the Chairman of the Village Council to ensure that proceedings in respect of offences against by-laws are instituted.

12. The High Commissioner may by order prescribe the categories of rates and taxes, including a poll-tax, and the maximum amounts of such rates and taxes which may be imposed by a Village Council.

Power of High Commissioner to prescribe rates and taxes.

13.—(1) Subject to the provisions of section 12 of this Ordinance, a Village Council may from time to time impose, take and receive such rates and taxes, including a poll-tax, as may be authorised by the District Commissioner.

Power of Village Council to levy rates and taxes.

— 6 —

(2) All rates and taxes so authorised, with the date or dates on which they become payable, shall be published by posting them in some conspicuous place in the village, and may also be notified by village crier.

(3) A certificate as to such publication by the District Commissioner or an Administrative Officer shall be conclusive proof of the due imposing and publication of any such rates or taxes.

Establishment, etc. of Village Fund.

14.—(1) The money raised under the provisions of section 13, together with all moneys otherwise received by the Village Council, shall be called the Village Fund.

(2) The Village Fund shall be in the custody and control of the Village Council.

(3) All moneys received by a Village Council in respect of the Village Fund shall be lodged for safe custody in such place as the District Commissioner may direct:

Provided that the Council may retain for the daily expenses of the Council such maximum sum as the Administrative Officer may authorise.

(4) All expenses to be paid on behalf of the Village Council shall be discharged out of the Village Fund.

(5) (i) The District Commissioner may require a Village Council to submit from time to time for approval estimates of its revenue and expenditure and where such estimates have been submitted no payment out of the Fund shall be made otherwise than as approved in such estimates save with the approval of the District Commissioner or of the Administrative Officer authorised by the District Commissioner to grant such approval.

(ii) Where no such estimates have been submitted and approved, no payment out of the Fund shall be made save with the approval of the District Commissioner or of the Administrative Officer authorised by the District Commissioner to grant such approval.

Audit of Village Fund.

15.—(1) The accounts of a Village Fund shall be audited annually by such person or persons as the District Commissioner shall appoint. The person or persons so appointed shall make a report to the District Commissioner. If, after the receipt of the report, it appears to the District Commissioner that any sum forming part of the Village Fund has been improperly expended, the District Commissioner shall order the person or persons who are in his opinion responsible for the improper expenditure, to refund the sum to the Village Fund, and the sum shall be recoverable as a debt due from such person or persons to the Village Council.

(2) An auditor may receive from the Village Fund such remuneration as the District Commissioner may approve.

Power of Village Council to raise loans.

16. A Village Council shall with the approval of the District Commissioner, but not otherwise, and subject to any terms and conditions which may be imposed by the District Commissioner, be entitled:—

(a) to borrow money from any person for any purpose approved by the District Commissioner and, in order to secure the payment of the principal and interest of any such loan, to mortgage any property or revenues of the Council to the lender;

(b) to borrow temporarily from a bank any sum or sums.

— 7 —

Part III—Village Courts.

17. The High Commissioner may, in his discretion, by order establish a Village Court in any village area for which a Village Council has been established and the area of jurisdiction of the Court shall be the village area including any lands of the Government of Palestine within the area.

Establishment of Village Court.

18.—(1) A Village Court shall consist of the Village Council: Provided that the Court shall not be properly constituted unless not less than three members of the Village Council are present.

(2) Unless the Administrative Officer shall otherwise direct, the Chairman of the Village Council or, in the absence of such Chairman, a member of the Court selected by the members present shall act as President of the Village Court.

Constitution of Village Court.

19.—(1) A Village Court constituted in manner provided by section 18 of this Ordinance shall have power and jurisdiction to try offences against by-laws made under Part II of this Ordinance and such cases or classes of cases, civil and criminal, as are from time to time assigned to such Court by order of the High Commissioner:

Provided, however, that it shall be lawful for the President of a Village Court before which any case shall be brought, or by which it shall be partially tried, to refer the case to a Court of a Magistrate having jurisdiction in the area in which the village is situated, if it shall appear to such President that the case is one which from its circumstances may more properly be tried by such Magistrate's Court, and the President shall refer any such case as aforesaid if so directed by the President of the District Court or by the District Commissioner or the Administrative Officer.

(2) An order of the High Commissioner made under subsection (1) of this section may impose such restrictions or limitations upon the exercise by the Village Court of jurisdiction in such cases or classes of cases, civil and criminal, as the High Commissioner thinks fit.

Jurisdiction.

20. The criminal jurisdiction of a Village Court shall extend, subject to the provisions of section 19 of this Ordinance, to the hearing, trial and determination of all criminal charges and matters in which any person is accused of having committed or been accessory to the committing of an offence wholly or in part within the area of the jurisdiction of the court:

Provided that the accused, if he is not ordinarily resident within the area, may, before the trial begins, declare his unwillingness to be tried before the Village Court and thereupon the Village Court shall not deal with the case but shall remit it to a Court of a Magistrate having jurisdiction in the area.

Criminal jurisdiction of Village Court.

21. The civil jurisdiction of a Village Court shall extend, subject to the provisions of section 19 of this Ordinance, to the hearing, trial and determination of all civil suits and matters in which the defendant is ordinarily resident within the area of the jurisdiction of the court or in which the cause of action shall have arisen within the said area.

Civil jurisdiction of Village Court.

22. A Village Court may order that any fine which it may impose shall be paid at such time or times and by such instalments or otherwise as it shall think just, and in default of the payment of any fine or of any instalment of the same when due, the court may order that

Recovery of fines.

the amount of the fine or of the instalment, as the case may be, shall be levied by the sale of any movable property belonging to the offender and situate within the area of the jurisdiction of the court.

Provisions as to imprisonment, fines and fees. No. 2 of 1940.	23.—(1) Subject to the provisions of any Ordinance other than this Ordinance, every person sentenced by a Village Court to imprisonment shall be detained in a prison established under the Prisons Ordinance, 1940.
	(2) Any fine imposed by a Village Court in exercise of its jurisdiction under this Ordinance and any court fees payable to a Village Court shall be paid into the Village Fund established under section 14 of this Ordinance.
Compensation to aggrieved persons.	24. A Village Court may direct any fine, or such part thereof as it shall deem fit, to be paid to the person injured or aggrieved by the act or omission in respect of which such fine has been imposed, on condition that such person, if he shall accept the same, shall not have or maintain any suit for the recovery of damage for the loss or injury sustained by him by reason of such act or omission.
Application of the Criminal Code Ordinance. No. 74 of 1936.	25. The provisions of section 22 of this Ordinance in relation to the levying of fines and the provisions of section 24 of this Ordinance relating to compensation shall be in lieu of the corresponding provisions of Chapter VII of the Criminal Code Ordinance, 1936.
Access to Village Court and records thereof.	26. The President of the District Court, the District Commissioner and the Administrative Officer shall each have access at all times to a Village Court and to the records thereof.
Review.	27—(1) The President of the District Court may at any time in his discretion either on the petition of a person concerned or of his own motion, do any of the following things, that is to say—

    (a) call for the record of any case in a Village Court;

    (b) refer any case pending before a Village Court to a Court of a Magistrate having jurisdiction in the area;

    (c) review any order or decision of a Village Court by cancelling or varying the same;

    (d) with or without cancelling or varying a previous order or decision of the Village Court, make any order or decision or give any direction in relation to the case which he may think just;

    (e) pending the exercise of any powers conferred by paragraphs (b), (c) or (d) of this subsection, make any interim order or decision or give any interim directions in relation to the case which he may think just.

(2) No order or decision shall be made under paragraph (c) or (d) of subsection (1)—

    (a) to the prejudice of an accused or convicted person in a criminal case unless that person has been given the opportunity of being heard;

    (b) to the prejudice of a party in a civil case unless that party has been given the opportunity of being heard.

(3) Save as provided in subsection (2), no person shall have the right to be heard by the President of the District Court but the President may in his discretion hear any person when exercising any power conferred by this section.

28.—(1) Save as otherwise provided in this Part an order or decision of a Village Court shall be final and shall not be called in question in any court.

(2) An order, direction or decision of the President of the District Court under section 27 of this Ordinance shall be final and shall not be called in question in any court.

Orders to be final.

29. No advocate may appear or act for any party before a Village Court: but a Village Court may permit the husband, or wife, or guardian of a party to appear and to act for such party.

Parties to appear in person.

30. Subject to the provisions of any rules made under section 46 of this Ordinance, the proceedings of Village Courts shall be free from the formalities of judicial proceedings, but it shall be the duty of any such courts to do substantial justice in respect of all questions coming before them without regard to matters of form.

Procedure of Village Courts.

PART IV—ARBITRATION.

31.—(1) A Village Council shall have power to appoint a committee of not less than three of its members for settlement by arbitration of any matter in dispute, or class of matters in dispute between parties ordinarily resident within the village area.

Arbitration by Village Council.

(2) The award of the committee upon any such arbitration shall be in writing. The award shall not have any force or effect unless confirmed in writing by the Administrative Officer but, upon such confirmation, shall be final and binding on all parties to the dispute and may be enforced and exercised as though it was a judgment of the Court of a Magistrate having jurisdiction in the area not subject to appeal.

32.—(1) An Administrative Officer shall have power to authorise a committee consisting of any number of persons to settle by arbitration any matter in dispute, or class of matters in dispute, between villages or parts of villages or between persons ordinarily resident in the same village or ordinarily resident in different villages.

General powers of arbitration.

(2) The powers conferred by this section may be exercised whether or not a Village Council has been established in any village concerned or in any part of any such village.

(3) In this section the powers conferred upon an Administrative Officer may, in the case of a dispute between different villages or parts of villages or between persons ordinarily resident in different villages, be exercised by the Administrative Officer of the sub-district or administrative sub-division in which any of the villages or parts of villages concerned are situated.

(4) The award of the committee upon any such arbitration shall be in writing. The award shall not have any force or effect unless confirmed in writing by the District Commissioner but, upon such confirmation, shall be final and binding on all parties to the dispute and may be enforced and executed as though it was a judgement of a Court of a Magistrate having jurisdiction in any of the villages or parts of villages or in the village (as the case may be), being a judgement not subject to appeal.

33. Notwithstanding the provisions of sections 31 and 32, a matter shall not be arbitrated under those sections unless—

General provisions as to arbitration.

(a) it has been approved by the District Commissioner as suitable for arbitration, or belongs to a class of matters approved by the

— 10 —

District Commissioner as suitable for arbitration, on the ground in either such case that matters of that class have customarily been submitted to arbitration; and

(*b*) a statement of the issues involved has been drawn up in writing and signed by all the parties to the dispute and by the Administrative Officer.

Parties to appear in person.

34. No advocate may appear or act for any party before an arbitration committee appointed under this Part of this Ordinance; but such a committee may permit the husband, or wife, or guardian of a party to appear and to act for such party.

Indemnity for acts lawfully done under order.

35. If any action or prosecution is brought, or any proceedings held against any person for any act done by him in lawful execution of an order for enforcement of an award made under section 31 or section 32 of this Ordinance, it shall be lawful for such person to plead that such act was done by him under the authority of such order and on the production of the order purporting to be signed by the District Commissioner, or the Administrative Officer, such person shall be entitled to a decision in his favour. No proof of the signature upon the order shall be necessary unless the Court before which such action, prosecution or proceedings are brought shall see reason to doubt its genuineness.

PART V—MUKHTARS.

Appointment of Mukhtars.

36.—(1) The District Commissioner shall appoint a Mukhtar or Mukhtars for every village and such other persons as Assistant Mukhtars as the size of the village or other circumstances may require.

(2) Any such appointment of a Mukhtar shall be notified in the *Gazette*.

No. 21 of 1942.

(3) Notwithstanding anything contained in the Mukhtars (Appointment) Ordinance, 1942, the appointment and dismissal of Mukhtars appointed under this Ordinance, and their duties, powers and conditions of service shall be subject to the provisions of this Ordinance.

First appointment of Mukhtars.

37. Upon the appointment under this Ordinance of a Mukhtar for any village, the Mukhtar of that village holding office at the time of such appointment shall cease to hold office.

Persons eligible for appointment as Mukhtars.

38. Any person ordinarily resident in a village who has attained the age of twenty one years shall be qualified to be Mukhtar in respect of such village.

Dismissal of Mukhtars and filling of vacancies, etc.

39.—(1) A Mukhtar shall be liable to be dismissed by the District Commissioner for misconduct or neglect of duty or any other sufficient reason, and, in case any Mukhtar shall die or become disqualified to act or incapable of acting or shall resign or shall be dismissed, the District Commissioner may forthwith appoint another person in the manner hereinbefore provided.

(2) In the temporary absence of the Mukhtar from his village his duties shall be performed by such person as may be nominated by such Mukhtar, unless the Administrative Officer otherwise directs.

(3) The death or termination of appointment of a Mukhtar shall be notified in the *Gazette*.

— 11 —

40. It shall be the duty of every Mukhtar:— **Duties of Mukhtars.**

(1) to keep the peace within the village of which he is the appointed Mukhtar and to give information to the police of any criminals or bad characters, strangers or suspicious persons found in such village or of any design to commit an offence which may come to his knowledge;

(2) to send information as soon as possible to the nearest Police Station of every serious offence or accident or death due to unnatural causes occurring in the village;

(3) to assist the officers of Government in the execution of their duty, including the collection of revenue;

(4) to publish within the village all such notices, proclamations and other official documents as may be sent to him for publication by the District Commissioner or by the Administrative Officer;

(5) to keep a seal as Mukhtar and to affix the same to all certificates and documents requiring the seal;

(6) to report to the Administrative Officer the death without heirs of any person possessed of or beneficially interested in immovable properties, together with a list of such properties;

(7) to report to the proper authority every case which shall come to his knowledge of the use of false or unjust weights or measures;

(8) to safeguard, to the best of his ability, and to report to the Administrative Officer or nearest Police Station damage to railways, telephone and telegraph communications, public highways, forests and other property of the Government;

(9) to report the discovery of antiquities and to conserve them and to safeguard scheduled historical monuments and sites;

(10) to maintain and safeguard or to safeguard such registers, records and statistics as the District Commissioner may direct;

(11) to report the outbreak or existence of pests or diseases affecting animals or crops;

(12) generally to carry into effect all the duties imposed upon or confided to him by law or custom.

41. A Mukhtar shall be deemed to be a public officer as defined in section 3 of the Interpretation Ordinance. **Mukhtar a public officer. Cap. 69.**

42. Every Mukhtar shall exercise all such powers, and have such privileges and immunities as belong to a police officer: Provided that he shall not act as a police officer beyond the village of which he is Mukhtar. **Mukhtars as police officers.**

43. Every person who shall without good and sufficient cause refuse or neglect when called upon to aid and assist a Mukhtar in the execution of his duty in keeping the peace or in the lawful arrest of any criminal or suspected person shall be guilty of an offence and shall be liable for each such offence to a fine not exceeding five pounds. **All persons to assist the Mukhtar in keeping the peace.**

44. Mukhtars appointed under this Ordinance shall be entitled to receive such fees or remuneration as the High Commissioner may by rule prescribe, in addition to such fees as they may be entitled to receive under any other law, and no Mukhtar shall be entitled to demand any fee that is not so prescribed or provided by any other law, and any **Payment of Mukhtars.**

— 12 —

Mukhtar receiving or so demanding such a fee or knowingly furnishing a false certificate shall be guilty of an offence and shall be liable for each such offence to a fine not exceeding ten pounds, without prejudice to any other penalty which he may have incurred.

PART VI—GENERAL.

Application to the Ordinance of the terms Mukhtar, etc., appearing in other Ordinances.

45. Upon the coming into operation of this Ordinance the terms:—
(a) Mukhtar;
(b) Notable, or elder;
(c) Mukhtar and elders, or mukhtar and notables:
(d) Village council, or village authority, or council of elders, or council of ancients, or local authority, or elders, or notables;

occurring in any other Ordinance or other law shall, unless the context otherwise requires, mean respectively:—

(a) Mukhtar;
and where a Village Council has been established,
(b) Member of a Village Council;
(c) Chairman and members of a Village Council;
(d) a Village Council established under this Ordinance.

Rules.

46. The High Commissioner may make rules for the purpose of carrying into effect this Ordinance and, in particular, and without prejudice to the generality of this power, such rules may be made—

(a) concerning the form and manner of proceeding to be observed by Village Councils and in cases before Village Courts;
(b) prescribing generally or specially that decisions of Village Councils or Village Courts shall be unanimous, or that they shall be by majority;
(c) conferring a casting vote generally or specially on the Chairman or Deputy Chairman of a Village Council or on the President of a Village Court;
(d) concerning the keeping of records by Village Councils and Village Courts;
(e) concerning the process to be issued by Village Courts and the mode of enforcing the same;
(f) prescribing the fees to be charged in Village Courts;
(g) providing for the execution of judgments of Village Courts by the seizure and delivery or sale of moveable property;
(h) providing, or delegating to District Commissioners power to provide, for the manner of collecting, recovering and accounting for rates and taxes imposed by virtue of this Ordinance.

Saving.

47. The provisions of this Ordinance and the powers conferred thereunder shall be in addition to and not in derogation of the provisions of and powers conferred under any other Ordinance or law regulating any of the matters regulated under this Ordinance.

HAROLD MACMICHAEL
High Commissioner.

12th August, 1944.

WEIGHTS AND MEASURES ORDINANCE, No. 24 OF 1944.

Officer Administering Government

WEIGHTS AND MEASURES ORDINANCE.
No. 24 of 1944.

An Ordinance to amend and consolidate the Law relating to Weights and Measures.

Be it enacted by the High Commissioner for Palestine, with the advice of the Advisory Council thereof:—

1. This Ordinance may be cited as the Weights and Measures Ordinance, 1944. — *Short title.*

2. In this Ordinance, unless the context otherwise requires— — *Interpretation.*

"inspection" means any examination and testing other than a verification, of any weight, measure or weighing machine;

"inspector" means an inspector of weights and measures under this Ordinance;

"metric weights and measures" means weights and measures specified in section 3 with their decimal multiples and divisions;

"prescribed" means prescribed by the rules contained in the Second Schedule or by rules made under section 17;

"verification" means the examination and testing of any weight, measure or weighing machine which—

(a) has not been stamped with a verification stamp in the prescribed manner, or

(b) is produced to the Keeper of the Standards under and in accordance with section 8(4);

"weighing machine" includes any balance, scale, beam, steelyard, and every other machine for determining weight.

3. The standards of weight and measure shall be— — *Standards of weight and measure.*

(a) the kilogramme as the standard of weight: the weight of the kilogramme is the weight of the standard international kilogramme;

(b) the litre as the standard of capacity: the capacity of the litre is the capacity of the standard international litre;

(c) the metre as the measure of length: the length of the metre is the length of the standard international metre;

(d) the square metre and the standard dunum, consisting of one thousand square metres, as the standard measures of surface.

4.—(1) The High Commissioner shall, as occasion may require, procure standard metric weights and measures which shall be verified at the Standards Department of the Board of Trade in England before being brought into use. — *Standards to be procured and kept.*

(2) The weights and measures so procured shall be the Palestine standards of weights and measures and shall, for all purposes, be conclusively deemed to be true and accurate.

(3) The standards shall be kept under the care of an officer to be appointed by the High Commissioner to be the Keeper of the Standards, and shall be re-verified at the Standards Department of the Board of Trade in England, from time to time, as the High Commissioner may direct.

5.—(1) The High Commissioner shall procure such copies of the standards, or any of them, as he may think fit, and shall provide for the verification and re-verification of such copies by the Keeper of the Standards or an inspector authorised in that behalf by the Keeper — *Secondary standards to be kept.*

— 2 —

of the Standards, and shall cause such copies to be authenticated as secondary standards in such manner as he may think fit.

(2) Judicial notice shall be taken of every secondary standard so authenticated.

(3) The High Commissioner may, at any time, cancel any secondary standard, and direct that it be no longer used as such.

(4) The secondary standards shall be kept in such place and used for such purposes as the Keeper of the Standards may, from time to time, determine.

Production of secondary standards.

6. The Keeper of the Standards shall, upon reasonable notice being given, and upon payment of the prescribed fees, produce the secondary standards to any person who makes written application for their production for the purpose of having any weight, measure or weighing machine compared or tested by the Keeper of the Standards, at the place where the secondary standards are kept, or, upon payment of any additional expense involved, at any other place which the Keeper of the Standards may deem suitable for that purpose.

Deputy Keeper of the Standards and inspectors of weights and measures.

7.—(1) The High Commissioner shall appoint a Deputy Keeper of the Standards, who may be authorised in writing by the Keeper of the Standards to exercise all or any of the powers, other than the power to make rules under section 17, and to perform all or any of the duties conferred or imposed upon the Keeper of the Standards under this Ordinance.

(2) The Keeper of the Standards and the Deputy Keeper of the Standards and any police officer authorised in writing by the Inspector General of Police and Prisons and any person appointed by the Keeper of the Standards with the approval of the Director of Medical Services shall have the powers of an inspector of weights and measures.

(3) An inspector may, at all reasonable times, inspect all weights, measures and weighing machines which are used by any person for trade, or are on any premises for use in trade, and may compare them with the secondary standards, and may seize and detain any such weight, measure or weighing machine which he deems to be used contrary to any of the provisions of this Ordinance.

(4) An inspector may, for the purpose of inspection, enter any place where he has reasonable cause to believe that any such weight, measure or weighing machine is kept for trade.

Verification of weights, measures and weighing machines.

8.—(1) An inspector shall examine every metric weight or measure and every weighing machine which is brought to him for the purpose of verification, and, subject to any instructions which the Keeper of the Standards may issue either generally, or in any particular case, he shall compare or test such weight, measure or weighing machine with the secondary standards, and, if he finds that it complies with the rules contained in the Second Schedule or any rules made under section 17 and is not already stamped, he shall stamp it in the prescribed manner.

(2) An inspector shall deliver to the person producing to him such weight, measure or weighing machine, a certificate of verification in the prescribed form. Such certificate shall be exhibited in a conspicuous place on the premises whereon such weight, measure or weighing machine is used, and the inspector shall keep a copy thereof for the purpose of control.

— 3 —

(3) The certificate of verification shall be signed and dated by the inspector and shall serve as a register of all weights, measures and weighing machines in the possession of any person for use in trade, and the inspector shall enter in such certificate the results of all verifications and inspections and all changes which may occur in the inventory of all weights, measures and weighing machines of a trader.

(4) Any person having in his possession for use in trade any weight, measure or weighing machine, shall produce it to the Keeper of the Standards for periodical verification at such intervals of time, being not less than one year each, and at such place and on such date as shall be notified by the Keeper of the Standards by notice in the *Gazette* or in such other manner as the Keeper of the Standards may deem fit.

(5) Any person having in his possession for use in trade, any weight, measure or weighing machine, shall immediately notify the Keeper of the Standards of any change in the inventory of all weights, measures and weighing machines in his posssession, and of any damage to any of such weights, measures or weighing machines.

(6) Such fees as may be prescribed shall be payable for verification and stamping of any weight, measure or weighing machine, whether on verification it is found to be correct or incorrect or defective.

(7) The inspector shall enter the payment of all fees in the certificate of verification.

9. Metric weights and measures shall be used for the purpose of all transactions entered into by any department of the Government or any municipal or local council, or other local authority. *Exclusive use of metric weights, etc.*

10. The area of any land concerning which any right, disposition, or contract shall be recorded in any register of the Government or any municipal or local council, or other local authority, shall be expressed therein in terms of the standard measure of surface: *Application to land transactions.*

Provided that nothing in this section shall affect the validity of any right, disposition or contract in or concerning land which was, at the date of the commencement of the Weights and Measures Ordinance, defined according to dunums other than standard dunums or according to any other measure of surface existing at the said date. *Cap. 150.*

11. The customary weights and measures in use at the date of the commencement of this Ordinance shall be deemed to be equivalent to the metric weights and measures according to the table contained in the First Schedule. *Comparison between customary and metric weights and measures.*

12.—(1) If, at any time, the High Commissioner in Council is of the opinion that it is desirable to prohibit the use of any weights or measures other than metric weights or measures, he may, by order, declare that, from a date to be specified in such order and with such reservations from, and exceptions to, the application of the metric system of weights or measures as may be specified in such order, the use of any weight or measure other than a metric weight or measure shall be unlawful, and thereupon any contract or dealing in any work or goods, disposition of land or other thing which is to be carried out, done or made by weight or measure and to which such order applies shall be deemed to be carried out, done or made according to metric weights or measures, as the case may be, and otherwise shall be void. *Power of High Commissioner in Council to make use of metric system compulsory.*

(2) If, at any time, the High Commissioner in Council is of the opinion that it is desirable to prohibit the use of any weight, measure

— 4 —

or weighing machine which has not been verified and stamped in accordance with the rules contained in the Second Schedule or any rule made under section 17 he may, by order, declare that, from a date to be specified in such order, and with such reservations or exceptions as may be specified in such order, the use of any weight, measure or weighing machine which has not been verified and stamped as aforesaid shall be unlawful.

(3) Any order made under subsection (1) or (2) may be applied only to all or any weights, or only to all or any measures, or only to all or any weighing machines, and either to the whole of Palestine or any part thereof.

Offences.

13.—(1) Any person who neglects or refuses to produce for inspection any weight, measure or weighing machine in his possession or on his premises, or refuses to admit an inspector to examine any such weight, measure or weighing machine, or otherwise obstructs or hinders the inspector, is guilty of an offence, and is liable to a fine of fifty pounds or to imprisonment for three months or both such penalties.

(2) Any person who uses for the purpose of any sale, contract or dealing, or has in his possession for use in trade, any weight, measure or weighing machine which is false or unjust is guilty of an offence and is liable to a fine of one hundred pounds or to imprisonment for six months or both such penalties.

(3) Any person who knowingly makes, or sells, or causes to be made or sold, any false or unjust weight, measure or weighing machine is guilty of an offence, and is liable to a fine of two hundred pounds or imprisonment for one year or both such penalties.

(4) Any person who forges, or counterfeits, or causes to be forged or counterfeited, or knowingly assists in forging or counterfeiting, any stamp or mark used for stamping or marking any weight, measure or weighing machine under this Ordinance is guilty of an offence and is liable to a fine of two hundred pounds or imprisonment for two years or both such penalties.

(5) Any person who knowingly uses, sells or disposes of any weight, measure or weighing machine with any forged or counterfeited stamp or mark thereon is guilty of an offence and is liable to a fine of two hundred pounds or imprisonment for two years or both such penalties.

(6) Any person who, on or after the date from which, by an order made under subsection (1) of section 12, the use, in any part of Palestine, of any weight or measure other than a metric weight or measure is declared to be unlawful, uses, in that part of Palestine, contrary to such order, any weight or measure other than a metric weight or measure, or any weighing machine fitted with any dial, indicator or graduation of any system other than the metric system, is guilty of an offence and is liable to a fine of fifty pounds.

(7) Any person who, on or after the date from which, by an order made under subsection (1) of section 12, the use, in any part of Palestine, of any weight or measure other than a metric weight or measure is declared to be unlawful, carries out, does or makes, in that part of Palestine, by any denomination of weight or measure other than metric, any contract or dealing in any work or goods, disposition of land or other thing which is to be carried out, done or made by weight or measure and to which such order applies is guilty of an offence and is liable to a fine of fifty pounds.

— 5 —

(8) Any person who, on or after the date from which, by an order made under subsection (2) of section 12, the use, in any part of Palestine, of any weight, measure or weighing machine which has not been verified and stamped in accordance with the rules contained in the Second Schedule or any rules made under section 17, is declared unlawful, uses, in that part of Palestine, contrary to such order, any such weight, measure or weighing machine which is not of the prescribed specification, composition, pattern or denomination, or has not been verified and stamped in the prescribed manner is guilty of an offence and is liable to a fine of fifty pounds or imprisonment for three months or both such penalties.

(9) Any person who, on or after the date from which, by an order made under subsection (2) of section 12, the use, in any part of Palestine, of any weight, measure or weighing machine, which has not been verified and stamped in accordance with the rules contained in the Second Schedule or any rules made under section 17, is declared unlawful, sells or otherwise disposes of, anywhere in Palestine, any such weight, measure or weighing machine which is not of the prescribed specification, composition, pattern or denomination, or has not been verified and stamped in the prescribed manner is guilty of an offence and is liable to a fine of fifty pounds or imprisonment for three months or both such penalties.

(10) Any person who knowingly commits or causes to be committed a fraud in using any weight, measure or weighing machine is guilty of an offence and is liable to a fine of two hundred pounds or imprisonment for two years or both such penalties.

(11) Any person who, without lawful authority, changes or causes to be changed any stamped weight, measure or weighing machine, thus making it false or unjust, and any person who knowingly uses, sells, or otherwise disposes of, such a changed weight, measure or weighing machine, which has been made false or unjust, is guilty of an offence and is liable to a fine of two hundred pounds or imprisonment for two years or both such penalties.

(12) Any person who neglects or refuses to produce any weight, measure or weighing machine in his possession for use in trade to the Keeper of the Standards at the date and place notified by the Keeper of the Standards is guilty of an offence and is liable to a fine of fifty pounds.

(13) Any person who neglects immediately to notify the Keeper of the Standards of any change in the inventory of all the weights, measures and weighing machines in his possession for use in trade, or of any damage to any of such weights, measures or weighing machines is guilty of an offence and is liable to a fine of twenty pounds.

14. Where any weight, measure or weighing machine is found in the possession of any person carrying on trade, or in or upon the premises of any person which are in use for trade, such person shall be deemed, until the contrary is proved, to have such weight, measure or weighing machine in his possession for use in trade. — *Presumption as to possession of weights, etc.*

15. Every weight, measure or weighing machine which has thereon any forged or counterfeited stamp or mark shall be forfeited and may at any time be seized by any inspector. — *Forfeiture of weights, etc.*

— 6 —

<small>Seizure of weights, etc. and forfeiture.</small>

16. Where an inspector has reasonable cause to believe that an offence against this Ordinance has been committed in respect of any weight, measure or weighing machine, he may seize such weight, measure or weighing machine and, upon conviction of any person of an offence in relation thereto, such weight, measure or weighing machine may be forfeited.

<small>Rules.</small>

17. The Keeper of the Standards may, with the approval of the High Commissioner, make rules for all or any of the following purposes:—
    (a) prescribing the specification, composition, pattern and denomination of weights, measures and weighing machines;
    (b) prescribing the procedure for verification, testing and inspection of weights, measures and weighing machines, and the adjustment and stamping thereof, including the design of the verification stamp;
    (c) prescribing the circumstances in which a verification stamp shall be obliterated and the manner of obliteration;
    (d) prescribing the limits of error to be allowed on verification or inspection, either generally or in respect of any trade;
    (e) restricting the use of marks on any weight, measure or weighing machine;
    (f) prescribing the fees to be paid for the verification, adjustment and stamping of weights, measures and weighing machines, and for the production of the secondary standards;
    (g) prescribing the form of a certificate of verification;
    (h) generally, for carrying the Ordinance into effect:

Provided that, until varied or revoked by any such rules, the rules contained in the Second Schedule shall be in force.

<small>By-laws relating to weights or measures.</small>

18. Notwithstanding anything contained in any other Ordinance or law, it shall not be lawful for any municipal or local council or other local authority to make any by-laws relating to weights or measures, and any such by-laws made by any municipal or local council or other local authority in force at the date of commencement of this Ordinance shall cease to have effect.

<small>Repeal. Cap. 150.</small>

19. The Weights and Measures Ordinance is hereby repealed.

FIRST SCHEDULE.
(Section 11).

CUSTOMARY WEIGHTS AND MEASURES WITH THEIR METRIC EQUIVALENTS.
(a) Weights.

(i) *Used throughout Palestine.*
  1 dram (dirhem) = 3.205 grammes.
  1 oqqa = 400 dirhems = 1.282 kilogrammes.
  1 kantar = 100 rotls.

(ii) *Used in northern Palestine.*
  1 oqia (northern) = 66.667 dirhems = 213.659 grammes.
  1 rotl (northern) = 12 oqias = 2 oqqas = 800 dirhems = 2.564 kilogrammes.
  1 kantar (northern) = 100 rotls = 200 oqqas = 256.400 kilogrammes.

(iii) *Used in southern Palestine, excluding Hebron.*
  1 oqia (southern) = 75 dirhems = 240.637 grammes.
  1 rotl (southern) = 12 oqias = 2.250 oqqas = 900 dirhems = 2.884 kilogrammes.
  1 kantar (southern) = 100 rotls = 225 oqqas = 288.450 kilogrammes.

— 7 —

(iv) *Used in Hebron*.
1 oqia (Hebron) = 83.333 dirhems = 267.073 grammes.
1 rotl (Hebron) = 12 oqias = 2.500 oqqas = 1000 dirhems = 3.205 kilogrammes.
1 kantar (Hebron) = 100 rotls = 250 oqqas = 320.489 kilogrammes.

(*b*) Measures of Length and Surface.

1 dra' = 24 qirats.
1 dra' or pic = 67.75 cm. (Cloth measure).
1 dra' or pic = 75.80 cm. (Building and land measure).
1 dunum (Turkish) = 1,600 sq. pics = 919.3 sq. metres.
1 dunum (Metric) = 1,000 sq. metres.

SECOND SCHEDULE.
(Section 17).

1. These Rules may be cited as the Weights and Measures (Metric Weights) Rules, 1944. — *Citation.*

2. Every metric weight shall be smooth on all its surfaces and free from flaws, and shall be made of such metal or metals and be of such pattern and denomination as is specified in these Rules. — *Specification.*

3. Every metric weight shall be made entirely of some metal other than lead, not being a soft metal or soft alloy, except where lead is inserted for the purpose of adjustment: — *Composition.*

Provided that a weight of a denomination of less than 100 grammes shall not be made of iron.

4.—(1) Every metric weight made of iron shall be hexagonal in form and shall have an adjusting hole, and every metric weight made of brass, or of any other metal other than iron, shall be cylindrical in form and may have an adjusting hole: — *Pattern.*

Provided that —

(i) no metric weight of a denomination of less than 50 grammes shall have an adjusting hole; and

(ii) a metric weight of a denomination of less than 1 gramme may be flat.

(2) (*a*) The adjusting hole in a metric weight shall be in the under-surface of the weight and shall be circular and undercut. The diameter of the hole shall, on the under-surface, be not less than 10 millimetres, and shall, in weights of a denomination not exceeding 200 grammes, not exceed one half of the maximum diameter of the under-surface, and in all other weights not exceed one third of the maximum diameter of the under-surface.

(*b*) The lead inserted in an adjusting hole shall cover the bottom of the hole and shall be not less than 5 millimetres thick. It shall be fixed quite immovable, and the distance of the lead from the under-surface shall, in weights of a denomination not exceeding 1 kilogramme, be not less than 4 millimetres, and in all other weights be not less than 8 millimetres.

5.—(1) The denomination of every metric weight other than a metric carat weight shall be a denomination set out in the first column of Appendix A to these Rules, and the denomination of every metric carat weight shall be a denomination set out in the first column of Appendix B to these Rules. — *Denomination.*

— 8 —

(2) The number and unit of the weight shall be indicated in a clear and unmistakeable manner, the letter "g" being used to indicate grammes, the letters "mg" to indicate milligrammes, the letters "kg" to indicate kilogrammes, and the letter "c" to indicate metric carats.

The number and unit shall be raised cast on the upper surface of a cast weight, and stamped on the upper surface of any other weight.

Verification of non-conforming weights.

6.—(1) Any metric weight which does not comply with the provisions of rules 4 and 5 may, with the prior written approval of the Keeper of the Standards, be verified and stamped, if —

(*a*) a clear and uninterrupted impression of the verification stamp can be made on the weight, and

(*b*) the denomination of the weight is a denomination set out in the first column of Appendix A to these Rules or in the first column of Appendix B to these Rules, and is indicated on the weight in a clear and unmistakeable manner.

(2) The Keeper of the Standards may, without assigning any reason for so doing, refuse the approval mentioned in sub-rule (1) or, having granted such approval, revoke it.

Testing in clean condition.

7. Every metric weight shall be tested in a clean condition, and, if necessary, the inspector shall call upon the owner or user of the weight to clean it, and such owner or user shall do so.

Verification.

8.—(1) No metric weight shall be stamped with a verification stamp unless and until the inspector is satisfied that such weight—

(*a*) complies with the provisions of these Rules, and

(*b*) is sufficiently strong to withstand the wear and tear of ordinary use in trade.

(2) The design of the verification stamp shall be the official design issued by the Government of Palestine, showing a crown between the letters "P" and "G" (representing Palestine Government) with the addition of an identification number.

(3) The verification stamp shall be stamped on the lead in the adjusting hole of the weight or, if the weight has no adjusting hole, on the under-surface of the weight:

Provided that flat weights of a denomination of less than 1 gramme may be stamped on the upper surface.

(4) The inspector shall, after verification, complete a certificate of verification in the form set out in Appendix C to these Rules.

Obliteration of verification stamp.

9.—(1) The inspector shall obliterate the verification stamp on any metric weight which —

(*a*) does not comply with the provisions of these Rules; or

(*b*) is broken, much indented, or otherwise damaged to an extent that does not allow of proper adjustment; or

(*c*) since the last stamping has been repaired or readjusted without authorisation by an inspector; or

(*d*) has an error other than an error allowed by rule 10: Provided that where such error is not in the inspector's judgment such as to require the immediate obliteration of the verification stamp, the inspector shall leave with the owner or user of the weight a notice calling upon him to have the weight corrected within such period, not exceeding one month, as is stated in such notice, and shall obliterate the stamp if the correction has not been made within such period.

(2) For obliterating stamps punches of suitable sizes showing a six-pointed star design, as shown in the illustration below, shall be used.

✶

10.—(1) The errors in excess to be allowed on verification or inspection of metric weights of the denominations set out in the first column of Appendix A to these Rules are those set out opposite each such denomination in the second or third column of Appendix A to these Rules, whichever is appropriate, and the errors to be allowed on verification or inspection of metric carat weights of the denominations set out in the first column of Appendix B to these Rules are those set out opposite each such denomination in the third column of Appendix B to these Rules. Limits of errors.

(2) The errors in deficiency to be allowed on inspection of metric weights of the denominations set out in the first column of Appendix A to these Rules are those set out opposite each such denomination in the fourth or fifth column of Appendix A to these Rules, whichever is appropriate, and the errors in deficiency to be allowed on inspection of metric carat weights of the denominations set out in the first column of Appendix B to these Rules are those set out opposite each such denomination in the fourth column of Appendix B to these Rules.

(3) No errors in deficiency are allowed on verification of any metric weight.

11. The fee payable for the production of a secondary standard in accordance with section 6 of the Ordinance shall be two hundred mils, and the fee payable for verification and stamping of a metric weight in accordance with section 8 of the Ordinance shall be twenty mils: Fees.

Provided that the fee payable for verification and stamping shall be fifteen mils if the verification and stamping are carried out on the premises of a manufacturer of weights and such manufacturer renders such assistance in the verification and stamping as the Keeper of the Standards may require.

12. No person shall mark, or permit any other person to mark, any metric weight with any mark, including any trade mark or manufacturer's name or initials, except in accordance with the provisions of these Rules. Restriction on marking.

13. Any person who either himself or by his servant, employee, or agent contravenes, or fails to comply with, any of the provisions of these Rules shall be guilty of an offence, and, upon conviction, shall, if no other penalty is provided for such offence, be liable to a fine not exceeding fifty pounds, or to imprisonment for a term not exceeding six months, or to both such penalties. Penalties.

— 10 —

Appendix A.

Denomination	Error allowed in excess on verification or inspection		Error allowed in deficiency on inspection	
	Precision Weights (Weights used by druggists, pharmacists, dealers in jewellery or dealers in precious metals, or as counterpoises)	Other Weights	Precision Weights (Weights used by druggists, pharmacists, dealers in jewellery or dealers in precious metals, or as counterpoises)	Other Weights
1 mg	0.1 mg	—	0.1 mg	—
2 mg	0.1 mg	—	0.1 mg	—
5 mg	0.1 mg	—	0.1 mg	—
10 mg	0.2 mg	—	0.1 mg	—
20 mg	0.2 mg	—	0.1 mg	—
50 mg	0.5 mg	—	0.2 mg	—
100 mg	1 mg	—	0.5 mg	—
200 mg	1 mg	—	0.5 mg	—
500 mg	2 mg	—	1 mg	—
1 g	3 mg	10 mg	1.5 mg	5 mg
2 g	4 mg	15 mg	2 mg	7 mg
5 g	6 mg	20 mg	3 mg	10 mg
10 g	8 mg	30 mg	4 mg	15 mg
20 g	10 mg	40 mg	5 mg	20 mg
50 g	15 mg	60 mg	7 mg	30 mg
100 g	30 mg	120 mg	15 mg	60 mg
200 g	50 mg	200 mg	25 mg	100 mg
500 g	120 mg	500 mg	60 mg	250 mg
1 kg	200 mg	800 mg	100 mg	400 mg
2 kg	350 mg	1.5 g	170 mg	750 mg
5 kg	600 mg	2.5 g	300 mg	1.2 g
10 kg	1 g	4 g	500 mg	2 g
20 kg	2 g	8 g	1 g	4 g
50 kg	5 g	20 g	2.5 g	10 g
100 kg	10 g	40 g	5 g	20 g

Appendix B.

Denomination (in metric carats)	Weight (in grammes)	Error allowed in excess on verification or inspection	Error allowed in deficiency on inspection
0.01	0.002	0.1 mg	0.1 mg
0.02	0.004	0.1 mg	0.1 mg
0.05	0.01	0.2 mg	0.1 mg
0.1	0.02	0.2 mg	0.1 mg
0.2	0.04	0.4 mg	0.2 mg
0.5	0.1	1 mg	0.5 mg
1	0.2	1 mg	0.5 mg
2	0.4	2 mg	1 mg
5	1	3 mg	1.5 mg
10	2	4 mg	2 mg
20	4	5 mg	2.5 mg
50	10	8 mg	4 mg
100	20	10 mg	5 mg

— 11 —

APPENDIX C.
WEIGHTS AND MEASURES ORDINANCE, 1944.

Number: District:

CERTIFICATE OF VERIFICATION.

Name of holder:
Kind of trade:
Address:

A. WEIGHTS.

Denomination, material, pattern:

1. *Verification.*

Date	Year	Number of weights	Fee (in mils)	Receipt of payment	
				Official stamp	Signature of inspector

Remarks of inspector. (Results of verification, defective weights, repairs).

2. *Inspection.*

Remarks of inspector. (Results of inspection, defective weights, repairs).

B. WEIGHING MACHINES.

Capacity, pattern, manufacturer, number of machine:

1. *Verification.*

Date	Year	Capacity and Number	Fee £P. mils	Receipt of payment	
				Official Stamp	Signature of inspector

Remarks of inspector. (Results of verification, defective machines, repairs).

2. *Inspection.*

Remarks of inspector. (Results of inspection, defective machines, repairs).

C. MEASURES OF LENGTH AND MEASURES OF CAPACITY.

Denomination, pattern (dry or liquid measure), material:

— 12 —

1. *Verification.*

Date	Year	Denomination	Fee (in mils)	Receipt of payment	
				Official Stamp	Signature of inspector

Remarks of inspector. (Results of verification, defective measures, repairs).

2. *Inspection.*

Remarks of inspector. (Results of inspection, defective measures, repairs).

HAROLD MACMICHAEL
High Commissioner

12th August, 1944.

LAND REGISTERS ORDINANCE, No. 30 OF 1944.

Officer Administering Government

LAND REGISTERS ORDINANCE,
No. 30 of 1944.

AN ORDINANCE TO PROVIDE FOR CASES IN WHICH LAND REGISTERS HAVE BECOME UNSERVICEABLE OR IN WHICH ENTRIES IN LAND REGISTERS HAVE BEEN DESTROYED OR RENDERED ILLEGIBLE AND FOR CERTAIN OTHER MATTERS.

BE IT ENACTED by the High Commissioner for Palestine, with the advice of the Advisory Council thereof :—

1. This Ordinance may be cited as the Land Registers Ordinance, 1944. *(Short title.)*

2. In this Ordinance, unless the context otherwise requires — *(Interpretation.)*

"authorised officer" means the Director of Land Registration or the Assistant Director of Land Registration or the Chief Inspector of Land Registration;

"Director" means the Director of Land Registration;

"entry" means an entry in a land register;

"land court" means a land court consisting of a president or relieving president of a district court;

"new entry" means an entry subsisting in a land register, which has been made in pursuance of powers conferred by this Ordinance.

3. Whenever an authorised officer is satisfied that any entries in a land register have been destroyed or rendered illegible in whole or in part and that such entries relate to subsisting interests, rights or obligations in respect of the land in question he may, in his absolute discretion, hold an enquiry as hereinafter provided. *(Power to hold enquiry.)*

4.—(1) Before holding such enquiry, an authorised officer shall, by a notice (hereinafter called "the preliminary notice") published in the *Gazette* or published in such newspaper circulating in Palestine as he may think fit, give notice of his intention to hold the enquiry. The preliminary notice shall describe the land in question and shall give such information as the authorised officer may deem appropriate as to the entries believed to be concerned and shall require any person who claims that he is interested in the reconstruction (as hereinafter provided) of any entries which have been destroyed or rendered illegible in whole or in part and that such entries relate to subsisting interests, rights or obligations in respect of the land to submit in writing to the authorised officer, within such period as is specified in the notice, a statement of his claim. *(Procedure for holding enquiry.)*

(2) After the expiry of the period specified in the preliminary notice, an authorised officer shall fix the time, date and place for the holding of the enquiry and shall cause a notice (hereinafter called "the notice of hearing") to be served on every person (hereinafter referred to as "an interested person") who has submitted a statement of his claim in accordance with the preliminary notice, and requiring such person to appear before an authorised officer at the time, date and place fixed for the holding of the enquiry.

(3) An interested person may appear at the enquiry either in person or by an agent authorised in writing or appointed before the authorised officer: where an agent so appointed is a member of the family of the person appointing him and is not an advocate, stamp duty

— 2 —

shall not be payable on the document authorising him to appear before the authorised officer.

(4) If any interested person upon whom a notice of hearing has been served fails to appear either in person or by an authorised agent, the enquiry may proceed in his absence.

Reconstruction of entries etc.

5.—(1) Upon the conclusion of the enquiry, the authorised officer may —

(a) if he is satisfied that there is sufficient material before him to enable him so to do, prepare new entries which are, as best he can ascertain, reconstructions of the entries to which the enquiry has related; or

(b) if he is not so satisfied, decline to prepare any such new entries.

(2) For the avoidance of doubt it is hereby declared that any new entry shall, as best the authorised officer can ascertain, be a reconstruction of the whole of the former entry, notwithstanding that a part only of the former entry has been destroyed or rendered illegible.

(3) When the authorised officer has prepared new entries as aforesaid, he shall endorse at the end of each entry a certificate substantially in form A in the Schedule to this Ordinance and shall sign and date such certificate.

(4) The authorised officer shall cause a notice to be served on every interested person giving the substance of his decision and, where the decision is to prepare any new entries, notify the interested person that he may inspect the new entries during office hours at such place as may be specified in the notice.

Further enquiries.

6.—(1) Where an enquiry has been held under the preceding section or under this section and an authorised officer is satisfied—

(a) that a person who was entitled to submit a statement of claim in connection with the last enquiry failed so to do for any reason other than his own neglect or default, or

(b) that evidence is available which was not before the authorised officer who held the last enquiry and could not reasonably have been given, produced or made available at that enquiry, but which had it been before the authorised officer who held that enquiry, might have led him to give a different decision in whole or in part,

he may decide to hold a further enquiry.

(2) The provisions of section 4 shall apply in relation to any such further enquiry as they apply in relation to enquiries held in pursuance of section 3: Provided that, in lieu of the matters required by subsection (1) of section 4 to be stated in a preliminary notice under that subsection, the preliminary notice of a further enquiry to be held under this section shall describe the land in question and shall give such information as the authorised officer may deem appropriate as to the new matters to be considered at the enquiry and shall require any person who claims that he is interested in the result of the enquiry to submit in writing to the authorised officer, within such period as is specified in the notice, a statement of his claim.

(3) Upon the conclusion of a further enquiry, an authorised officer may—

(a) if he is satisfied that there is sufficient material before him to enable him to do so, prepare new entries which are, as best he can

— 3 —

ascertain, reconstructions of entries to which the enquiry has related, and, if necessary, cancel any previous new entry, or

(b) if he is not so satisfied, decline to do any of such things.

(4) Subsection (2) of section 5 shall apply in relation to any new entry prepared under this section.

(5) When a new entry is cancelled under this section, the authorised officer shall endorse at the end thereof a certificate of cancellation substantially in the form B in the Schedule to this Ordinance. When a new entry is prepared under this section, the authorised officer shall endorse at the end thereof a certificate substantially in the form C or D (whichever is appropriate) in the Schedule to this Ordinance. The authorised officer shall sign and date any such certificate.

(6) The authorised officer who has held an enquiry under this section shall cause a notice to be served on every interested person and, where the decision is to prepare a new entry, notify the interested person that he may inspect the same during office hours at such place as may be specified in the notice.

7.—(1) Any interested person who is aggrieved by a decision of an authorised officer under section 5 or 6 may, within thirty days after service of the notice of such decision upon him, appeal against the decision to the land court in whose jurisdiction the land affected is situated. Appeal.

(2) The land court shall determine the appeal and shall make such order thereon as may appear to the court to be just.

(3) The authorised officer shall give effect to any decision on appeal and, without prejudice to the generality of this direction, may prepare any new entry or cancel any new entry or do both such things, as may be appropriate, and the provisions of subsection (3) of section 5 and subsection (5) of section 6 shall apply *mutatis mutandis* in relation to any such new entry or cancellation: Provided that any certificate of the Director shall quote the reference to the appeal case.

(4) The Chief Justice may, with the concurrence of the High Commissioner, make rules of court for regulating the practice and procedure in appeals under this section and, without prejudice to the generality of this power, any such rules may provide for the forms to be used and the fees to be payable.

8. A new entry prepared under the provisions of this Ordinance shall, as from the date of the certificate of the authorised officer thereon, have the same force and effect as the entry of which it is a reconstruction. Effect of certificate of authorised officer.

9. A notice under this Ordinance may be served on an interested person by— Service of notices.

(a) serving it upon him personally; or
(b) leaving it for him at his last known address; or
(c) sending it by registered post addressed to him at his last known address.

10.—(1) Whenever, in the opinion of the Director, the whole or any part of any land register is, or is likely to become, unserviceable, by reason of its age or of damage or otherwise, the Director may cause a copy of such land register or part thereof to be prepared. Preparation of copies of land registers.

— 4 —

(2) Copies prepared under this section shall be checked by such persons and in such manner as the Director may deem appropriate.

(3) The Director may cause any copy prepared in accordance with this section to be bound as a separate land register, or to be substituted in an existing land register for any part of which it is a copy.

(4) Whenever, in accordance with the provisions of this section, a copy of a land register or any part thereof has been prepared and checked, an authorised officer shall endorse against the last entry on each folio a certificate substantially in form E in the Schedule to this Ordinance.

(5) An authorised officer shall sign and date every certificate endorsed under this section.

(6) With effect from the date of any certificate endorsed in accordance with the provisions of this section the copy to which it relates shall have the same force and effect for all purposes as the register or part thereof of which it is a copy and such register or part thereof shall cease to have any force or effect and may be destroyed by the Director.

(7) When a certificate of an authorised officer has been endorsed in accordance with this section it shall be presumed, unless the contrary is proved, that all things required by this section were duly done prior to the endorsement of the certificate.

Power of Director to hold enquiry regarding certain documents.
Cap. 81.
Cap. 135.

11. Where the Director is satisfied that—

(a) (i) any person has applied to the Director for the grant, under section 4 of the Land Transfer Ordinance, of his consent to the disposition of any immovable property; or

(ii) any person claiming to be entitled to any share in any immovable property forming part of a succession has applied to the Director, under section 25 of the Succession Ordinance, for the registration of his name upon a land register in respect of his interest in such immovable property; and

(b) such application, and all or any of the documents or any part thereof submitted with such application, have been destroyed or rendered illegible in whole or in part whilst in the custody of the Director; and

(c) similar documents, or documents having the same force and effect, cannot be obtained by such person for production to the Director,

the Director may appoint an authorised officer to hold an enquiry for the purpose of ascertaining any facts which he may desire to ascertain before giving his decision.

Power of Director to postpone certain transactions.
Cap. 81.

Cap. 135.

12. In the following cases, namely—

(a) where any person applies or has applied to the Director for the grant, under section 4 of the Land Transfer Ordinance, of his consent to the disposition of any immovable property; or

(b) where any person claiming to be entitled to any share in any immovable property forming part of a succession, applies or has applied to the Director, under section 25 of the Succession Ordinance, for the registration of his name upon a land register in respect of his interest in such immovable property, and the Director is satisfied that it is desirable to postpone his decision until any enquiry under this Ordinance has been held, he may postpone his decision accordingly.

13. An officer holding an enquiry under this Ordinance shall have the following powers:— Powers of officer when holding enquiry.

(a) to procure all such evidence, written or oral, and to examine all such persons as witnesses as he may think it necessary or desirable to procure or examine;

(b) to require the evidence (whether written or oral) of any witness to be given on oath or otherwise, such oath to be that which could be required of the witness if he were giving evidence in a court of law;

(c) to summon any person residing in Palestine to attend before him to give evidence or produce any document in the possession of such person and to examine such person as a witness or require him to produce any document in his possession, subject to all just exceptions;

(d) to issue a warrant to compel the attendance of any person who, after having been summoned to attend, fails to do so, and does not excuse such failure to the satisfaction of the officer, and to order him to pay all costs which may have been occasioned in compelling his attendance or by reason of his refusal to obey the summons, and also to fine such person a sum not exceeding five pounds;

(e) to fine in a sum not exceeding five pounds any person who, being required by the officer to give evidence on oath or otherwise or to produce a document, refuses to do so and does not excuse such refusal to the satisfaction of the officer:

Provided always that, if any witness objects to answer any question on the ground that it will tend to incriminate him, he shall not be required to answer the question nor be liable to any penalties for refusing so to answer;

(f) to admit any evidence, whether written or oral, which might be inadmissible in civil or criminal proceedings;

(g) to take account of any documents in the custody of the Director;

(h) to order any person who, in the opinion of the officer—

(i) has made a false representation in consequence of which an enquiry has been held under this Ordinance; or

(ii) in connection with an enquiry held under this Ordinance, has made a frivolous claim,

to pay such sum as in the opinion of the officer represents the cost to Government of holding such enquiry, or the cost of holding such part of such enquiry as was due to such frivolous claim, as the case may be.

14.—(1) Any fine imposed under section 13 shall be recoverable in the same manner as a fine imposed by a court of law. Recovery of fines and other moneys.

(2) Where any person is ordered to pay any amount under section 13, such amount shall be a debt due from such person to the Government of Palestine and shall be recoverable accordingly.

15. The Director may, with the approval of the High Commissioner, make rules for the better carrying into effect of the provisions of this Ordinance. Without prejudice to the generality of the power conferred Rules.

— 6 —

by this section, any such rules may, subject to the provisions of section 7, provide for the forms to be used under this Ordinance, the fees to be payable in relation to things done thereunder and the granting of exemptions from the payment of any such fees.

Saving.   16. Nothing in this Ordinance shall prejudice or affect any right which would exist if this Ordinance had not been enacted.

SCHEDULE.

Form A.

Prepared under section 5(1)(a) of the Land Registers Ordinance, 1944.
Dated this   day of

Authorised Officer.

Form B.

Cancelled under section 6(3)(a) of the Land Registers Ordinance, 1944.
Dated this   day of

Authorised Officer.

Form C.

Prepared under section 6(3)(a) of the Land Registers Ordinance, 1944.
Dated this   day of

Authorised Officer.

Form D.

Prepared under section 6(3)(a) of the Land Registers Ordinance, 1944, in substitution for new entry at
Dated this   day of

Authorised Officer.

Form E.

Copy prepared under section 9(1) of the Land Registers Ordinance, 1944.
Dated this   day of

Authorised Officer.

13th September, 1944.

J. V. W. SHAW
Officer Administering the Government.

LAND COURTS (AMENDMENT) ORDINANCE, No. 39 OF 1944.

High Commissioner

LAND COURTS (AMENDMENT) ORDINANCE,
No. 39 of 1944.

AN ORDINANCE TO AMEND THE LAND COURTS ORDINANCE.

BE IT ENACTED by the High Commissioner for Palestine, with the advice of the Advisory Council thereof:—

1. This Ordinance may be cited as the Land Courts (Amendment) Ordinance, 1944, and shall be read as one with the Land Courts Ordinance, hereinafter referred to as "the principal Ordinance". *Short title. Cap. 75.*

2. The following heading and section shall be added at the end of the principal Ordinance:— *Insertion of new heading and section in the principal Ordinance.*

"*Vesting Orders.*

"Land Court may not make vesting orders in certain cases. 12. Where by any Ordinance there is conferred upon any court, other than a Land Court, jurisdiction to make a vesting order in respect of land, the Land Court shall not have jurisdiction to make such a vesting order."

3. Where before the commencement of this Ordinance a vesting order in respect of land has been made by any court, other than a Land Court, in exercise of the powers so to do purported to be conferred upon such Court by any Ordinance, such vesting order shall be deemed to have been validly made if it would have been validly made had this Ordinance been in force at the time such vesting order was made. *Validation.*

GORT
High Commissioner.

20th December. 1944.

Section 27: 1945

**RURAL PROPERTY TAX (AMENDMENT) ORDINANCE,
No. 8 OF 1945.**

High Commissioner

RURAL PROPERTY TAX (AMENDMENT) ORDINANCE,
No. 8 OF 1945.

AN ORDINANCE TO AMEND THE RURAL PROPERTY TAX ORDINANCE, 1942.

BE IT ENACTED by the High Commissioner for Palestine with the advice of the Advisory Council thereof:—

1. This Ordinance may be cited as the Rural Property Tax (Amendment) Ordinance, 1945, and shall be read as one with the Rural Property Tax Ordinance, 1942, hereinafter referred to as "the principal Ordinance". *Short title. No. 5 of 1942.*

2.—(1) Section 4 of the principal Ordinance shall be amended — *Amendment of section 4 of the principal Ordinance.*

(*a*) by the insertion of the word "or" after the comma at the end of paragraph (iii) of the proviso to subsection (1) thereof; and

(*b*) by the insertion, immediately after paragraph (iii) of the proviso to subsection (1) thereof, of the following paragraph:—

"(iv) remit payment of any rural property tax due, or about to fall due, in respect of any land, or direct the refund of any rural property tax paid in respect of any land."

(2) This section shall be deemed to have come into force on the date of the commencement of the principal Ordinance.

3. Section 6 of the principal Ordinance shall be amended by the repeal of subsections (3) and (4) thereof, and by the renumbering of subsections (5), (6) and (7) thereof as subsections (3), (4) and (5) respectively. *Amendment of section 6 of the principal Ordinance.*

4. If any rural property tax payable before the first day of April, 1944, is not paid on or before the first day of June, 1945, a sum equal to twenty per centum of the amount of such tax shall be added thereto, and the provisions of the principal Ordinance relating to the collection and recovery of rural property tax shall apply to the collection and recovery of such sum: *Penalty for non-payment of certain arrears of tax.*

Provided that a District Commissioner may for any good cause shown direct the recovery of any sum less than the full penalty and may enhance the sum so directed to be recovered from time to time in the case of a continuing default, so, however, that the total sum so directed to be recovered shall not exceed twenty per centum of the amount of such tax.

5. This Ordinance shall be deemed to have come into force on the first day of April, 1945. *Commencement.*

20th March, 1945.

GORT
High Commissioner.

LAND TRANSFER (FEES) RULES (AMENDMENT) ORDINANCE,
No. 34 OF 1945.

High Commissioner

LAND TRANSFER (FEES) RULES (AMENDMENT) ORDINANCE, No. 34 of 1945.

An Ordinance to repeal the Land Transfer (Fees) Rules (Amendment) Ordinance, 1941, and to amend the Land Transfer (Fees) Rules, 1939.

Be it enacted by the High Commissioner for Palestine, with the advice of the Advisory Council thereof:—

1. This Ordinance may be cited as the Land Transfer (Fees) Rules (Amendment) Ordinance, 1945. *Short title.*

2. The Land Transfer (Fees) Rules (Amendment) Ordinance, 1941, is hereby repealed. *Repeal of Ordinance No. 11 of 1941.*

3.—(1) The Land Transfer (Fees) Rules, 1939, as from time to time amended (which rules as so amended are hereinafter referred to as "the principal Rules") are hereby further amended in accordance with the directions set forth in the Schedule hereto. *Amendment of the Land Transfer (Fees) Rules, 1939. Gaz: 26.12.39, p. 1477.*

(2) For the avoidance of doubt it is hereby declared that the principal Rules as amended by this Ordinance may be further amended or may be revoked, in whole or in part, by rules made by the High Commissioner under section 16 of the Land Transfer Ordinance. *Cap. 81.*

THE SCHEDULE.

Amendments of the principal Rules effected by this Ordinance.

Rule		Amendment
3(1)		Substitute the following:—
		"(1) Transfer by sale, gift or bequest.
	Cap. 80.	(a) If the land has been registered in accordance with the provisions of section 36 of the Land (Settlement of Title) Ordinance — 5% on the market value of the land.
		(b) If the land has not been registered as specified in paragraph (a) of this sub-rule —
		(i) where the land is situated within an urban area — 5% on the market value of the land;
		(ii) where the land is not situated within an urban area — 3% on the market value of the land:
		Provided that wherever the land is situated the fee shall in no case be less than 500 mils."
3(2)		Substitute the following:—
		"(2) Exchange.
	Cap. 80.	(a) If all of the lands exchanged have been registered in accordance with the provisions of section 36 of the Land (Settlement of Title) Ordinance — 5% on one half of the aggregate market value of the lands exchanged, provided that such fee shall in no case be less than 500 mils and that the exchange is of land approximately equal in value. If the lands being exchanged are not approximately equal in value, the fee of 5% shall be calculated upon the market value of whichever of the lands is the higher in value.
		(b) If all of the lands exchanged have not been registered as specified in paragraph (a) of this sub-rule —

Rule	Amendment
	(i) where any of the lands exchanged is situated within an urban area — 5% on one half of the aggregate market value of the lands exchanged, provided that such fee shall in no case be less than 500 mils and that the exchange is of lands approximately equal in value. If the lands being exchanged are not approximately equal in value, the fee of 5% shall be calculated upon the market value of whichever of the lands is the higher in value;
	(ii) where none of the lands exchanged is situated within an urban area — 3% on one half of the aggregate market value of the lands exchanged, provided that such fee shall in no case be less than 500 mils and that the exchange is of lands approximately equal in value. If the lands being exchanged are not approximately equal in value, the fee of 3% shall be calculated upon the market value of whichever of the lands is the higher in value."
3(7)	Substitute the following:—
	"(7) *Sale by auction of mortgaged property in execution proceedings at the request of the mortgagee.*
	The appropriate fee specified in sub-rule (1) shall be paid.
	For the purposes of this sub-rule and of sub-rule (1), a sale shall be deemed to take place when a mortgagee becomes entitled to have the mortgaged property provisionally registered in his name under the provisions of section 10 of the Credit Banks Ordinance or section 3 of the Mortgage Law (Amendment) Ordinance:
Cap. 29. Cap. 95.	
	Provided that if, after the mortgaged property has been provisionally registered in the name of the mortgagee, the mortgagee re-transfers the mortgaged property into the name of the mortgagor in accordance with the said provisions, the fee paid on such provisional registration of the mortgaged property in the name of the mortgagee shall be refunded to him."
3(18)	Substitute the following:—
	"(18) *Transfer by Company, Other Corporate Body or Partnership.*
	The appropriate fee specified in sub-rule (1) shall be paid on the transfer of any land by any company or other corporate body or partnership (whether in liquidation or not) to any member, contributory, debenture holder or creditor of such company, corporate body or partnership or to any other person."

3rd September, 1945

J. V. W. SHAW
Officer Administering the Government.